Praise for *Theology in Motion*

Given the dangerous political divisions in this country, the churches have a justice-oriented responsibility toward one of its main causes: immigration. Aimee Hein argues with power, passion, and plenty of examples that American Christians can and should repair and restore immigration, and that migrants and Indigenous peoples too are "capable agents" leading immigration reform. This book is exceptionally timely, well-researched, culture-critical, and yet hopeful. It will give courage and energy to anyone at a loss to see how our immigration problem can be solved, or what the churches can really do about it.

—Lisa Sowle Cahill, J. Donald Monan, S.J.,
Professor of Theology, Boston College

This incisive book grapples with the history that shapes and misshapes how US Christians conceive of border enforcement. Hein offers a piercing theological-ethical reflection on the demands that our past places on the relationships that bind immigrants and citizens today, deepening migration ethics' ability to provide an expansive vision that takes us beyond communitarian and cosmopolitan views to discern a more just future.

—Victor Carmona, associate professor of theology
and religious studies, University of San Diego

Aimee Hein provides a compelling and bold ecumenical agenda for the urgent challenges posed by forced migration in our day. Her integration of Indigenous studies with Christian theological ethics and practice yields an account of citizens' responsibilities in justice that will be of great service to disciples and citizens alike. Interrogating the function and costs of our nation's founding myths, she challenges US citizens to remember rightly, repent, and repair, advancing a valuable responsibility framework for migration ethics today.

—Kristin E. Heyer, professor of theological ethics, Boston College

Aimee Hein's new book draws on a synthesis of US history, theologies of responsibility, and ethics of immigration in order to argue that the United States and its Christian churches have specific responsibilities of repair to immigrant communities. In this context, being a disciple means learning new histories and stories. Hein shows us that a just response to immigration includes changes at the level of law, policy, churches, communities, and human hearts. Essential reading for any study not only of the theology and ethics of migration, but of justice and the ethics of memory.

—Tisha M. Rajendra, associate professor of Christian ethics,
Loyola University Chicago

THEOLOGY IN MOTION

AIMEE ALLISON HEIN

THEOLOGY IN MOTION

Migration, History, and Responsibility

FORTRESS PRESS
Minneapolis

THEOLOGY IN MOTION
Migration, History, and Responsibility

29 28 27 26 25 24 1 2 3 4 5 6 7 8 9

Library of Congress Control Number: 2024935610 (print)

Cover image: Statue of Liberty seen through window of Staten Island Ferry in Hudson River; compilation of photos from Getty Images
Cover design: Brice Hemmer

Print ISBN: 978-1-5064-9157-8
eBook ISBN: 978-1-5064-9158-5

CONTENTS

ACKNOWLEDGMENTS

There are so many people who have been vital to the development of this book. I would like to thank Kristin Heyer, my doctoral director, who nurtured the earliest versions of this project. Kristin, you have been an invaluable conversation partner throughout this process. Your energy, dedication, and patience have made this project stronger and have helped make me a better scholar. I am also deeply indebted to my dissertation committee members: Lisa Sowle Cahill and O. Ernesto Valiente. Lisa and Neto, your insightful feedback and generosity are so appreciated. You have contributed immeasurably to this work, and I am beyond grateful.

I would also like to thank the academic communities that have stimulated and supported my growth as a theologian and the development of this book. Thank you to the Boston College Theology Department, especially Ken Himes, Andrea Vicini, Jim Keenan, David Vanderhooft, and John Makransky. Thank you to my cohort, Nicholas Hayes-Mota and Rohan Oberai, for your friendship and support as partners on this journey; my comps buddy, Andy Vink, for inspiration, commiseration, and coffee (special shout-out to Bobby!); and also Sara Bernard-Hoverstad, Michael DePue, Maria Howe, Xavier Montecel, Peter Fay, Jen Lamson-Scribner, Annie Selak, Stephanie Edwards, Kim Humphrey, and Craig Ford.

Thank you to the Boston College School of Theology and Ministry, especially Colleen Griffith, Andrew Davis, Barb Quinn, Nancy Pineda-Madrid, and Francine Cardman. Thank you also to my classmates and friends: Ali Carroll, Rachel Nagengast, Amy Northrop, Martha Ligas, Brian Taber, Megan Kush, and Megan Colford. To my Encuentro companions, thank you for allowing me to share in that journey with you.

I would also like to thank my professors at St. Ben's and St. John's, especially Kathy Cox, Vincent Smiles, Kelly Kraemer, and Ron Pagnucco, and my friend Chelsea Parker. Thank you also to Hanna Kaufman, who is always in my heart.

Thank you to my colleagues Amy Maxey, Kristopher Seaman, August Higgins, Jerry McCarthy, Rhodora Beaton, John Markey, Bob Wright, and Rodolfo Luna.

Thank you to my editor, Ryan Hemmer, and the team at Fortress Press for taking such care with this book. Working with you has been a joy.

Special thanks is also due to the community who so inspired this project, especially Ana, Erika, and Briana, as well as Kris, Gaby, Nestor, and Alfredo. You have all taught me so much.

To my San Antonio community, who welcomed me into a new city and gave me a beautiful life there. My love to Becca, Bug, Riley, and Andrew; to Marquetta, Ari, Daniel, Lizzie, and Toni; to Michaela, Iris, Chris, Myles, Gabel, Ellen, and Emma Rose; to Reagan and Julian.

To my Boston friends, especially Tom, Corrie, Sophie, and Joni. Your friendship has helped keep me grounded through this process, and I am grateful for each one of you.

To Lacie, who has been my friend through so many eras of my life. I love you forever.

To my parents, Tom and Barbara, I cannot find the words to describe how much you have given me over the years. Thank you, thank you, thank you for giving me the space to become, for reading to me, for always believing in me, and for loving me whether I succeed or fail. I have never had to question it. I am so lucky to have you as role models and friends. Jack, I am forever in awe of your spirit, your ferocity, and your vulnerability. You inspire me to be wholly myself, and I cannot imagine doing life without you. Thank you to my grandmothers, Nancy and Lois, in whose footsteps I follow.

To Hannah and Ryan, my darling friends without pretense, knowing you is one of the great joys of my life. I am eternally grateful for you. To Rory. Being your godmother is an honor and a joy. I hope we leave this world better than we found it for you.

Finally, to Sara, Walt, and Derek. Thank you for making me a home, together in Boston and across the country. I could not do this without you. I love you with every bit of myself.

INTRODUCTION

In the summer of 2021, the US military withdrew from Afghanistan, capturing the attention of the world. Images of the airport in Kabul, filled with thousands of Afghans desperate to evacuate alongside US troops, flooded the news and social media. In some, people chased and even clung to planes as they took off for the United States. These images of desperation weighed heavily on the consciences of many US citizens. One unfolding story that garnered particular attention and concern was that of the many Afghan translators, people who had put their lives at risk in order to aid US troops throughout the United States' presence in Afghanistan, who were unable to make it out of the country as the United States withdrew.

In the two decades of US-led conflict in Afghanistan, tens of thousands of Afghans worked with the US military, often as translators. The International Rescue Committee puts the number of Afghans who provided official aid at no less than 263,000.[1] In June 2021, as the United States prepared to withdraw, approximately 18,000 of these Afghan nationals were reportedly waiting on the US visas promised to them in exchange for their service. Working with the US military in this capacity can be extremely dangerous, not just by placing these contractors in active war zones but by making them and their families potential targets for retaliation by the Taliban. Many feel they have a very real reason to fear for their lives and for the safety of their loved ones, especially as the US withdrawal made way for the Taliban to gain increasing control of the country. Some even report receiving threatening phone calls and letters from the Taliban, forcing them into hiding.[2] Reports indicate that in recent years the Taliban has killed several hundred Afghans who worked with the US military.[3]

---

1. International Rescue Committee, "Evacuations from Afghanistan: What Is the Afghan Special Immigrant Visa (SIV) Program?," August 2, 2021, https://tinyurl.com/2zcb9zxy.

2. Martha Raddatz, Cindy Smith, and Conor Finnegan, "Afghan Translators, Contractors Fear for Their Lives amid Taliban Offensives, US Withdrawal," ABC News, June 23, 2021, https://abcnews.go.com/Politics/afghan-translators-contractors-fear-lives-amid-taliban-offensives/story?id=78422573.

3. Greg Palkot, "Afghan Translators, Families Fear Taliban Takeover as They Try Escaping to US," Fox News, August 4, 2021, https://www.foxnews.com/world/afghan-translators-families-fear-taliban-takeover-try-escaping-us.

In the weeks following the evacuation, officials estimated that the majority of these translators and other contractors had been left behind, resulting in public outcry in both Afghanistan and the United States.[4] By October 2021 it was reported that 28,000 visa applicants were waiting in the pipeline, with under a third of those applicants and their families having successfully left Afghanistan.[5] A year after the withdrawal, multiple sources reported that more than 160,000 special visa–eligible Afghans were still in Afghanistan.[6] Many citizens and lawmakers alike were furious, feeling that people who had taken such risks to aid the United States had been unjustly abandoned.[7] This outrage hinges on an assumption that the United States had a responsibility to these translators, a responsibility to which the nation failed to adhere.

Concern for what is owed to Afghan translators and other contractors is not new to the 2021 evacuation. It has been a topic of concern for almost as long as the United States has been in Afghanistan. Beginning in 2006, Congress sought to address the danger faced by those willing to help the US military by making special immigrant visas (SIVs) available for Afghan (and Iraqi) translators and other contractors facing threats related to their service. In doing so, Congress acknowledged that the nation has some degree of responsibility to protect those put in danger by partnering with US troops. By law, this process is meant to take nine months, but in reality it takes an average of four years, sometimes longer.[8] Due to increasing issues of backlogs and the pending military evacuation, in July 2021 Congress increased the number of SIVs available to Afghan applicants by eight thousand and made moves to streamline the process.[9] Even so, the number

4. Elsie Foley, "U.S. Left Most Afghans Who Helped Americans Behind," Huffington Post, September 1, 2021, https://www.huffpost.com/entry/afghanistan-siv-applicants_n_612fc097e4b0aac9c011d73b.

5. Mike Brest, "Estimated 450 Americans and Thousands of SIV Applicants Remain in Afghanistan: Defense Official," *Washington Examiner*, October 26, 2021, https://www.washingtonexaminer.com/policy/defense-national-security/estimated-450-americans-and-thousands-of-siv-applicants-remain-in-afghanistan-defense-official.

6. Kim Staffieri, Matt Zeller, and Michael Trudeau, "The Left Behind Afghans One Year Later," Association of Wartime Allies, August 15, 2022, https://tinyurl.com/mr4a5wy6; Tevah Gevelber, "Stuck While the World Moves On: Upwards of 160,000 Afghans Remain in Limbo," Responsible Statecraft, June 14, 2022, https://responsiblestatecraft.org/2022/06/14/stuck-while-the-world-moves-on-160000-afghans-remain-in-limbo/.

7. Raddatz, Smith, and Finnegan, ""Afghan Translators, Contractors."

8. Raddatz, Smith, and Finnegan, ""Afghan Translators, Contractors."

9. "Special Immigrant Visas for Afghans—Who Were Employed by/on Behalf of the U.S. Government," Immigrate, U.S. Department of State—Bureau of Consular Affairs, accessed October 19, 2022, https://travel.state.gov/content/travel/en/us-visas/immigrate/special-immg-visa-afghans-employed-us-gov.html.

of eligible Afghans still waiting remains significant. Other efforts come from the nonprofit sector. In 2013, one Afghan interpreter cofounded No One Left Behind, a nonprofit organization dedicated to assisting SIV-eligible Afghan and Iraqi nationals as they seek resettlement in the United States.[10] The International Rescue League and the Association of Wartime Allies have also participated in efforts to assist these and other Afghan nationals in dire need of safety.[11]

Others receive aid from the soldiers they worked alongside. One former translator, Abdulhaq Sodais, repeatedly sought asylum in the United States. After his initial 2013 application for a US visa was denied, Sodais appealed four times. He was denied each time despite facing death threats for his work aiding the United States and the fact that another of his platoon's translators, Sayed Masoud, had been killed by the Taliban in 2017. Finally, following the beheading of his uncle and the shooting of a neighbor who had also worked for the military, Sodais fled Afghanistan, traveling for seven months through numerous countries before ending up in Germany. A veteran from his platoon, Spencer Sullivan, assisted him in his fight for asylum, providing photos and records as well as emotional support. Sullivan is just one of many US veterans who have been left with the burden of rescuing the Afghans who served alongside them in the absence of efficient US intervention. In September 2021 Sodais was finally granted asylum in Germany.[12]

For Sullivan, the United States has failed. "I made a promise to [Sodais] just as America made a promise to him to protect him and save his life," he said in an interview. "I mean how can you turn your back on that promise? I don't think the answer is more complicated than that. I think it's actually very simple." Sullivan reports that his experiences losing Masoud and then fighting to help Sodais gain asylum taught him that the US government is capable of betrayal, of failing to do something as basic as keeping a promise. [13] In going to war and seeking assistance from locals, the United States created dangerous situations for which it bore responsibility. The nation acknowledged this responsibility by promising visas and by making some efforts in recent months to address

10. No One Left Behind, "About Us," accessed October 19, 2022, https://www.nooneleft.org/about.

11. International Rescue Committee, "Evacuations from Afghanistan"; Association of Wartime Allies, "Our Story," accessed October 19, 2022, https://www.wartimeallies.co/about.

12. Julie Watson, "US Soldier Wins Long Fight to Get Afghan Translator Asylum," Fox 29, September 22, 2021, https://www.wboy.com/news/national/us-soldier-wins-long-fight-to-get-afghan-translator-asylum/.

13. Julie Watson and Andrea Rosa, "US Soldier Loses One Afghan Translator; Fights to Save Another," Army Times, August 27, 2021, https://www.armytimes.com/news/your-army/2021/08/27/us-soldier-loses-one-afghan-translator-fights-to-save-another/.

the massive backlog of applicants. Despite these efforts, a staggering number of applicants are still waiting.

Cases of translators and contractors abandoned for months or years in dangerous situations, often finding reprieve only through the luck of being connected to dedicated friends or a nonprofit, are especially poignant examples of how a nation might have and fail to live up to responsibilities based on its choices at home and abroad. Stories like Sodais and Sullivan's tug at our hearts because they have such a deeply personal element to them: two men whose friendship was forged in war now working together against a looming threat and an unjust system. These stories are effective because they are relatively straightforward, people who fought with "us" on the "right side" of a war and were promised a level of protection for taking those risks have been left behind, in many ways abandoned. It is easy to see the responsibility the United States has and the ways it has not lived up to that responsibility.

Other ways the United States might have responsibility, and particularly responsibility to create adequate channels for migrants in need to find refuge within US borders, can be a bit less clear. As this book will argue, however, this responsibility is no less vital to the lives of migrants and to the moral health of the nation. It is to these stories that I seek to call attention.

An Overview

In recent years the United States has entered into increasingly heated debates about who should be let into the country and under what circumstances, how to respond to the presence of undocumented immigrants, and the best approach to border security. In these debates Christian scholars, church leaders, and religious citizens have all weighed in with their takes on the proper way to approach questions of immigration from a Christian worldview. These responses generally prioritize either Christian obligations to care for all people or the importance of upholding the rule of law and protecting national sovereignty. These priorities usually signal one of two frameworks: a communitarian approach, which begins with a concern for law and sovereignty, or a cosmopolitan approach, which begins with a particular focus on human dignity. Both offer important values and considerations that can help Christians think about the morally relevant features of migration and the US immigration system. Both, however, also tend to lack a sufficient grounding in history, a consideration of how we got to the situation we are in nationally and globally and what that history might teach us about our ethical responsibilities as Christians, as US citizens, and as a nation. Put another way, both frameworks have failed to attend to the human relationships at the heart of migration.

This book aims to bring those relationships to the fore. It responds to the prevalence of communitarian and cosmopolitan framings of migration in

Christian ethics but is particularly in conversation with works such as *Kinship across Borders: A Christian Ethic of Immigration* by Kristin Heyer (Georgetown University Press, 2012), *Migrants and Citizens: Justice and Responsibility in the Ethics of Immigration* by Tisha Rajendra (Eerdmans, 2017), and *Humanity in Crisis: Ethical and Religious Response to Refugees* by David Hollenbach, SJ (Georgetown University Press, 2020). These theologians have begun to shift Christian migration ethics away from a debate between human rights and national sovereignty and toward a more relationship-focused set of questions. In line with this shift, the specific contributions of this book include offering a responsibility ethics approach as a framework for addressing the relational concerns raised by these thinkers, and considering what role churches and other communities of faith might play in responding to those concerns. Additionally, the book brings Indigenous studies and the perspectives of Indigenous thinkers to the forefront, intentionally expanding the network of relationships to which Christian migration ethics is responsible and the perspectives the field considers formative.

Entering into this conversation as a white US citizen, I am conscious of the potential dangers to which my work is open. At the same time, I believe this is a conversation white people and US citizens need to be having. We need to reflect on how the United States has arrived where it is today, how we have benefited from a history of oppression and violence, and what obligations might exist for us today based on this history. Therefore, I locate myself in this conversation as an ethicist considering what responsibilities my communities and my country might have. Given the strong focus on relationships and responsibility in my work and in this book, I have striven to be conscious of how my choices as a scholar may be responsible or irresponsible, and contribute to good or bad patterns of relationality. This has influenced my methodological and stylistic choices in several ways. First, I have intentionally foregrounded the perspectives of people from communities most harmed by the dynamics of US imperialism. In doing so, I have tried to be a respectful conversation partner, hoping to engage them in a way that does not co-opt their perspectives.

Second, writer Khairani Barokka argues compellingly that italicization of non-English words can reinforce the hegemony of English culture, operating as a sort of "linguistic gatekeeping."[14] Because the tendency to normalize and prioritize Anglo-American experience and culture is a dynamic of US history with which this book is especially concerned, I have chosen not to italicize words in other languages. Third, I am conscious that much of the language used to name those with shared Latin American heritage is contested. I have chosen to use

---

14. Khairani Barokka, "The Case against Italicizing 'Foreign' Words," Catapult, February 11, 2020, https://catapult-prod.herokuapp.com/stories/column-the-case-against-italicizing-foreign-words-khairani-barokka.

"Latine" throughout not in an effort to weigh in on this debate (which is not my debate to have) but in a spirit of inclusivity and with every intention of respect for language and cultural experiences that are not my own.

The book proceeds in the following manner. Chapter 1 examines the founding of the United States, considering how ideologies such as the doctrine of discovery shaped the earliest European encounters with this continent as well as the nation the United States would become. It tracks the further evolution of myths and practices that developed out of this origin as the new nation expanded westward. This chapter pays particular attention to how these myths and practices developed in connection to the removal of Indigenous peoples from their land. In doing so, it seeks to broaden the perspectives through which we understand US history and lays the groundwork for identifying the responsibility the United States has to migrants now. This chapter also offers a consideration of social sin, which serves as a framework for understanding the legacy of the myths and practices outlined in this chapter and helps prepare the reader for the theology presented in chapters 3–6.

Chapter 2 considers the impact of these early decades, illustrating how the process outlined in chapter 1 shaped US foreign policy and immigration policy as well as national discourse around both topics. This history calls us to consider who and what our current immigration system actually protects. The chapter focuses in particular on the way the world beyond the United States is cast as a threat, leading to aggressive foreign policy, militarized borders, and a posture of defense and isolation rather than collaboration and friendship. The legacy of the myths and practices outlined in chapter 1 can also be seen in common migratory patterns into the United States, patterns that were in many ways caused by US colonialism.

Chapter 3 draws on the work of H. Richard Niebuhr and Charles Curran to propose a responsibility ethics framework for responding to the history outlined in chapters 1–2, connecting this framework to the biblical injunction to be a good neighbor. Responsibility ethics frames our moral actions as taking place within an ongoing dialogue with those with whom we are in relationship. Acting ethically requires being accountable to what has come before and to what might result from our choices. The chapter argues that the United States must reckon with its founding mythologies and repent for the harm they have caused, and that US immigration policy ought to reflect the nation's culpability in the creation of a world in which people are forced to migrate.

Chapter 4 underscores the responsibility framework proposed in chapter 3 through a consideration of reparative justice. Responsibility ethics provides a framework for thinking about our moral decision-making and for identifying how we have failed to act well. Having thus identified the harms caused, reparative justice provides a way forward, focusing on how building true accountability, reciprocity, and mutuality can move us toward justice in the wake of that harm. The chapter frames this work of concrete repair as consistent with the radical love of Jesus and as integral to the kin-dom of God. Repair is the proper work of the church. Christians therefore ought to consider questions of immigration through the lens of how we might repair global relationships that have been broken or unjust.

Chapter 5 provides a bridge between conceptual work and practical proposals by considering how the work of the church is framed and directed by the relationship between Christology and ecclesiology. How does what we believe about Jesus shape how we understand the role of the church in the world? With particular attention to the christological and ecclesiological contributions of Indigenous and Latine theologians, this chapter identifies four qualities churches ought to cultivate as they engage in the work of responsible repair: community building, listening, solidarity, and flexibility.

Chapter 6 concludes with proposals for how Christian communities can live out the ecclesiological vision of the previous chapters and foster more just relationships with migrants. What can and should individuals and churches do in the face of US responsibility to migrants? It does this primarily by considering four case studies that highlight concrete examples of how the themes outlined in chapter 5 might be lived out. These examples are intentionally diverse. They highlight a variety of tactics that might be taken in different contexts and based on particular strengths and resources. Christian communities are encouraged not to mimic these cases but to allow them to inspire and direct their own particular, contextual work of radical love in service of the kin-dom of God.

CHAPTER ONE

Discovery

> *That sunny day in early 2017, we marched behind Tongva drummers, the original people of what is currently Los Angeles. We held placards that read "No Ban On Stolen Land!" protesting Donald Trump's executive order barring travel to the United States from seven Muslim-majority countries in Africa and the Middle East. This defiance is the living legacy of centuries of Indigenous resistance: the active refusal to cede moral authority over who belongs and who doesn't to a settler nation.*
>
> —Nick Estes, "Go Back Where You Came From"

ALTHOUGH IT HAS come under increasingly widespread scrutiny in recent years, the notion that the Americas were discovered is one of the most prevailing and foundational myths influencing US identity to this day. It is the basis on which Columbus Day remains a federal holiday observed by many (though there have been not insignificant movements toward the alternative celebration of Indigenous Peoples' Day[1]), and it provides the conceptual framework that has allowed for the United States to form into the nation it is today. For much of US history and up to today, the collective memory of this nation has been of a European discovery beginning in 1492. The problem, as this chapter will highlight, is that we are remembering poorly.

Memory plays an important role in moral decision-making. Moral theologian William C. Mattison identifies memory as a subvirtue essential for the practicing of prudence. This is not simply about whether we remember something but how we remember it, the story we tell. Mattison argues that as humans we are prone to remember things in ways that are beneficial to ourselves. When communities do this, our collective memories skew the truth in our favor. This matters for ethics in particular because remembering history in an inaccurate or incomplete manner inhibits our ability to act well and make

1. As of October 2019, at least ten states officially shifted from celebrating Columbus Day to some form of Indigenous People's Day. See Leila Fadal, "Columbus Day or Indigenous Peoples' Day," National Public Radio, October 14, 2019, https://www.npr.org/2019/10/14/769083847/columbus-day-or-indigenous-peoples-day.

prudent choices.[2] Remembering the initial European settling of the United States as a discovery shapes the way we think about the nation and its rights. It is often taken for granted that nations have a right to defend their borders, but we too rarely stop to consider how those borders came to be, who might have been harmed in the process, and what that harm might bring to bear on the question of just or ethical immigration law and policy today. When dealing with systems, such as the immigration system in the United States, morality requires we work to remember well. We cannot debate the potential ethics of any system without looking at how that system currently functions concretely and how that system came to be. I contend that providing a fuller account of the European "discovery" of the Americas (and the subsequent establishment of colonies and later the US) ought to substantially shift the way we understand and approach the question of immigration and border control. This chapter seeks to unsettle the conceptual foundation and worldview on which the very right to exclude is built, particularly when that right rests in the hands of the US government.

Illuminating the importance of remembering well, German theologian Marianne Heimbach-Steins employs a postcolonial lens in order to understand and frame contemporary migration patterns.[3] Though she directs her attention specifically to the European context, the principles of her approach can be applied to the United States as well. For Heimbach-Steins, the approaches of modern European nations to immigration policy are rooted in Europe's colonial history. In particular, "Fortress Europe," a term that describes the impulse to tighten borders against increased immigration from outside Europe, represents "a new type of neo-colonialism." In order to understand the present situation in Europe, she argues, we must recognize that European colonialism did two important things. First, it shaped "long term international relationships and lasting unequal opportunities" and access to resources. The relationships and inequality colonialism created have a direct impact on migration patterns today. People migrate in part because of an inequitable distribution of global resources that colonialism perpetuated, and the places to which those with fewer resources choose to migrate are often directly related to historic colonial relationships. Second, colonial structures "also created culturalist patterns, ideologies of domination and subordination which continue to influence the way international migrants are treated in legal systems, political decision making, and economic

2. William C. Mattison, *Introducing Moral Theology: True Happiness and Virtue* (Grand Rapids: Brazos, 2008), 103.

3. Marianne Heimbach-Steins, "Migration in a Post-colonial World," in *Religious and Ethical Perspectives on Global Migration*, ed. Elizabeth W. Collier and Charles R. Strain (Lanham, MD: Lexington Books, 2014), 87–108.

and social practices of the societies they live in or want to immigrate to."[4] In other words, the ideologies on which colonialism was based and that it perpetuated—racist ideas of superiority and inferiority—have had lasting effects on how Europeans perceive the foreigners among them. These perceptions then directly affect immigration policy and the treatment of migrants and potential migrants more broadly.

Similar dynamics can be seen in the US context. It is no accident who shows up at the US border seeking entry. Many migrants "are here because [we] were there."[5] This chapter therefore offers a reframing of US history in order to provide a fuller understanding of the nation's imperialist tendencies and how they developed. This account of history will help to highlight how the development of US imperialism has shaped US responses to migration and driven the migration patterns we see today. In particular, this chapter explores how US imperialism has been supported by national myths that have become embedded in US foreign policy. These founding myths must therefore be identified and deconstructed in order to facilitate movement toward more just immigration policy in the United States. The historical account offered in this chapter identifies and tracks these myths in order to help us remember well so that we may approach immigration ethics more prudently.

Historian Roxanne Dunbar-Ortiz insists that founding myths matter because "origin narratives form the vital core of a people's unifying identity and the values that guide them."[6] They are what orient us in the world, and they therefore warrant serious consideration for a project such as the formation of a Christian ethical response to migration. We cannot contemplate how we ought to live if we do not first consider how our past (and the way it has been told to us) has shaped our relationship to our nation and the world. The way we remember matters. We must remember well in order to act prudently. This is especially true given this book's focus on responsibility. To be prudent, responsible actors responding well to immigration in the United States, we must understand how we got here so that we might identify what in our past

---

4. Heimbach-Steins, "Migration in a Post-colonial World," 91–93.

5. Ambalavaner Sivanandan, cited in Gary Younge, "Ambalavaner Sivanandan Obituary," *The Guardian*, February 7, 2018, https://www.theguardian.com/world/2018/feb/07/ambalavaner-sivanandan.

6. Roxanne Dunbar-Ortiz, *An Indigenous Peoples' History of the United States*, ReVisioning History (Boston: Beacon, 2014), 3. Dunbar-Ortiz's discussion of history and origin narratives can be related to Johann Baptist Metz's work on memory. While this book does not engage Metz in any detail, his work is a strong analogue to be considered in conversation with this book. See, for example, Johann Baptist Metz, *Faith in History and Society: Toward a Practical Fundamental Theology* (New York: Seabury, 1979).

may create responsibilities for the United States now.[7] Constructing a more accurate history of the United States is therefore essential to the formation of an adequate immigration ethic.

Settler Colonialism: The Origins of US Identity

While the fifteenth-century encounter with and subsequent settling of the Americas by Europeans has historically been characterized as discovery, in reality the Americas were not discovered at all, at least not by Europeans. When Columbus landed in North America in 1492 he found not "virgin wilderness" populated by wandering nomads but a complex network of Indigenous nations.[8] Human societies have existed in both North and South America for thousands of years. The peoples of these continents developed innovative agricultural systems, unique forms of game management, and complex, civilized societies. In other words, "by the time of European invasions, Indigenous peoples had occupied and shaped every part of the Americas, established extensive trade networks and roads, and were sustaining their populations by adapting to specific natural environments."[9] These peoples had complex and diverse cultures and governments, and they interacted with one another as independent and self-governing nations on generally equal footing with one another.[10] Bearing this history in mind reframes the way the precontact era is often understood in the United States. Christopher Columbus and subsequent European explorers did not discover the Americas; they invaded and then systematically displaced sovereign Indigenous nations.

That the peoples of the Americas were recognizable, sovereign, and independent nations is to a degree reflected in Euro-America dealings with them from the earliest settlers to today. The existence of over 370 treaties between

7. This question of responsibility will be dealt with more fully in later chapters, but the reconstruction of US history offered in this chapter sets the groundwork for the responsibility framework I am building.

8. Dunbar-Ortiz, *Indigenous Peoples' History*, 30–31.

9. Dunbar-Ortiz, *Indigenous Peoples' History*, 27. See also Matthew Klingle, "Frontier Ghosts along the Urban Pacific Slope," in *Frontier Cities: Encounters at the Crossroads of Empire*, ed. Jay Gitlin, Barbara Berglund, and Adam Arenson (Philadelphia: University of Pennsylvania Press, 2012), 124.

10. Dunbar-Ortiz, *Indigenous Peoples' History*, 25–27. It is also worth noting that these nations also warred with and at times even conquered one another. As this book is written with the aim of considering the history of attitudes and behaviors that shaped US identity, policy, and discourse, it is beyond the scope of this project to analyze this Indigenous warfare and conquest. What is important for us to consider here is not whether Indigenous nations always related justly to one another but rather how the US has behaved and what the consequences of that behavior might be.

the United States and the various Native nations within its borders stands as unequivocal legal evidence that "the United States formally recognized the fully sovereign national status and character of North American Indigenous governments during the period following the American Revolution."[11] The reality of Indigenous sovereignty has, however, consistently been at odds with Euro-American interests and so has been subverted in numerous ways.

The doctrine of discovery provided legal and conceptual grounding for this undermining of Indigenous sovereignty in service of the interests of European settlers. The doctrine finds its basis in the Roman legal notion of territorium (res) nullius, which holds that something that is not currently owned may become the property of anyone who seizes it. With the establishment of the Holy Roman Empire, this idea was expanded to include the legal right to occupy a discovered territory. Eventually the European notion of a fundamental distinction between Christians and "infidels" was embedded in this legal practice. This notion allowed for the expansion of Christianity through the "discovery" and claiming of sovereignty over lands inhabited by "infidel" societies. These lands were considered legally subject to reconquest due to the unwillingness of their inhabitants to accept Christianity.[12] This idea was first applied to the Americas in the papal bulls of Pope Alexander VI, who confirmed the rights of the sovereigns of Castille and Aragon (modern-day Spain) to "acquire and Christianize" this "New World."[13] It therefore came to be that European colonizers considered themselves to have acquired legal title to lands already inhabited by Indigenous nations because these nations' "natural claims" to the land were forfeit upon European "discovery." Dunbar-Ortiz denounces this as "legal cover for theft," which set the stage for "Euro-American wars of conquest and settler colonialism [which] devastated Indigenous nations and communities, ripping their territories away from them and transforming their land into private property."[14] This

11. Rebecca L. Robbins, "Self-Determination and Subordination: The Past, Present, and Future of American Indian Governance," in *The State of Native America: Genocide, Colonization, and Resistance*, ed. M. Annette Jaimes (Boston: South End, 1992), 89.

12. Glenn T. Morris, "International Law and Politics: Toward a Right to Self-Determination for Indigenous Peoples," in James, *State of Native America*, 58.

13. Morris, "International Law and Politics," 59. It is worth noting that in March 2023 the Vatican formally repudiated the Doctrine of Discovery, arguing that the notion fails to properly recognize the human dignity inherent in all people, including Indigenous peoples. See Elisabetta Povoledo, "Vatican Repudiates 'Doctrine of Discovery,' Used as Justification for Colonization," *New York Times*, March 30, 2023, https://tinyurl.com/33adm96t.

14. Dunbar-Ortiz, *Indigenous Peoples' History*, 198. It is precisely because non-European nations such as those inhabiting the Americas at the time of European "discovery" were recognizable as sovereign nations with legitimate claims to their land that the Doctrine of Discovery became necessary to uphold the expansionist interests of imperial powers from Europe.

is the beginning of a sustained Euro-American effort to undermine Indigenous sovereignty and promote colonial interests, particularly in the form of land acquisition, through the intentional manipulation of the rule of law.

The doctrine of discovery is deeply embedded in the founding of the United States. Simply put, without this doctrine the fight for Euro-American independence from Britain makes little sense. It is only because the British crown had claimed sovereignty over the land in order to establish colonies there in the first place that these colonies were later able to claim an independent right to govern themselves on that land. Further, in the early years of US independence, Thomas Jefferson, as secretary of state, claimed that the doctrine was applicable to US action beyond its newly established borders. The Supreme Court later upheld this idea in an 1823 majority opinion on a case involving a land dispute, in which the court affirmed that while "Indigenous people could continue to live on the land, the title resided with the discovering power, the United States."[15] This provides the conceptual basis for centuries of masking the theft of Indigenous land by giving it the appearance of legal legitimacy.

We can see that from the beginning the United States was founded on settler colonialism. Unlike other forms of colonialism, in which control of a territory is largely handled from a distance, settler colonialism seeks specifically to remove Indigenous populations in order to replace them with settlers.[16] According to Dunbar-Ortiz, "the objective of settler colonialism is to terminate Indigenous peoples as nations and communities with land bases in order to make the land available to European settlers."[17] This project of terminating Indigenous land-holding nations is overtly genocidal in nature. Genocide is defined by the United Nations as one or more specified acts undertaken with the "intent to destroy, in whole or in part, a national, ethnical, racial, or religious group."[18] Such actions can include killing or causing serious bodily or mental harm to members or the group, deliberately creating conditions meant to cause the destruction of the group, preventing births, and the forceful removal of children from the group.[19] In order to gain access to and control over the land inhabited and claimed by Indigenous nations, European settlers undertook actions such as these, actions

15. Dunbar-Ortiz, *Indigenous Peoples' History*, 200.

16. Amanda Morris, "What Is Settler-Colonialism?," Learning for Justice, January 22, 2019, https://www.learningforjustice.org/magazine/what-is-settlercolonialism.

17. Roxanne Dunbar-Ortiz, *Not "A Nation of Immigrants": Settler Colonialism, White Supremacy, and a History of Erasure and Exclusion* (Boston: Beacon, 2021), 23.

18. United Nations Office on Genocide Prevention and the Responsibility to Protect, "Genocide," accessed July 1, 2023, https://www.un.org/en/genocideprevention/genocide.shtml.

19. Dunbar-Ortiz, *Not "A Nation of Immigrants,"* 23.

directly intended to undermine and destroy these peoples. In fact, when considering the ratification of the Genocide Convention, US senators expressed concerns that the treaty might be used to classify the nation's treatment of Indigenous people as genocide. This is one reason the United States did not ratify the convention until 1988, almost four decades after it was adopted by the United Nations.[20] Dunbar-Ortiz writes, "The shadow of genocide lies in the Doctrine of Discovery."[21] Considering the genocidal actions undertaken by the United States in order to secure the nation's claim to this "discovered" land, it is hard to disagree.

Alongside the explicit use of the doctrine of discovery as justification, the practices and worldviews that fostered this European colonial project in the Americas were formed centuries before Columbus set sail. A brief consideration of the history of European Christian Crusades highlights this development of colonial ideology, the legacy of which the United States inherited and continues. The Crusades, while supported by a deadly religious zeal to Christianize the world, were explicitly linked to economic goals. In part this is because they were intended to result in European control of lucrative trade routes. The Crusades also, however, provided opportunity for soldiers to advance themselves economically and socially by acquiring wealth through the sacking and looting of Muslim cities, which would in turn grant them a degree of prestige upon their return home. Further, the late thirteenth century saw the papacy begin to turn this crusading energy against domestic enemies, in particular heretics, pagans, commoners, and especially women. This became a way for knights and noblemen to seize land and, having done so, force a situation of servitude onto those commoners who were already living on that land.[22]

This is important for understanding the formation of US myths and identity for two reasons. First, US history is a story of the seizure of land and exploitation of labor in service of increasing the wealth of the few. It is important to highlight the origins of this practice here. In short, "the rise of the modern state in Europe was based on the accumulation of wealth by means of exploiting human labor and displacing millions of subsistence producers from their lands,"[23] practices that were continued in the founding and expansion of the United States. Second, the displacement of European peasantry that began in this period has an even more direct relationship to the settling of the Americas. Dunbar-Ortiz shows that in the centuries after knights and noblemen began claiming land and forcing

20. Dunbar-Ortiz, *Not "A Nation of Immigrants,"* 24.

21. Dunbar-Ortiz, *Not "A Nation of Immigrants,"* 32.

22. Dunbar-Ortiz, *Indigenous Peoples' History*, 32–34.

23. Dunbar-Ortiz, *Indigenous Peoples' History*, 33.

the inhabitants of that land into servitude, the notion of land as private property began to gain popularity alongside the practice of enclosure, the privatization of land that had previously been commons. The peasantry who had traditionally used the commons as pasture for sheep and cows, and as a source of water, food, medicinal plants, firewood, and more, were evicted and rendered unable to provide for themselves as the land was turned over to private commercial use.[24] This privatization of land and mass displacement of people created a population ready to "serve as settlers in North American British colonies."[25] The people suddenly denied access to the common land that allowed them to make a living became prime candidates for settling the Americas because their situation made them especially vulnerable to draws of indentured servitude, which provided a means of living and the promise of future prosperity in the New World. After completing the terms of their servitude, these settlers "were free to squat on Indigenous land and become farmers again."[26]

Thus, Dunbar-Ortiz argues that "by the time Spain, Portugal, and Britain arrived to colonize the Americas, their methods of eradicating peoples or forcing them into dependency and servitude were ingrained, streamlined, and effective."[27] This became embedded into US practice and self-understanding. After gaining its independence, the nation embarked on a project of expansion dependent on continual seizure of Indigenous territory. This seizure of land was violent and bloody, and it utilized and manipulated the legal system in order to gain legitimacy and achieve its ends. The decades following US independence were a "nightmarish" period of extreme and unrestrained violence and increased colonization of Indigenous lands as the United States proceeded to make its way across the continent, utilizing a program of "scorched earth and annihilation" as it went.[28]

In the early period of US independence, alliances were formed between Indigenous nations in order to fend off settler encroachment. The Washington administration determined that the promotion of US interests required breaking up these alliances. Moreover, the administration insisted that war, rather than diplomacy, was the best method for achieving this goal. Here we can begin to see the continued legacy of the classes who had made their way to the New World

---

24. Dunbar-Ortiz, *Indigenous Peoples' History*, 34–35. Again, we encounter a pattern of land seizure for profit that influenced the actions of the Euro-American settlers, who spent the next few centuries similarly taking forceful control of land, disregarding the livelihoods and well-being of the people already inhabiting it.

25. Dunbar-Ortiz, *Indigenous Peoples' History*, 35.

26. Dunbar-Ortiz, *Indigenous Peoples' History*, 35.

27. Dunbar-Ortiz, *Indigenous Peoples' History*, 40.

28. Dunbar-Ortiz, *Indigenous Peoples' History*, 78–79.

by way of indentured servitude in order to find access to the land and livelihood that had been taken from them in Europe. Not only did these people and their descendants provide bodies to populate the colonies and the new nation they later formed, but they also provided a ready-made army desperate for land or profit and willing to go to extreme means to gain it. Dunbar-Ortiz notes that although the armies who fought Indigenous nations to expand US borders were led by federal officers, by and large the soldiers populating these armies were squatter settlers: less well-off settlers squatting on Indigenous land who were "unaccustomed to military discipline but fearless and willing to kill to get a piece of land to grab or some scalps for bounty."[29] Thus the colonial legacy of unjust land acquisition and the relentless quest for profit, inherited from Europe, continued to develop in the new settler nation.

This period of war against the Indigenous peoples relied on the use of "vicious killers to terrorize the region, thereby annexing land that could be sold to settlers," a primary source of revenue for the burgeoning government.[30] The military strategy developed in this period was aimed at destroying the enemy's will or capacity to resist by utilizing any means necessary. Called "irregular warfare," this method continued to be prevalent even after the official founding of the professional US Army in the early 1800s. The main characteristic of irregular warfare was the use of extreme violence against civilians, including outright physical attacks as well as efforts to undermine the systems on which they relied for survival.[31]

Alongside these overtly violent forms of genocide, legal tactics emerged, including the practice of treaty making. As noted above, this practice was necessary because the United States recognized, at least in some capacity, the Indigenous nations of the continent as sovereign nations having some legally legitimate claim to the land.[32] These treaties often came at the end of violent assaults against Indigenous nations as a way of formalizing the conquest of Indigenous territory. For example, the 1795 Treaty of Greenville, which redrew the lines between Indigenous and US territory and limited Indian Country to northwestern Ohio, formalized a US victory based on a sustained period of irregular warfare.[33] Andrew Jackson and his infamous Trail of Tears provides

29. Dunbar-Ortiz, *Indigenous Peoples' History*, 81.

30. Dunbar-Ortiz, *Indigenous Peoples' History*, 82.

31. Dunbar-Ortiz, *Indigenous Peoples' History*, 56–60, 81–102.

32. The US Constitution names the power "to regulate commerce with foreign Nations . . . and with Indian Tribes" as a power of the federal government. See "Commerce Clause," Cornell Law School, accessed February 20, 2020, https://www.law.cornell.edu/wex/commerce_clause.

33. Dunbar-Ortiz, *Indigenous Peoples' History*, 83.

another example. Jackson built his political career off an exceptionally brutal military one, largely spent annihilating Indigenous peoples, especially the Muscogee Nation and the Seminoles.[34] Jackson's brutalities included the indiscriminate killing of civilians, even those seeking refuge and shelter; the fashioning of reins for horses using "leather" created from the skin of defeated Muscogees; and the collection of other souvenirs from the bodies of the dead. Violently coerced by this brutal campaign, the Muscogee Nation signed the Treaty of Fort Jackson in 1814, a treaty of Muscogee surrender for which Andrew Jackson was the only US negotiator and which stated that the Muscogee people had lost in an honorable war. The treaty further stated that their loss and subsequent ceding of land was a matter of national justice. Jackson insisted on the Muscogee Nation's complete destruction, a move the Muscogee negotiators had no leverage against or power to negotiate. The treaty obligated them to move west to the remnants of a small portion of their original homeland.[35]

This military career led directly to Jackson's presidency and its defining project: the "elimination of all the Indigenous communities east of the Mississippi through forced removal."[36] As soon as he was elected, Jackson began using his office to displace Indigenous farmers and destroy their towns in the South. The state of Georgia considered his election to be a green light to begin claiming as public land the coveted territory of Cherokee Nation. While the Cherokees took Georgia to court over this and the Supreme Court ultimately ruled in their favor, Jackson ignored the court's decision, insisting that it was unenforceable, as Jackson had control of an army and the court did not. During this time, gold was discovered in Georgia,[37] bringing tens of thousands of gold seekers into the state, who proceeded to squat on Indigenous land, destroy their fields and game parks, loot their towns, and kill their people. Finally, under the authority of the Indian Removal Act of 1830, the Treaty of New Echota was negotiated and signed by a group of Cherokees hand-selected by the US government.[38] This treaty ceded all Cherokee territory to the US in exchange for land in "Indian Territory" in

34. Dunbar-Ortiz, *Indigenous Peoples' History*, 96–97.

35. Dunbar-Ortiz, *Indigenous Peoples' History*, 99–100.

36. Dunbar-Ortiz, *Indigenous Peoples' History*, 98.

37. Note again here the connection between the seizure of land and the quest for profit.

38. Alongside violent irregular warfare, the US also imprisoned Cherokee leaders and closed their printing press in order to coerce the people into signing the treaty. These practices (imprisoning or assassinating leaders, cutting off lines of communication, destabilizing traditional forms of government, etc.) are typical tactics utilized by the US throughout its history to undermine Indigenous sovereignty, create dependency, and ultimately further US interests. For examples, see Dunbar-Ortiz, *Indigenous Peoples' History*, 107–10, 117–61.

the west.[39] Including this treaty, the Jacksonian period saw eighty-six treaties forcing land succession, including removal to Indian Territory, made between Indigenous peoples and the United States. During this time seventy thousand people, nearly all the Indigenous nations east of the Mississippi, were forcibly relocated to Indian Territory by means of bloody irregular warfare and coerced treaties. Thousands died. Other communities chose to flee to Canada and Mexico rather than face forced removal to Indian Territory.[40]

There is a risk here, in naming the particular brutality, bloodlust, and sociopathic quest for land obvious in this account of Jackson's life and presidency, that it is implied that the fault lies mostly with him and his administration or that he was a reprehensible outlier in an otherwise less violent past. It should therefore be emphasized that not only did Jackson not carry out any of his military campaigns or political goals alone, but his actions also grew out of and were sanctioned by the culture around him. As he was born to settlers squatting on Indigenous land, "his life followed the trajectory of continental imperialism" he inherited from his sociopolitical location.[41] The following section explores in more depth the mythology and ideology of this period. For now, it is important to note that Jackson was born into this cultural milieu and should not be thought of as separate from it.

Furthermore, many tie Jackson directly to Thomas Jefferson's explicit philosophy and his goals for the nation, calling Jefferson the thinker and Jackson the doer in the project of "forging populist democracy for full participation in the fruits of colonialism based on opportunity available to Anglo settlers."[42] The Cherokees Jackson forcibly removed had been under pressure to relocate since the time of the Jefferson administration. Jackson simply finally got the job done. Before he was elected president, Jackson's methods of warfare against Indigenous people earned him a commission as major general from President Madison. Jackson was also wildly popular among rural, land-poor, white US

---

39. Dunbar-Ortiz, *Indigenous Peoples' History*, 109–10. The story of the Cherokee signers of this treaty is a complicated and contested one. For another perspective on these "handpicked" Cherokees, see Cherokee writer Rebecca Nagle's analysis of Major Ridge, John Ridge, and their roles in the signing of the treaty on her podcast *This Land*, episode 4, "The Treaty," June 24, 2019, https://crooked.com/podcast-series/this-land/. Here Indian Territory, or Indian Country, refers to the lands (especially Oklahoma) Indigenous peoples were removed to by the US government. More broadly, "Indian Country" is a term used to refer to reservations, informal reservations, dependent Indigenous communities, and allotments or land titles possessed by Indigenous people. See "What Is Indian Country," Tribal Jurisdiction, accessed February 20, 2020, https://tribaljurisdiction.tripod.com/id7.html.

40. Dunbar-Ortiz, *Indigenous Peoples' History*, 110–13.

41. Dunbar-Ortiz, *Indigenous Peoples' History*, 114.

42. Dunbar-Ortiz, *Indigenous Peoples' History*, 107.

citizens, and he was the most popular president the United States had yet to see.[43] It is clear that Jackson exemplified a widespread anti-Indigenous ideology as well as the types of brutal tactics utilized to rid desirable land of Indigenous people in order to make way for US expansion.[44]

Besides using treaty making to formalize violent conquests, the United States also began concerted efforts to establish Indigenous dependency on US benevolence and the US economy very early on. For example, in the early 1800s the Choctaw and Chickasaw peoples of the US Southeast were cut off from trade with the Spanish in Florida, trapping them in the US trade world. In this world they quickly accumulated debt they had no means of paying and thus became beholden to creditors, often agents of the US government, to whom they were forced to cede land in order to pay off debt. The Choctaws ultimately relinquished most of their lands, while the Chickasaws were forced to cede all of their territory north of the Tennessee River. As a result many Chickasaws and Choctaws were plunged into landless poverty, pushing them into participation in the plantation economy and the continual accrual of further debt and dependency.[45]

This result was by no means accidental or unavoidable. Thomas Jefferson, Dunbar-Ortiz reports, not only foresaw this outcome of debt leading to the ceding of Indigenous land but fully encouraged it in the name of US interests.[46] Later, as the US continued to expand westward into the territory of the Plains Nations, economic dependency was intentionally fostered by again cutting the people off from an important resource, this time the buffalo, which had traditionally provided an economic base for these nations. The US Army was directed to destroy this resource, killing tens of millions of buffalo in a few short decades and leaving only a few hundred, not nearly enough to sustain the independent economies of the Plains Nations.[47]

---

43. Dunbar-Ortiz, *Indigenous Peoples' History*, 111, 100, 108–9, 97.

44. For an in depth consideration of Andrew Jackson and his context, see Paul Michael Rogin, *Fathers and Children: Andrew Jackson and the Subjugation of the American Indian* (New York: Knopf, 1975).

45. It is worth noting here that some Indigenous nations, including the Chickasaws and Choctaws, participated in the buying, owning, and selling of enslaved Africans. This history of Indigenous slaveholding, and subsequent relationships between the descendants of these groups, is complex and important but ultimately beyond the scope of this project. See Barbara Krauthamer, *Black Slaves, Indian Masters: Slavery, Emancipation, and Citizenship in the Native American South* (Chapel Hill: University of North Carolina Press, 2013).

46. Dunbar-Ortiz, *Indigenous Peoples' History*, 97.

47. Dunbar-Ortiz, *Indigenous Peoples' History*, 142–43.

Systems of law and government have also been similarly utilized throughout the history of the United States in order to seize Indigenous land, create Indigenous dependency on the United States, and ultimately eliminate as many vestiges of Indigeneity from the nation as possible.[48] While there is not space in this chapter to detail the entire history of the United States' genocidal actions against Indigenous people, a brief exploration of a few examples will help to illuminate how the United States came to control its current territory. Doing so will bring to the fore how the rule of law has taken particular shape in the United States. Proponents of stricter immigration policy and enforcement often cite the protection of the rule of law.[49] Understanding the history of how the rule of law has developed and functioned complicates these arguments. That the rule of law may be important for a functioning society does not mean specific manifestations of the law are necessarily worth protecting. As many have noted, the Holocaust offers a prime example of the ways in which the legal systems of a nation may be used to perpetuate horrors against people, including segments of a nation's own citizens. Yet, there is no need to cross the ocean to find examples of this sort of strategic misuse of law and order. US history offers a surplus of examples of how legal systems can be manipulated in order to protect or promote the interests of some people at the direct expense of others.

Some such US actions came under the guise of help. In the late 1800s wealthy and influential advocates who understood themselves to be "friends of the Indians" developed an assimilation-based policy that was later formulated into an act of Congress by Senator Henry Dawes. The 1887 General Allotment Act (or the Dawes Act) divided up collectively held Native land: reservations where Indigenous survivors of US conquest and expansion had been relocated. Allotment divided this land among the people so that it was no longer commonly held but rather individually owned private property.[50] Senator Dawes argued that

---

48. As we will continue to see going forward, this elimination of Indigeneity, physically violent and otherwise, meets the United Nations definition of genocide.

49. For example, see Mark Amstutz, *Just Immigration: American Policy in Christian Perspective* (Grand Rapids: Eerdmans, 2017); James Hoffmeier, *The Immigration Crisis: Immigrants, Aliens, and the Bible* (Wheaton, IL: Crossway, 2009); "A Restitution-Based Immigration Reform," Evangelical Immigration Table, accessed November 12, 2019, http://evangelicalimmigrationtable.com/a-restitution-based-immigration-reform/; Tal Kopan, "Sessions Criticizes Immigrants' Attorneys before Immigration Judges," CNN, September 10, 2018, https://tinyurl.com/3cphzfpf.

50. It is beyond the scope of this chapter to consider the theological ramifications of sacred land being made into private property, but this is an area worthy of further exploration and study. It is important to keep in mind that what Indigenous communities have lost is not just land to be used but sacred land to which these communities often had deep, specific spiritual and religious connections.

allotment was in the best interests of Native peoples, insisting that the reservation system was socialist and defective because it lacked the ability to motivate people to make their homes better than others'. These communities, he insisted, lacked selfishness, and selfishness was the foundation of civilization. Each Native person needed to own their own land in order for them to progress as people. In reality, allotment succeeded only in significantly reducing the Indigenous land base, cutting it in half. It also established further Indigenous poverty and dependency on the United States. In 1889 territory left over from this allotment process, called "Unassigned Lands" by the US government, became open to US settlers looking for land.[51]

Other land in Indian Territory, however, was not available to be opened up in this way. Because of the terms of the treaties they signed, the five Indigenous nations removed from the South, including the Muscogee Nation and the Cherokee Nation, remained legally sovereign nations inhabiting their own land rather than reservations. Therefore, their territories could not be broken up by allotment. The discovery of oil in this territory heightened US interest in gaining access to it, and so in 1898 Congress passed the Curtis Act. Breaking the terms of the removal treaties signed between the United States and these nations, the Curtis Act "unilaterally deposed the sovereignty of those nations and mandated allotment of their lands."[52] By breaking up these nation's lands and assigning 160-acre allotments to each person, the government again significantly reduced Indigenous land holds as the sum of their allotments totaled less than the land granted to them in their treaties. The remaining land, as with the Dawes Act, was "declared surplus and opened to homesteading."[53] The Dawes and Curtis Acts combined dispossessed Native people of three-quarters of their land base and left many individuals without any land at all. Indian Territory was then considered to be dissolved when Oklahoma became an official state in 1907.[54]

51. Dunbar-Ortiz, *Indigenous Peoples' History*, 157–58. The Dawes Act can most generously be labeled misguided paternalism, an effort to help without taking into account the actual wants and needs of the people being "helped." The end result of freeing up significant portions of Indigenous lands to Anglo settlers, however, suggests that the motives behind the act may have been less altruistic.

52. Dunbar-Ortiz, *Indigenous Peoples' History*, 158.

53. Dunbar-Ortiz, *Indigenous Peoples' History*, 158.

54. Interestingly, in the summer of 2019 the US Supreme Court heard a case, *Carpenter v. Murphy*, in which jurisdiction in an Oklahoma murder case was disputed. Mr. Murphy committed a murder on land that was historically Indigenous land. The question for the court was whether Oklahoma's statehood, declared in 1907, abrogated Indigenous sovereignty in that land. In the summer of 2020, the Court voted 5–4 that a treaty signed in 1832 was still valid, despite Oklahoma's statehood. Therefore, the contested land is still legally Indigenous land. See Allison Herrera, "U.S. Supreme Court Sides with Tribes in Stunning 5-4 Ruling," KGOU, July 9, 2020,

Allotment ended in 1934 with the passing of the Indigenous Reorganization Act, but the land taken was never returned and the people never reimbursed or compensated for their losses.[55]

Other examples include efforts to stamp out Indigenous cultures through forced assimilation, especially in Indigenous boarding schools, where students were punished for speaking their native languages or dressing in ways befitting their traditional cultures. This removal of Indigenous children from their communities meets the United Nations' criteria for genocide.[56] The United States also unilaterally forced US citizenship onto Indigenous peoples, confusing their loyalties, undermining their sovereignty and systems of government, and making them legally beholden to the obligations of US citizenship.[57] It becomes evident, then, that the United States gained its present territory through the combined means of violent irregular warfare, coerced treaties, the manipulation of systems of law and government, and the violation of the terms of the treaties signed between the government and Indigenous peoples. The United States exists as it does today because of invasion and settler colonialism.

This exploration of US settler colonialism and the seizure of Indigenous land may seem out of place in a consideration of immigration ethics. It is, however, directly relevant on several fronts. This will become more evident in later chapters but warrants highlighting here. First, the ideologies that drove this genocidal conquest of the continent are deeply embedded in US identity, and this has had a profound impact on the way immigration policy and border enforcement has developed, as we will see in chapter 2. It is important to highlight the ways

---

https://www.kgou.org/politics-and-government/2020-07-09/u-s-supreme-court-sides-with-tribes-in-stunning-5-4-ruling; Adam Liptak, "Is Half of Oklahoma an Indian Reservation? The Supreme Court Sifts the Merits," *New York Times*, November 27, 2018, https://www.nytimes.com/2018/11/27/us/politics/oklahoma-indian-territory-supreme-court.html; Rebecca Nagle, *This Land* (podcast), June 3–July 22, 2019, https://crooked.com/podcast-series/this-land/.

55. Dunbar-Ortiz, *Indigenous Peoples' History*, 158–59. This is not the only time the US passed laws that broke treaties made with Indigenous nations in this way. For example, the 1862 Homestead Act and Morrill Act were also US land grabs that similarly broke the terms of treaties (see Dunbar-Ortiz, *Indigenous Peoples' History*, 140).

56. Dunbar-Ortiz, *Indigenous Peoples' History*, 151.

57. M. Annette Jaimes, "Federal Indian Identification Policy: A Usurpation of Indigenous Sovereignty in North America," in Jaimes, *State of Native America*, 127–28. The effects of coercive citizenship here prove to be ultimately quite similar to those of exclusion from citizenship. The power dynamics are the same. Coercive belonging and exclusion from belonging are both tools that function to keep the control of resources in certain hands and out of others. Whether people are being coerced into relinquishing resources because they are citizens who must contribute to the nation's good or being denied access to resources based on a lack of citizenship, the outcome is the same. Some benefit while others pay the price.

this ideology affected and continues to affect not only those who come to the United States from abroad but also those whose presence on this continent predates European invasion.[58] Second, the practices highlighted here, such as irregular warfare and tactics meant to destabilize governments, become hallmarks of US foreign policy and directly affect migration to the United States. The period of US history explored in this section represents a defining moment for this country, its military, and the relationship between the military and US economic interests. I will also address this legacy in more depth in chapter 2. Third, Dunbar-Ortiz writes that the birth of the United States was caused and defined by "the colonialist settler-state's willingness to eliminate whole civilizations of people in order to possess their land."[59] This will continue to be an important theme going forward. This book argues that the United States has acted and continues to act in such a way as to make itself and its citizens deeply culpable in the suffering and instability of many people, and that this culpability establishes relationships of responsibility including but not limited to the sharing of US resources by way of more open immigration policies. Therefore, establishing these patterns in US history is an important element of the central argument.

Fourth, making moral choices concretely requires an adequate understanding of the context in which those decisions are being made, including the historical events that lead to the present context. To this end, understanding the context of immigration in the United States requires an understanding of US history. This history "cannot be understood and accounted for without acknowledging the genocide that the United States committed against the Native nations and enslaved Africans, both of whose descendants survive in US-claimed boundaries under conditions that constitute genocide."[60] How precisely the United States came to be in control of its borders is extremely relevant for a consideration of immigration ethics. We must remember well in order to act prudently and justly.

This leads to the final purpose of this exploration of history. The history of this continent ought to significantly reframe the national conversation about immigration into the United States. Understanding how the United States utilized brutal military force and coercion to establish its current borders raises many questions about what right the government now has to enforce these borders. If US claims to this land are morally tenuous, as I argue in this section, what

58. This ideology also affected and continues to affect those who were brought here by force. Later in this chapter and in the next, I will also address the connections between immigration, US mythology, and the treatment of enslaved Africans, their descendants, and other Black people in the US.

59. Dunbar-Ortiz, *Indigenous Peoples' History*, 96.

60. Dunbar-Ortiz, *Not "A Nation of Immigrants,"* 28.

moral authority does the US government have over who can and cannot be here? This book does not ultimately argue that the United States ought (or ought not) to cede its authority over its borders entirely.[61] Rather, the point is to unsettle the certainty with which politicians, scholars, and citizens often consider the right of a state to control its borders. Understanding the history of conquest on this continent destabilizes this argument, and it is a reality with which any argument for strong US border control must reckon. It is also important to note the ways in which systems of law and government were manipulated and weaponized against Indigenous peoples in order to secure US interests (particularly the interests of the wealthy). This highlights why commitments to upholding the rule of law require further scrutiny.

The way history is told matters a great deal.[62] Dunbar-Ortiz insists that the formation of a more accurate historical narrative

> requires rethinking the consensual national narrative. That [current national] narrative is wrong or deficient, not in its facts, dates, or details but rather in its essence. Inherent in the myth we've been taught is an embrace of settler colonialism and genocide. The myth persists, not for lack of free speech or poverty of information but rather for an absence of motivations to ask questions that challenge the core of the scripted narrative of the origin story.[63]

She goes on to argue that "awareness of the settler-colonialist context of U.S. history writing is essential if one is to avoid the laziness of the default position and the trap of an unconscious belief in Manifest Destiny."[64] Unmasking and shifting away from this default position is precisely what this chapter aims at, and the brief history of US settler colonialism presented in this section is one piece of that puzzle. This retrieval of a fuller US history helps to establish a more accurate narrative and bring to light the responsibilities this history imparts on US citizens and the government. With this in mind, it is therefore to the mythological, unconscious belief in manifest destiny to which we now turn.

61. The manner in which Indigenous rights to this land ought to be honored is an ongoing discussion. A full consideration of this topic is beyond the scope of this book, as it would require a much more in-depth examination of US settler colonialism, the history of treaties (and the breaking of treaties), Indigenous sovereignty, and the desires and interests of modern Indigenous peoples than this project can provide. This is an important conversation that intersects with immigration and so is raised but not fully explored here.

62. I will consider this more fully in chapter 3.

63. Dunbar-Ortiz, *Indigenous Peoples' History*, 2.

64. Dunbar-Ortiz, *Indigenous Peoples' History*, 6.

Manifest Destiny, the Myth of the Frontier, and the Forging of US Identity

Early European colonial invasion of the Americas wrested control of the land from Indigenous peoples. The result was that the previously cultivated landscape became densely forested, giving it an appearance of being wildly untamed and underdeveloped when later colonial settlers arrived. These later settlers were often also unable to recognize the Indigenous methods of land cultivation and management that they did witness. These realities led them to conclude that the people native to the continent were unskilled at using the land to its full potential.[65] As Dunbar-Ortiz writes,

> In the founding myth of the United States, the colonists acquired a vast expanse of land from a scattering of benighted peoples who were hardly using it—an unforgivable offense to the Puritan work ethic. The historical record is clear, however, that European colonists shoved aside large networks of small and large nations whose governments, commerce, arts, sciences, agriculture, technologies, theologies, philosophies, and institutions were intricately developed, nations that maintained sophisticated relations with one another and with the environments that supported them.[66]

The United States' founding and violent westward expansion, as outlined in the previous section, was legitimized through the creation and maintenance of this type of foundational mythology. This mythology has roots in European colonialist narratives and the Protestant work ethic[67] but takes on a distinctive form in the land that became the United States. It relies on this notion that the land was in some fundamental way virgin: uncultivated, underused, and very lightly populated by uncivilized groups of Native people.[68] The previous section highlighted the ways in which the doctrine of discovery was used to legitimize European claims to the continent, resulting in a genocidal campaign of conquest. The idea that land could be claimed because its inhabitants were

---

65. Dunbar-Ortiz, *Indigenous Peoples' History*, 45.

66. Dunbar-Ortiz, *Indigenous Peoples' History*, 46. Moreover, far from taming an uncultivated virgin landscape, European settlers benefited from what existed through their appropriation of the ready-made roads, cultivated farmlands, and knowledge of the land provided by captured Natives. See also Adam Gomez, "Deus Vult: John L. O'Sullivan, Manifest Destiny, and American Democratic Messianism," *American Political Thought* 1, no. 2 (2012): 236–62.

67. See Max Weber, *The Protestant Ethic and the Spirit of Capitalism* (London: Routledge, 2001).

68. Dunbar-Ortiz, *Indigenous Peoples' History*, 45–47.

non-Christian or resistant to Christianity connects directly to this notion that the land was being improperly utilized by uncivilized Native nations. Particular understandings of civilization, religion, and the land are deeply intertwined in US founding mythology.[69]

The United States is unique in that it is one of the only nations founded on the biblical notion of God's covenant people (or a Christian appropriation thereof).[70] The early settlers of the American colonies understood themselves to be a new Israel gifted a new promised land by God. Despite this religious self-understanding, the United States is not a theocracy but rather understands itself to be a nation of faithful citizens who freely join together to form a godly society, pledging commitment to each other and their God, who will in turn ensure prosperity in the new land. While this does not always manifest in explicitly religious ways throughout all of US history, there is often a prevailing sense of providence, destiny, or exceptionalism directly tied to this idea. Dunbar-Ortiz roots this notion in Calvinist theology and the idea of a God-ordained elect.[71] While it is not possible in Calvinism to be certain whether someone is a member of this elect, there are outward signs such as good fortune and material wealth that indicate one is elect. Bad fortune or poverty are therefore signs of not being of the elect. This plays well into a colonialist mindset, particularly when paired with an inherited sense of the doctrine of discovery, as the successful conquest of

69. This discussion of the development of US identity and mythology intersects with and relies on a larger academic discussion of civil religion in the United States. The contemporary discourse on these ideas has considered a variety of angles and questions, including how to think about this so-called American civil religion, what its contours and origins are, whether it is helpful or harmful to the nation, and what the relationship between churches, theology, and civil religion is or ought to be. This chapter is concerned with the development of US mythology that shaped the nation's identity and practice. This mythology and its impact can be considered a form or part of US civil religion. See Robert N. Bellah, "Civil Religion in America," *Daedalus* 96, no. 1 (1967): 1–21; James Mathisen, "Twenty Years after Bellah: Whatever Happened to American Civil Religion?," *Sociological Analysis* 50, no. 2 (1989): 129–46, https://doi.org/10.2307/3710983; Bellah, "Comment: [Twenty Years after Bellah: Whatever Happened to American Civil Religion?]," *Sociological Analysis* 50, no. 2 (1989): 147, https://doi.org/10.2307/3710984; Phillip E. Hammond, "The Sociology of American Civil Religion: A Bibliographical Essay," *Sociological Analysis* 37, no. 2 (1976): 169–82, https://doi.org/10.2307/3709692; E. Harold Breitenberg, "To Tell the Truth: Will the Real Public Theology Please Stand Up?," *Journal of the Society of Christian Ethics* 23, no. 2 (2003): 55–96, https://doi.org/10.5840/jsce20032325; Philip Gorski, *American Covenant: A History of Civil Religion from the Puritans to the Present* (Princeton, NJ: Princeton University Press, 2019); Rogers M. Smith, *Civic Ideals: Conflicting Visions of Citizenship in U.S. History* (New Haven, CT: Yale University Press, 1997).

70. Dunbar-Ortiz, *Indigenous Peoples' History*, 46.

71. Dunbar-Ortiz, *Indigenous Peoples' History*, 48.

(especially darker-skinned[72]) Native people can be viewed as a natural outcome of one group being elect and the other being marked for damnation. The founders of the colonies had a deep sense of being placed in a providential moment, an opportunity for God-ordained success, and the founders of the United States fell right in line with this ideology.[73]

This sense of providence and of success ordained and granted by God led the settlers and the early United States to believe that it was not only their right but their duty to take over the continent. The result is a strong and prevailing belief that Euro-American settlers had a God-given right to the land and a mission to conquer and civilize it. This mentality is perhaps best exemplified by John L. O'Sullivan, who coined the phrase "manifest destiny" to refer to his belief that God's revealed plan for the United States was for it to spread across the continent. Rooted in a Euro-American tradition of thinking on providence, O'Sullivan considered the United States to be the hand of God on earth. His work emphasized the moral superiority of the United States and the sin that existed beyond its borders. Importantly, for him the United States' sinlessness was based on its perfect system of government.[74] O'Sullivan believed that while the United States was not perfect (he in fact devoted significant time to advocating various social reforms, such as the abolition of the death penalty), it was also not sinful. Sin, for him, was what violated the holy democratic principle, because democracy was a godly form of government. Therefore the United States could be viewed as religiously pure (sinless) because of its governmental structure, even if it was in need of social reforms. This decoupling of religious and moral purity meant that he could view the United States as imperfect in practical matters but still maintain that its system of democratic government was "spiritually unstained" and a "radical break with world history."[75]

Importantly, O'Sullivan believed that democracy, like religious faith, was something that must be held, not simply believed in. While he purported to believe in a basic equality between all people, O'Sullivan insisted that certain people were capable of actively embracing democracy while others were not. True equality in practice, he argued, depended on one's ability to be truly free, and not all people had that ability. Enslaved (and formerly enslaved) people, Indigenous

72. Dark skin was also seen as a sign of damnation (Dunbar-Ortiz, *Indigenous Peoples' History*, 49).

73. Dunbar-Ortiz, *Indigenous Peoples' History*, 47–49.

74. Gomez, "Deus Vult: John L. O'Sullivan," 239–40.

75. Gomez, "Deus Vult: John L. O'Sullivan," 240, 250–52. This notion of the US having radically broken from history (and especially from the sins of history) contributes to American exceptionalism, and its legacy diminishes US ability to conceive of itself as culpable for the sins of history.

people, and Mexicans were among those O'Sullivan believed to be incapable of such freedom and self-legislation, and therefore he believed that these were peoples rightly governed by those who had more democratic capacity, even if they did not consent to be so governed.[76] Basically, he believed that "to hold the democratic principle bestows equality with those who can grasp it, while granting superiority, moral and otherwise, over those who cannot or will not."[77] It was therefore the holy duty of the United States to spread freedom and democracy wherever it could, by means of coercion if necessary.[78] For O'Sullivan, because this system of governance was so radically different from others, its mission of expansion was extremely important. In this worldview, enemies of the United States, for example those who oppose US expansion into their territory, become enemies of God and are dealt with as such.[79]

O'Sullivan's tying the will of the United States so firmly to the will of God in this way finds its roots in the Puritan belief that their settlements in the New World would transform everything, the whole planet.[80] This sense of mission and providence, while not always so explicit as O'Sullivan makes it, is pervasive throughout US history. The United States has been shaped by people who "believed (or pretended to believe) that they were a new chosen people in a new promised land. They believed (or pretended to believe) that their destiny was to spawn the freest, happiest, richest commonwealth in the world. They believed (or pretended to believe) that their history was a continuing revelation of God's purpose."[81] The legacy of this cannot be understated. Political scientist Adam Gomez

76. Gomez, Gomez, "Deus Vult: John L. O'Sullivan," 240–41, 247–48.

77. Gomez, "Deus Vult: John L. O'Sullivan," 250.

78. Note here the connections between O'Sullivan's thinking and the doctrine of discovery. Both justify conquest and coercion by insisting that some people are suited for governing and controlling land and others are less suited for such things. That only certain types of people are suited to US democratic ideals will continue to be an important factor in immigration discourse and policy. I explore this more later in this chapter and the next.

79. Gomez, "Deus Vult: John L. O'Sullivan," 240, 250–52.

80. Gomez, "Deus Vult: John L. O'Sullivan," 238.

81. Walter A. McDougall, *The Tragedy of U.S. Foreign Policy: How America's Civil Religion Betrayed the National Interest* (New Haven, CT: Yale University Press, 2016), 72–73. The caveat that those who shaped the US may have "pretended to believe" that they were aligned with God's purpose for the world is important. There is some debate over whether motivations such as racism and religious mission were the primary factors driving US behavior regarding atrocities such as chattel slavery and Indigenous genocide, or whether practical motivations such as a desire for wealth and power lead to the development of convenient supporting ideologies. Whichever motivations were primary, racism and religious exceptionalism have left an indelible mark on US history and self-understanding. I will consider the long-term effect of this more fully in chapter 2.

writes, "The belief that the United States has an exceptional moral standing in world history and an obligation to spread democracy and the experience of international politics through the lens of a conflict between good and evil remain prominent in contemporary American politics" across party lines.[82] Manifest destiny has in this way remained pervasively influential in the Euro-American psyche,[83] and it has profoundly shaped US self-understanding.

"Playing Indian": Dealing with the Contradictions of Democratic Colonialism

Manifest destiny paints the colonization of the Americas and the westward expansion of US borders as both inevitable and justified. According to this narrative, the United States had a preordained shape and size that it has since reached in fulfillment of its destiny.[84] The preceding section outlined some of the ways in which the United States went about expanding its borders. While it was a force against which no amount of Indigenous resistance was able to gain much large-scale, sustainable traction,[85] in reality the way the United States reached its current borders was in no way inevitable or preordained. Rather, US imperialism was achieved largely by small groups of counterinsurgents made up of squatter frontiersmen, backed up by the US Army and the government (by way of law and treaty), running roughshod over the continent in search of land and profit.[86] The conquest of the continent was brought about by intentional, imperialist actions, first by European colonists and later by the fledgling US government and its citizens. Manifest destiny "normalizes the successive invasions and occupations of Indigenous nations and Mexico as not being colonialist or imperialist, rather simply ordained progress."[87]

It is very important to the formation and maintenance of the United States and to US self-understanding that manifest destiny cast otherwise overtly

82. Gomez, "Deus Vult: John L. O'Sullivan," 255.

83. Gomez, "Deus Vult: John L. O'Sullivan," 256.

84. Dunbar-Ortiz, *Indigenous Peoples' History*, 118.

85. Dunbar-Ortiz highlights the many ways Indigenous peoples resisted colonization, as well as the ways in which their resistance, while it generally did not succeed in fending off US seizure of their land, makes possible the continued existence of modern Indigenous peoples and their own resistance movements (*Indigenous Peoples' History*, 129). See also Steven Charleston, "Articulating a Native American Theological Theory," in *Full Circle: Constructing Native Christian Theology*, ed. Steven Charleston and Elaine A. Robinson (Minneapolis: Augsburg Fortress, 2015), 12.

86. Dunbar-Ortiz, *Indigenous Peoples' History*, 220.

87. Dunbar-Ortiz, *Indigenous Peoples' History*, 118.

imperialist actions in this way. Most often, when people think of US identity or the nation's founding values, it is the high ideals of the Declaration of Independence or the Constitution that are likely to come to mind. In reality, however, freedom, equality, and justice are standards up to which this nation has rarely lived. The idea that US identity is based in these ideals becomes difficult to argue convincingly in a country that has committed genocide, has enslaved millions, and to this day systematically denies the basic rights and dignity of significant portions of even its citizen population. This tension between the purported ideals and the actual practices of the United States is not new. As Dunbar-Ortiz writes, "Democracy, equality, and equal rights do not fit well with dominance of one race by another, much less with genocide, settler colonialism, and empire."[88]

The United States, for all its pontificating about the importance of democracy, equality, and justice, had ambitions for size, influence, and wealth, as well as an exaggerated sense of its own importance, inherited from its European forebears. Like the British before them, the founders of the United States had imperialistic designs. The difference is that US imperialism was framed, in the words of Thomas Jefferson, as an "empire for liberty," imperialism with a higher moral purpose.[89] The tension between these ideals required the development of a mythology that could reconcile rhetoric and reality, liberty and empire. Historian Paul Michael Rogin also identifies this tension, arguing that the origin of the United States is one rife with sinful "acts of force and fraud," noting that statesmen of the time were "preoccupied" with the problem of how to reconcile this reality with democratic ideals.[90] O'Sullivan's insistence that some people were incapable of true freedom represents one attempt to reckon with this problem, but his is far from the only attempt.

Dunbar-Ortiz calls the process through which Euro-American settlers sought to reconcile this tension "settler self-indigenizing."[91] Through this self-indigenizing came the creation of "a new people born of the merger of the best of both worlds, the Native and the European."[92] She names James Fenimore Cooper as one of the "initial scribes" of this mythological new race of people, and she argues that his novel *The Last of the Mohicans* became the official origin story of that new race. In the novel, Dunbar-Ortiz writes,

---

88. Dunbar-Ortiz, *Indigenous Peoples' History*, 103.

89. Dunbar-Ortiz, *Not "A Nation of Immigrants,"* 18–19.

90. Rogin, *Fathers and Children*, 3–9.

91. Dunbar-Ortiz, *Not "A Nation of Immigrants,"* 35.

92. Dunbar-Ortiz, *Not "A Nation of Immigrants,"* 36.

> Cooper devised a fictional counterpoint of celebration to the dark underbelly of the new American nation—the birth of something new and wondrous, literally, the US American race, a new people born of the merger between the best of both worlds, the Native and the European, not biological merger but something more ephemeral, involving the dissolving of the Indian. In the novel, Cooper has the last of the "noble" and "pure" Natives die off as nature would have it, with the "last Mohican" handing the continent over to Hawkeye, the nativized settler, his adopted son. This convenient fantasy could be seen as quaint at best if it were not for its deadly staying power. Cooper had much to do with creating the US origin myth to which generations of historians have dedicated themselves.[93]

In reality, of course, there was no "last noble Native," because Indigenous people continue to survive and live on this continent to this day. They never handed over the land in any definitive way and in fact continue to contest the United States' claim to the land. US expansion across the continent was far less inevitable and far more violent than Cooper suggests. The notion that Euro-Americans lacked some sort of fundamental historical connection to the land and that their conquest of it was a serious violation of their purported ideals, however, led to precisely this sort of rewriting of history in order to paint a happier picture of how the United States came to be and to claim a more Indigenous connection to the land.

Yankton Dakota historian Philip Deloria argues that this tension is at the very heart of US identity. Appropriating Indigenous identity, as exemplified in the choice of dress during the Boston Tea Party or in the activities of groups such as Tammany societies, became a popular way of wrestling with this tension, erasing real Indigenous people and replacing them with fictitious, idealized stereotypes. This allowed Euro-Americans to participate in Indigeneity, however false, and take on a sense of real American-ness while simultaneously explaining away the atrocities committed against real Indigenous people and using them as a foil against which civilization could be defined.[94] Deloria writes, "Savage Indians served Americans as oppositional figures against whom one might find a civilized national Self. Coded as freedom, however, wild Indianness proved equally attractive, setting up a 'have-the-cake-and-eat-it-too' dialectic of

---

93. Rogin, *Fathers and Children*, 104.

94. Philip Joseph Deloria, *Playing Indian* (New Haven, CT: Yale University Press, 1998), 10–70. See also Klingle, "Frontier Ghosts along the Urban Pacific Slope."

simultaneous desire and repulsion."[95] Similarly, Rogin argues that in attempting to reconcile with the violence of their conquest and expansion on the American continent, Euro-Americans began to claim Indigenous people as their brethren and "inner double," arguing that many of the nation's most important families had Indigenous ancestry of some kind and putting on a mask of Indigeneity by way of costumes and cultural appropriation.[96] All of this took place alongside the casting of actual Indigenous people as lesser in some way, seeing them as helpless benefactors of US benevolence and superiority or as incapable of utilizing the continent to its full potential.[97]

This mythology was picked up by countless historians and writers and pervades US consciousness to this day. It includes an almost complete erasure of Indigenous peoples except to cast them as foils for US civilization, incompetent villains against whom the settlers had to struggle in order to win rightful control of the continent, or as mythical ancestors who helped shape national identity and then handed the continent over to Anglo settlers. From this, American exceptionalism is bred, through either the belief that a unique form of civilized life was carved out in this struggle or the belief that success in this struggle was divinely granted to a chosen people. Either way, colonization becomes both less and more than it is: less brutal and violent, more destined and profound, full of adventure.[98] Novelist Wallace Stegner captured this well when he wrote of the US frontier: "With a continent to take over and Manifest Destiny to goad us, we could not have avoided being footloose."[99] Bloody, imperialist conquest becomes the footloose wandering of a people destined to explore. Stories such as *The Last of the Mohicans* were "instrumental in nullifying guilt related to genocide," setting a pattern that influences US self understanding to this day.[100]

95. Deloria, *Playing Indian*, 3. See also Klingle, "Frontier Ghosts along the Urban Pacific Slope," 121–22.

96. Rogin, *Fathers and Children*, 5.

97. Rogin, *Fathers and Children*, 4, 6, 8. Note again the connection to both O'Sullivan and the doctrine of discovery, as well as the glossing over of how precisely Indigenous nations came to be poor and indebted.

98. Dunbar-Ortiz, *Indigenous Peoples' History*, 103–5.

99. Dunbar-Ortiz, *Indigenous Peoples' History*, 105.

100. Dunbar-Ortiz, *Indigenous Peoples' History*, 105–7.

The Frontier: Drawing Battle Lines and Creating Enemies

For US Latino systematic theologian Roberto Goizueta, the United States' founding mythology is all about the frontier. Like Dunbar-Ortiz, he is interested in uncovering the unconscious mythology that drives US self-understanding and action, both historically and today. Goizueta argues that while Western civilization has produced indisputable literary, intellectual, and human-rights advances, underlying those positive contributions to the world there are "disturbing signs of another reality," evident in everything from the corpses of the Shoah to the existence of permanent underclasses of people.[101] In order to understand this other reality, we must understand the frontier myth, which Goizueta calls "the foundational myth of modernity" and "our creation myth."[102] Fundamentally, the frontier myth is about conquest. The frontier describes what is at the edge of our progress, where civilization meets savagery.[103] The idea that what lies beyond US borders must be made civilized was part of what drove the nation ever more westward, trampling over people and planet in its way.[104]

Notably, this casting of US identity had an impact on the way the US War for Independence was fought. Generally speaking, groups fighting wars for independence from colonizing forces include and work together with Indigenous people. In the Mexican war for independence, for example, a majority of the insurgents were Indigenous people. The US War for Independence is in stark contrast to this trend; US independence fighters saw Indigenous nations as enemies and targeted them as such.[105] For their part, most Indigenous nations concluded that a colonizing power that was an ocean away was preferable to the settlers fighting for independence on their land. They largely supported the

---

101. Roberto Goizueta, "Beyond the Frontier Myth," in *Hispanic Christian Thought at the Dawn of the 21st Century*, ed. Justo J. González et al. (Nashville: Abingdon, 2005), 150.

102. Goizueta, "Beyond the Frontier Myth," 152.

103. Due to the modern misappropriation of the word *savage*, my use of it here may require justification. Today it is generally used to denote an action which is particularly ruthless or for which a person shows no remorse. Many Indigenous people decry this usage as failing to acknowledge the history of the word, used against Indigenous people to dehumanize them and normalize their violent removal from the land. I use it here in order to highlight that original usage and how this casting of Indigenous people as savage played into foundational US mythology and self-understanding.

104. Goizueta, "Beyond the Frontier Myth," 152.

105. Dunbar-Ortiz, *Indigenous Peoples' History*, 120.

British efforts.[106] Hence, from the earliest moments, US identity was built in contrast to and in a state of enmity with Indigenous peoples. The United States has always defined itself as a civilization in contrast to the original peoples of this land.[107]

Goizueta is not alone in identifying the importance of the frontier in US history. Rogin considers it foundational to US identity that the nation was "continually beginning again on the frontier," and he notes that "as it expanded across the continent, it killed, removed, and drove into extinction one tribe after another."[108] Ted Morgan similarly identifies the frontier as a "battle line" that shaped the earliest decades of the United States and argues that "the idea of a great expanse of land waiting to be filled is central to the spirit of America."[109] He considers this availability of space, so different from crowded Europe, as a fundamental inspiration for Euro-American ideals of democracy and equality. It was only in a place where such availability of land existed and anyone (anyone white and male, that is) could access it, he argues, that these ideals could have any real foothold. Of course, this necessitated the removal of the former inhabitants of the land. Indigenous removal, therefore, became part and parcel of Euro-American freedom and democracy.[110]

It is important to highlight that for frontier mythology, what lies beyond the borders of society (or "civilization") is something savage. At the edges of civilization lies that which is dark (civilization, after all, being fundamentally white), something wild and untamed, fundamentally lesser than those on the inside. At best, it needs to be brought into the fold and assimilated into civilization. At worst, it is a danger that must be conquered, pushed out, or kept at bay at all costs.[111] US history is full of examples of both. Dunbar-Ortiz uses similar language of "subjugation or expulsion" to define the goals of violence and irregular warfare against Indigenous peoples in US history.[112]

---

106. Dunbar-Ortiz, *Indigenous Peoples' History*, 74–76, 79, 81.

107. For an in-depth look at the various frontiers and borderlands of the young US and their role in shaping national identity, see Andrew K. Frank and Glenn A. Crothers, eds., *Borderland Narratives: Negotiation and Accommodation in North America's Contested Spaces, 1500–1850* (Gainesville: University Press of Florida, 2017).

108. Rogin, *Fathers and Children*, 3.

109. Ted Morgan, *Wilderness at Dawn: The Settling of the North American Continent* (New York: Simon & Schuster, 1993), 12–13.

110. Morgan, *Wilderness at Dawn*, 482–88.

111. Goizueta, "Beyond the Frontier Myth," 153.

112. Dunbar-Ortiz, *Indigenous Peoples' History*, 71.

It is also worth clarifying that while frontier mythology has long influenced US thinking about and actions at concrete geographical borders, this distinction between civilization and savagery is ultimately not about geography. Rather, it is about how the United States has understood and developed its sense of national identity and belonging. These boundaries of belonging have long been drawn along the lines of socially constructed notions of whiteness. Those who can be considered white can belong to US civilization. Those who cannot be considered white cannot. Philosopher José Jorge Mendoza notes that one's ability to be fully included in US society and membership has long been tied to a distinction between white and nonwhite—from the Naturalization Act of 1790, which explicitly stipulated that people who were not white could not become naturalized US citizens, through the Civil War amendments that opened up naturalization to Black people without ridding the law of the whiteness clause, and beyond.[113]

Recall O'Sullivan's argument that the United States was God's hand on earth, tasked with enacting divine will by spreading democracy and governing those who were deemed incapable of governing themselves well. This, along with his subsequent casting of those opposed to the United States as enemies of God, is directly related to the frontier mythology Goizueta is identifying. According to the frontier myth worldview, "to be civilized is to extend the frontier, to expand, to seek new opportunities, to dominate, to conquer."[114] It is how one acts virtuously, properly. For O'Sullivan, it is how the will of God is lived out. Those who are opposed to this stand not only in the way of progress and civilization but in contrast to God. This is in part how people end up willing to massacre others for the simple crime of already being on a desired area of land. Everything that lies beyond a narrow understanding of proper civilization, everything that is beyond US borders, is fundamentally other, less than human, in need of being made

113. José Jorge Mendoza, "Illegal: White Supremacy and Immigration Status," in *The Ethics and Politics of Immigration: Core Issues and Emerging Trends*, ed. Alex Sager (Lanham, MD: Rowman & Littlefield International, 2016), 208–19. Mendoza goes on to argue that this has created a state of "perpetual foreignness" that hangs over people who are categorized into nonwhiteness and thus barred from full inclusion, even if the law no longer explicitly ties membership to whiteness. Moreover, he argues that use of the term *illegal* to refer to undocumented (or potentially undocumented) migrants carries on this raced conception of belonging as proper only to those who are white (207).

114. Roxanne Dunbar-Ortiz, *Indigenous Peoples' History*, 153. It should be noted that of course such acts of conquering aggression from the other side of the frontier, from the "savage," would not be read in this view as a legitimate act of civilization but as a hostile invasion. One cannot help but to see that race plays an important part in how civilization is defined. It is only proper for white people to expand and conquer in this way, only a sign or act of civilization when done by those already defined as civilized.

useful through assimilation or enslavement, or kept safely beyond the nation's ever-expanding borders.

Frontier myth, like manifest destiny, casts white settlers in the role of just conquerors, taking control of what was rightfully theirs, defending certain God-given goods understood to exist in their civilization and in their very identities, and subduing or eliminating threats to God's plan on earth. Sin becomes easier to commit and harder to notice in this environment because the sinful activities of genocide and conquest are cast as the right thing to do. Truly good choices are harder to make because the wrong choices—complicity with or outright participation in evil—are understood as good and right, as God-ordained.

Sin as Social: Analytical Tools for Understanding Culpability

This understanding of manifest destiny, frontier myth, and their roles in the formation of the United States can be further illuminated by viewing sin as deeply social. Theologian and ethicist Kristin Heyer describes social sin as that which "encompasses the unjust structures, distorted consciousness, and collective actions and inaction that facilitate injustice and dehumanization."[115] This view of sin takes up the Pauline and Johannine understanding of sin as a condition rather than as discrete acts of disobedience and highlights the ways "the social situation of original sin" establishes a milieu in which individual sinfulness becomes more likely.[116] That is to say, it attends to the more nonvoluntary nature of some sin, the way people become conditioned to certain attitudes and behaviors, affecting individual agency.[117] Catholic theologian Gregory Baum notes that while sinful social structures cannot be separated from the concrete, sinful actions of individuals, there is also an "unconscious, nonvoluntary, quasi-automatic dimension of social sin."[118] What Baum and Heyer are articulating is the reality that humans participate in ideologies and behaviors that can properly be called sin without necessarily consciously intending to sin or to cause harm to others.

It can perhaps not be said that social sin *causes* individual sin directly. Rather, a certain atmosphere or environment is created in which individual sin is harder

115. Kristin Heyer, "Social Sin and Immigration: Good Fences Make Bad Neighbors," *TS* 71 (2010): 412, https://doi.org/10.1177/004056391007100207.

116. Heyer, "Social Sin and Immigration," 414.

117. Heyer, "Social Sin and Immigration," 418.

118. Gregory Baum, "Structures of Sin," in *The Logic of Solidarity: Commentaries on Pope John Paul II's Encyclical on Social Concern*, ed. Gregory Baum and Robert Ellsberg (Maryknoll, NY: Orbis, 1989), 115.

to avoid and good choices are more difficult to make.[119] This environment forms and is formed by the ideologies and habits that shape people's consciousness: the worldviews, narratives, and frameworks for understanding that so influence a person's approach to the world that they act sinfully, more or less without consciously intending to, and thus shape the way they think and act. Social sin is self-justifying; it happens because the environment is such that we have been convinced (or have convinced ourselves) that what we are doing is not only not wrong, but it is the right choice, proper and good.[120] Sinful structures legitimate themselves by building a culture in which the harms caused by our systems and structures are hidden, masked by good intentions or practicality.[121] When we understand or view our situation or our world in a particular way, certain responses or actions seem obvious. Social sin can convince us we are acting correctly, obscuring our sin and cutting us off from repentance and growth.

Furthermore, understanding social sin can help us articulate another angle of the relationship between the individual and the social. Not only are individuals made more prone to sin by sinful structures, but we can also see that these sinful structures are upheld precisely by these individuals participating in certain ideologies or behaviors. Sinful structures work to create and uphold sinful ideologies, and sinful ideologies also create and uphold structural sin. In this way, social sin is self-sustaining and self-perpetuating. Sinful structures do not, however, operate without individuals who buy into these ideologies, who support them in direct and indirect ways.

It is important to highlight that social sin does not deny the existence of individual sin and intentionality. Rather, social sin seeks to highlight that individual intention is not the whole story, that there is much more going on to which we will have to attend if we want to offer a sufficient response to the situation of immigration in the United States. It may be illuminating to return briefly to Andrew Jackson. As argued above, Jackson was by no means an outlier but rather a product of and participant in a larger anti-Indigenous culture. His predilection for conquest and land seizure by any means necessary did not arise in a vacuum. Rather, we can think of everything we have been outlining thus far about US history as a situation of rampant social sin, baked into the very foundations of this nation and certainly affecting how Jackson saw and understood the world and his role in it vis-à-vis Indigenous people and the land. To say Jackson's "life followed the trajectory of imperialism"[122] is to say that his life fell in line with the

119. Heyer, "Social Sin and Immigration," 419.

120. Baum, "Structures of Sin," 114.

121. Heyer, "Social Sin and Immigration," 113–14.

122. Dunbar-Ortiz, *Indigenous Peoples' History*, 114.

situation of social sin into which he was born. He was predisposed by his birth and his upbringing to view Indigenous peoples as inferior and to view the land as the rightful, God-ordained property of the United States. This outlook was further fostered during his military career when, far from being questioned on his violent military tactics, he was lauded for his successful campaigns against Indigenous nations. Moreover, his participation in this sinful way of viewing the world further perpetuated precisely that worldview, especially as he continued to gain power and influence. Recall that his election to president green-lighted Georgia's seizure of Cherokee land. This was sin fostering sin. From the position of president, he was able to further inscribe this sinful ideology into US law with the Indian Removal Act. This is how social sin works. It both encourages and is caused by the actions and views of people like Jackson as well as every person who, while possibly less violent than he or even in disagreement with his policies, implicitly or explicitly sanctioned his actions and the worldview in which they were rooted. Thus, while Jackson is guilty of egregious sins for which he is responsible as an individual, his individual actions are not the whole story and need to be fully understood in the context of the sin that they were caused by as well as the further sin they caused.

Recall also the formation of the US military on the basis of methods of irregular warfare. Dunbar-Ortiz reports that this extreme violence fostered more widespread racism against Indigenous people. While those who fought in these wars were killing women, children, and the elderly, combatants and noncombatants alike, they were lauded as heroes. The killing of Indigenous people became an important element of US identity and patriotism.[123] This was true for those participating in these actions, those supporting those actions, and those raised to believe that this was the correct way of the world, and it is precisely how the sinful ideology of the frontier myth fosters further sin. It builds an identity based on differentiating those who belong as good and those who do not as bad. People who fight against these bad outsiders are cast as heroic defenders, breeding increased loyalty and patriotism founded on the idea that those who belong to our nation are good and that those who do not are somehow less than human, threatening and needing to be eradicated.

It is important to highlight this reality of social sin for two related reasons. First, without casting US history in this light, there is a danger of understanding this history as a story of the occasional, individual sinful actions of individual sinful actors. We are instead articulating something sinful at the heart of US identity and practice. Understanding sin as social allows us to see these more pervasive dynamics at work throughout US history. Relatedly, the purpose of this chapter and its exploration of US history is to build toward the

123. Dunbar-Ortiz, *Indigenous Peoples' History*, 59.

claim that the United States has responsibilities it is not fulfilling, responsibilities linked to its ongoing patterns of sinful behavior. Social sin, in that it shows how sin perpetuates further sin, can help us connect the sins of the past to today and will thus be a helpful tool for establishing responsibility now for the past actions of others. When we participate in sinful structures, behaviors, or attitudes, we are culpable in the harm that they cause. I will address this more fully in chapter 3.

Alongside this consideration of how these founding myths participate in and perpetuate social sin, it is important to make especially clear the role Christianity has played in their development. Explicitly Christian ideas are at the heart of manifest destiny and the frontier myth. Manifest destiny, in that it casts Anglo settlers as the new Israel, chosen by God to tame the Americas, roots itself in a misuse of Hebrew Scriptures. The frontier myth similarly often views civilization as something Christian and God-ordained, in an ongoing battle with the godless frontier. The role Christian theology and the use of Scripture have played in supporting and motivating colonial projects, in particular the conquest of the Americas by way of seizing Indigenous land and undermining Indigenous sovereignty, makes clear that Christians today have a responsibility for the way our Scriptures, teachings, and theologies have been utilized to perpetuate harm.

Expanding Empire: Mexico, Latin America, and the United States

For the United States, driven by the sinful ideology of a manifest destiny to conquer the frontier, Mexico became "just another Indian nation to be crushed."[124] Journalist Juan Gonzalez reports that "proponents of Manifest Destiny saw Latin Americans as inferior in cultural makeup and bereft of democratic institutions."[125] Mexico was in fact in many ways Indigenous territory, colonized by the Spanish rather than the British. The territory underwent a series of its own wars for independence, and like in the United States, the relationship between the Native people of the land and those who arrived by way of colonization continued to be oppressive after independence from the original colonizing force (Spain).[126] From the beginning the United States had its sights set on portions of

124. Dunbar-Ortiz, *Indigenous Peoples' History*, 118.

125. Juan Gonzalez, *Harvest of Empire: A History of Latinos in America* (New York: Penguin Books, 2000), 43.

126. For a fuller exploration of the history of the land now considered Latin America, see Gonzalez, *Harvest of Empire*; Paul Ortiz, *An African American and Latinx History of the United States* (Boston: Beacon, 2018); Gabriel B. Paquette and Matthew Brown, *Connections after Colonialism: Europe and Latin America in the 1820s* (Tuscaloosa: University of Alabama Press, 2013); Jerome Branche, *Race, Colonialism, and Social Transformation in Latin America*

this Spanish territory. This had repercussions for how the nation's borders took shape and for the developing relationships between the United States and the peoples of Latin America (official governments and otherwise). Two examples of US expansion into this Spanish or formerly Spanish territory will help highlight how these relationships began to take shape: Florida and Texas.

Spurred in part by the success of the US colonies in declaring independence from Britain, Latin American peoples began declaring their own independent nations, moving over time toward the countries we recognize today. Some of these revolutions anticipated US support and were surprised to find that their neighbors to the north were at best ambivalent, passive spectators to their struggles for liberty and self-determination. This is in large part due to US interest in maintaining a good relationship with Spain, against whom these revolutionaries were struggling, in order to gain access to Spain's colonial territories and further expand US borders.[127] In particular, the United States had a strong interest in acquiring Florida. Florida was an especially desirable piece of land for Anglo-settlers because the Spanish settlers who lived there had created strong ties to the Indigenous nations of the Southeast, including the Cherokees, Creek, Choctaws, and Chickasaws, with whom the United States was at war and whose territory it wanted control over. Florida provided a place of refuge for fighters from these nations, and was furthermore serving as refuge for enslaved Africans who escaped, a direct contrast to the interests of the plantation economy.

Unlike the purchasing of Louisiana from the French, Gonzalez describes the treaty through which the United States gained Florida as "more akin to a street corner holdup."[128] The Adams-Onis Treaty, which transferred Florida from Spain to the United States, was the result of two decades of constant pressure on the Spanish. Anglo settlers began moving into Florida at such a rate that they were soon beyond the control of the Spanish soldiers. Spain legalized these settlers in return for the settlers' pledge of allegiance to the Spanish Crown in an effort to reassert their control, but this only succeeded in making settler immigration into Florida easier. Bands of these settlers eventually began forming, capturing towns and territories, declaring their own republics, and further undermining Spanish authority. Andrew Jackson led one of these groups of "filibusteros,"

and the Caribbean (Gainesville: University Press of Florida, 2008). There are ongoing tensions and dynamics of colonialism left over from the Spanish invasion of this territory, which, as with the US, often results in situations of subjugation for Indigenous peoples in these countries. There are simultaneous dynamics of US colonialism in and against Latin American nations, and these nations' own continued colonial relationship with certain portions of their populations. Dynamics of race, class, and privilege factor heavily into this complicated situation. This is named here because it is important, but it is beyond the scope of this project to fully address.

127. Gonzalez, *Harvest of Empire*, 30–34.

128. Gonzalez, *Harvest of Empire*, 35.

capturing Pensacola in 1814.[129] Eventually the Spanish were left with little choice but to sell Florida to the United States for the paltry sum of $5 million. Then, in 1822, President Monroe changed the official US stance on Latin America, becoming the first world leader to recognize Mexican independence. The next year his famous Monroe Doctrine declared the Americas to be off-limits to further European colonization. Subsequently, US presidents following Monroe used this doctrine to turn much of Latin America "into a virtual U.S. sphere of influence," and his words have been used in the twentieth century to "justify repeated military occupations of Latin American nations."[130]

Texas provides another helpful example of how US expansion into a formerly Spanish territory shapes the relationship between Latin America and the United States. Mexico gained independence in 1821, and in the decades that followed the United States repeatedly annexed portions of the newly independent nation's territory. Anglo settlers began pouring into the Texas region in particular in the 1820s, many of them purchasing cheap land through fraudulent sales conducted by speculators who had no legal title to it. These squatters, like their counterparts in Florida, began seizing territory and declaring independence from Mexico. In an effort to control the settlers, the Mexican government barred further immigration into the territory. Mexico also worked to abolish slavery, officially outlawing it in 1829.[131] In the years that followed and up through emancipation, Mexico became a destination and a source of hope for enslaved people. Thousands of formerly enslaved people fled to the area,[132] to the great frustration of the United States, which was committed to expanding slavery and its dominance as a nation.

This was particularly troubling for many of the Anglo settlers in the Texas region, especially those who owned enslaved people and had no plans to abandon the practice. If Mexico hoped abolishing slavery would have the added benefits of deterring further Anglo settlement and cutting the settlers already on Mexican land off from the plantation economy, they soon found that this was not the case. Settlers continued to pour into Texas, and when General Santa Anna removed

129. This further highlights the significant relationship between the conquest of Indigenous territory and the conquest of Spanish or formerly Spanish land. Furthermore, Jackson used this opportunity to increase his own wealth by buying stock in Chickasaw land, forcing the Chickasaws to renegotiate their treaty and open their land to white settlers, and then selling his investment at a rate much higher than that at which he had purchased it (Gonzalez, *Harvest of Empire*, 36).

130. Gonzalez, *Harvest of Empire*, 30–39.

131. Gonzalez, *Harvest of Empire*, 39–42.

132. John Burnett, "A Chapter in U.S. History Often Ignored: The Flight of Runaway Slaves to Mexico," NPR, February 28, 2021, https://tinyurl.com/2y9hymm7.

their tax exemptions and attempted to enforce antislavery laws, these settlers called it tyranny and broke away from Mexico. Gonzalez calls the Texas War of Independence a pivotal part of US mythology, casting the defenders of the Alamo as martyred heroes when in reality they were men who openly defended slavery and were not even actually US citizens but rather Mexican citizens committing treason.[133]

Dunbar-Ortiz reports that this period of occupation and annexation of Mexican territory was a time of great joy for many in the United States. This continual expansion of US borders caught the imagination of the nation's citizens and fit well into the ideologies of the frontier myth and manifest destiny. Expansion was something to be proud of, proof of the nation's continued excellence and superiority. Heroism became a popular topic of writing as the men fighting to expand US control and influence became immortalized. Walt Whitman believed the war to be bolstering US pride and self-respect, and President James K. Polk saw the war as evidence that democracy was capable of as much vigor in war as any authoritarian government.[134] Dunbar-Ortiz insists that "it was the fast and irregular military action against the Indians . . . that shaped the nature of American Nationalism."[135] This method of warfare, settler squatting, and land seizure became part and parcel of what it meant to be a US citizen, an identity fundamentally shaped by opposition to those beyond the borders of white civilization.

Lucas Alaman, Mexican secretary of state during the annexation of Texas, noted that while most nations invaded with armies, the United States sent settler colonists in their place.[136] These settler squatters were no less effective than imperialist armies. Prior to US annexation of Mexican territory, Mexico and the United States were similar in size and population.[137] By the end, the United

133. Gonzalez, *Harvest of Empire*, 39–42. One of these men, Sam Houston, had previously been a member of Andrew Jackson's White House. Houston plotted rebellion and war while Jackson offered to purchase Texas from Mexico, again highlighting this double tactic of open aggression paired with the use of treaties. Some even speculated that Houston was a secret agent for Jackson, secretly doing his bidding in Texas. Gonzalez calls Houston Jackson's disciple. We can see here again the strong ties between the seizure of Indigenous land and the developing relationship between the US and Latin America. These elements of US history and identity are two sides of the same coin (42). For a more in depth exploration of the history of Texas, the Alamo, and the myth building around this event, see Bryan Burrough, Chris Tomlinson, and Jason Stanford, *Forget the Alamo: The Rise and Fall of an American Myth* (New York: Penguin, 2021).

134. Dunbar-Ortiz, *Indigenous Peoples' History*, 130–31.

135. Dunbar-Ortiz, *Indigenous Peoples' History*, 221.

136. Gonzalez, *Harvest of Empire*, 41.

137. Gonzalez, *Harvest of Empire*, 39.

States had annexed more than half of Mexico's territory.[138] Mexico also lost three-quarters of its mineral resources in this loss of land, and in the coming decades Latin Americans were reduced in the US imagination to a source of cheap labor and the Caribbean basin to a "permanent target of Yankee exploitation and intervention."[139] I will explore this more recent history of labor, exploitation, and intervention in chapter 2. For now, I am establishing a pattern of US settler colonialism and annexation of territories already inhabited and governed by sovereign nations, spurred on by manifest destiny and the frontier myth. The conquest of these territories, Indigenous and Mexican, was (and is) understood to be the right and sacred duty of the United States.

Furthermore, we can identify the early development of an unjust relationship between the United States and Latin America based on theft of land and resources and the strategic use of foreign policy to promote US interests, no matter the cost to others. The way the United States ignored revolutionary efforts in Latin America in order to maintain its relationship with Spain, only to do an about-face and support Mexico and ban further European colonization when it suited US interests to do so, is a prime example of the self-serving one-sidedness of US foreign policy. Finally, before people from Latin America began moving across the southern US border in the migration patterns we recognize today, the border moved across people. While nothing about them fundamentally changed, people in formerly Mexican territories suddenly found themselves to be within the United States and beholden to its laws and systems of government. Traditional familial and cultural ties had a new border drawn right through them. People on the Mexican side of the line suddenly found themselves cut off from resources and land they might previously have had access to. The arbitrariness of these lines we draw on maps to denote who controls what territory and has rights to what resources, as well as the unjust tactics that were used to gain access to those lands and resources, continues to unsettle the assumptions on which much immigration policy and discourse is based. This will continue to be an important theme moving forward.

As with the seizure of Indigenous land and resources outlined above, the annexation of Florida and Texas represented overt acts of imperialism that do not fit well with the nation's own purported ideals of liberty and equality. Neither does the United States' ambivalent and passive response to Latin American revolutionary efforts. Manifest destiny and the myth of the frontier normalized violent conquest and the blatant promotion of US interests at the expense of others, actions that might otherwise have stood out as

138. Dunbar-Ortiz, *Indigenous Peoples' History*, 131. This land also included communally held Indigenous land.

139. Gonzalez, *Harvest of Empire*, 28.

intolerably contrary to the ideals the country was supposed to be defending.[140] The United States, with its democracy and its constitution, distinguished itself from European empires, which conquered peoples and lands in order to enslave them, by insisting that its own conquest was the work of a free nation spreading liberty and bestowing freedom on others.[141] In reality, US interests were not that pure. The liberty the United States was interested in spreading was the liberty it could control, that is, the expansion of its own borders and influence. This is social sin. This is the way these origin stories and founding mythologies justify sinful and unjust behavior and predispose us to continue to behave in sinful and unjust ways.

Concluding Thoughts

The account of US history provided in this chapter is intended to problematize the assumptions on which much immigration policy and discourse has been grounded. Proponents of strict immigration policies often take for granted the borders and nations that currently exist, as they currently exist, without a sufficient consideration of how to reconcile the way these nations got here and the legitimate claims other peoples might have to the land and resources that currently exist within the borders of colonizing (or former colonizing) powers. They also fail to sufficiently take into account that these nations' very existence relies on centuries of colonization and theft, which has created rampant inequality. As we will see in chapter 2, this history of colonization has played a vital role in shaping the migratory patterns we see today.

This chapter has also introduced founding mythologies that have fundamentally shaped US identity and US actions throughout the nation's history. Chapter 2 will consider the legacy of these mythologies, especially in relation to US immigration policy and practice throughout history and up to today.

140. Dunbar-Ortiz, *Indigenous Peoples' History*, 146–47.

141. Dunbar-Ortiz, *Indigenous Peoples' History*, 105. Note the echoes of O'Sullivan here.

CHAPTER TWO

Legacy

Conquest of the continent, including the military conquest of Mexico, which ceded half its territory to the United States, was only the beginning of US imperialism. Native nations were the first subjects of US empire, but not the last. When the founders were writing the constitution, Indian affairs were a central site of nation-state formation, establishing a template for later imperial projects.

—Roxanne Dunbar-Ortiz, *Not "A Nation of Immigrants": Settler Colonialism, White Supremacy, and a History of Erasure and Exclusion*

ROXANNE DUNBAR-ORTIZ ARGUES that the pervasive desire for Indigenous landholdings outlined in the previous chapter helped form the US federal government into a "fiscal-military state," a term she uses to denote "a state primarily designed for war."[1] Historian Max Edling contends that the United States' ability to expand as it did in the first century or so of its existence was dependent on the creation of such a state, modeled after the fiscal-military states of eighteenth-century Europe, states designed especially to finance and conduct wars. While manifest destiny paints a picture of inevitable (predestined) US expansion, Edling argues that in reality the federal government worked very intentionally to acquire the territory we now recognize as the United States, and this acquisition required the ability to wage war against other European nations in the Americas and against Indigenous nations. This required federal powers that the Articles of the Confederation did not fully include, essentially curtailing the ability of the federal government to wage war and leaving the new nation vulnerable and less able to expand its territory. The US Constitution would therefore need to address this issue.[2]

Similarly, legal scholar Gregory Ablavsky reports that when drafting the Constitution, the Continental Congress faced the dual issues of an empty treasury and looming wars on the frontier. Of particular concern was the reality

1. Dunbar-Ortiz, *Not "A Nation of Immigrants,"* 12.

2. Max Edling, "The US Fiscal-Military State and the Conquest of a Continent, 1783–1900," in *The Cambridge History of America and the World*, ed. Kristin Hoganson and Jay Sexton (Cambridge: Cambridge University Press, 2021), 220–24.

that much of the land labeled on maps as the United States was in fact owned and governed by Indigenous nations. That Congress lacked sufficient power to exercise the authority it had on paper and build the nation the founders envisioned therefore became a central issue to be addressed during the drafting and ratification process. There were, by and large, two schools of thought on how to address this issue. Madisonians believed the problem was primarily an issue of state interference with federal treaty-making and favored a centralization solution that expanded federal power to restrain states (and Indigenous nations) from intruding on federal policy.[3] Hamiltonians, on the other hand, sought a solution that married military power and national wealth concentration.[4] Concerned especially with potential external threats to US power, they argued that the military was too weak to defend the nation against "savages" and therefore needed to be strengthened. Their solution was ultimately the creation of a fiscal-military state with the power to dominate the frontier and shore up US interests (economic and otherwise). The Hamiltonian vision won out, and the Federalists' repeated invocations of a "savage" threat were central in helping them gain vital support.[5] The result, Ablavsky argues, is that the conquest of Indigenous peoples and land was elevated "to a constitutional principle,"[6] influencing US law for centuries to come.

Edling finds that the Constitution's changes to the legal structure of the new nation finally gave the federal government the ability to pursue its vision, namely, continental conquest. Therefore, the "small but expandable" US version of the fiscal-military state played a key role in the development of the United States into the nation we know today. The ability this gave the nation to pursue and achieve rapid economic and geographic expansion provided "the material basis for the United States to rise to world power status" in the twentieth century. Ablavsky notes that Federalists "had sold the Constitution by promising to use federal power against Indians," resulting in "the disposition and settlement of western lands [becoming] one of the central projects of the new federal state."[7]

3. Gregory Ablavsky, "The Savage Constitution," *Duke Law Journal* 63, no. 5 (2014): 1006–7, link.gale.com/apps/doc/A360474541/AONE?u=txshracd2799&sid=bookmark-AONE&xid=f2013f83.

4. Dunbar-Ortiz, *Not "A Nation of Immigrants,"* 15–17.

5. Ablavsky, "Savage Constitution," 1003–8. In particular, this argument helped Federalists to sway Georgia, as the state hoped to secure military aid in its ongoing war for control of Indigenous land.

6. Ablavsky, "Savage Constitution," 1008.

7. Edling, "US Fiscal-Military State," 224, 221–22, 243–44.

Going forward, encounters with Indigenous nations offered the new nation a template for how to encounter cultures other than their own, with the prevailing goal of ensuring domination over them (predicated on their supposed inferiority) and gaining their land. Ablavsky writes, "The strategic deployment of the rhetoric of savagery anticipated future debates, as Indians became the stock template for America's subsequent cross-cultural encounters, their supposed primitiveness evolving into a free-floating discourse to justify rule over other purportedly inferior peoples."[8] The invocation of a dangerous or savage threat becomes a template for the justification of the use and/or expansion of federal power, especially for the purposes of war or defense.[9]

Over two centuries after these constitutional debates, on April 11, 2017, then–US Attorney General Jeff Sessions delivered prepared remarks on national security at the United States border in Nogales, Arizona. Among his statements that day were the following striking lines:

> Here, along our nation's southwest border, is ground zero in this fight. Here, under the Arizona sun, ranchers work the land to make an honest living, and law-abiding citizens seek to provide for their families. But it is also here, along this border, that transnational gangs like MS-13 and international cartels flood our country with drugs and leave death and violence in their wake. And it is here that criminal aliens and the coyotes and the document-forgers seek to overthrow our system of lawful immigration. . . . It is here, on this sliver of land, where we first take our stand against this filth.[10]

When Sessions called the border the place where we "take our stand," this was no accident, and it was not new. Striking though his words may be, they do not represent the uniquely racist ideology of an administration that has thrown off all decorum and convention and turned away from the American way. The imagery Sessions invoked draws on and in many ways exemplifies ideologies that have been embedded in the United States from its conception. It is the same imagery Federalists employed to secure support for a more dominant military. Following our discussion in chapter 1, we can see that Sessions's words are in fact precisely in line with the creation myths of this nation and the self-understanding the United

8. Ablavsky, "Savage Constitution," 1083.

9. Dunbar-Ortiz, *Not "A Nation of Immigrants,"* 15.

10. Department of Justice, "Remarks Announcing the Department of Justice's Renewed Commitment to Criminal Immigration Enforcement" (speech, Nogales, AZ, April 11, 2017), https://www.justice.gov/opa/speech/attorney-general-jeff-sessions-delivers-remarks-announcing-department-justice-s-renewed.

States has always had, especially in relation to who or what lies beyond the border and might want to come in. This mentality is what Goizueta and Dunbar-Ortiz identify in the founding and development of the United States. For Sessions, the border is where "our stand" should be taken because it is where civilization and savagery meet. All that is beyond it is dangerous. All (or most, depending on how it is defined[11]) that is within is good and worth preserving. The border, then, represents a very real place of conflict between the good and the untamed, the safe and the dangerous, the godly and the ungodly. It therefore must be militarized, in the same way the frontier was militarized, in order to shore up US interests and to defend the nation against threats both real and imagined.

It is also no accident that it is the *southern* border where this stand will be taken. Historically, of course, there are many reasons why the undocumented border crossing with which Sessions is concerned comes primarily through Mexico and not Canada. We will explore some of these reasons later in the chapter. But it is also important to note, with the frontier myth and manifest destiny in view and with all the ways they cast whiteness as civilized and anything darker as a savage danger firmly in mind, that we can see that it is of course a dark-skinned threat that has so captured the nation's psyche. If civilization is cast as white, it is then dark-skinned people against whom "we take our stand" and whom it will require a wall and the deployment of the National Guard to keep at bay.[12]

Theologian and ethicist Tisha Rajendra writes, "Every ethics of migration, every immigration policy proposal, and every public discourse about migrants implicitly draw on narratives about migrants: who they are, why they left home, and why they came to their new country."[13] Narratives help us make sense of the world around us. Because of this, our moral analysis of a topic such as migration is always filtered through narrative, through the stories we believe to be true. US narratives about who migrants are and why they come here (and why we might need to be worried about their presence) are shaped in many ways by the mythologies outlined in chapter 1. The narrative Sessions offered in 2017 has specific

11. There are, of course, many who are within the borders of society but not granted full belonging in civilization. Think, for example, of the continued legacy of slavery and anti-Black racism in the United States, and how Black people, especially Black men, are considered dangerous, a sort of enemy within, barred in many ways from full access to "civilization." See, for example, Michelle Alexander, *The New Jim Crow: Mass Incarceration in the Age of Colorblindness* (New York: New Press, 2012); Ortiz, *African American and Latinx History*.

12. For a related exploration of the history and development of this notion of taking a stand and its relationship to race, see Kelly Brown Douglas, *Stand Your Ground: Black Bodies and the Justice of God* (Maryknoll, NY: Orbis Books, 2015).

13. Tisha M. Rajendra, *Migrants and Citizens: Justice and Responsibility in the Ethics of Immigration* (Grand Rapids: Eerdmans, 2017), 54.

historical roots embedded deep in this nation's origin stories. Understanding the legacy of these founding myths, especially as that legacy pertains to immigration, can help us better understand the narratives that drive public discourse and policy proposals in this country. Understanding these narratives in this way can then help us to move forward toward a more just situation for migrants. To that end, this chapter examines the legacy of the mythologies identified in the previous chapter as they have developed over time in order to illuminate their particular impact on modern immigration.

The Legacy of Conquest

As powerful as manifest destiny and the desire to conquer the frontier were in the US imagination, the nation did eventually stop moving west. The Atlantic Ocean is, at least for the time being, generally resistant to conquering.[14] However, "myths do not easily die when historical conditions change."[15] Manifest destiny and the frontier myth were so fundamentally a part of how US identity had developed that they did not simply disappear once the nation reached its present borders. Rather, the myths adapted. Goizueta argues that the frontier myth's vision of society, its ideals and goals, and its caricature of what lies beyond all persist in the US psyche. The frontier myth's fundamental characteristic, its imagining of the frontier as the place where civilization meets savagery, is preserved. That is to say, the idea that there is an important, definable line between that which is good and civilized and that which is dangerous still holds sway in the US imagination. That line still needs to be defended. The difference is that the location of this line is no longer the western frontier as such but rather the border. Particularly, as evident in Sessions's proclamation, it is the southern border between the United States and Mexico. This grafting of frontier mythology and the mandate to expand and civilize onto the southern border is rooted first in already established patterns of expansion. After all, as we saw in chapter 1, westward expansion already included a massive conquest of Mexican land. Later, as we will see in this chapter, economic conquest and domination replaced the outright seizure of land.[16] Furthermore, the southern border fits

14. Of course, we might call our use of the ocean and its resources a form of conquest. This discussion, however important, is beyond the scope of this project, but the connection between the conquest of land/water and the domination of people should not be overlooked. Matthew Klingle writes that "dominating nature and dominating people [are] reciprocal and concomitant parts of frontier evolution" ("Frontier Ghosts along the Urban Pacific Slope," 123). Similarly, Goizueta's argument that frontier mythology evolved points to the fact that the same mentality is behind the exploitation of people and the extractive mistreatment of the rest of the natural world.

15. Goizueta, "Beyond the Frontier Myth," 152.

16. Gonzalez, *Harvest of Empire*, 58.

comfortably into a raced understanding of the division between savagery and civilization. Those who are considered to be outside civilization generally remain darker-skinned than those on the inside.[17]

Frontier mythology conceives of belonging in terms of civilization. That is to say, one belongs insofar as one is able to assimilate or conform to Anglo-American civilization.[18] The treatment of both enslaved and free Africans and the continual removal of Indigenous communities from the earliest days of British settlement in this country speak to the deep sense that there are some people who are in a meaningful way incompatible with this civilization. They can be made useful, as was the case with slavery, or they must be removed, as was largely the case with Indigenous peoples. The border-based incarnation of the frontier myth adjusts this notion of belonging insofar as it shifts the geographical location of belonging from being "within civilization" to being on the proper side of a national border, but this idea that what is within this border is in some important way good and civilized, while that which lies beyond is a threat, remains. Moreover, the racism that has always undergirded this worldview persists.[19] Those who live beyond our southern border are understood to pose a potential threat in part and precisely because they are or are imagined to be darker-skinned than "us."[20]

17. Gonzalez, *Harvest of Empire*, 153–54. The southern border becomes the primary physical location of this mythological battle between civilization and savagery in the US imagination, but we should also keep in mind the way a more conceptual border exists to keep out those who are unwanted, particularly in recent decades (especially post-9/11) when this has meant people from Muslim-majority countries. These migrants may not cross along the southern border as frequently, but their crossing into US territory, however it occurs, comes to represent the same threat to Anglo-American civilization. That US involvement in many of these countries (discussed briefly later in this chapter) has in many ways mirrored US involvement in Latin America and US treatment of Indigenous peoples should be noted. Goizueta's argument that frontier myth was grafted onto the southern border and has influenced US foreign policy in Latin America should not be seen to exclude its being grafted onto other ports of entry and broader US foreign policy as well.

18. Recall O'Sullivan here.

19. Klingle, "Frontier Ghosts along the Urban Pacific Slope," 154. Klingle also notes another evolution of the frontier. As space to expand ran out and the west began to modernize in cities such as Seattle, he notes that Euro-Americans sought to draw a hard line between their rougher frontier past and their new urban life. This included the expelling of "uncivilized" people, particularly Indigenous and Latine people and Asian migrants, as they were seen as "reminders of the outmoded frontier" (122–23).

20. This is not to deny the existence or legitimacy of white Latine people but rather to make the point that the way those who live south of the border are conceived of in the American imagination is inextricably tied to race.

Beyond this general casting of that which is beyond the border as threatening and that which is within it as worthy of protection, we can see several examples of how the specific ideologies and logic of the frontier myth and manifest destiny have been grafted onto the way immigration is conceived of in the United States today.

Meritocracy

Manifest destiny and the myth of the frontier are fundamentally about human worth. According to a belief in manifest destiny, one group is chosen by God, destined to settle and tame the Americas. This group is believed to be particularly worthy in God's eyes. O'Sullivan's notion that there are people who have the capacity to hold democracy and those who do not inscribes an implicit less-than-worthiness on those who are believed to be incapable (unworthy) of self-governance. In the worldview of frontier mythology, those inside Anglo civilization are believed to be inherently superior to those outside it. Both ascribe worth to US membership and identity. That these founding ideologies eventually give way to more generalized forms of American exceptionalism, to beliefs that the United States is special, particularly worth defending, or that it has a duty to spread democracy and freedom (as it conceives of them) around the world, is, then, not especially surprising.[21] This relates to modern immigration not simply because the means the United States has used to "spread freedom and democracy" have destabilized entire regions and contributed to the global flow of migrants,[22] but also because of a pervasive notion that immigration policy should in some way be dictated by merit. If the United States is in some fundamental way special or superior, it stands to reason (or so the argument goes) that those welcomed into US society should have some merits that make them worthy.[23]

One argument prominent within the national discourse on immigration suggests just that, that we ought to reserve visas for those who "deserve" them, whether because they are deemed more worthy of or amenable to US culture or because they have particularly desirable skills. Data shows that just over half of the population, 53 percent, supports the adoption of a merit-based

21. Recall Adam Gomez's argument that "the belief that the United States has an exceptional moral standing in world history and an obligation to spread democracy and the experience of international politics through the lens of a conflict between good and evil remain prominent in contemporary American politics." Gomez, "Deus Vult: John L. O'Sullivan," 255.

22. We will see examples of this below.

23. Think of O'Sullivan's insistence that not everyone was equally capable of true freedom and self-governance. The idea that "American-ness" is incompatible with certain peoples or ways of life has influenced US immigration discourse and policy since the earliest immigration laws.

immigration system.[24] The Pew Research Center reports that 78 percent of the US public supports encouraging "highly skilled people" to immigrate to the United States.[25] In comparison, 10 percent less (68 percent) consider taking in civilian refugees fleeing war and violence to be an important goal, with only 28 percent designating it as very important.[26] Stronger support for "highly skilled" migrants compared to refugees indicates that there remains a sense that migrants should merit entry, especially by being beneficial to the United States.

During his presidency, Donald Trump joined with several senators to advocate for a merit-based point system that would prioritize migrants with desirable skills.[27] The former president's subsequent comments suggesting that Norwegian migrants would be more preferable to those from Africa or Latin America[28] represent precisely the mindset that certain people are better or more deserving of immigrating to the United States, or at least more desirable. That these notions of merit still often fall along racialized lines (Norway vs. Africa and Latin America) is consistent with manifest destiny and the frontier myth.

Law and Order

The role of law-and-order rhetoric must also be addressed. Many supporters of US immigration policy cite the importance of upholding the rule of law. For example, evangelical political scientist Mark Amstutz cites Romans 13, arguing that our sinful reality renders the coercive power of the state necessary to ensure justice and the protection and advancement of human rights. In order to achieve this,

24. "Polling Update: Americans Continue to Resist Negative Messages about Immigrants, but Partisan Differences Continue to Grow," National Immigration Forum, September 18, 2020, https://immigrationforum.org/article/polling-update-americans-continue-to-resist-negative-messages-about-immigrants-but-partisan-differences-continue-to-grow/.

25. Phillip Connor and Neil G. Ruiz, "Majority of U.S. Public Supports High-Skilled Immigration," Pew Research Center, January 22, 2019, https://www.pewresearch.org/global/2019/01/22/majority-of-u-s-public-supports-high-skilled-immigration/.

26. J. Baxter Oliphant and Andy Cerda, "Republicans and Democrats Have Different Top Priorities for US Immigration Policy," Pew Research Center, September 8, 2022, https://www.pewresearch.org/short-reads/2022/09/08/republicans-and-democrats-have-different-top-priorities-for-u-s-immigration-policy/.

27. Alan Semuels, "The Last Time the U.S. Seriously Considered Merit-Based Immigration," *Atlantic*, August 4, 2017, https://www.theatlantic.com/business/archive/2017/08/immigrants-merit-based/535974/.

28. Nurith Aizenman, "Trump Wishes We Had More Immigrants from Norway. Turns Out We Once Did," National Public Radio, January 12, 2018, https://www.npr.org/sections/goatsandsoda/2018/01/12/577673191/trump-wishes-we-had-more-immigrants-from-norway-turns-out-we-once-did.

governments must maintain a strong and enforceable rule of law. Preserving the sovereignty of nation states therefore becomes important for Amstutz because it is the sovereign state that has the coercive power necessary to enforce the laws that protect these rights. Without the systems and laws that protect sovereignty, Amstutz argues, states cease to exist, and without the state, it is not possible to enforce laws. If laws are unenforceable, human rights cannot be protected.[29] The events of history that make many wary of nationalism, he argues, are actually often the result of an insufficient respect for national sovereignty. Nazism, for example, was an imperial project "that refused to recognize the sovereignty of non-Germanic peoples."[30] That Nazism was also a failure of a nation to take care of its own people, instead utilizing the coercive rule of law to systematically marginalize and massacre millions of people, German and otherwise, does not factor significantly into Amstutz's analysis.

Evangelical Bible scholar James K. Hoffmeier also roots his response to immigration in Romans 13. He is adamant that in this passage Christians are called to submit to the laws and to the authorities of the land in which they live, and that this is true even if the laws are unfair or inconvenient or if we do not like them. "Based on this clear instruction," he concludes, "citizens and foreigners should be subject to a nation's laws, and this applies to immigration laws and how one enters a country and becomes a legal resident (or citizen.)" Christians, he argues, are bound to respect the law and submit to authority because it is ordained by God. Accordingly, Christians must therefore take stances on immigration that uphold the law and ought to encourage others to do the same. Hoffmeier will grant that there are some "clear" cases in which human law directly contradicts God's law and that in such cases one may be called to break the law. He insists, however, that US immigration laws do not conflict with God's laws. As he finds "nothing in scripture that would abrogate current immigration laws," the breaking of these laws must be understood as improper for Christians.[31]

In chapter 1 we discussed the role of Calvinist predestination theology in justifying and motivating conquest. Calvinists also believed that "a person's

29. Amstutz, *Just Immigration*, 104.

30. Mark Amstutz, "Two Theories of Immigration," *First Things: A Monthly Journal of Religion and Public Life*, no. 258 (2015): https://www.firstthings.com/article/2015/12/two-theories-of-immigration

31. Hoffmeier, *Immigration Crisis*, 139–52. Both Hoffmeier and Amstutz offer a rather narrow interpretation of Rom 13 and its meaning for Christian life. For a richer interpretation of this passage, see M. Daniel Carroll R., *Christians at the Border: Immigration, the Church, and the Bible* (Grand Rapids: Brazos, 2013). Among other things, Carroll highlights that Rom 13 must be read in context with chapter 12, in which Christians are called to resist conforming to the patterns of the world and to be influenced instead by the will of God.

ability to abide by the laws of a well-ordered society" could be evidence of membership in the elect, as Christian citizens have an obligation to obey authority.[32] This belief becomes especially insidious as the laws of the "civilized" society (the US) are utilized to deprive Indigenous peoples of land, power, and culture. The same can be said about slavery and fugitive slave laws. Resistance to these laws on the part of Black and Indigenous people becomes evidence of their lack of civilization and need to be conquered. Social sin is self-justifying. Their resistance to US laws becomes evidence for the necessity of those laws. Moreover, many US citizens are motivated by this belief system to support these laws, as it is their duty as Christians and part of what it means to be a member of civilized society. Hoffmeier's insistence that to be Christian calls us to respect and obey the law and authority is directly related. People who break immigration law (often with good reason) are levied as justification for stronger immigration laws and harsher border enforcement, and US citizens are called to be good citizens by supporting efforts to uphold the rule of law against lawless encroachers.

Commitments to the rule of law such as these seek to protect important goods such as human rights and cultural diversity. What these arguments too often fail to take into account, however, is the ways the rule of law actually functions in history. Amstutz's depiction of Nazism as a failure to respect the sovereignty of other European nations obscures the ways the Nazis utilized the rule of law against German citizens, highlighting precisely why appeals to the rule of law fall flat. In chapter 1 we saw that systems of law and government can be weaponized against people, as with the use of these systems to undermine Indigenous sovereignty and foster their removal from their lands. That these systems can be and so often are manipulated against some in order to preserve or promote the interests of others calls them into serious question and highlights important weaknesses in rule of law–based arguments.

The administration of law and order is also often unequally imposed. We may think, for example, of how the criminal justice system disproportionately works against people of color and people with less financial means.[33] Similarly, while Indigenous resistance to laws against their interests was condemned, white citizens who broke laws and harmed Indigenous peoples were often not punished. In 1864 John Chivington led a group of seven hundred onto a reservation in which Cheyenne and Arapaho captives and displaced people were being held. Chivington and his men proceeded to attack these captives. This unprovoked attack initially killed over 130 people, mostly women and children. Chivington and his volunteers later returned and killed more people, burned their homes, stole their horses, and mutilated their corpses. While this incident

32. Dunbar-Ortiz, *Indigenous Peoples' History*, 49.

33. See Alexander, *New Jim Crow*.

was investigated by the Congressional Joint Committee on the Conduct of the War, which provided a detailed report of the atrocities, Chivington and his men were not prosecuted or even officially reprimanded. Dunbar-Ortiz writes that this lack of punishment signaled that the extralegal killing of Indigenous peoples was open to all.[34]

Today, we see this same pattern in the immigration system. Amstutz himself admits that a shortcoming of the immigration system in the United States is that its application is often discretionary, left up to the priorities of individual government administrators who must choose what to do with limited resources. This results in a troubling lack of consistency in the interpretation and application of immigration law, meaning that it often does not apply equally to all people.[35] We might also consider former President Donald Trump's pardoning of Arizona sheriff Joe Arpaio. A statement from the White House on the pardoning alleged that controversial (illegal) tactics Arpaio used were justified for the protection of the United States against the "scourge" of undocumented immigration.[36] In doing so, Trump and his administration normalized such harsh tactics, placing people such as Arpaio outside the confines of the law in the name of protecting the nation from a criminal threat.[37] This double standard, that Arpaio's lawbreaking was justified and permissible but undocumented border crossing is irredeemably criminal, shows that the law continues to be applied unequally, to the benefit of some and at the expense of others.

Appeals to the rule of law and the preservation of law and order are common throughout US history and remain common today, especially in reference to immigration. The history of this nation shows the way these appeals can serve, intentionally or unintentionally, to preserve a status quo that is unjust. The rule of law has always functioned unequally in the United States, often to preserve the nation's interests, at the expense of those who have limited power to oppose it. Migrants are too often modern victims of this long-standing tendency.

Military Strategy

The Federalists' successful use of the "savage" threat in order to garner support for their proposal for a stronger military set a precedent in US politics. Jeff Sessions's

34. Dunbar-Ortiz, *Indigenous Peoples' History*, 136–38.

35. Amstutz, *Just Immigration*, 63–64. To his credit, Amstutz recognizes that this calls the rule of law into question.

36. Note the legacy of the frontier myth here. Arpiao's tactics are necessary because the nation must be defended against a "savage" other.

37. Kevin Liptak, Danielle Diaz, and Sophie Tatum, "Trump Pardons Former Sheriff Joe Arpaio," CNN, August 27, 2017, https://www.cnn.com/2017/08/25/politics/sheriff-joe-arpaio-donald-trump-pardon/index.html.

words at the border in 2017 are one example, as is the White House statement in reference to Joe Arpaio. Ablavsky also notes that "the U.S. Justice Department has claimed that precedent from nineteenth century Indian wars legitimizes current practices in the War on Terror." The purpose the federalists envisioned for the US military, expansion of empire and protection from savage enemies, continues to drive the military today, even as the primary enemy has changed from Indigenous nations to terrorists. The military even used the name of a nineteenth-century Apache leader, Geronimo, as the codename for the mission to assassinate Osama bin Laden.[38] This use of Indigenous names by the US military is fairly common. Dunbar-Ortiz notes in particular the use of the phrase "Indian Country" to denote enemy territory. This is not slang or a mere insensitive slur; it is an official, technical term used regularly and found in military training manuals. In this sense, it is similar to "collateral damage" or "ordnance." The military often also uses Indigenous names such as Mohawk, Apache, or Thunderbird to label both missions and machinery.[39] The war on terror is a modern-day continuation of the "Indian Wars," as can clearly be seen in the Justice Department's use of precedent and in the language chosen by the military.

Edling argues that the United States' political and military power, which made it a dominant global force in the twentieth century, was "tested and improved" in early battles against Indigenous nations.[40] Ablavsky writes, "Natives were among the first subjects of [US] empire, but they were not the last."[41] Dunbar-Ortiz similarly argues that "the way of war largely devised and enacted by settlers" in the early decades of the United States "formed the basis for the founding ideology and colonialist military strategy of the independent United States." She draws strong connections between the tactics and military worldview developed in these formative years and military beliefs and behavior today. Today, tactics of irregular warfare first used against Indigenous peoples in Massachusetts and Virginia, such as the targeting of civilians or their systems of livelihood (food, supplies, etc.), are called "special operations" or "low intensity conflict."[42] Dunbar-Ortiz writes,

> The army of the West was a colonial army with all the problems of colonial armies and foreign occupation, principally being hated by the people living under occupation. It is no surprise that the US military

38. Ablavsky, "Savage Constitution," 1085–86.

39. Dunbar-Ortiz, *Indigenous Peoples' History*, 56–58.

40. Edling, "US Fiscal-Military State," 243–44.

41. Ablavsky, "Savage Constitution," 1083.

42. Dunbar-Ortiz, *Indigenous Peoples' History*, 56–58.

> uses the term "Indian Country" to refer to what it considers enemy territory. Much as in the Vietnam War, the 1980s covert wars in Central America, and the wars of the early twenty-first century in Muslim countries, counterinsurgent army volunteers in the late nineteenth century West had to rely heavily on intelligence from those native to the land, informers and scouts. Many of these were double agents, reporting back to their own people, having joined the US Army for that purpose. Failing to find guerrilla fighters, the army resorted to scorched-earth campaigns, starvation, attacks and removals of civilian populations—the weapons of counterinsurgency warfare.[43]

This connection Dunbar-Ortiz, Ablavsky, and Edling draw between the Indian Wars in the West and more modern military conflicts is an important one. Understanding this connection is especially relevant for creating a just and responsible ethic of immigration because it helps highlight the ways in which the United States remains responsible for creating paths of migration. It will be helpful here to recall Heimbach-Steins's discussion of the role of colonial relationships in creating and sustaining migration, as well as Goizueta's argument that frontier mythology was grafted onto the border and our relationship with countries to its south. With this in mind, we will turn to a consideration of how these tactics can be seen throughout the history of US foreign policy and how these foreign actions have contributed to the global migration patterns we see today.

Expanding Empire: Tactics for Colonization

One frequent target for the tactics first developed in battles with Indigenous nations has been Latin America. The development of the relationship between Latin America and the United States is complex and cannot be fully explored here. We can, however, identify key moments that highlight both the connection between the Indian Wars and US foreign policy, and between US foreign action and the creation of migratory patterns.

We have already established how the seizure and annexation of Mexican land relates directly to manifest destiny, settler colonialism, and the frontier myth. Evangelical Anglican theologian Robert Heimburger rightfully notes that this annexation of Mexican land and resources "remains in the collective Mexican memory," and therefore it should come as no surprise that "it is to this triangle of land the United States wrested from Mexico that most Mexican immigrants to

43. Dunbar-Ortiz, *Indigenous Peoples' History*, 148–49.

the United States have come."[44] Before Mexicans crossed the border, the border crossed Mexicans, not only leaving formerly Mexican citizens now inhabiting US land in a state of limbo but also leaving in collective memory some sense of ancestral claim to the land and resources claimed forcefully and unjustly by the United States.[45] We can see here a connection between US military policies born out of the Indian Wars and the formation of migratory patterns. The United States treated Mexico as it did Indigenous territory farther north and east, and in doing so it dictated the paths many migrants would take when fleeing economic instability and violence (also due in part to US action[46]) decades later.

Another helpful example of the connection between the Indian Wars and the southern border can be identified in US action in Central America. The final decades of the twentieth century saw the Central American migrant population in the United States, previously virtually nonexistent, expand exponentially. As Juan Gonzalez writes, this sudden influx of migrants "did not originate with some newfound collective desire for the material benefits of U.S. society; rather, vicious civil wars and the social chaos those wars engendered forced the region's people to flee."[47] Furthermore, this violence and instability was the direct result of US action in these countries. Nicaragua, for example, began the twentieth century as a stable and prosperous nation, due in large part to José Santos Zelaya, who served as president from 1893–1909. Zelaya came into conflict with US interests by favoring Nicaraguan businesses and refusing to give special treatment to foreign ones. This did not endear him to the US executives who owned mining, mahogany, and banana concessions in Nicaragua, granted to them before Zelaya's presidency. Zelaya's popularity, nationalism, and financial independence irked US powers who wished to gain increasing control over Central America by refinancing Central American debt through transferring the holdings from European investment bankers to US companies, by way of military force if necessary.[48] In 1909, Liberal Nicaraguan army officer Juan Estrada and Conservative Emiliano Chamorro launched a rebellion against Zelaya. This rebellion was backed by the United States, not only through a media campaign that vilified the president but also through the dispatching of Anglo soldiers who fought on the side of the rebels. According to Gonzalez, the rebellion was planned not in

44. Robert W. Heimburger, *God and the Illegal Alien: United States Immigration Law and a Theology of Politics* (Cambridge: Cambridge University Press, 2018), 167.

45. Heimburger, *God and the Illegal Alien*, 167.

46. For examples, see Gonzalez, *Harvest of Empire*, 96–107.

47. Gonzalez, *Harvest of Empire*, 129.

48. This type of foreign action is precisely what Goizueta refers to when he describes the grafting of the frontier myth onto the southern border and our relationship with countries to its south.

Nicaragua but in New Orleans, and it was financed by US companies. When Zelaya sentenced several of these Anglo rebels to death, President Taft seized the excuse to break diplomatic relations and begin a full campaign against Zelaya. This added US pressure soon forced his hand, and Zelaya resigned.[49]

Zelaya was succeeded by US picks for power, Estrada and Alfonso Díaz, who "dutifully carried out all the 'reforms' [US secretary of state] Knox wanted," including the refinancing of Nicaraguan debt to US companies and the installation of US overseers and US troops in Nicaragua.[50] When Nicaraguans voted Liberal Juan Sacasa into the presidency and General Chamorro attempted to reinstall Díaz instead, US marines backed Díaz against the Nicaraguan peasants, led by Augusto César Sandino, who had taken up arms in support of Sacasa. Sacasa was reelected president in 1932, and US troops were forced to withdraw, but not before they trained "a new National Guard and [installed] its English-speaking commander, Anastasio Somoza García." Two years later, Somoza's soldiers assassinated Sandino and ousted Sacasa. Somoza's sons succeeded him, and the family gained long-standing control over the region.[51] During the Somozas' rule they received US backing, including the training of Nicaraguan military officers by the US Army at the School of the Americas. When the Sandinista National Liberation Front arose in the 1970s and rebelled against continued Somoza rule, the United States continued to back the Somozas. The popular uprising eventually succeeded in overthrowing the Somozas and bringing the Sandinistas into power, and while the Carter White House initially sought to work peacefully with the them, it was succeeded by a Reagan administration that "immediately authorized the CIA to arm, train, and finance many of the former Somoza soldiers and henchmen into the infamous Contra army."[52] The resultant ongoing war between the new government and the CIA-backed Contras (supported by both the Reagan and Bush administrations, which worked to isolate the Sandinistas on the international stage) caused many Nicaraguans to flee north in search of safety.[53]

Similarly, in El Salvador, civil war and ongoing violence caused many to flee to the United States in the latter decades of the twentieth century. The origins of this war can be found in the reign of General Maximiliano

---

49. Gonzalez, *Harvest of Empire*, 73–75.

50. Gonzalez, *Harvest of Empire*, 75.

51. Gonzalez, *Harvest of Empire*, 75–76.

52. Gonzalez, *Harvest of Empire*, 132.

53. For a fuller consideration of US involvement in Nicaragua, see Michel Gobat, *Empire by Invitation: William Walker and Manifest Destiny in Central America* (Cambridge, MA: Harvard University Press, 2018).

Hernández Martínez, who seized power through a military coup. Hernández represents one example of "pliant pro-U.S. dictators" supported by US diplomats who used them to control the region. This approach to Latin America became popular during the presidency of Franklin D. Roosevelt as the more overt tactics of earlier decades, such as military occupation, largely ended.[54] In 1932, Hernández orchestrated the slaughter of thirty thousand Pipil, a people of the nation's Izalco region who had rebelled against the nation's landlords and organized a revolt. This massacre largely stamped out such popular uprisings and opposition for the next four decades. Hernández had US backing until 1944, when he was ousted by army subordinates unhappy with his methods of ruling. After Hernández, power alternated between members of the Salvadoran oligarchy and military generals. Between 1961 and 1975 the number of people without land in El Salvador quadrupled as the oligarchy seized control of coffee farms. These landless Salvadorans initially sought refuge in Honduras, where work on banana plantations could be found, but Honduras soon became overwhelmed by the number of refugees fleeing across its borders and began mass deportations. Those migrants who were returned to El Salvador were largely unable to find jobs or land to work and began resorting to demonstrations against the nation's rulers.

As it had during under Hernández, the government responded with violence against the people in the form of military death squads. As the popular uprising grew, the oligarchy's rigging of elections to maintain power became increasingly blatant. When a coup terminated the results of a democratic election in 1979, the country descended into civil war. For their part, both the Bush and Reagan administrations largely ignored public outcry against the horrors being done in El Salvador because they relied on the oligarchy to be an anticommunist force in the region. Instead of decrying the violence of the ruling class, the United States made El Salvador the largest recipient of US weaponry and military aid in an effort to keep the oligarchy in power. This led increasing numbers of Salvadorans to flee the country. By 1984, five hundred thousand Salvadorans had crossed into the United States.[55]

While it is fairly obvious that US action in the region contributed directly to the increased numbers of Central Americans crossing the southern border into the United States, the Reagan and Bush administrations failed to take responsibility for these refugees fleeing US-sponsored violence. While Nicaraguans were largely welcomed because it suited the US narrative (the violence in Nicaragua could be blamed on the Sandinista government, which Washington was actively

---

54. Gonzalez, *Harvest of Empire*, 76, 133.

55. Gonzalez, *Harvest of Empire*, 133–35, 138.

trying to help overthrow),[56] Salvadoran refugees were largely denied asylum. Gonzalez argues that this is because these administrations were bent on battling communism and thus supported violent anticommunist governments such as that of the oligarchy in El Salvador.[57] Conflicts in Latin America became proxy wars in the Cold War between the United States and the Soviet Union. It would be contrary to US interests to grant asylum to those fleeing governments the US government actively supported.

Under the Carter administration, Congress enacted the 1980 Refugee Act, which intended to end discrimination of refugees and asylum seekers based on country of origin, which may have curtailed this practice of accepting migrants based on US political interests, but "before the law could take effect, Ronald Reagan assumed the presidency and reasserted the fight against Central America's 'Communists' as a linchpin of his foreign policy."[58] One result of this change in approach was that in 1981 all undocumented Central American migrants began to be held in detention. This quickly resulted in overpopulation of detention centers, and new, makeshift holdings were built. Eventually, migrants fleeing violence in El Salvador and Guatemala (a government also backed by US interests) realized their chances of being granted asylum were extremely low. Many subsequently concluded that the better path was to avoid capture by Border Patrol and to live in the United States without documentation.[59]

It is also worth noting that some young Salvadoran migrants, living in poverty and segregation in the United States, turned to the "protection and camaraderie" provided by gangs.[60] Under the Illegal Immigration Reform and Immigrant Responsibility Act, signed by President Clinton in 1996, gang membership made these migrants particular targets for deportation back to El Salvador, a country they barely knew.[61] These gangs then turned into

56. The US granted 25.2 percent of asylum requests to Nicaraguan applicants between 1983 and 1990, a significantly larger percentage than those fleeing regimes the US supported (El Salvador, Guatemala, etc.). In addition, even when Nicaraguans were denied asylum, they were rarely deported. Thirty-one thousand were denied in the '80s, while only 750 were deported (Gonzalez, *Harvest of Empire*, 131).

57. Gonzalez, *Harvest of Empire*, 131.

58. Gonzalez, *Harvest of Empire*, 138–39.

59. Gonzalez, *Harvest of Empire*, 135–139.

60. Daniel Denvir, "Deporting People Made Central America's Gangs. More Deportation Won't Help," *Washington Post*, July 20, 2017, https://www.washingtonpost.com/news/posteverything/wp/2017/07/20/deporting-people-made-central-americas-gangs-more-deportation-wont-help/.

61. According to Denvir, these deportations have also been aided by the INS Violent Gang Task Force (1992) and US Immigration and Custom Enforcement's Operation Community Shield (2005).

cross-border enterprises, placing immense burdens on a postwar Salvadoran nation that was not equipped to handle them. When the United States sent gang members "to El Salvador and its neighbors in Central America's northern triangle, Guatemala and Honduras," these deportees "arrived in war-torn, unstable countries whose conditions helped to perpetuate a legacy of U.S.-fomented violence," thus creating a new generation of migration fleeing this violence.[62] Traveling north, these migrants face a US immigration system that remains unequipped or unwilling to provide refuge from a problem it helped create. Journalist Daniel Denvir puts it succinctly, writing that the United States "has exported violence, time and again, to Central America," violence for which the nation has not taken responsibility.[63]

We can see, then, that not only did Anglo-American conquest of Latin America boomerang back into the United States in the form of mass migration,[64] but also the United States' own policies and mismanagement contributed to an increased presence of undocumented migrants living in the country and to the formation of the very gangs that became the scapegoats used to defend harsher immigration policies that continue to impede the people trying to flee this US-exported violence.[65] The connections between US action in Latin America and Anglo seizure of Indigenous land and undermining of Indigenous sovereignty are also evident. Anglo settlers infiltrated the region by way of bogus land claims and squatter violence, and eventually created economic dependency on US businesses.[66] US actors fostered divisions that weakened Latin American nations and installed governments and leaders with whom they were more able to negotiate or who would act as puppets to support their interests. The United States has repeatedly violated the sovereignty of Latin American nations while insisting on the right to defend its own borders, just as it did with Indigenous nations. The United States has long used such tactics to lay claim to land and

62. Denvir, "Deporting People."

63. Denvir, "Deporting People."

64. Gonzalez, *Harvest of Empire*, 78.

65. See also Ortiz, *African American and Latinx History*; David Bacon, *The Right to Stay Home: How US Policy Drives Mexican Migration* (Boston: Beacon, 2013); Felipe Fernández-Armesto, *Our America: A Hispanic History of the United States* (New York: Norton, 2014); Alan L. McPherson, *Encyclopedia of U.S. Military Interventions in Latin America* (Santa Barbara, CA: ABC-CLIO, 2013); Peter S. Michaels, "Lawless Intervention: United States Foreign Policy in El Salvador and Nicaragua," *Boston College Third World Law Journal* 7, no. 2 (1987): 223; Cynthia McKinney, *How the US Creates "Sh*thole" Countries* (Atlanta: Clarity, 2018); Ronald Cox, *Power and Profits: U.S. Policy in Central America* (Lexington: University Press of Kentucky, 2015).

66. Gonzalez, *Harvest of Empire*, 47–52.

resources and assert US interests, and its methods for doing so were first refined against Indigenous people in the land that would become the United States.

We can also see the continued relationship between the US military and US business interests. Just as the US military was called in and utilized to aid Anglo settlers in gaining control of Indigenous land for business ventures and economic development, so too was the US military deployed in Latin America to secure US business interests therein and to ensure that governments in these nations remained amiable to the needs of these US businesses. Dunbar-Ortiz reports that the extension of the US military into new territories is usually "not militarism for its own sake" but rather "all about securing markets and natural resources, developing imperialist power to protect and extend corporate wealth."[67] This is the fiscal military state, operating as the Federalists intended: utilizing military force for US economic gain and doing so by spreading fear of a savage threat.

As with the seizure of Indigenous land farther north, explicitly racist justifications for Anglo rights to Latin American land were levied, including the work of phrenologists who studied skulls and concluded that various races had different, innate capacities for knowledge, and the general casting of the peoples of Latin America as a "mongrel" race whose land and resources could be availed by the superior "Northmen."[68] Echoes of settler-colonists' insistence that they were God's chosen people entrusted with the civilizing of the Americas, and that the Indigenous peoples of the region were not capable of utilizing its full potential, are evident here.[69] This makes clear the connection between anti-Indigenous settler-colonial action and US action in Latin America. All of this is rooted in the explicitly racist worldview of the frontier myth and manifest destiny. When Goizueta argues that the frontier myth was grafted onto the southern border of the United States, this is what he is identifying. Everything that drove Anglo settlers to "civilize" the continent and root out all vestiges of Indigeneity that stood in their way, everything that told them the land was rightfully theirs and that the people outside their Anglo civilization were not only inherently dangerous but also inherently lesser in intelligence and moral capacity, influences US action in Latin America because this mentality becomes embedded in US identity and especially in the self-understanding of the US military sent out to the front lines of this battle on the frontier.

This also directly affects the US approach to the border itself. The overmilitarization of the southern US border is another example of how the presence of imperialist, settler-colonialist sensibilities at the heart of the development of the

67. Dunbar-Ortiz, *Indigenous Peoples' History*, 167.

68. Gonzalez, *Harvest of Empire*, 43, 49.

69. For example, recall O'Sullivan's arguments.

US military continues to affect our modern world,[70] particularly as related to immigration. Above, I argued that Jeff Sessions's identification of the southern border as a place of conflict between good and evil is a modern incarnation of the frontier myth and the Federalists' "savage" threat. Manifest destiny and frontier mythology construct a US identity based on differentiating those who belong as good and those who do not as dangerous, potential threats. The border serves in this way to draw a line not only between those who are US citizens and those who are not but between those who are deemed worthy of being US citizens and those who are not. Those who are deemed unworthy are cast as a potential threat, against whom we must deploy our military forces. This sense of the border as a battleground lends support to the US government's treatment of it as a war zone.[71]

Dunbar-Ortiz describes how highly respected military analyst Robert D. Kaplan presents the successful achievement of "continental dominance in North America by means of counterinsurgency and employing total and unlimited war" as a guide for continued military success in the present day. He considers the modern war on terror to be a "taming" of the frontier. Kaplan opposes belief in manifest destiny because it veils the actual actions that accomplished US conquest, which he wishes to unveil in order to better learn from these tactics so that modern military campaigns can be similarly successful.[72] Kaplan highlights a central argument of this chapter: the frontier mentality, which casts the United States as a civilization that needs to be spread and protected, and that which is outside the boundaries of this civilization (the enemy) as needing to be tamed, continues to have a direct impact on US foreign action. It is foundational to how the military developed and how the relationship between the military and US civilians developed. We still set our military to the task of taming Indian Country, at home and abroad, to make it safe and useful for US needs.

This legacy of the colonization of the Americas by the United States shapes this nation's self-understanding, its military, and its foreign policy. It has directly influenced the US actions that have shaped the migration flows we see today.[73] It has also shaped immigration policy, particularly at the border.

---

70. Dunbar-Ortiz, *Indigenous Peoples' History*, 56–57.

71. See, for example, Tony Payan, *The Three U.S.-Mexico Border Wars: Drugs, Immigration, and Homeland Security* (Santa Barbara, CA: Praeger, 2016).

72. Dunbar-Ortiz, *Indigenous Peoples' History*, 219–21.

73. Consider Kaplan's notion that the war on terror is simply another taming of the frontier. As with US action in Latin America, the war on terror has resulted in an increase in migrants into the US from the nations in which this war is being fought, making clear the connections this chapter has been naming.

The border, like the frontier, becomes a line the United States can cross in order to expand its influence, but one that outsiders deemed undesirable or unworthy may not cross, necessitating military-style defenses. With this in mind, it will be worthwhile to consider two central and related elements of US immigration policy and practice: exclusion and expulsion. If a central function of the border is to hold this line between civilization and savagery, it is necessary to consider how the legal practice of excluding (or expelling) the undesirable took shape.

Exclusion and Expulsion in "A Nation of Immigrants"

Like Dunbar-Ortiz and Goizueta, legal scholar Daniel Kanstroom also identifies an ugly alternate reality beneath the surface of US success and idealism. He writes, "Buried within the proud history of our nation of immigrants, shrouded but always present, there exists a distinct system" giving the US government the power to detain and deport migrants.[74] While the country has often been labeled a nation of immigrants, the reality is much more complicated. In part, this is because of what we have been outlining: the very existence of the United States is dependent on a history of sustained imperialism and settler colonialism. The United States is at its foundations a nation of invasion more than it is a nation of immigrants. Dunbar-Ortiz calls the idea that the United States is a nation of immigrants "a mid-twentieth century revisionist origin story." In the wake of World War II and in the beginning of the Cold War, the nation-of-immigrants myth replaced manifest destiny and the frontier as the ideological vision of the nation. Less explicitly racist than its forebears, the myth offers a vision of the United States that is much more palatable for the human-rights era. However, it also obscures the reality that this is a nation built on the backs of enslaved people, people brought here not by immigration but in chains, on land forcefully and unjustly stolen from Indigenous people and nations.[75]

Certainly there is a long history of people immigrating into the United States. Dunbar-Ortiz reminds us that "from its beginning the United States has welcomed—indeed, often solicited, even bribed—immigrants to repopulate conquered territories 'cleansed' of their Indigenous inhabitants."[76] However, this

---

74. Daniel Kanstroom, *Deportation Nation: Outsiders in American History* (Cambridge, MA: Harvard University Press, 2010), 2.

75. Dunbar-Ortiz, *Not "A Nation of Immigrants,"* xi–xxvii.

76. Dunbar-Ortiz, *Indigenous Peoples' History,* 51. This idea that the land was cleansed of Indigeneity ties directly into the notions of civilization foundational to the frontier myth. There is sense that the land is being cleansed and made fit for civilization as US borders expand westward. What is inside the borders of civilization is clean, pure. What is beyond the frontier is dirty and dangerous. Cleansing also ties directly into the idea that the land was not being used

is settler colonialism more than it is the type of immigration the nation-of-immigrants myth implies. Furthermore, this nation's relationship to actual immigration, and especially to the presence, near or within its borders, of those deemed less desirable or dangerous, has always been tumultuous, as we have seen in this and the previous chapter. For many migrants (and others[77]), this nation of immigrants has more often been a nation of exclusion and expulsion. This section brings this reality to the fore, outlining the development of practices of exclusion and expulsion that shaped US immigration and border policy, highlighting particularly important moments and themes in that development in order to show how current policy came to be and why it is so deeply flawed.

Kanstroom argues that the nation-of-immigrants myth has always come with and worked to obscure concerns that immigrants be decent, that they merit inclusion, and that they be capable of assimilating or, in Goizueta's terms, capable of becoming civilized.[78] The nation's republican vision, based in self-evident and natural rights and principles, has throughout the history of debate on immigration conflicted with concerns about national identity and security. Because of this, there is a deep tension at the heart of US immigration policy. In particular, practices of exclusion and expulsion, necessary if a nation is concerned with allowing only the "right types" of immigrants, are in tension with the principle of jus soli, by which citizenship rights are predicated on the location of one's birth, and later also with US aspirations toward being and understanding of itself as a nation of immigrants.[79]

It is in dealing with this tension that one of the earliest identifiable practices of (US) exclusion occurred in the mid-1700s, when liberal naturalization policies for European immigrants met with some discomfort and debate in the colonies. Concerns were raised that the "the full rights of Englishmen would be granted to certain immigrants" who would not yet know how to make proper

---

to its full potential prior to Euro-American invasion. Race, religion, and capitalistic enterprise are all at the heart of the frontier myth worldview.

77. As we will see below, many of the earliest people who were excluded or expelled were not immigrants but people who were already here (Indigenous nations) or people who were brought here in chains (enslaved Africans).

78. Dunbar-Ortiz, *Indigenous Peoples' History*, 21.

79. Kanstroom, *Deportation Nation*, 23–24. Given this tension, it is perhaps no surprise that in a time when suspicion and fearmongering about dangerous or unsavory migrants are once again extremely prevalent, we are also seeing calls to end birthright citizenship. See, for example, Ed Kilgore, "DeSantis Joins Trump's Call to End Birthright Citizenship," *New York Magazine*, June 27, 2023, https://nymag.com/intelligencer/2023/06/desantis-joins-trumps-call-to-end-birthright-citizenship.html.

use of those rights.[80] In this fear we can identify parallels to the worldview the frontier myth fostered. If civilization is understood as existing primarily or only within particular borders (geographical or conceptual), and if it takes a certain degree of internalized civilization to make "proper use" of the rights afforded to the civilized, there is reason to believe that those coming from without, even those who are white Westerners, ought to be subject to suspicion. This inclination toward exclusion went hand in hand with a practice of expulsion. In the colonies "it was widely assumed that the right to exclude," which was presumed, "included a right to admit prospective inhabitants on specific conditions."[81] This meant that migrants were admitted on the condition that they behave within the parameters of certain expectations. Legal mechanisms for dealing with those who did not meet these expectations could include banishment from the colony. Kanstroom identifies these practices as "the functional forebears" of substantial portions of the modern US deportation system.[82] Expulsion, then, is built into some of the earliest American self-understandings.[83]

Dunbar-Ortiz similarly traces this suspicion about the uncivilizability of certain immigrants, and the desire to exclude or expel them, to the early years of the United States, especially to Alexander Hamilton and the Federalist party. While the hit musical that bears his name portrays Hamilton as a scrappy immigrant who defied the odds, in reality he was a citizen of Great Britain who moved from one British colony (Nevis) to another (New York). Such freedom of movement was the right of British citizens and does not as such make one an immigrant. Later, as a US citizen and founding father, Hamilton was deeply suspicious of immigrants. He and the Federalist party were instrumental in pushing through portions of the Alien and Sedition Acts, which "restricted the activities of foreign

80. Kilgore, "DeSantis Joins Trump's Call," 25. O'Sullivan's belief that not all people are capable of true freedom and holding democracy correctly echoes these early concerns.

81. Kanstroom, *Deportation Nation*, 29.

82. Kanstroom, *Deportation Nation*, 29, 34–36.

83. Sociologist Saskia Sassen uses the term "expulsion" to refer to the various ways in which socioeconomic and environmental causes of migration are connected. Identifying this pattern as expulsion highlights the brutality of this system and draws attention to its causes—expulsion implies an expeller. Sassen's identification of systems of expulsion as a problematic form of late capitalism is helpful for articulating the historical dynamics with which this chapter is concerned, as well as their connection to profit, and will be helpful for building a responsibility framework in the next chapter. "Expulsion" is therefore used from this point forward in this book to refer to various forms of explicit expulsion, deportation, or exclusion, building on Sassen's usage. See Sassen, *Expulsions: Brutality and Complexity in the Global Economy* (Cambridge, MA: Belknap, 2014).

residents in the country."[84] It was his opinion that, with a few exceptions, "the mass [of aliens] ought to be obliged to leave the country."[85] Suspicion of immigrants led to a desire not only to exclude but to forcefully expel. Dunbar-Ortiz argues that Hamilton and the Federalists were concerned with preserving a particular, homogenous ideology of US citizenship, especially in the context of revolution in France and a voter base concerned with the potential influence of French universalism.[86] According to historian Douglas Bradburn, "The Federalists crafted that legislation on the back of broad popular mobilization that demanded a national vision of American citizenship, one that celebrated and defended a homogeneous American nation against the threat of international revolution posed by French universalism."[87] In Goizueta's terms, this is a concern about certain immigrants being unable to properly civilize, to fit into the conceptual borders of US society. If they could not fit into the homogenized ideal purported by the Federalists, Hamilton and others saw expulsion as the best course of action for preserving US interests.[88]

From these early impulses to exclude or expel unwanted immigrants, we can trace three main patterns of expulsion within the United States, patterns that relate directly to manifest destiny and the frontier myth, both in their original forms and in their modern incarnations, especially as they relate to migration in the modern world. These are the exclusion of the poor, the exclusion of the criminal, and the exclusion of people of color.

Exclusion of the Poor

Kanstroom contends that many of the mechanisms of the modern deportation system can be traced back to the treatment of poor people in early US history.

---

84. Dunbar-Ortiz, *Not "A Nation of Immigrants,"* 1–4.

85. Alexander Hamilton to Timothy Pickering, June 7, 1798, Pickering Papers (Massachusetts Historical Society), XXII, 19, quoted in James Morton Smith, "Alexander Hamilton, the Alien Law, and Seditious Libels," *The Review of Politics* 16, no. 3 (1954): 305–33, and Dunbar-Ortiz, *Not "A Nation of Immigrants,"* 5.

86. Dunbar-Ortiz, *Not "A Nation of Immigrants,"* 5–6.

87. Douglas M. Bradburn, "'True Americans' and 'Hordes of Foreigners': Nationalism, Ethnicity and the Problem of Citizenship in the United States, 1789–1800," *Historical Reflections / Réflexions Historiques* 29, no. 1 (Spring 2003): 19–41.

88. That the Federalists' understanding of US interests aligned with their own desires to stay in power highlights an important point about whose interests are reflected in appeals to US interests. We have tracked the ways those in power shore up their own interests at the expense of those outside the borders as well as those within them who are deemed inferior (people of color, Indigenous people, women, the poor, etc.). US interests as such rarely reflect a full understanding of the good or interests of all people within the United States, or even all citizens.

More precisely, they can be traced back to practices that forced the poor to relocate. As early as the sixteenth century, policies were in place allowing officials to expel beggars and force them from place to place until they returned to the location of their birth. Furthermore, laws existed that based admission into a community on the condition that a person prove that they would not become a public charge or a burden on the community, and a person's lack of wealth or land made them much more susceptible to practices of warning out, a proto-deportation system through which people were made to leave a community. Like many parts of the modern immigration and deportation system in America, the enforcement of this practice was discretionary, making its application in practice highly unequal and resulting in the poor, especially poor people of color, being more frequently warned out and more harshly dealt with than wealthier whites who might have otherwise been warned out.[89]

The disproportionate impact of this practice on poorer individuals and families echoes throughout US history. As with the US legal system in general, lack of money can be a barrier to successful immigration or asylum cases, and access to legal representation in immigration proceedings can make a huge impact on the success of one's case. For example, Human Rights First reports that asylum seekers who have legal representation are over three times more likely to be granted asylum than those without.[90] Free or reduced-price representation can be difficult to access due to high demand, and costs for the legal process are often high.[91] Money makes a difference in the modern deportation system, just as it did in early expulsion practices.

Furthermore, the Pew Research Center reports that 73 percent of US citizens believe that undocumented immigrants should be prevented from accessing social services and public benefits "if they are not qualified to receive them."[92] This demonstrates a concern about immigrants becoming a burden on the

---

89. Kanstroom, *Deportation Nation*, 33–35, 37.

90. Rebecca Gendelman, "Inadequate Access to Legal Representation, Rushed Timelines Impede Meaningful Opportunity to Seek Asylum under New Asylum Processing Rule," Human Rights First, September 14, 2022, https://humanrightsfirst.org/library/inadequate-access-to-legal-representation-rushed-timelines-impede-meaningful-opportunity-to-seek-asylum-under-new-asylum-processing-rule/.

91. "Applying for U.S. Asylum: How Much Will It Cost," NOLO, accessed July 4, 2023, https://www.nolo.com/legal-encyclopedia/how-expensive-obtain-asylum-the-us.html; "How Much Does an Immigration Lawyer Cost?," Upcounsel, accessed July 4, 2023, https://www.upcounsel.com/immigration-attorney-fees.

92. Rob Suls, "Less than Half the Public Views Border Wall as an Important Goal for U.S. Immigration Policy," Pew Research Center, January 6, 2017, https://www.pewresearch.org/short-reads/2017/01/06/less-than-half-the-public-views-border-wall-as-an-important-goal-for-u-s-immigration-policy/.

community in which they settle, similar to the public-charge concern that Kanstroom identifies in the early colonies. "Public charge" remains grounds for inadmissibility into the United States and can prevent people from receiving a green card or a visa, or prevent them from being admitted into the country altogether.[93] Additionally, in January 2020 the US Supreme Court upheld an effort by the Trump administration to add new barriers for low-income green card applicants. The effect of this ruling is that those who are judged more likely to rely on governmental aid and social services will have an even more difficult time gaining permanent residency in the United States.[94]

Kanstroom notes that practices of warning out also often resulted in the separation of families and involved "little apparent concern for the effects of such separation on children."[95] This bears striking similarity to modern deportation practices, which often result in the separation of families and cause immense harm, especially to children.[96] Most infamously, fifty-five hundred children were separated from their families under the Trump administration's "zero tolerance" policy.[97] It is worth noting, however, that the separation of families is not unique to the Trump administration.[98] As we will see in later sections, shifting policies and practices regarding the porousness of US borders have long made it difficult for families to stay together, especially families with mixed immigration statuses.[99]

---

93. "Public Charge," Immigrant Legal Resource Center, accessed July 4, 2023, https://www.ilrc.org/public-charge.

94. Joel Rose, "Supreme Court Allows Trump Administration Rule for Immigrants on Public Benefits," National Public Radio, January 27, 2020, https://www.npr.org/2020/01/27/800158106/supreme-court-allows-trump-administration-rule-for-immigrants-on-public-benefits.

95. Kanstroom, *Deportation Nation*, 37–38.

96. "US: Family Separation Harming Children, Families," Human Rights Watch, July 11, 2019, https://www.hrw.org/news/2019/07/11/us-family-separation-harming-children-families. We might also think of the practice of removing Indigenous children from their families and communities and forcing them to attend residential boarding schools in order to anglicize them. Family separation tactics can be seen throughout US history as a way of dealing with those deemed undesirable.

97. Jasmine Aguilera, "Here's What to Know about the Status of Family Separation at the U.S. Border, Which Isn't Nearly Over," *Time*, September 20, 2019, https://time.com/5678313/trump-administration-family-separation-lawsuits/.

98. Kate Morrissey, "Family Separations at the Border Continue under Biden," *San Diego Union-Tribune*, August 16, 2022, https://www.sandiegouniontribune.com/news/immigration/story/2022-08-16/family-separations-at-the-border-continue-under-biden.

99. Cassaundra Rodriguez, "Seven Things to Know about Mixed-Status Families," Medium, June 5, 2018, https://medium.com/national-center-for-institutional-diversity

We can see, then, that there is a rather direct evolutionary line from such historical practices to the modern practice of deportation[100] and its impact on the poor, especially as deportation is used as a response to undocumented immigration.

Exclusion of the Criminal

Expulsion based on criminality can perhaps best be understood as rooted in English practices of expelling people convicted of crimes. The English legal system dealt harshly with crime, responding to even minor theft with the death penalty. This harsh punishment could be avoided through royal pardon or the pleading of clergy, in which case the convicted person would instead be exiled and sent to the colonies. Tensions around this form of expulsion existed from the beginning. On the one hand, criminals sent from England met real labor needs in the colonies. On the other hand, fear and distrust surrounded these foreigners. The American colonies' opposition to being sent expelled criminals eventually resulted in expulsions to Australia instead. Conversations also began regarding the potential for the American colonies to forcibly send their own criminals abroad.[101]

We can see, then, that the idea that those who commit crimes are subject to expulsion is built into the foundations of this nation. Moreover, from early on, there has been a link between immigration and crime, the fear of crime, and the need for deportation practices in response to or as prevention of crime. Crime continues to be a major factor in how people think about immigration and especially undocumented immigration. There is a pervasive perception that less harsh border enforcement or immigration laws may allow the easy entry of nefarious people with criminal aims. Migrants who cross into the country, both legally and illegally, are often under suspicion of criminality. Undocumented immigrants, because they have technically broken US law just by being here, are further shrouded in a perception of criminality.[102] These links to criminality both

/seven-things-to-know-about-mixed-status-families-92a18a714bb5; Mohamad Moslimani, "Around Four-in-Ten Latinos in U.S. Worry They or Someone They Know Could Be Deported," Pew Research Center, February 14, 2022, https://www.pewresearch.org/short-reads/2022/02/14/around-four-in-ten-latinos-in-u-s-worry-that-they-or-someone-close-to-them-could-be-deported/.

100. Kanstroom, *Deportation Nation*, 38.

101. Kanstroom, *Deportation Nation*, 39–42.

102. This link to crime was further exacerbated by the Trump administration with the implementation of a weekly list of crimes committed by noncitizens. Consider, for example, the language used by Jeff Sessions in his speech at the border. In his worldview, those who would cross unauthorized are criminals to be dealt with and little more. Deportation can be justified more

play into and are supported by the way frontier mythology casts those outside "civilization" as a savage threat. Social sin, recall, is self-perpetuating.[103]

Exclusion of People of Color

We must also consider the ways in which expulsion in the United States has always been tied to race. As the conquest of this continent and the forced removal of Indigenous peoples outlined above indicate, the frontier myth and manifest destiny are raced understandings of the world. This removal was based on the idea that white settlers had a right to the land because it was their God-given mission to civilize it and because they had won the land in conquest against members of a supposedly inferior race.[104] Indigenous peoples were displaced and forced out of their lands from the beginning of English invasion. This practice continued vigorously through the Civil War, but eventually, when there was nowhere left to remove Indigenous people to, attempts at incorporation and "civilization" were made instead.[105] This impulse to control what cannot be deported (and, conversely, to deport what cannot be controlled or homogenized) remains prevalent in conversations about the perceived incompatibility of migrants, especially Latine people and those from Middle Eastern countries, as a factor that contributes to US attitudes toward immigration.

Chattel slavery is another arena in which the United States first began to establish practices of removal based on race. From the time the first enslaved people were brought to Virginia in 1619 through the first century of the United States' independent existence, the prevalence of slavery increased significantly. This was in some ways because membership in the community (and the rights that entailed) could be easily denied to Black people. Journalist and author Ta-Nehisi Coates reports, "As life spans increased in the colony, the Virginia

easily when someone is labeled a criminal. See, Muzaffar Chishti, Sarah Pierce, and Jessica Bolter, "Muscular Public Relations Strategy to Paint Immigrants and Immigration as Negatives Embedded Deep within Trump Executive Orders," Migration Policy Institute, March 22, 2017, https://www.migrationpolicy.org/article/muscular-public-relations-strategy-paint-immigrants-and-immigration-negatives-embedded-deep; and Leo R. Chavez, *The Latino Threat: Constructing Immigrants, Citizens, and the Nation* (Stanford, CA: Stanford University Press, 2013), 27.

103. For more on the link between perceptions of criminality and migration, and especially the criminalization of migration, see César Cuauhtémoc García Hernández, *Migrating to Prison: America's Obsession with Locking Up Immigrants* (New York: New Press, 2019).

104. Kanstroom, *Deportation Nation*, 63–65. The racialization of Indigenous peoples is a fraught practice that continues in many ways today. For further analysis, see: Kim Tallbear, "DNA, Blood, and Racializing the Tribe," *Wicazo Sa Review* 18, no. 1 (Spring 2003): 81–107.

105. Kanstroom, *Deportation Nation*, 70; Chavez, *Latino Threat*, 71–72.

planters found in the enslaved Africans an even more efficient source of cheap labor. Whereas indentured servants were still legal subjects of the English crown and thus entitled to certain protections, African slaves entered the colonies as aliens. Exempted from the protections of the crown, they became early America's indispensable working class—fit for maximum exploitation, capable of only minimal resistance."[106] In other words, the practice of slavery increased in part because Black people were considered alien and therefore more easily exploitable. Exclusion of Black people from the community of rights-bearers was a foundation of chattel slavery and highlights the race-based dynamics of exclusion and expulsion present in the earliest years of this nation.

From independence onward through "the next 250 years, American law worked to reduce black people to a class of untouchables and raise all white men to the level of citizens."[107] Excluding Black people from full membership in the community in this way paved the way for practices of expulsion and forced movement. Kanstroom identifies the slavery-linked restrictions around the entry, movement, and residence of Black people in the United States as "fundamentally related to the development of the post-Civil War deportation system."[108] Fugitive slave laws provide one clear example of this. The legal battles surrounding the writing of these laws set important precedent for the forced movement of people across state and national borders, and set in place policies for hunting for people suspected of being where they were not authorized to be. This created the ideological groundwork that later legitimized immigration and deportation policy that formed in the nineteenth and twentieth centuries, and allowed for Congress and the Supreme Court to adopt procedural aspects of these laws in those deportation policies.[109] Furthermore, the removability of a person based on race and legal status has obvious correlations to modern deportation practices. We may think, for example, of the policies that allow for law enforcement officials to question anyone they suspect of being undocumented and how those policies overwhelmingly affect people of color.[110] In fugitive slave laws, the presumption that a person had or may have broken the law based

106. Ta-Nehisi Coates, "The Case for Reparations," *Atlantic*, June 2014, https://www.theatlantic.com/magazine/archive/2014/06/the-case-for-reparations/361631/.

107. Coates, "Case for Reparations."

108. Kanstroom, *Deportation Nation*, 74.

109. Chavez, *Latino Threat*, 81, 83.

110. Consider, for example, Arizona's SB 1070 law, which required police to demand the immigration documents of anyone suspected of being undocumented, a practice that advocates for immigrants' rights decried for its inherent racial profiling. Latine people in Arizona were at a much higher risk of having their papers demanded under this law than white people. Nigel Dura, "Arizona's Once-Feared Immigration Law, SB 1070, Loses Most of Its Power in Settlement,"

solely on the color of their skin found its legal and ideological precedent and entrenched itself into the US psyche.[111]

Beyond the measures set in place to control the movement of Black people already in America, Black people from other countries seeking to enter the United States could be denied entry based solely on race. White people quite clearly feared the free movement of Black people, particularly *free* Black people. These fears are linked to concerns of an internal revolt. White people were afraid that the unrestricted movement of Black people would result in the creation of a unified "enemy within," a force of people who could rise up and topple their carefully ordered social systems.[112] These fears were further linked to concerns that Black people and white people were in some way fundamentally incompatible, that Black people could not assimilate and therefore could not become properly American. We can look, for example, at the multiple very serious proposals for the mass deportation of freed Black people, especially after the Civil War.[113] Abraham Lincoln's attempt to purchase land in Central America on which to settle formerly enslaved people, based in concerns that Black and white people would never be able to live together and a belief that the United States required an homogenized people,[114] is a clear example of this. That which cannot be civilized must be made useful and controlled, or it must be expelled. Free Black people thus needed to be very controlled or they needed to be removed for the country altogether.

One way in which this was achieved was the pitting Black and Native people against each other. At the end of the Civil War, many Black soldiers stayed in the army as a way of ensuring access to food, shelter, and security. Called "buffalo soldiers," these men were assigned to segregated regiments and deployed west to fight against Indigenous resistance. This served a dual purpose for white US citizens: it kept these Black soldiers out of their communities and labor pools, and it put them to work ridding the land of Indigenous people. Dunbar-Ortiz reports that despite what is portrayed in glamorized Westerns that depict noble white cavalries laying claim to the West, in reality it was armies of Black men as well as German and Irish immigrants—unwanted immigrants—who were put to work cleansing the West of its Indigenous peoples and making it fit for

---

Los Angeles Times, September 15, 2016, https://www.latimes.com/nation/la-na-arizona-law-20160915-snap-story.html.

111. Kanstroom, *Deportation Nation*, 75. The first clue a person may be a fugitive slave was after all their Blackness.

112. Kanstroom, *Deportation Nation*, 76, 74.

113. Dunbar-Ortiz, *Indigenous Peoples' History*, 83–90.

114. Dunbar-Ortiz, *Indigenous Peoples' History*, 86–87.

Anglo purposes. In this way the demands of the frontier myth were fulfilled: unwanted populations (Black, Irish, German), were made useful to and kept out of the way of Anglo-Americans, while those deemed unable to be civilized (Indigenous peoples) were eradicated. This is also a classic tactic of oppressive classes: pitting oppressed groups against each other so as to avoid their coming together to overthrow the shared oppressor.[115]

Another example of how expulsion developed as a raced practice can be seen by tracking how the United States went from withholding rights from those who were alien to considering aliens people whose presence itself could be unlawful.[116] In the early decades of the United States, immigration policy and enforcement was largely handled by state governments. The shift to federal control of immigration came in the mid-nineteenth century. Both the building of a transcontinental railroad system and the ending of US chattel slavery meant the United States saw a large increase in labor needs, needs that began to be filled especially by Chinese immigrants. At first, this migration was welcomed, but as numbers increased and the national mood shifted, restrictions of Chinese migration began to be put in place on a federal level.[117] This culminated in the Chinese Exclusion Act of 1882, which marked "a turning point in American history," after which lawmakers used "restrictive, racist legislation" in response to the perceived race problems facing the nation.[118] The point of the Chinese Exclusion Act was to keep out a particular ethnic group deemed unsuitable for membership in the US community and/or a threat to US interests. In other words, it was about the exclusion and expulsion of people based explicitly on race. The impact of the act cannot be overstated. Its passing "set the standard for how Americans would both frame the immigration debate in the years that followed and come to accept greater and greater restrictions on foreigners seeking refuge and freedom in the United States."[119]

In particular, two Supreme Court cases dealing with the act's aftermath helped shape federal authority to exclude and deport, authority that to this day

115. Dunbar-Ortiz, *Indigenous Peoples' History*, 146–48.

116. See Heimburger, *God and the Illegal Alien*, especially 72–81.

117. Kanstroom, *Deportation Nation*, 91–93.

118. Andrew Gyory, *Closing the Gate: Race, Politics, and the Chinese Exclusion Act* (Chapel Hill: University of North Carolina Press, 1998), 6, 16.

119. Gyory, *Closing the Gate*, 259. It should also be noted that proponents of the act, such as Representative Addison McClure, included the idea that Chinese people were pagans as one reason that Chinese migrants were thoroughly un-American (see Gyory, *Closing the Gate*, 5). The connection evident here between US identity and religious identity points to the role of Christianity in shaping US identity and mythology. This is important to keep in mind as we consider the culpability, responsibility, and role of the church in the coming chapters.

remains largely unrestricted.[120] In the first of these cases, *Chae Chan Ping v. United States*, the court argued that the United States had the right to exclude. Ping, a man previously allowed to reside in the United States, was denied admittance at a port of entry, which the court determined the United States had the right to do. The court rooted this right in national sovereignty and in doing so established that the regulation of immigration is extraconstitutional, meaning that it need not be "justified by reference to a specific source of constitutional authority."[121] In another case, *Fong Yue Ting v. United States*, the court insisted that the authority of a nation to expel certain immigrants already within its borders (to deport) was the same as the right to exclude. That is, it was a matter of national sovereignty, fundamental to the nation's ability to protect itself, its way of life, and the public welfare.[122] This establishes that the right to deport is essentially the same as the right to exclude from entry, key precedent for later deportation law. It also establishes that deportation is not a punishment for crime, an important qualification as this kept deportation from being in direct conflict with the Bill of Rights.[123] Kanstroom calls the effect of this decision "staggering," and he argues that this case "left deportation law in the harsh, anomalous state in which we still find it today."[124] Thus, these cases granted the federal government vast authority over immigration and laid the legal precedent and the conceptual foundation for current immigration law, and did so on explicitly raced lines.[125]

Space here does not permit this chapter to cover the entire history of race-based forced movement and expulsion in the United States. We could speak, for example, of Jim Crow laws or practices such as redlining, which have also restricted the movement of Black people.[126] What is important to note is that

120. David A. Martin, Daniel Kanstroom, and Peter H. Schuck, *Immigration Stories* (New York: Foundation, 2005), 7.

121. Martin, Kanstroom, and Schuck, *Immigration Stories*, 14–15, Kanstroom, *Deportation Nation*, 114.

122. Martin, Kanstroom, and Schuck, *Immigration Stories*, 18; Heimburger, *God and the Illegal Alien*, 78–81.

123. Martin, Kanstroom, and Schuck, *Immigration Stories*, 20; Kanstroom, *Deportation Nation*, 118–20.

124. Kanstroom, *Deportation Nation*, 120, 130.

125. Here we also see connections between US labor needs and migration. In particular, we can see how labor needs drive migration patterns, and how US immigration policy has consistently failed to reflect US labor needs. This will continue to be a theme moving forward.

126. For further analysis of race-based forced movement in the US, see Ortiz, *African American and Latinx History*; Alexander, *New Jim Crow*.

alongside the development of a US identity that defined itself as a civilizing force in battle with a savage frontier, there was also the development of policies and practices that exclude or expel based on economic status, perceptions of criminality, and racism. As we will see in the following section, these patterns continued to influence immigration policy and US identity as they developed.

Modern Immigration Policies: Roots and Impact

We have been mapping the development of ideologies and practices that shape modern immigration discourse and policy. This final section highlights several important developments in immigration policy in the twentieth and twenty-first centuries. This exploration serves two main purposes. First, we can begin to see how these developments fit into the legacy of the frontier myth, manifest destiny, and the patterns of expulsion outlined in the previous section. Second, the policies examined below continue to show how specific migration patterns have developed as a direct result of US action. This will be important as we move into the responsibility framework offered in chapter 3.

The first immigration policy vital for understanding modern immigration is the Bracero Program. In the twentieth century, migration from Mexico increased exponentially. This was due to many factors, including the earlier US seizure of Mexican land and resources, US intervention in Mexico that destabilized and fundamentally changed the Mexican economy, and the privatization of land and mechanization of agriculture under the presidency of Porfirio Díaz (1876–1911), which left many Mexicans without land or work.[127] Furthermore, as the migration of workers from China and Japan was halted, a need for labor developed as those jobs were largely unable to be filled by willing US citizens. Restrictions in 1917 limiting migration across the US-Mexico border exempted Mexican workers precisely because they met important labor needs. Undocumented presence in the United States was made illegal in 1924, and when the demand for laborers slowed during the Great Depression, many Mexican workers were deported. However, with the onset of World War II and the deployment of many young US men to war, the need for cheap Mexican labor was reignited. In 1942 the Roosevelt administration negotiated an agreement with Mexico that would bring braceros, so named for the brazos (arms) with which they would work US fields, to the United States with promises of fair wages and good living and working conditions. Hundreds of thousands of Mexican laborers came to

127. For a fuller consideration of US intervention in Mexico, see, Bacon, *Right to Stay Home*; Payan, *Three U.S.-Mexico Border Wars*; Jason Ruiz, *Americans in the Treasure House: Travel to Porfirian Mexico and the Cultural Politics of Empire* (Austin: University of Texas Press, 2014); Jaime Suchlicki, *Mexico: From Montezuma to NAFTA, and Beyond* (New Brunswick, NJ: Transaction, 2000).

the United States through this program. The United States, for its part, did not uphold its side of the treaty, doing little to enforce the requirement for fair wages and good living and working conditions.[128]

This program continued into the 1950s, and many more migrants were encouraged to migrate illegally in order to find similar work outside the stipulations of the program, enticed by the prosperity promised by recruiters and the ever-present US need for more labor. This was initially met with little concern by US policymakers, especially as labor needs spiked during World War II.[129] Eventually, however, the US government sought to limit undocumented migration from Mexico. One way this was done was by excluding migrants from "contiguous countries" such as Mexico from the 1952 McCarran-Walter Act. This act provided a means for undocumented migrants of good standing who were long-term US residents to gain legal residence if deportation would lead to undue hardship for them or their families. Meant as a deterrent against future undocumented migration, the exclusion of Mexicans from the effects of this act made it increasingly difficult for undocumented Mexican migrants already here to legalize their status.[130] Daniel J. Tichenor argues that this act represents an effort to maintain "returnable" Mexican migration, an important labor source, while avoiding more permanent migration from Mexico.[131]

In 1954 the US government went forward with a large-scale deportation effort called Operation Wetback, named after the racial slur used to describe those who entered the United States by crossing the Rio Grande. Over a million undocumented migrants were rounded up and deported through this program.[132] Despite these efforts, undocumented migrants continued to cross the border into the United States, where they were nevertheless welcomed readily by US employers and a US economy dependent on them for cheap and exploitable labor. The Bracero Program officially ended in 1964, due in large part to the lobbying of religious groups concerned about the inhuman treatment of migrant laborers as well as groups claiming this cheap source of labor was harmful to the interests

128. John H. Barnhill, "Bracero Program," in *Multicultural America: A Multimedia Encyclopedia*, ed. Carlos E. Cortés (Thousand Oaks, CA: SAGE, 2013), 389–90; Daniel J. Tichenor, *Dividing Lines: the Politics of Immigration Control in America* (Princeton, NJ: Princeton University Press, 2002), 173–74.

129. Tichenor, *Dividing Lines*, 172–73.

130. Aristide R. Zolberg, *A Nation by Design: Immigration Policy in the Fashioning of America* (Cambridge, MA: Harvard University Press, 2006), 313.

131. Tichenor, *Dividing Lines*, 193.

132. Paul López, "Operation Wetback," in Cortés, *Multicultural America*, 1652–53.

of US citizen farmworkers.[133] The effects of the program, however, live on, and the US economy continues to be dependent on the labor of migrants, discouraged from crossing the border by official policy but encouraged by the needs of US employers as well as their own needs to provide for themselves and their families.[134] We begin to see here, then, the inconsistencies and contradictions embedded in US policy and practice as well as the failures of US immigration policy to adequately address US labor needs and the needs of migrants recruited to this country.[135]

The twentieth century also saw the implementation of immigration quotas in the United States. Beginning in 1921, the first immigration quotas ushered in a new era in US immigration policy, in which limits were placed on the number of immigrants who could enter the United States from various countries around the world. The first move toward this system came in the form of emergency quotas, put in place to limit migration from the Eastern Hemisphere. Rooted in racist pseudoscience that divided peoples into types based on notions of racial superiority, including inherent mental and moral advantages supposedly found in some races and not in others, these emergency quotas divided potential migrants into race-based categories that assigned varying levels of desirability and ability to assimilate to a US way of life. This, it must be noted, is a rather natural outgrowth of manifest destiny and frontier mythology, which deem people worthy or unworthy of belonging on explicitly raced lines. Furthermore, the quota system came on the heels of earlier immigration restrictions such as the use of literacy tests, implemented in 1917 with the aim of encouraging the immigration of those deemed desirable and discouraging the immigration of those who were thought to imperil the nation (at the time, those from eastern and southern Europe). The Immigration Act of 1924 and later quotas implemented in 1929 arose in response to a US desire for immigration policy that would prioritize the types of migrants the nation desired and block the migration of those deemed less

133. Barnhill, "Bracero Program."

134. Heimburger, *God and the Illegal Alien*, 168–73.

135. Tichenor also notes that this moment in US history coincided with a new turn outward. After World War II, he argues, the nation was no longer able to ignore the ways in which global affairs affected it, especially in terms of national security. Emerging as "an uneasy superpower," the US continued to develop its foreign policy while struggling to adapt its borders and immigration policies to its changing role in the world. Increasing concerns for national security, especially during the Cold War, made this especially difficult (*Dividing Lines*, 216–17). The tension that exists between the US's interventionist approach to being a global superpower and its notable resistance to opening its doors to the migrants created in part by those interventionist policies thus continues to develop and will be important to track moving forward.

desirable. Created with the help of experts in eugenics, these early quotas further embedded a deeply discriminatory way of thinking into US law and policy.[136]

The effect of these early quotas was that the only races allowed to join US society were those who were thought to be superior, those who resembled earlier generations of US citizens. In this way we can see the legacies of the frontier myth and manifest destiny. In the twentieth century, US identity continued to be defined by explicitly racist ideas about protecting US civilization from some threatening other, now defined especially as migrants from Asia as well as southern and eastern Europe. Maintaining a particular cultural makeup in the US population by restricting certain migration flows allowed this racialized understanding of US identity to continue. There is also an inherent exceptionalism in the eugenics and other racist pseudosciences that inspired the earliest versions of the quota system. This is a modernization of the manifest destiny mindset. Instead of citing a God-ordained right to the land as God's new chosen people, Anglo-Americans were now turning to science to justify their racist notions of superiority and sense of inherent right to land and resources. The same patterns of thinking that caused Anglo settler colonists to condemn Indigenous peoples for not using the land to its "full potential" can be seen in insistences that certain races possess superior moral and intellectual abilities, or in the implementation of immigration requirements such as literacy tests.

There was, however, an important exception to the quotas of the 1920s. Migrants from the Western Hemisphere were initially excluded from the quota system and free to migrate without such restrictions. In large part, this was due to lobbying by those in the south and west of the United States who relied on cheap labor from Mexico.[137] Later, as the economy became increasingly dependent on the cheap and expendable source of labor Mexican migrants represented, farm lobbyists and lawmakers from southern and western states most immediately dependent on this labor source worked to maintain this exemption from the quota system. This exclusion of Mexico from quotas is also in a way rooted in the ideas of the frontier myth, which casts anything outside Anglo civilization as needing to be assimilated, eradicated, or made useful. Mexican migrants were allowed to migrate more freely because they were useful. Arguments against including the Western Hemisphere in the quota system also explicitly maintained that these migrants posed no threat to Anglo civilization because they were rendered powerless, were temporary, and were a people more suited to farm labor than to supervisory roles and thus would not take jobs from superior US citizens.[138]

---

136. Tichenor, *Dividing Lines*, 130–31, 140–49.

137. Tichenor, *Dividing Lines*, 146.

138. Tichenor, *Dividing Lines*, 170–72.

The United States' complicated relationship with migrants from south of the border is evident here. These migrants were welcomed into the United States because racist beliefs in their inherent inferiority allowed them to be framed as unthreatening, meaning they could be made useful rather than simply excluded from society entirely. However, even with this sense of US superiority, we see that the sense that their otherness might make them a danger never fully goes away. Even those who can be made useful (enslaved Africans, Chinese and Mexican workers) have the potential to become a threat, especially as their population grows larger. When that happens, the United States responds by way of exclusion and expulsion. Migrant workers from Mexico, initially framed as unthreatening, became increasingly perceived as a threat to US society as these migrants increased in number and longevity.[139]

The exemption of the Western Hemisphere from the quota system came under increasing fire as ideals of equality pricked the consciences of many US citizens and began to weigh on certain lawmakers. Robert Heimburger cites in particular a 1953 report commissioned by President Truman, *Whom We Shall Welcome.* This report condemns the state of the quota system and US immigration policy in general as failing to live up to US ideals.[140] If we truly believe that all people are children of God created equally worthy of dignity, that this essential equality is unalienable, this must affect how we conceive of and apply immigration policy. As a senator, John F. Kennedy had similarly critiqued the quota system, arguing that as a whole the US immigration system was undemocratic and lacking in reason. As president, he argued that the accident of where someone was born ought not to affect one's chances of admittance into the United States.

The Immigration Act of 1965 followed this trajectory and shifted the US approach to immigration. The act identified "special immigrants" such as family members of US citizens and desired workers but sought to end discrimination based on country of origin by ending the Western Hemisphere's exemption from the quota system. Additionally, a 1976 amendment extended the cap of twenty thousand migrants from each state, already applied to states in the Eastern Hemisphere, to the Western Hemisphere, meaning that Mexico and Canada were no longer able to fill the majority of the 120,000 spots granted to the Western Hemisphere as a whole. This necessitated a significant drop in legal

139. See Chavez, *Latino Threat,* for an exploration of how Latine migrants became increasingly seen as a threat to US identity and interests.

140. The US has repeatedly failed to live up to the ideals on which it claims to base itself. While liberty, equality, and justice are the values the US claims in its founding documents, settler colonialism, manifest destiny, and the frontier myth are much closer to its actual founding ideals. In this sense, immigration policy in this nation, insofar as it has developed in direct relationship to these ideologies and systems of oppression, is and has been very consistent with the US's most foundational values.

migration from these two countries. In 1978 another amendment adjusted the quota numbers so that the Western and Eastern Hemispheres would share a total cap on migration, meaning the Western Hemisphere lost its higher quotas and was subjected to the same limits as the Eastern Hemisphere.[141]

Heimburger condemns this later implementation of quotas as failure to be good neighbors to Mexico and to honor the historic and ongoing relationship between Mexico and the United States. He argues that in applying such abstract notions of equality, the quota system treats Mexico as if it were any other nation when in fact Mexico and the United States have always had a particular relationship that must be recognized as such.[142] Heimburger's attention to the ways the particular relationships between people or nations may obligate us in specific ways is an important caution. Arguments in favor of more open immigration policies tend to rely heavily on notions of the equality and inherent dignity of all people. Insistence on equal dignity is not misplaced, especially as it is often so easy to show that US immigration policy and practice run contrary to that inherent human dignity. As the quota systems put in place in the 1960s show, however, it is not enough to simply insist on equal treatment, and in fact this approach can cause or perpetuate harm. Insisting on treating migrants from the Western Hemisphere the same as those from elsewhere sounds fine in theory, but in practice it represents a failure to understand history, migratory flows, and US labor needs. That is to say, it is a failure to attend to the particulars of the relationships between the United States and the countries to its south, particularly Mexico. Justice is not simply about equal treatment.

Heimburger is not alone in noting the disparity between the demands of migration, especially from Mexico, and the allowances of the quota system. Kristin Heyer also draws attention to this problem and the long visa backlogs it causes. Heyer argues that insufficient visa availability breaks up families, especially as family members of those migrants whose residence was legalized due to Immigration Reform and Control Act of 1986 try to join their family members in the United States. The visas allocated to countries like Mexico do not come close to meeting the demand.[143] Heyer and Heimburger provide two examples of how, by treating countries like Mexico "equally," the quota system failed to attend to the reality of migration between the United States and Mexico. We might also consider the failures of the Reagan and Bush administrations to take responsibility for migration from nations such as El Salvador and Guatemala, migration the United States had a heavy hand in causing. Nations like El Salvador

141. Heimburger, *God and the Illegal Alien*, 158–63.

142. Heimburger, *God and the Illegal Alien*, 190–208.

143. Kristin Heyer, *Kinship across Borders: a Christian Ethic of Immigration* (Washington, DC: Georgetown University Press, 2012), 65–66, 147.

or Mexico are not just nations that ought to be treated equally, like any other nation, but rather nations with whom the United States has a particular history. As I will argue in chapter 3, justice requires attention to the particulars of these relationships, not flat attempts at equality that deny the differences of history and circumstance.

The migratory paths originally created and encouraged by US policy and labor needs continue to foster migration in higher numbers than US laws allow for, resulting in "an explosion of undocumented migration."[144] The reality for many migrants is there is no viable line to join to migrate legally. Migrants wishing to reunite with their family members or in need of safety or a way to make a living find themselves with too few legal options.[145] Many conclude that their best chance is to cross the border without documentation. This drastic increase in undocumented migration has been encouraged by the fact that the United States has a history of tacitly allowing such migratory practices, primarily because they were understood to suit US interests. Historically, the border between the United States and Mexico has been considered too large to effectively prevent undocumented border crossing, and a general understanding prevailed in Congress that undocumented migration supplied an important labor force on which US employers relied. The United States developed a habit of largely ignoring undocumented migration, forbidding it by law but largely failing to enforce those laws.[146]

We have seen that alongside the legal migration allowed by the Bracero Program, large numbers of undocumented migrants also came from Mexico and were in many ways encouraged to do so by a US economy that relied on their labor and a government that largely ignored their presence. This was initially a temporary and circular pattern of undocumented migration. Migrants came, worked, and then returned home with increased means of providing for their families. In 1986 the Immigration Reform and Control Act legalized some of these undocumented migrants, but it also implemented increased border enforcement policies that made more traditional, circular migration difficult. The result was that migrants were more likely to stay in the United States long term rather than returning to their families, as there was an increased danger that they would be unable to cross the border multiple times.[147] A consequence of this was that it became increasingly likely that the families of these once temporary migrant workers would follow them to the United States. However,

144. Heimburger, *God and the Illegal Alien*, 174.

145. Heyer, *Kinship across Borders*, 66.

146. Heimburger, *God and the Illegal Alien*, 156, 173.

147. Heimburger, *God and the Illegal Alien*, 176.

because the act "failed to provide status to family members of IRCA beneficiaries," even the families of legal residents were left with few options for reunification. This has resulted in increased undocumented migration, especially of women, as families have sought extralegal ways to reunify and also as more women have taken on roles as head of household and migrated with and without their families.[148]

As the United States began to focus more on limiting the migration of people across its borders, it also worked to increase the movement of goods and business across those same borders through the North American Free Trade Agreement (NAFTA). NAFTA destabilized the Mexican economy and caused massive migration by forcing Mexican farmers, unable to compete with imported and US-subsidized goods, off their land to seek livelihoods elsewhere.[149] While NAFTA was facilitating the movement of goods and money across borders and displacing Mexican farmers, it did nothing to simultaneously provide options for those displaced people, nor did it coincide with any efforts to make space for this newly displaced population in the US immigration system. On the contrary, NAFTA coincided instead with the beginning of Operation Gatekeeper and its efforts to deter undocumented migration by forcing migrants away from cities and onto rougher, far more dangerous terrain. Meant as a deterrent, Operation Gatekeeper relied on the danger of these routes to discourage people from undocumented migration. In practice, it resulted in more than two thousand deaths in its first decade.[150] A 1993 report by the Government Accounting Office anticipated that the impacts of NAFTA on the Mexican economy, especially the displacement

148. Heyer, *Kinship across Borders*, 62, 65.

149. One element of NAFTA was that it forced Mexico to amend its constitution, Article 27 of which had stated that much communal land and natural resources could not be bought by or sold to foreigners. By making this land and these resources commodities to be gobbled up by US businesses, NAFTA fundamentally changed the Mexican economy and way of life. See Jeff Veteto, "Foreign Land Ownership on Mexico's Coasts: The Proposed Amendment to Article 27 of the Mexican Constitution," *Law and Business Review of the Americas* 20, no. 2 (Spring 2014): 325–34.

150. Heyer, *Kinship across Borders*, 9–11. It is worth noting that the extreme cost of life related to this policy alone is enough to draw into question Hoffmeier's insistence that nothing in Scripture abrogates US immigration policy. Whatever position may be argued about a nation's rights to defend its borders or the right of a nation to take a human life if that person breaks the law or represents a threat, policies such as Operation Gatekeeper, with the explicit purpose of putting human life in danger in order to deter undocumented migration, are a clear assault on human dignity. Further, as will become more evident in coming chapters, the failure of the US to live in just relationship with its neighbors to the south is evidence of a deep disconnect between US society and the values of Scripture. These values will be considered more fully below.

of farmers, would result in a spike in migration from Mexico to the United States, as Mexico would be unable to provide work for everyone who would need it.[151] This is to say that the effects of NAFTA on Mexico, and the resultant migration north, were not unforeseen, and yet little was done to provide space or mitigate harm.[152]

Heimburger argues that one of the biggest problems with the US immigration system is that the government's power to exclude and deport is largely unchecked. Any true tie between US law and a larger moral framework or outside standard of justice has been severed. It is basically up to the nation to decide what is right and just and to judge for itself what it ought to do. National interests drive the laws, and any true consideration of justice is rendered toothless and unbinding.[153] Relatedly, Ablavsky notes that the constitutional structures created for the purpose of removing Indigenous peoples from their land formed the basis for the nation's global empire in the decades and centuries that followed. These structures included in particular "federal territorial plenary power" and "the exclusion of subject peoples from the privileges of representation and citizenship."[154] In doing so, the crafters of the Constitution gave the federal government of the United States incredible power, which it has consistently used to advance its own interests at the expense of people it chooses not to care about, while refusing to take any substantial or meaningful responsibility for the problems it causes. A result is that the modern US immigration system has functioned and in many ways continues to function to protect the rights and interests of some at the expense of others. How to respond to this sinful reality will be the task of the forthcoming chapters.

151. US Government Accounting Office, "North American Free Trade Agreement; Assessment of Major Issues," vol. 2, GAO/GGD-93-137, September 9, 1993, https://www.gao.gov/products/GGD-93-137.

152. For a more in-depth look at NAFTA and the broader socioeconomic relationship between the US and Mexico, see Ralph Haughwout Folsom, *NAFTA, Free Trade and Foreign Investment in the Americas in a Nutshell* (St. Paul, MN: West Academic, 2014); John Perkins, *The New Confessions of an Economic Hit Man* (San Francisco: Berrett-Koehler, 2016); John Carlos Frey, *Sand and Blood: America's Stealth War on the Mexico Border* (New York: Bold Type Books, 2019); Nancy Pineda-Madrid, *Suffering and Salvation in Ciudad Juárez* (Minneapolis: Fortress, 2011); Kathryn Kopinak, *Desert Capitalism: Maquiladoras in North America's Western Industrial Corridor* (Tucson: University of Arizona Press, 1996).

153. Heimburger, *God and the Illegal Alien*, 86–94.

154. Ablavsky, "Savage Constitution," 1083–84. Federal plenary power gives the federal government the "power to dispose of and make all needful Rules and Regulations respecting the Territory or other Property belonging to the United States." Constitution of the United States, article IV, section, 3 clause 2.3.

Concluding Thoughts

This chapter has mapped the development of ideologies and practices that have shaped US identity, foreign policy, and immigration policy and discourse. We can see that immigration discourse and policy in the United States is rooted in the sinful mythologies of settler colonialism, embedded deep in the heart of US identity and self-understanding. This has not only fundamentally shaped the nation's approach to immigration directly but has had a considerable impact on foreign policy, resulting in unjust action within, beyond, and at US borders. This has also directly affected migration, as migratory patterns into the United States were in many ways caused by US imperialism. US immigration policy too often fails to reflect this culpability.

Dunbar-Ortiz writes that "under the crust of that portion of the Earth called the United States of America—'from California . . . to the Gulf Stream waters'—are interred the bones, villages, fields, and sacred objects of American Indians."[155] We might add to this account the immense amounts of harm the nation has done beyond its borders. This history must be reckoned with. There can be no sufficient ethics of immigration that does not account for how the United States came to be the nation it is, what impact this historical development has had on the rest of the world, and how this might be factored into the creation of just immigration policy. The building of a more just world requires articulating and acknowledging past wrongs in order to begin attending to these injustices and their continued impact on the world. We must find ways to repair the damage unjust relationships have caused.

What is needed is a framework that highlights relationships as a central focal point for navigating ethical questions. To this end, chapter 3 takes the patterns identified in chapters 1–2 and applies them to a responsibility ethics framework in order to argue that this history obligates the United States to migrants and the countries from which they come. I will argue that US immigration policy ought to reflect its culpability in the creation of a world in which people are forced to migrate and that it can do so by creating tangible reparations. We will also consider how the United States might reckon with its founding mythologies and repent for the harm they have caused.

155. Dunbar-Ortiz, *Indigenous Peoples' History*, 1.

CHAPTER THREE

Responsibility

To support his claims about the importance of defending sovereignty in order to preserve the rule of law, Mark Amstutz points to the current migration trends in Europe, in which most migrants are refugees fleeing conflict. These refugees, he argues, are "victims of failed states—a reminder of the importance of well governed societies for any global system of justice."[1] Framing migration in this way implies that these "failed states" are solely responsible for their situation and thus for the production of refugees. What his account does not address is how these nations came to be failed in the first place. In contrast, Marianne Heimbach-Steins's postcolonial lens shows the way migration patterns in Europe have often been the result of colonial relationships.[2] In other words, while all states bear the responsibility for providing (or failing to provide) their people with adequate access to and protection of their human rights, placing responsibility solely on the failure of individual nation states to provide their citizens with rights befitting their human dignity belies the global dynamics that drive migration and ignores the fact that nations do not become failed states alone in a vacuum.

Focusing primarily or solely on the failure of sending countries to adequately provide for their citizens provides a one-dimensional account of a multidimensional reality. In reality, migration is driven by a number of factors that include but cannot be limited to the choices and failures of sending nations.[3] Often, the colonialist expansionism of nations such as Britain and the United States (and later the expansionism of corporations[4]) contributed significantly to the instability of what Amstutz labels failed states. Amstutz would do well to acknowledge the role "stable" nations have played in destabilizing the failed states he charges with driving migration into Europe. When we miss this vital context, the story of migration becomes one in which sending states, unwilling or unable to take responsibility, burden host nations with picking up the slack. Taking in or providing aid to migrants becomes an act of generosity on the part of these host nations rather than

1. Amstutz, "Two Theories of Immigration."

2. Heimbach-Steins, "Migration in a Post-colonial World."

3. Sociologist Saskia Sassen provides a helpful account of the multifaceted dynamics that contribute to migration flows worldwide (*Expulsions*).

4. See, for example, Heyer, *Kinship across Borders*, 100–104.

an acknowledgment of the role these nations have often played in creating the conditions under which people migrate. Our understanding of history, our stories about what has happened and what is happening now in our own nations and more globally, influence how we think about who is responsible for responding to migration.[5]

Herein lies the importance of the account of history highlighted in the preceding chapters. In its divergence from more dominant accounts of US history, it makes evident that the telling of history is never a neutral, objective activity. History can always only ever be told as narrative, and narratives always have a point of view. A dominant, Eurocentric perspective has tended to be taught in US schools while the perspectives uplifted in the previous chapter have largely gone unnoticed and untaught. This results in a US populace insufficiently versed in the uglier side of US history or the role the United States has played in creating the present status quo and in driving global migration. This narrative serves the status quo, keeping US power structures largely intact by making them seem natural and good rather than the result of centuries of unjust action.[6] Historical narratives and their biases matter. "Those whose voices are ignored or forgotten are those whose perspectives are most often left out of social narratives."[7] It is therefore particularly important to hear the perspectives of those whose voices have been silenced or ignored, especially the voices of those who have been harmed in the process of establishing or maintaining the status quo. Justice requires accurate narratives,[8] and we do not get an accurate narrative without paying attention to those who have been harmed.

Understanding the realities of how the United States gained control of its present borders, or the ways in which US policy has contributed to migration flows, ought to influence how we think about what just immigration policy entails. The previous chapters have shown that throughout its history, the United States has forged unjust relationships for which it has not taken responsibility.

5. Rajendra, *Migrants and Citizens*, 129.

6. Indeed, in recent years there has been a concerted effort to exclude from schools any account of history that paints the US in a less than positive light. Terry Gross, "From Slavery to Socialism, New Legislation Restricts What Teachers Can Discuss," NPR, February 3, 2022, https://tinyurl.com/3svpww52; Brian Lopez, "Republican Bill That Limits How Race, Slavery and History Are Taught in Texas Schools Becomes Law," *Texas Tribune*, December 2, 2021, https://www.texastribune.org/2021/12/02/texas-critical-race-theory-law/; Olivia B. Waxman, "Anti-'Critical Race Theory' Laws Are Working. Teachers Are Thinking Twice about How They Talk about Race," *Time*, June 30, 2022, https://time.com/6192708/critical-race-theory-teachers-racism/.

7. Rajendra, *Migrants and Citizens*, 115.

8. Rajendra, *Migrants and Citizens*, 109.

This chapter therefore offers an ethical framework that might help bring these dynamics to the fore and allow us to think more concretely about the specific responsibilities host nations such as the United States might have to migrants. I will argue that this framework can help us take the biblical account of justice seriously in our ethical decision-making.

Beyond Communitarianism and Cosmopolitanism: The Third Way

In general, approaches to immigration have tended to fall into one of two major moral frameworks. The first of these frameworks is communitarianism.[9] In the immigration debate, communitarians often consider themselves political realists. They insist that the Westphalian nation-state system is the world that we have and within which we must work. Communitarians tend to emphasize the importance of the goods this system makes possible. In particular, they argue that human rights are best promoted by strong, sovereign states, and thus sovereignty must be protected. This tends to lead to a strong emphasis on upholding the rule of law, such as we saw from Amstutz and Hoffmeier in chapter 2. While most communitarians grant that there is an ultimate higher authority that sometimes puts us at odds with human law, the instances in which they see this actually happening are considerably limited, and so the law should in general be followed and respected. Overall, communitarian perspectives tend to focus on the importance of national sovereignty, protecting the particularity of nations and communities, defending and promoting the rule of law.[10]

Conversely, others enter the immigration debate from a cosmopolitan perspective. Cosmopolitans tend to emphasize the moral obligation to care for all of humanity. They believe that whatever our local or national ties may be, we are all connected and responsible to each other as one human family under God. Human dignity, often rooted in our creation in God's image, is one foundational basis for this approach. Cosmopolitans are generally more hesitant to take the status quo for granted and often see fit to challenge it based on their cosmopolitan understanding of Christian or biblical values and what they understand to be God's vision for the world. Cosmopolitans tend to center themes such as

9. My use of the language of communitarianism (and cosmopolitanism) is consistent with much recent migration discourse. It is important, for clarity, to distinguish this particular use of this language from how these terms are sometimes used outside the field of migration ethics. For a helpful example of how these terms have been used in migration discourse, see Amstutz, *Just Immigration*, 80–109.

10. See Nigel Biggar, *Between Kin and Cosmopolis: An Ethic of the Nation* (Cambridge: Clarke, 2014); Amstutz, *Just Immigration*; Hoffmeier, *Immigration Crisis*.

human dignity, global solidarity, hospitality, and the preferential option for the poor and oppressed.[11]

In summary, Kristin Heyer reports that in migration ethics communitarian arguments begin "from a more narrowly circumscribed understanding of belonging" and "root defense of membership restrictions in the duties of states to preserve particular cultures or political identities," while "for those who subscribe to cosmopolitan approaches, national boundaries require moral justification."[12] Basically, communitarian ethics "begins at home,"[13] assuming a need to protect what is good about local communities first and foremost, while cosmopolitan ethics begin more broadly, concerned first with considering what justice is owed to all people before attending to more local concerns.

Both approaches raise important questions, moral principles, and goods we should seek to protect. My own understanding of immigration and the ethical concerns related to it is deeply indebted to thinkers from both perspectives. However, both approaches are limited. Communitarians too often take the status quo for granted and offer little in terms of guidance for reckoning with historical injustices that status quo has caused or through which the status quo has been achieved. Cosmopolitans offer important insights into how a just world ought to look but do not usually provide sufficient guidance for responding ethically in the aftermath of injustice. In order to take the account of US history provided in chapters 1–2 seriously, therefore, a different framework is needed. It is this need to which the present chapter responds.

A number of philosophers and theologians have undertaken the important tasks of both bridging the gaps between communitarian and cosmopolitan approaches in order to uphold the important commitments each identifies and, importantly, moving beyond the boundaries of that dichotomy in order to identify what both approaches miss. For example, philosopher Kwame Anthony

---

11. See Daniel G. Groody, "Crossing the Divide: Foundations of a Theology of Migration and Refugees," *TS* 70, no. 3 (2009): 638–67; Groody, "Jesus and the Undocumented Immigrant: A Spiritual Geography of a Crucified People," *TS* 70, no. 2 (2009): 298–316; Groody, "Migration: A Theological Vision," in *Intersections of Religion and Migration: Issues at the Global Crossroads*, ed. Jennifer B. Saunders, Elena Fiddian-Qasmiyeh, and Susanna Snyder (New York: Palgrave Macmillan, 2016), 225–40; Elizabeth W. Collier and Charles R. Strain, *Religious and Ethical Perspectives on Global Migration* (Lanham, MD: Lexington Books, 2014); Fleur S. Houston, *You Shall Love the Stranger as Yourself: The Bible, Refugees, and Asylum* (New York: Routledge, 2015); Heimburger, *God and the Illegal Alien*.

12. Heyer, *Kinship across Borders*, 111.

13. William O'Neill, "The Place of Displacement: Ethics of Migration in the United States," in *Living with(out) Borders*, ed. Agnes Brazal and Maria Teresa Davila (Maryknoll, NY: Orbis, 2016), 68.

Appiah proposes what he calls "rooted cosmopolitanism." In response to criticisms that cosmopolitanism is ungrounded and unpatriotic, he insists that while it may be opposed to nationalism, cosmopolitanism does not preclude patriotism or loyalty to one's community or nation. If patriotism is a sentiment, a certain pride in or love for our local or national community, there is nothing inherent in it that goes against cosmopolitan views. Likewise, cosmopolitanism, as a sentiment of loyalty to or care for all of humanity, does not preclude care for those closest to us, nor does it necessarily deny specific responsibilities to those with whom we have more direct relationships.[14] We can see, then, that Appiah finds a middle ground. His work is rooted in cosmopolitan ideals but also takes seriously the importance of the specific responsibilities we may have to those to whom we are most closely related. Appiah's work shows that there is possibility beyond the starkly divided cosmopolitan/communitarian debate and that both approaches lift up goods worth defending. Recognizing that these goods might not be mutually exclusive is an important first step toward approximating a better migration ethic.

William O'Neill similarly resists the communitarian/cosmopolitan binary. He insists that the communitarian approach often leaves migrants virtually "[expelled] from humanity altogether," while cosmopolitan (which he calls "The Liberal Abstract Citizen") approaches lack the specificity to foster actual obligation among host nations.[15] In response, he turns instead to Catholic social teaching to uplift the virtues of both approaches while moving beyond their limited scope. Catholic social teaching, he argues, seeks balance between the importance of individual rights and the demands of the common good, making it a strong bridge between the two major approaches to migration. Unlike communitarianism's "members and citizens" and cosmopolitanism's "abstract citizen," O'Neill insists, the church relies on the idea of neighbors, both near and distant, as a grounding metaphor for thinking about our relationship to the global community. The social teaching of the Catholic Church, he argues, calls people to be neighborly to all people, regardless of distance.

At first glance, this may seem like basic cosmopolitanism. What O'Neill seeks, however, is a more concrete balance between the demands of the common good and subsidiarity (in other words, between global and local

14. Kwame Anthony Appiah, "Cosmopolitan Patriotism," in *For Love of Country*, ed. Martha Nussbaum (Boston: Beacon, 2002), 619–22. Conversely, Appiah labels nationalism an ideology, one he argues is incompatible with cosmopolitan sentiments.

15. William O'Neill, "Rights of Passage: The Ethics of Forced Displacement," *Journal of the Society of Christian Ethics* 27, no. 1 (2007): 116. He cites Hannah Arendt, "The Perplexities of the Rights of Man," *Headline Series* 318 (Winter 1998): 88.

responsibilities).[16] Recognizing the stranger as neighbor establishes solidarity with all people. For O'Neill, this makes possible "equitable policies of voluntary repatriation, reintegration, rehabilitation, and reconstruction" as well as hospitable treatment of migrants.[17] In other words, seeing people as near and distant neighbors rather than, for example, citizens and migrants, helps citizens of host nations to view migrants as proper recipients of concrete care, people we must take into consideration. The imagery of near and distant neighbors allows space for differentiating those with whom we have greater proximity (we will consider what proximity means below) and those with whom we have lesser, without abolishing the concrete responsibility to be neighborly to all people (even if that may look different in different situations).

For O'Neill, in this motif of near and distant neighbors the Catholic tradition offers a model in which a universal respect for all humans can be applied to concrete others rather than as an abstract ideal.[18] That is, in this model appeals to universal human dignity are given actual specificity and weight in real encounters with concrete, actual human individuals with specific needs and relationships. The migrant at US borders is not a generalized other worthy of some lofty ideal summarized in the phrase "human dignity" but an actual neighbor with specific needs to whom a response is owed in accordance with their concrete human dignity. The migrant is someone we must treat in a neighborly way. This turn to a more specifically Christian key for framing the immigration discourse represents an important move away from the confines of the dominant binary. In following chapters, I will move this insight further by considering how the biblical notion of a neighbor directs us not only to provide for each other's concrete needs but to build just relationships with one another.

O'Neill finds that while the Catholic tradition takes seriously the rights of all people to seek lives worthy of their dignity as persons, and the responsibility of states to care for those who are most vulnerable (including refugees and migrants), these teachings are simply aspirational if they do not include concrete ways of prioritizing our responsibilities to near and distant neighbors. One method he offers for determining the obligations of specific states to specific migrants is by considering "special relationships with refugees or migrants:

16. William O'Neill and William Spohn, "Rights of Passage: The Ethics of Immigration and Refugee Policy," *TS* 59, no. 1 (1998): 84–106.

17. William O'Neill, "What We Owe to Refugees and IDPs: An Inquiry into the Rights of the Forcibly Displaced," in *Refugee Rights: Ethics, Advocacy, and Africa*, ed. David Hollenbach (Washington, DC: Georgetown University Press, 2008), 37–38.

18. O'Neill, "Rights of Passage," 113–36.

familial relationship, complicity of the host country in generating immigration/refugee flows, and historical or cultural affiliations (e.g. patterns of migration)."[19] This call for countries to consider their own complicity in the creation of global migration is a recurring theme in O'Neill's work,[20] representing a shift toward a more responsibility-based approach to migration ethics. He further insists that the moral commitments of the Catholic tradition call for a continual revision of social structures and ordering of society in order to ensure that the rights of all people, especially those most vulnerable, are being protected and no one is left behind.[21] He insists that the eschatological vision Christians are called to live into in this life is one in which hospitality is extended especially to those who are vulnerable and in need. If this is to be the Christian eschatological understanding of kinship, then it ought to inform Christian understandings of membership and solidarity now.[22]

David Hollenbach argues that in general a cosmopolitan approach that casts the scope of responsibility more widely and focuses on the needs and rights of all humanity is perhaps the most helpful overall worldview for addressing migration. While he agrees with Appiah that this must not preclude diversity and local responsibilities, he nevertheless finds the cosmopolitan ideal important for challenging the adequacy of our present systems.[23] However, Hollenbach also views national sovereignty as a vital good to be protected and argues that as a general rule, sovereignty ought to be respected.[24] This dual concern for the rights of all people and for the importance of sovereignty leads him to consider the circumstances under which a nation's obligation to care for migrants might take moral priority over that nation's sovereignty.[25] In response, Hollenbach offers the Kew Gardens principle as a

19. O'Neill and Spohn, "Rights of Passage."

20. See, for example, O'Neill, "Rights of Passage," 122.

21. O'Neill and Spohn, "Rights of Passage."

22. William O'Neill, "The Place of Displacement: A Theological Locus," *Colloquium* 46, no. 1 (May 2014): 104.

23. David Hollenbach, "Internally Displaced People, Sovereignty, and the Responsibility to Protect," in Hollenbach, *Refugee Rights*, 184–85.

24. David Hollenbach, "A Future beyond Borders: Reimagining the Nation-State and the Church," in Brazal and Dávila, *Living with(out) Borders*, 227; David Hollenbach, *Humanity in Crisis: Ethical and Religious Response to Refugees* (Washington, DC: Georgetown University Press, 2020).

25. Hollenbach, "Internally Displaced People," 177–91.

guide for considering what obligations might be said to outweigh a nation's right to sovereign borders.[26]

A universal responsibility to all people does not mean that responsibility to each person looks the same. Rather, various communal bonds and forms of relationship can make us more specifically or immediately responsible to certain people. To all people, humans have responsibilities to, for example, do no harm. More specifically, Hollenbach argues that people may understand themselves to be responsible to respond to the needs of others when a critical need exists, they are in proximity to that need, they have some capacity to address that need, and when there are no other sources of aid likely to be available. He warns that this system cannot be applied in a mechanical fashion but suggests instead that it is meant to guide the consideration of global responsibility. He further qualifies that proximity ought not to be thought of merely in terms of physical distance but rather primarily in terms of knowledge of a need.[27] If we are aware of a need, we are in closer proximity to it than someone who is unaware. He has also suggested that a nation's participation in the creation of refugees, such as military action in the sending country, might create moral obligation, another form of proximity.[28] Like O'Neill, he also argues that nations have obligations to particular people based on existing cross-border relationships.[29] In his later work on the topic, Hollenbach more fully picks up the question of the root causes of migration and the role those root causes might have in delegating responsibility to migrants.

While laying out the usefulness of the Kew Gardens principle, Hollenbach notes that in complex political situations, the principle of last resort may be difficult to determine definitively. He therefore calls for the creation of global systems of response in order that the global community may reliably and regularly respond quickly to a given need.[30] This system of global partnership must divide responsibility and cost fairly, depending on various nations' abilities to provide

26. The Kew Gardens principle originated in the assault and murder of Kitty Genovese in Kew Gardens, New York City, during which a reported 38 people witnessed her distress and failed to aid her. While it has since come to light that this initial report is not entirely factual, the case gave rise to much consideration about the moral duty to aid those in need. The principle argues that agents have responsibility based on critical need, proximity, capacity, and likelihood of being a last resort. See David Hollenbach, "Borders and Duties to the Displaced: Ethical Perspectives on the Refugee Protection System," *Journal on Migration and Human Security* 4, no. 3 (2016): 156.

27. Hollenbach, "Internally Displaced People," 186–89.

28. Hollenbach, "Future beyond Borders," 231.

29. David Hollenbach, *Driven from Home: Protecting the Rights of Forced Migrants* (Washington, DC: Georgetown University Press, 2010, 6).

30. Hollenbach, "Internally Displaced People," 189.

different types of aid, so that the burdens or costs of aid to migrants in need does not disproportionately fall on nations with less capacity while other nations contribute little.[31] Hollenbach names the consideration of how to achieve such fairness "perhaps the greatest ethical challenge facing the humanitarian movement today."[32] He draws attention to the importance of structural change rather than just temporary emergency aid (although he notes that this will always play an important role) in building a more just world in which fewer people are forced to migrate, which is for him the ultimate goal. Hollenbach suggests three areas of focus for this structural work: the reduction of conflict, the promotion of development globally, and the significant reduction of human-caused climate change.[33] His attention to cross-border relationships, root causes, and the need for structural change raises important themes for the development of a responsibility-based approach to immigration.

Heyer has also made significant moves toward a more relational model for migration ethics. Both cosmopolitan and communitarian approaches, she argues, "fall short of providing meaningful protections" to migrants.[34] She writes,

> Whereas communitarian and cosmopolitan models tend to focus on rights to movement and reception alone, categories like justice-in-relation, the global common good, or restorative justice contextualize the individual acts of migrants and underscore social dimensions of justice and sinful complicity alike. Relational frameworks rightly signal it is not merely those who overstay visas or unscrupulous employers who bear responsibility for an undocumented presence; they orient analyses toward root causes of displacement and shared accountability.[35]

31. Consider, for example, the burdens that have fallen on Turkey as refugees have fled across their borders and other nations have failed to step up and help shoulder that responsibility, even if their capacity to provide aid is arguably greater than Turkey's. Luke McGee, "A Migration Crisis and Disagreement with Turkey Is the Last Thing Europe Needs Right Now," CNN, March 2, 2020, https://www.cnn.com/2020/03/02/europe/turkey-migrant-crisis-european-union-intl/index.html. This is precisely the form of unequal sharing of responsibility Hollenbach seeks to prevent.

32. Hollenbach, *Humanity in Crisis*, 112.

33. Hollenbach, *Humanity in Crisis*, 130–54.

34. Kristin Heyer, "Migrants Feared and Forsaken: A Catholic Ethic of Social Responsibility," *Interdisciplinary Journal for Religion and Transformation in Contemporary Society* 6, no. 1 (2020): 160, https://doi.org/10.30965/23642807-00601010.

35. Kristin E. Heyer, "Internalized Borders: Immigration Ethics in the Age of Trump," *TS* 79, no. 1 (2018): 157.

Heyer's approach centers on the themes of social sin and human relationships, highlighting the ways in which contemporary policy and discourse fail to protect families or honor global relationships.[36] Her insight that the current US immigration system operates in direct contrast to Christian values because of the way it separates, puts undue stress on, or otherwise harms families is a helpful example of how a more relationship-focused approach to migration ethics highlights the sinfulness of the contemporary situation.[37]

More directly relevant for the present project, however, is her focus on social sin and global relationships, through which she identifies how neoliberal capitalist systems have produced massive global inequality, both within and between nations. This inequality, spurred by the global extension of corporate power (exemplified by the effects of NAFTA, as outlined in chapter 2), turns migration to countries such as the United States into "a strategy for survival" for those globalization has left behind or exploited.[38] Naming this a situation of social sin (consistent with the account provided above in chapter 1), Heyer links increased global migration to this situation of corporate expansion, an important development for establishing relationships between host nations and migrants in order to determine a responsibility to care. In this way, her work helps bring the less visible relationships between migrants and host countries to the fore, an important counternarrative pushing back against the laying of blame solely on "failed states." Like O'Neill, she turns to a more specifically Catholic Christian lens, arguing that "the Catholic tradition's social anthropology, understanding of social sin, and commitment to a global common good are poised to reorient responsibility," opening up a more robust understanding of global relationships and cross-border responsibilities.[39]

In drawing attention to the dynamics of social sin at play in the push and pull of global migration, Heyer makes space for the important consideration of the ideologies that support and perpetuate sinful social structures.[40] As was evident in chapters 1–2, more attention is due to the relationship between the founding ideologies of the United States—manifest destiny and the frontier myth—and the nation's approach to foreign policy and immigration law. Heyer shifts the conversation away from debates of states' rights versus human rights, drawing attention instead to an interrogation of host nations' hostilities toward

36. Heyer, *Kinship across Borders*, 4; see also Heyer, "Internalized Borders," 146–64.

37. Heyer, *Kinship across Borders*, 61–88. This also once again makes clear that Hoffmeier offers insufficient evidence that the present US immigration system does not contrast biblical values.

38. Heyer, *Kinship across Borders*, 100–104.

39. Heyer, "Migrants Feared and Forsaken," 158.

40. Heyer, "Migrants Feared and Forsaken," 165–67.

migrants, raising this up as important for ethical consideration. Not only does this open a new and important area of consideration, but also understanding the situation more fully through the lens of social sin in this way can prompt US citizens to better consider their own role and complicity in the injustices of US foreign and immigration policies. This also provides space for a fuller consideration of what the situation of global migration calls nations and individuals to. In moving emphasis away from simple defense of human rights toward a more robust consideration of what is needed for the "unmasking of complex structures and ideologies" that abet injustice, for which all citizens are responsible,[41] Heyer therefore offers an important reframing of immigration as a topic for Christian ethics, providing a theological lens through which to consider the structural issues to which she and Hollenbach have drawn particular attention.

The language of sin Heyer uses is especially helpful here. In Christian theology, having sinned necessitates certain responses for the sinner, specifically recognition, repentance, and repair. Moreover, sin has often been understood in terms of relationship: most notably the relationship between humans and God but also relationships between humans. Sin represents a breaking of these relationships. The recognition that we have sinned, then, calls us to repent and repair the relationship that has been broken. While the language of injustice might signify the same dynamics identified with the terms "social sin" or "structural sin," "sin" carries a particular connotation that can help drive the focus on repairing relationships for which this book ultimately argues. Labeling US history and policies as social and structural sin in which all US citizens participate therefore has the power to draw attention to our own culpability and to call us into the work of repair. The importance of this work of repair will be outlined in chapter 4.

Heyer also connects this situation of global social sin and the root ideologies that abet that sin to a consideration of the rule of law, arguing that "when the present system fails to protect fundamental human rights in these ways, it does not itself honor the rule of law,"[42] helping to articulate why unnuanced or ahistorical appeals to the rule of law are insufficient. She argues that many in the United States have been lulled by national ideology into equating obedience to the rule of law with just living.[43] Her work emphasizes that responsibility lies primarily with the systems that fail to protect and promote human dignity (and those who support these systems), not with humans seeking to survive within and in spite of those systems. She shows how "the U.S. criminal justice system and Christian churches alike" have failed to take seriously enough

41. Heyer, "Migrants Feared and Forsaken," 165.

42. Heyer, *Kinship across Borders*, 137.

43. Heyer, "Social Sin and Immigration," 429.

the ways in which our systems and structures abet lawbreaking and constrain human agency.[44]

In response to this, Heyer calls us to a "subversive hospitality" that breaks through the ideologies that shape our understanding of migrants and refuses to reduce justice to obedience to human law. She argues that what is needed is an approach to migration "committed to truth-telling regarding the nation's historical confrontations with immigrant waves and repentance regarding its complicity in generating push and pull factors" in order to "move the debate beyond amnesic scapegoating."[45] Furthermore, in her later work Heyer draws attention to the ways increased divisiveness and isolationist tendencies on the part of the United States pose a serious problem to the development of a more just immigration system. What is needed, she argues, is a rebuilding of public trust in which a broader sense of community can be established. This will allow for greater accountability as citizens learn to take their responsibilities to migrants more seriously.[46] Heyer's themes of truth telling, accountability, and repentance are key for the framework this chapter is building.

Tisha Rajendra argues that while Christian appeals to human dignity, the option for the poor, and the call to welcome strangers are of course relevant and important, they remain insufficient because they do not sufficiently allocate responsibility and thus fail to adequately address the needs of migrants or help us navigate the proper response to these needs. Instead of these too-general appeals to Christian values, Rajendra argues that "the relationships between citizens and migrants that initiated and sustain migration systems must be at the heart of the Christian ethics of migration."[47] In other words, the pivotal question for migration ethics is not about the proper balance between states' rights and human rights but about the relationships between citizens and migrants—how those relationships have formed, where they have been unjust, and what responsibilities might exist within and because of these relationships.

Rajendra highlights the ways that this relationship based approach is consistent with the biblical account of migration. She shows that in Scripture, justice is rooted in specific relationships, especially Israel's relationship to God, and is thus best understood as fidelity to the demands of specific relationships. Furthermore, Israel is given specific commands on how to behave toward others, most particularly toward the foreigners among them, based on their history as oppressed foreigners in Egypt. God draws for Israel a specific relationship of

44. Heyer, *Kinship across Borders*, 156–57.

45. Heyer, *Kinship across Borders*, 145, 142.

46. Heyer, "Internalized Borders," 162–63.

47. Rajendra, *Migrants and Citizens*, 12, 52.

responsibility between themselves and migrants in their midst by connecting them in the common experience of being foreigners in a strange land. Israel is to treat the foreigners among them well so that they do not become like Egypt to them.[48] Biblically speaking, then, we can see that the consideration of just treatment of migrants need not be predicated on the good but insufficiently particular ideals of human dignity and welcoming the stranger but rather can be thought of in terms of the way specific histories and relationships involve certain responsibilities.[49] Working out of this biblical analysis, Rajendra proposes a framework for considering immigration that is based on specific relationships of responsibility.[50]

As an example, Rajendra highlights the history of European guest-worker programs to show how relationships of responsibility ought to be understood. These programs cooperated with foreign governments to recruit foreign workers to fill temporary labor needs. The explicit intention of these programs was that the migration be temporary. These programs were considered good for the host country because as noncitizens these migrants' rights were limited. The belief was that such workers would accept lower standards of labor and lower wages than citizens, could be provided with fewer benefits, and would either leave of their own accord or could be deported when their labor was no longer necessary. Rajendra points out that this program hinged precisely on the difference between citizens and migrants, relying on the ability to treat those with no citizenship status differently because of that lack of status. Ultimately, "these programs were premised on relationships in which citizens commodified the guest workers," using them as sources of labor but keeping them separate from the social and political community and the rights that community enjoys. In reality, these programs ended up resulting in much more permanent migration than they were intended to. Rajendra writes, "The guest workers were human beings with family ties who made decisions within the context of the larger macro- and mesostructures of guest-worker programs, family reunification policies, and their

48. Rajendra, *Migrants and Citizens*, 94–109.

49. Importantly, the land that is entrusted to Israel by God is given on the condition that they are just, that is, that they fulfill the demands of their relationship with God, which include just treatment of foreigners. Although this is not the major point I want to draw from Rajendra's analysis, it is interesting to consider this in light of manifest destiny. If America really believed in any serious way that this land is God-given or entrusted, might we also say from Jewish and Christian perspectives that the very entrustment of that land is conditional and that we are meant to treat others justly, not remove them when they get in our way. There is, I think, a real danger in playing into the myth of manifest destiny in this way, so I am cautious of it. However, I also think it is important to reach people with language they can relate to, and I wonder whether this idea could provide a stepping stone out of the sinful structures I have outlined in this book.

50. Rajendra, *Migrants and Citizens*, 72–75.

own social networks."[51] As much as these programs tried to reduce migrants to their labor, in reality they arrived as full human beings with a full array of human needs.

Over time, this disconnect between the host countries' desires and the humanity of guest workers led to increased undocumented populations in host countries and to higher desire for families to migrate as well to join their relatives. In other words, while the programs tried to keep guest workers at arm's length, firmly defined only by their capacity to provide cheap labor, in reality they became part of Europe.[52] A Christian ethic of migration must, according to Rajendra, take the historical creation of these relationships seriously and allocate responsibility to migrants accordingly. Host countries may not have intended to forge relationships with full human beings who came with full human needs, but their actions did so anyway. The responsibility this creates between host country and migrant must be attended to in order to move toward more just immigration discourse and policy.

Moving Forward

These thinkers offer vital contributions to the field of Christian migration ethics, and the present project is deeply indebted to them. There is, however, more work to be done. Drawing especially from Heyer and Rajenra's accounts of culpability and responsibility, this project looks closely at the notion that justice is concerned not only with how we ought to treat one another but also especially with what must be done to mend a broken relationship. The United States has obligations because it has specifically and repeatedly failed to live in just relationship with other countries. O'Neill calls for the consideration of the "complicity of the host country in generating immigration/refugee flows."[53] Together with the historical account provided in chapters 1–2, this chapter considers such US complicity and argues that framing justice in terms of taking responsibility for this complicity garners a more productive set of questions and considerations than do broader questions of the just treatment of strangers or foreigners. It frames the discussion of migration as a discussion of what the United States owes to others because of past and ongoing US action at home and abroad, of what might be offered by the United States in order to begin to repair the damaged and unjust relationships it has created. To ask how the United States might be more just is to ask how the

51. Rajendra, *Migrants and Citizens*, 58–61.

52. Rajendra, *Migrants and Citizens*, 60–63.

53. O'Neill, "Rights of Passage," 122.

United States might increase fidelity to the relationships it has forged and work for repair where those relationships have been broken.

To that end, I offer a responsibility-ethics framework with the hope that it can help guide our actions as we seek to take seriously the relational dynamics highlighted by these thinkers.

Responsibility as an Ethical Framework: Niebuhr and Curran

The life and ministry of Jesus was marked by a particular care for human relationality. Mujerista theologian Ada Maria Isasi-Díaz argues that the kin-dom of God hinged on Jesus's fostering patterns of kinship and community within his disciples that actively rejected hierarchy and division in favor of mutuality and justice. His ministry centered ways of relating that were opposed to "the elitist and authoritarian characteristics of kingdoms and empires and focuse[d] instead on relationality and mutuality."[54] Likewise, womanist theologian M. Shawn Copeland argues that Jesus's work centered on calling ordinary people to the work of building egalitarian socioeconomic relationships.[55] Jesus cared deeply for how people related to one another. He built a community around himself that stood in the face of the division and oppression of the Roman Empire, a community that was intentionally inclusive and in which members cared for each other and shared their lives together.[56] In other words, in a context in which unjust relationship patterns were the norm, Jesus presented an alternative in which justice was expected and encouraged.

The analyses of Isasi-Díaz and Copeland, along with the work of the thinkers profiled above, direct Christian reflection on migration toward a fuller consideration of relationships. This will not only allow us to better respond to US history as outlined in chapters 1 and 2 but will also more firmly situate our responses

---

54. Ada Maria Isasi-Díaz, "Kin-dom of God: A Mujerista Proposal," in *In Our Own Voices: Latino/a Renditions of Theology*, ed. Benjamin Valentin (Maryknoll, NY: Orbis, 2010), 186. Isasi-Díaz uses "kin-dom" to avoid what she sees as the elitist undertones in "kingdom" language and in order to emphasize Jesus's focus on community building and relationships. Similarly, I make use of "kin-dom" in this book because the language of kinship is helpful for highlighting the inherently relational dimensions of Jesus's ministry and the Christian life. See Isasi-Díaz, "Kin-dom of God," 179–86.

55. M. Shawn Copeland, "Marking the Body of Jesus, the Body of Christ," in *The Strength of Her Witness: Jesus Christ in the Global Voices of Women*, ed. Elizabeth Johnson (Maryknoll, NY: Orbis, 2016), 61.

56. M. Shawn Copeland, *Enfleshing Freedom: Body, Race and Being* (Minneapolis: Fortress, 2010), 55–84.

within Christian commitments to just relationality. Responsibility ethics provides a fruitful framework for moving forward from this basic insight to address the current situation of migration and to determine what obligations can and should be placed on receiving countries such as the United States. As this is an intentionally ecumenical project, I turn to H. Richard Niebuhr and Charles Curran for insights into how both the Catholic and Protestant moral traditions interact with the notion of responsibility. This approach creates a foundation for a responsibility-based approach to migration that is compatible with Catholic and Protestant approaches to theology. As both Niebuhr and Curran situate their approaches within their respective traditions and in conversation with other thinkers from those traditions, they are well suited to this goal.

Niebuhr is particularly helpful to this project because he views his responsibility ethic as applicable outside Christianity.[57] As migration is a topic very much in the public sphere, providing a framework that is intelligible outside Christian circles is important. Curran is a beneficial Catholic interlocutor for Niebuhr in part because he responds directly to Niebuhr.[58] He also brings a responsibility ethics framework more fully into the social sphere, writing on the relationship between the individual responsible person and the "responsible society" and embracing the "communion ecclesiology" of the Second Vatican Council.[59] Consistent with his interest in creating a framework for ethics applicable beyond Christianity, Niebuhr's approach is grounded in philosophy. He does not devote much time to considering a thick theological account of responsibility, offering instead a philosophical framework in order to invite diversity. This philosophical framework he presents, however, can be put in conversation with more explicitly theological concerns and themes.[60] Curran's approach is more robustly theological. His openness to diversity and inclusion is explicitly rooted in his commitment to Catholicism,[61] and thus he concerns himself more fully and explicitly with theology. In this way, Curran helps begin the process of fleshing out the theological underpinnings in Niebuhr's philosophical framework in a way that does not damage the intentional inclusivity for which Niebuhr strove.

---

57. H. Richard Niebuhr, *The Responsible Self* (New York: Harper & Row, 1963), 45.

58. Charles Curran, "Responsibility in Moral Theology: Centrality, Foundations, and Implications for Ecclesiology," *The Jurist* 31, no. 1 (1971): 116.

59. Curran, "Responsibility in Moral Theology," 124–28, 136; Linda Hogan, "Formative and Transformative," *JRE* 41, no. 2 (2013): 364, https://doi.org/10.1111/jore.12017.

60. Chapter 5 in particular takes up this work, developing the theological themes that are present in his work with the help of Indigenous and Latine theologians.

61. Hogan, "Formative and Transformative," 360, 362–65, 373.

H. Richard Niebuhr: A Protestant Understanding of the Human Person as Responsible

Niebuhr proposes four distinct elements of responsibility. These elements are the basis for his understanding of responsibility as an ethical framework. The four elements are response, interpretation, accountability, and social solidarity. Understanding these elements will help us move toward a framework for responding to migration in the United States based on US history.

Niebuhr begins by insisting that all human action is a "response to an action upon us." Every time we act, we are responding in some way to something. We either do this directly, as in responding to something someone does to or asks of us, or more indirectly, as when we act in response to the world as we encounter it (e.g., I make a choice to drive to work not so much in response to any one thing someone has done but in response to my context, to the city I live in, and the transportation options available to me in that city). Our action, our response, elicits more responses from others, to which we might again respond, and so on. In this way, through our choices we take part in a sort of conversation.[62]

These responsive actions are moral actions, Niebuhr holds, when they are interpreted and intended rather than reflexive, knee jerk–type actions over which we have little control and through which we do not convey meaning or intent. For Niebuhr, actions are moral actions when they are "accompanied and infused, as it were, with interpretation." By this he means that we interpret actions based on larger systems of meaning, that is, as parts of a larger narrative by which we make sense of the world. These larger narratives, or patterns of interpretation, determine—though, he cautions, not in a mechanical sort of way—what our responsive moral action looks like. They influence how we understand the things to which we are responding, the field of conceivable responses we believe ourselves to have, and what those possible responses mean to us. When we act as moral agents, we do so based on how we interpret actions (both our own and those we are responding to). This is true for groups and for individuals. In his own context of the early 1960s, Niebuhr uses the example of the United States and Russia to make his point. Neither nation, he argues, acts or confronts the other as "those who are reflexively reacting to the manufacture of bombs and missiles" and so on, but, crucially, "as two communities that are interpreting each other's actions and doing so with the aid of ideas about what is in the other's mind."[63] Moral actions are always undertaken within the context of interpretation.

Niebuhr argues that these interpretations are "not simply an affair of our conscious, and rational, mind but also of the deep memories that are buried within us, of feelings and intuitions that are only partly under our immediate

62. Niebuhr, *Responsible Self*, 61–64.

63. Niebuhr, *Responsible Self*, 61–62.

control." The contexts in which we live and develop as agents instill in us certain narratives and systems of meaning that inform how we interpret the world around us and things that happen within that world. This runs deeper than our conscious understanding of the world, relying also on communal memory, on a history of interpretation and response we inherit, sometimes unconsciously, as members of certain communities. As moral agents, our responses "are guided largely by the remembered a priori patterns" through which we seek "to interpret each new occasion by assimilating it to an old encounter," meaning that we tend to respond in the present in the ways we always have, the ways we have learned to respond from our own past and from the history of our communities.[64] The importance is evident, then, of liberating the narratives that shape our process of meaning making from the influence of social sin. Responses based in social sin are likely to perpetuate sin.

Relatedly, Niebuhr's second element is interpretation. Responsible moral action responds "in accordance with our interpretation of the question to which answer is being given." Before we can determine our proper response in any situation, we must first identify what precisely is going on. Niebuhr poses this identification of what is going on in place of questions of ultimate law (which a deontologist might ask) or ultimate end (which teleology might prompt us to ask). For him, the proper moral question to consider is, "To what am I responding?" The United States might, for example, ask itself how it interprets and understands migration. Niebuhr expands on this by situating the moral agent firmly in history, insisting that all people are historical and "time-full." The future and the past, he argues, are "extensions of the present," that is, "the still-present" and the "already-present."[65] The past is not left behind as we move forward in time. Rather, it is still-present in our habits and in our memories, conscious and unconscious, individual and communal.

Niebuhr writes that nations are communities of people both living and dead. The community of the dead include heroes and founders, especially those to whom we still make appeals in defense of ideals or values or when supporting our position. These founders and heroes are symbols. They represent causes that are deeply entrenched in our national identity. These representatives become almost sacramental in nature, revelatory of something beyond themselves. Children are formed in the image of these representatives when taught to be responsible citizens. These figures serve as touchpoints and models so that as developing citizens these children can begin to "interpret the actions of their fellow citizens in the context of the national intention." In other words, national founders and heroes present to us a vision of what it means to be properly American, the types

64. Niebuhr, *Responsible Self,* 63, 96.

65. Niebuhr, *Responsible Self,* 63, 90, 93.

of people US citizens ought to strive to be if they are to be good citizens. When we form children into responsible citizens based on historical representatives of national values, we influence the way they interpret the world around them. Niebuhr writes, "My conscience represents . . . the ethos of my society," meaning that we are formed as moral agents by our society and therefore respond based on what we have learned, consciously and unconsciously, from that society.[66] This is to say, we are formed as moral agents to interpret the world around us and respond accordingly based on the myths and ideologies of our communities, whether we are consciously aware of their influence or not and whether those myths and ideologies are good or not. We can begin to see, then, why it matters how history is taught. If figures such as Andrew Jackson or others influenced by manifest destiny and the frontier myth are presented as models for responsible US citizenship, we form people in their image.

Just as the past is not truly left behind, the future is not solely ahead of us. It is also present now in our expectations, hopes, worries, and commitments. Niebuhr argues that humans live forward, into the future. This is part of what it means to be self.[67] How we see the future, as individuals and as communities, influences our moral actions. We act in part based on our hopes, our fears or what we anticipate happening. We might try, for example, to build an immigration system that seeks to be in line with what we hope to be as a "nation of immigrants." Or, we might choose policies aimed at limiting migration out of fear for how that migration might change or endanger the nation. In either case, the future is present in our actions, helping to shape them. Furthermore, the self that responds time-fully in this way responds to actions in the present based on interpretations that are in themselves time-full. As moral agents, we respond based on interpretations inherited from societies "which [have] taught [us] a language with names and explicit or implicit metaphors and with implicit logic" that inform our understanding of the world and the actions we encounter in it.[68] These metaphors and interpretations have a history and are aimed toward the future. They are time-full.

The notion that the present also contains the not-yet (or the already-present) leads to Niebuhr's third element of responsibility: accountability. By this Niebuhr means that when acting responsibly we not only have to consider the action we are responding to but also anticipate the response to our response. We have already established that the future is present in the now in our hopes, fears, and expectations. Responsible action takes into account not only the future toward which we are aiming by our actions but also the responses our actions may elicit.

66. Niebuhr, *Responsible Self*, 84–86, 79.

67. Niebuhr, *Responsible Self*, 93.

68. Niebuhr, *Responsible Self*, 96.

Niebuhr conceives of our moral choices as parts of a broader conversation in which we are one participant among many.[69] Our responses to actions upon us are not the final word; they continue that conversation. Therefore, responsible action must be done in anticipation of the coming response(s). This applies to both personal and communal action. Of the latter Niebuhr writes,

> Thus, a political action, in this sense, is responsible not only when it is responsible to a prior deed but when it is so made that the agent anticipates the reactions to his action. So considered, no action taken as an atomic unit is responsible. Responsibility lies in the agent who stays with his action, who accepts the consequences in the form of reactions and looks forward in a present deed to the continued interaction.[70]

We can see, then, that acting responsibly requires backward and forward thinking. It necessitates not only properly interpreting the action to which we are responding, conscious of all the things that influence our interpretation, but also a thorough consideration of the possible and probable responses to our response. Responsible action is accountable to the responses it provokes, and responsible actors take this seriously *before* they act. We might say, then, that the United States had a responsibility to anticipate the impacts of NAFTA and the responses that impact would prompt. Failure to do so represents a serious lack of moral responsibility.[71]

Finally, Niebuhr insists that responsible action also includes social solidarity. By this he means that "our action is responsible . . . when it is a response to action upon us in a continuing discourse or interaction among beings forming a continuing society." Personal responsibility, he writes, means that one's response is not and cannot be rooted in a context that is completely disconnected from that from which the action to which one is responding comes. Responsibility demands a degree of continuity, a "relatively consistent scheme of interpretations" in which one is interpreting and reacting.[72] We have to respond to our context, within our context, in a way that is intelligible within that context. Recall that Niebuhr thinks of moral action as part of a continuous conversation. We do not converse simply with ourselves but rather with others who are also

69. Niebuhr, *Responsible Self*, 63–64.

70. Niebuhr, *Responsible Self*, 64.

71. We saw in chapter 2 that some impacts of and responses to NAFTA were in fact anticipated. Because these responses were anticipated but not adequately addressed (either before or after NAFTA), we can say that the US acted irresponsibly, based on Niebuhr's framework.

72. Niebuhr, *Responsible Self*, 65.

in conversation with still more others, and so on. Responsible action takes this communal web of conversations into serious consideration. Some shared sense of meaning, interpretation, and understanding makes our conversations and our moral choices intelligible to ourselves and, crucially, to others.

When we act, we respond as people formed by "the words, categories, and relations supplied by [our] society."[73] The very language we use when thinking or speaking about a situation to which we are responding and about our possible responses carries meaning, for us and for our communities. That meaning shapes the way we think about the situation and our responses, and it shapes the way others think (or will think) about the situation and about our actions. Here Niebuhr's fourth element relates closely to the second. All moral action is a response based on an interpretation of an action upon us. This interpretation, as we have said, is informed by society. These interpretations shape our actions and also the actions of those around us. When we think about migrants, for example, the very word "migrant" carries with it meanings and connotations received from (and often shared with) our communities. Responsible action therefore needs not only to be aware of those interpretations and their influence but is in an important way responsible to the society from which those interpretations came. Social solidarity means that we are responsible for the direction the communal conversation takes, and we ought to work to shape it into a just conversation.

Being responsible to society may take a number of forms, including being consistent with society and its existing interpretations. In the case of migration, we might understand and respond to migration in ways consistent with how our community has understood and responded to migration historically. On the other hand, we might intentionally and thoughtfully dissent. Here we respond in opposition or contrast to the interpretations and manner of conversation as they presently stand. For example, we might come to understand migrants differently than our community has and therefore respond to them differently. In doing so, however, it is still important to consider the broader context responsibly. If our community understands migrants to be a threat, and we come to think differently, we should of course not respond to migrants as a threat, but we should also not ignore the reality that many in our community still see them that way. To do so would be irresponsible to the migrants to whom we are trying to respond well, and it would be a failure to take responsibility for our communities. When considering how to act responsibly, we act best when we consider the whole context in which we are acting and consider what it might mean to be responsible to and for that context.

Responsible action is social action, and it is responsible to multiple other actors and communities. In fact, ultimately Niebuhr calls us to recognize that we

73. Niebuhr, *Responsible Self*, 80–81.

are responsible to the whole of creation. He writes, "The responsible self is driven as it were by the movement of the social process to respond and be accountable in nothing less than a universal community."[74] Of course, as finite beings we cannot take every person and every community into account every time we act. But we can begin to think about the world in terms of these interlocking webs of relationships of which we are a part. We can aim to act in ways that are responsible to those relationships instead of acting as if in a vacuum or as if our immediate context were the only context worth considering.

In summary, Niebuhr defines the idea of responsibility as a moral agent responding to actions based on the agent's (well-informed) interpretation of that action and what the agent anticipates as a likely response to their choice. These choices are undertaken in light of just, prudent goals. The process takes place within a continuous community of responsibilities and relationships, all of which must be brought to bear in this process of interpretation, anticipation, and action. Responsible moral agents must ask themselves to whom or to what they are properly responsible within their communities of responsibility and interpretation.[75] In other words, we cannot make responsible, moral choices without being aware of and careful with how we interpret the world around us, who we are in relationship with and thus have direct responsibilities to, and how our actions might prompt certain responses from others. More universally, we act well when we understand ourselves as situated within and responsible to interlocking webs of relationships. Responsibility ethics, as Niebuhr conceives of it, considers where moral agents are situated in various relationships, making it especially capable of responding to the situation we are in now, in view of the history that got us here and in view of our responsibility based on our relationship to God and to God's creation.

Charles Curran: A Catholic Understanding of the Human Person as Responsible

Charles Curran accepts Niebuhr's basic understanding of responsibility, including his account of responsibility's four elements. He does, however, modify Niebuhr's approach by "calling on persons to initiate action as well as respond to the actions of others."[76] Arguably, this is a disagreement of semantics. Is it possible, we might ask, to initiate action that is entirely new and in no way a response to the actions of others? This chapter does not seek to answer this question. What

74. Niebuhr, *Responsible Self*, 88.

75. Niebuhr, *Responsible Self*, 65, 68.

76. Charles Curran, *The Catholic Moral Tradition Today: A Synthesis* (Washington, DC: Georgetown University Press, 1999), 73.

is important is that Curran's modification emphasizes the possibility and necessity of individual creativity and nonconformity that is perhaps underdeveloped in Niebuhr's account. As we consider the need to identify and break down the harmful interpretations and patterns out of which the United States responds to migration, this need for new and creative action will be especially important.

For Curran, relationships are central themes in Scripture and theology. He notes that in Scripture, our relationship to God and to one another are not only consistently repeated topics but are also explicitly connected, as in Matthew 25.[77] Scripture also emphasizes our relationship to the rest of creation. Further, Curran lifts up the Catholic tradition's focus on our relationships to ourselves and the need for self-love. Therefore, he argues, it is natural that we take these various relationships—to God, others, self, and creation—seriously in our ethical considerations. In other words, attention to these relationships can provide a sort of ethical guide. He calls this model "the relationality-responsibility model." Importantly, he also argues that Catholic social teaching has moved toward this model over time, though not explicitly.[78] For Curran, responsibility ethics is a deeply Christian and deeply Catholic endeavor. It represents an attempt to be more in line with the tradition, not a turn away from it.

For Curran, the relationality-responsibility model takes seriously that "the individual lives in a network of different relationships in which there can be no minutely codified plans of conduct, but in a creative way the individual determines, by properly responding to all these demands upon [them], the way in which [they] should respond and live [their] life."[79] This leads Curran to three areas of emphasis that are especially relevant for our project. First, Curran's understanding of responsibility shapes (and is shaped by) his understanding of human freedom. Human freedom and dignity, he notes, are cornerstones in contemporary ethics. These are vitally important values and certainly worth upholding. However, Curran notes that there is a danger in overemphasizing personal, individualistic freedom.[80] We do well not to think of freedom in terms

77. Matthew 25 is also exemplary of the type of relationships Scripture is concerned with: relationships with those who are marginalized, oppressed, or in need. The next chapter considers how Jesus's love and community building prioritized the good of the marginalized in order to establish justice and equity. Here we can understand Curran's reading of the biblical emphasis on relationships through the lens of the preferential option for the poor. We might also say that Niebuhr's philosophy is consistent with this approach insofar as responding rightly to oppression would entail ending it and establishing more equitable relationships, but this is not explicit in Niebuhr's work.

78. Curran, *Catholic Moral Tradition Today*, 73–74, 77–78.

79. Curran, "Responsibility in Moral Theology," 115.

80. Curran, "Responsibility in Moral Theology," 125.

of self-indulgence and absolutely unconstrained free choice.[81] Instead, he speaks of freedom in relationship to and with responsibility.[82] Especially in the face of the dangers of individualistic liberalism, Curran calls us to remember that all individual people live in relationship—with God, with each other, with creation. Individual freedom is not absolute, because the free individual "exists in a relationship of responsibility with others and with the whole world."[83]

Curran notes that there are "numerous" ways to understand or define freedom.[84] It may therefore be helpful here to briefly consider what precisely we mean by freedom. First, the Catholic tradition generally defines free action as intentional action undertaken in service of a particular goal. When we make a specific choice for a specific purpose, that is a free act.[85]

Additionally, we can think of freedom as framed in one of two ways: "freedom of indifference" or "freedom for excellence."[86] Freedom of indifference understands freedom as an absence of constraints, our ability to do whatever we choose. True freedom means being unconstrained and able to make a choice. Any intentional choice, directed at any goal, is truly free so long as it is unconstrained. Freedom for excellence, on the other hand, considers what the ultimate purpose of freedom is or ought to be. Why are we free, or why is it good for us to be free? Is the point freedom for freedom's sake, or is there a greater purpose freedom allows us to pursue? What sorts of intentions and goals should direct our choices? In the Christian tradition, freedom has most often been framed as freedom for excellence, the freedom of being released from sin not so that we might do whatever we want but specifically so that we might embrace our ultimate ends as human beings and live creatively in line with the will of God. Freedom of indifference holds that we are free whenever we make an unconstrained choice. Freedom for excellence, in a Christian view, holds that we are truly free when we are released from the powers of sin and able to make good choices that affirm our humanity. Choices that do not affirm

81. In fact, Curran notes that unconstrained free choice is impossible, in part because one choice we make will constrain or limit other choices we might later make. As contextually situated people who have already made choices, our present choices are never unlimited. Charles Curran, *Christian Morality Today: The Renewal of Moral Theology* (Notre Dame, IN: Fides, 1966), 31.

82. Curran, *Christian Morality Today*, 29–32.

83. Curran, "Responsibility in Moral Theology," 125.

84. Curran, *Christian Morality Today*, 31.

85. Mattison, *Introducing Moral Theology*, 47–48.

86. These terms are borrowed from Mattison, *Introducing Moral Theology*, 51–52.

our humanity, even if we understand them to be unconstrained, are not truly free because they are influenced by sin.[87]

Freedom and responsibility go hand in hand for Curran because he understands freedom not in terms of self-indulgence and an unconstrained ability to make any choice we want but as "the spontaneous creativity of the human person to realize [oneself] . . . as a creature of God." This is freedom for excellence. Freedom is about our ability, redeemed by the God who provides us a release from the grips of sin, to live in ways that affirm our deep humanity. Created in the image of the triune God, to be human is to be, at our core, deeply relational. Affirming our humanity means affirming this relationality by striving to make these relationships good and just. Sin constrains our ability to do this. God sets us free from this constraint. For Curran, a Christian understanding of human freedom properly formed is deeply connected to the will of God and involves "the responsibility of opening oneself to the demands of the Spirit."[88] True freedom coexists with and is bound by responsibilities to God, to others, and to ourselves. This balance of freedom with responsibility is a central component of the Christian moral tradition, and Curran's emphasis of it is helpful, especially in a US context in which freedom is so often framed in highly individual terms.

This idea of the free human subject called to constrain their freedom in order to act out of responsibility for relationships, Curran argues, provides a basic model for a Christian responsibility ethic. In this way, the emphasis on the dignity and freedom of individual people found in contemporary Christian ethics is consistent with, not opposed to, a relationality-responsibility approach. In fact, Curran argues that a responsible society is meant to protect and promote individual freedom and dignity, even as responsibility to society and each other may constrain our freedom. Human freedom, properly formed, is a responsible freedom.[89]

Second, the turn to responsibility prompts Curran to significantly consider the role of the human conscience in ethics. Curran writes that "for the Christian who has made a commensurate effort to form his conscience correctly, *the dictate of conscience is an infallible norm of conduct*." Working from a Thomistic anthropology, Curran insists that a person's "moral activity demands a great responsibility, the responsibility of determining one's actions according to the

87. Mattison, *Introducing Moral Theology*, 50–55.

88. Curran, *Christian Morality Today*, 31.

89. Curran, *Christian Morality Today*, 31, 127–28. For Curran, it is important that the demands of responsibility go both ways: we are responsible to society and community, and society is then responsible for us as individuals. The mutuality of this protects human dignity and ensures that responsibility does not become one-sided or abusive.

true and good."[90] Conscience, properly formed, helps people determine what they ought to do in a given situation. This "ought," Curran insists, is rooted in our being. Our moral action is meant to affirm who we are as humans, created by God, at a deep level. This is related to Curran's account of freedom, which is deeply linked to a relationship with and responsibility to God, and to the reality of humans as people in various relationships to which we are properly responsible. Conscience is meant to help people live more authentically as humans in relationship with God and others, helping them to determine behavior that is right for and responsible to those relationships. Curran writes, "The greatest possible freedom and the greatest possible happiness for [people] consist[s] in the fulfillment of [their] own being."[91]

Furthermore, Curran insists that a well-formed conscience is about more than knowledge of laws and ethical formulas. Rather, consistent with his focus on responsibility and relationships, he writes that Christian morality is primarily about love, rooted in the loving relationship between God and humans. The foundation of right behavior is the love between humans and God, God's love for us and our loving response. The formation of conscience is meant to prepare people to hear and answer God's call to love in concrete circumstances. Curran concludes that conscience leads people "to participate ever more deeply in Christian love and freedom until the Christian reaches [their] final destiny where love, joy, freedom, and conformity with God's will are one."[92] A well-formed conscience prepares us not to obey laws but to love God, and out of that love for God, to love others, ourselves, and the rest of creation.

Finally, Curran emphasizes the importance of historical consciousness. In philosophy, historical consciousness includes a strong emphasis on change, on the evolution of the historical situation over time. Similarly, Curran argues, contemporary approaches that seek to make use of responsibility as a motif for ethics must be conscious of historicity. Rather than deductive approaches that conceive of moral action as adherence to a priori norms, relationality-responsibility approaches understand such norms to be culturally and historically conditioned. Adherence to these norms has too often been given too much priority, often with the result of maintaining the status quo by conflating it with the will of God. Curran notes that this system has tended to perpetuate injustice, promoting the interests of some at the expense of others.[93] This does not mean Curran calls

90. Curran, *Christian Morality Today*, 21 (emphasis added), 34–35.

91. Curran, *Christian Morality Today*, 17–18.

92. Curran, *Christian Morality Today*, 20–22.

93. Curran, "Responsibility in Moral Theology," 128–32. We saw this dynamic in chapters 1–2. Conflating the US's ambitions for expansion with the will of God resulted in advantages

for an abandonment of concrete norms.[94] Rather, a relationality-responsibility approach takes seriously the role context has in shaping the norms by which we order society and so resists too firm an enshrinement of those norms within moral thinking. It is more "open to a less structured understanding of reality in that it seems to allow for more dynamism, tension and interplay."[95] Norms, as historically and contextually situated ideas, are always open for reevaluation and revision.

Taking the historically rooted nature of laws and norms seriously can help inform our understanding of the proper role of human laws, an important element of immigration ethics. Positive human law is based on changing circumstances. These laws are good insofar as they help direct society toward good goals or help us protect and promote good values. They are not good simply because they are laws, even if we believe societies need laws to function. Because of this, Curran emphasizes the virtue of epieikeia. Related to the virtue of justice, epieikeia is the virtue that aims to address the gap between justice and human law. It is necessary, Curran argues, because human law is imperfect by nature.[96] Because human law cannot account for every circumstance in which we might find ourselves, and because it aims at but never fully encompasses the demands of justice, epieikeia holds that we might, in certain circumstances, not follow a law or a norm if doing so would be contrary to justice (or contrary to the good spirit or intention of the law itself). Curran sees epieikeia as "the response to the demands of a higher law in a particular situation."[97] This virtue can aid in breaking down the notion that the most relevant factor in undocumented border crossing is the act of lawbreaking. With Heyer, we can consider that perhaps, because in this circumstance the rule of law is unjust, it is the law and not the action of the lawbreaker that most needs to be changed.

Curran's account offers theological flesh for Niebuhr's more philosophical framework. As such, it allows for a more concrete consideration of the content of biblical relationality and Christian love. Rooted in Catholic social teaching, Curran's work begins to highlight what a specifically Christian responsibility ethic has to offer. With Niebuhr's framework and Curran's theological grounding, we are beginning to develop tools that can help guide Christians

---

for the elite and immense harm to many others, including most prominently enslaved Black people and Indigenous people.

94. Curran's own approach is, after all, deeply rooted in and committed to the norms of Catholic social teaching.

95. Curran, "Responsibility in Moral Theology," 130.

96. Curran, *Christian Morality Today*, 35–37.

97. Curran, *Christian Morality Today*, 38.

as they consider what it might mean to respond to migration in the United States as Christians, shaped by a particular set of commitments, values, and traditions.

Having thus considered the basic framework of Niebuhr's and Curran's responsibility ethics and how they relate to each other, we now turn to how they each understand sin and salvation in relation to responsibility.

Sin and Salvation: The Failure of Responsibility and Learning to Live in Relationship

Heyer's account of global migration highlights the importance of a robust understanding of social and structural sin, without which we risk underplaying the harm done by the US immigration system and missing the ways in which we are all culpable and therefore responsible for the work of repair. It is therefore helpful to consider Niebuhr's and Curran's accounts of sin and salvation as they relate to the responsibility motif. Doing so will allow us to more fully articulate the situation of sin in the United States and consider what proper responses to that sin might be. We have seen that in the Bible and in the Christian tradition, sin is understood to involve a breaking down of relationships and therefore creates responsibilities to repair those relationships. By highlighting how Niebuhr and Curran conceive of sin, we can begin to see how specifically they understand sin to break relationships, thus providing a thicker understanding of what right or just relationships look like in contrast. An understanding of sin, then, matters greatly for how responsibility is understood.

For Niebuhr, our responses as moral agents are either fitting or unfitting. Humans act rightly not simply by considering what is objectively right or wrong but rather by taking into consideration how an action fits or does not fit into the whole, ongoing conversation in which they are participating as actors.[98] Sin therefore is best understood as a failure to act fittingly. Niebuhr writes,

> The responsible self we see in Christ and which we believe is being elicited in all our race is a universally and eternally responsive I, answering in universal society and in time without end, in all actions upon it, to the action of the One who heals all our diseases, forgives all our iniquities, saves our lives from destruction, and crowns us with everlasting mercy. The action we see in such a life is obedient to law, but goes beyond all laws; it is form-giving but even more form-receiving; it is fitting action. It is action which is fitted into the context of universal, eternal, life-giving action by the One. It is infinitely responsible in an

98. Niebuhr, *Responsible Self*, 97.

> infinite universe to the hidden yet manifest principle of its being and its salvation.[99]

Fitting therefore is not just about what is happening, about responding properly to the context one is in with an adequate understanding of the action to which one is responding and accountability to the response one's response is likely to trigger. We must also take into consideration a more universal context, a cosmic-scale worldview. For Niebuhr, people are always in conversation not only with each other and their contexts but also with the "One," that is, with God. We are always ultimately acting in response to the act of creation by which we exist. Here Niebuhr is perhaps most explicitly theological in his account of responsibility. In a state of sin, Niebuhr says, we interpret God as an ultimate enemy, and we respond out of that enmity with God in all our other responsive actions. He argues, "Deep in our minds is the myth, the interpretive pattern of the metahistory, within which all our histories and biographies are enacted." In a state of sin, "the great overarching myth" leaves us with a sense of barrenness and of intense battle with good and evil in which we strive only for survival. Niebuhr finds that because we so often operate out of this sense of ultimate enmity, modern social ethics can largely be defined as an "ethic of self-defense," in which we are ruled by death and our first priority is self-preservation.[100] It is easy to see how this might lead to exclusionary, fear-based responses to migration. If we are operating from an ethic of self-defense, the primary or ultimate moral good to be promoted becomes the survival of the nation, whether or not that makes us good neighbors or responsible participants in the global community.

In this context of sin, freedom is a matter of "the self's ability in its present to change its past and its future and to achieve or receive *a new understanding of its ultimate historical context.*" Importantly, this is not about forgetting the past, as if we could pluck ourselves out of our social and historical context and somehow start fresh. The past remains with and in us; we cannot abandon it. Rather, we must accept and reinterpret the past, coming to a new, better understanding by remembering it more fully and reorganizing our understanding of it.[101] This was the primary task of chapters 1–2. For Niebuhr, this reinterpretation of the past means in particular a reframing of our understanding of our ultimate relationship with the One (God). We try to better understand the past—in a universal sense, the story of the universe—specifically and especially with the aim of moving away from a state of enmity with God and a defensive ethic of

---

99. Niebuhr, *Responsible Self,* 144–45.

100. Niebuhr, *Responsible Self,* 111–12, 139–42, 106–7, 99–100.

101. Niebuhr, *Responsible Self,* 101 (emphasis added), 102–3.

self-preservation. Salvation for Niebuhr is ultimately a shift away from enmity and toward love. This shift reorients all of our relationships and our responses as moral agents. Salvation involves a rejection of the mythology of death in order to embrace life, which then allows us the space to respond out of something other than fear and defensiveness.[102]

I want to be clear that concern for our own safety is not sinful. Loving and taking care of ourselves is good and properly Christian.[103] One of the relationships we ought to be responsible to is our relationship with ourselves. Niebuhr calls us to embrace life. There is a difference between loving and caring for ourselves, and acting out of an ethic of self-defense. Under the ethic of self-defense, we view ourselves as under constant threat, either consciously or more unconsciously. This sense of threat causes us to turn inward, into a defensive stance, and this shapes the way we respond to the world and to other people. Salvation entails shifting to trust in God, to reconceptualizing our understanding of ultimate history and reality. The mythology of death gives way to a "history of life," changing our understanding of what a fitting response ought to entail. For Niebuhr, situating all of our moral decisions within the history of life, rather than the mythology of death, allows us to respond more fittingly to God and therefore to respond more fittingly in all of our relationships.[104]

For Christians, this means responding ultimately to the One, to God, by thinking through our actions and how they might fit into the broader context in which God's vision for the world must factor. This means considering our telos, our eschatology, what we believe about our ultimate destiny, as well as recognizing that the work of reconciliation between God and humanity has begun and then finding ways to live into that telos through our actions in the present. Further, Niebuhr writes that Christianity presents moral actors with two questions: "How can they become free from being dominated by inherited images?" and "How can they respond in the present not only to their fellow men . . . but to Jesus Christ and to God, with reconstructed interpretations instead of with merely customary symbols and emotions?"[105] Reinterpreting our past and our ultimate context in such a way opens the possibility for new responses to actions on us in the present. Niebuhr argues that we all have a choice to respond to God out of distrust or trust. A state of sin is a state of distrust. Salvation means

102. Niebuhr, *Responsible Self*, 142–43, 107.

103. See, for example, James Keenan, "Proposing Cardinal Virtues," *TS* 56, no. 4 (1995): 709–29, https://doi.org/10.1177/004056399505600405.

104. Niebuhr, *Responsible Self*, 107.

105. Niebuhr, *Responsible Self*, 123–26, 144, 103. These questions will be of particular importance in chapter 5 when we consider Niebuhr's ecclesiology and his understanding of the role of the church.

responding to God from a place of ultimate trust.[106] This is all to say that for Niebuhr, salvation comes with making right our relationship with God, which opens up the possibility of new and more fitting responses to actions upon us. We become free to respond creatively rather than out of ingrained and habitual responses learned from a sinful society.

Niebuhr is perhaps open to charges of individualism here. Attention to the dynamics of social sin becomes key for avoiding a completely individual understanding of sin and salvation. We respond to God out of fear or trust always as members of communities, habituated to particular responses. Our turn from the ethic of self-defense to the freedom of a trusting relationship with God must also somehow involve these communities. Importantly, Niebuhr also conceives of sin as a communal state of being closed off from the world. He writes, "Responsive and responsible to each other in our closed societies, we are irresponsible to the larger world that includes us."[107] As the self turns inward out of a sense of enmity with God and lives an ethic of self-defense, so too do communities turn inward and ignore their connections and responsibilities to those beyond their borders. A truly fitting and therefore not sinful way of living in the world requires acknowledgment of and responsibility to the global community. Understanding the social and structural dynamics of sin calls us to consider the social and structural dynamics of salvation. Social and structural salvation implies just community building.

Curran's understanding of sin is related to Niebuhr's. He insists that sin is basically "selfishness and egoism."[108] Curran roots this understanding in Scripture, arguing that from Genesis onward, Scripture repeatedly depicts sin in deeply relational terms. The story of the fall of humanity in Genesis tells the story of evil entering the world through human sin. Curran understands this sin, as depicted in Genesis 1–2, to be a failure on the part of humans to accept their given, dependent relationship on God. In wanting to be like God, Adam and Eve fundamentally break their relationship with God, and this sends ripple effects through history. Their relationships with themselves, with each other, and with nature are all negatively affected by sin. We can see, then, that "Genesis shows us that sin is really a relational term; it affects our

106. Niebuhr, *Responsible Self*, 104, 121, 125–26.

107. Niebuhr, *Responsible Self*, 138.

108. Curran, *Christian Morality Today*, 31. It is worth noting the criticisms of a too narrow framing of sin and the human condition levied by theologians such as Valerie Saving Goldstein, Nikki Young, and others from feminist, womanist, and queer perspectives. Selfishness is perhaps most suited to name the sins of those with power, although certainly we may all be prone to it at times. Valerie Saiving Goldstein, "The Human Situation: A Feminine View," *JR* 40, no. 2 (1960): 100–112, https://doi.org/10.1086/485231; Thelathia "Nikki" Young, "Queering 'The Human Situation,'" *JFSR* 28, no. 1 (2012): 126–31, https://doi.org/10.2979/jfemistudreli.28.1.126.

multiple relationships with God, neighbor, world, and self."[109] The writer(s) of Genesis offer an account of sin as a breaking of relationships that begets more broken relationships. From this, Curran understands sin to be fundamentally about a failure to be in right relationship. This insight is especially helpful for identifying the sins of the United States. The nation has repeatedly failed to be a good global neighbor or to foster just relationships. In doing so, the nation has sinned.

Curran also links sin more directly to responsibility, insisting that "one of the most important sins of [humanity] is precisely the failure to take responsibility for [oneself] and [one's] world." He argues that every person is responsible for protecting the dignity of other persons, and failure to live up to that responsibility is sinful.[110] This is deeply related to his relationality-focused understanding of sin. If sin is about a failure to be in right relationships, it stands to reason that it also consists of a failure to take responsibility in those relationships—with ourselves, our world, and God. Like Niebuhr, Curran calls our attention to our broad, global relationships and our responsibility to them. Like all relationships, these global relationships are varied and unique. Being responsible to them will not look the same as being responsible to our relationship with our parents or with citizens of our town. The goal is not that every relationship look the same but rather that we be responsible to each relationship, however that responsibility may be defined based on the specifics of the relationship. Sin can helpfully be defined "in terms of a fundamental option or core project of [a person's] existence in which the person affirms [themselves] in [their] multiple relations with God, neighbor, self and the world. The individual in the very core of [their] being accepts responsibility for [their] life and existence."[111] A failure to take responsibility in these relationships is sinful.

As with Niebuhr, Curran's relationality-responsibility model also influences his understanding of salvation. It, too, is profoundly relational. He writes, "The fundamental Christian understanding of grace and the divine-human relationship calls for a relational model. God's grace is a gracious gift. We are called to respond." Our response is good when it affirms and is responsible to our relationships. So, if sin in Genesis is a failure to be in a dependent relationship with God, accepting and surrendering ourselves to that dependence is a moment of salvation. Similarly, if sin caused Adam and Eve to turn on each other, a return to an "intimate relationship of love and life" mends that harm. The salvation God offers, to which we are called to respond, puts our relationships back in

109. Curran, *Catholic Moral Tradition Today*, 74–76.

110. Curran, "Responsibility in Moral Theology," 122, 127.

111. Curran, "Responsibility in Moral Theology," 126, 89.

order. This requires openness. Curran insists that people who are closed off and turned inward cannot hear the prompting of the Spirit.[112]

Salvation, as a repairing of our most fundamental orientation to God and the world, has everything to do with our relationships. We are called to cooperate with salvation. Curran argues that this takes place in part through the acquiring of virtues, many of which are themselves fundamentally relational in nature. Because redemption is a fundamentally already/not-yet reality, however, our cooperation with God also requires work to tangibly improve that which is "not yet," the realities of the present world that stand in contradiction to salvation. For Curran, "sin is both personal and structural" and therefore "involves liberation at all levels—political, economic, cultural, social, and religious."[113] We participate in salvation by working to make the world more just and humane. This work is as political and socioeconomic as it is religious.

Finally, it is important to remember that, for Curran, salvation takes place primarily in community. Curran reminds us that God's covenantal relationship was with Israel as a community, not as individual people. Salvation comes "not directly and immediately from God to the individual but in and through the community of God's people."[114] We cannot and were never meant to do this work alone. Salvation comes in, through, and alongside community. When we cooperate with God in the work for liberation, we move toward being in right relationship with one another, and when we move toward being in right relationship with each other, we are cooperating with God in the work for liberation.[115]

Before continuing, it is worth returning to and considering the different theological starting points out of which Niebuhr and Curran are operating. While not always especially theological in nature, Niebuhr's approach is distinctly theocentric in character, centered on responding ultimately to God and highlighting each moral agent's responsibility to God and to God's creation.[116]

112. Curran, *Catholic Moral Tradition Today*, 75–76, 119. Here again, there is a vulnerability to charges of individualism. The Rahnerian notion of a fundamental option puts salvation in personal terms. But if sin is about broken relationships, salvation must be about repairing those relationships. This perhaps starts with each person's fundamental option but must necessarily also include the formation of communities that foster justice and responsibility. Curran moves in the right direction by insisting the salvation puts relationships back in order, but he has not done enough to fill out an account of how relational salvation operates. The thinkers profiled in chapter 5 offer helpful insights for this question.

113. Curran, *Catholic Moral Tradition Today*, 91, 110–33, 34, 46.

114. Curran, *Catholic Moral Tradition Today*, 76.

115. More so than Niebuhr, Curran begins moving toward a social and structural understanding of salvation here. This groundwork will be important in the following chapters.

116. Curran, *Catholic Moral Tradition Today*, 40.

This theocentric approach seeks to "correct for the subjectivist tendency in much liberal theology" while avoiding "the exclusivistic tendency of strongly Christocentric theology."[117] His work "captures the theologically important notion that agency is situated in relation to pre-existing goods—a good creation which is directed by a benevolent God."[118] Moreover, Niebuhr finds that a theocentric approach frames all of God's creation as the proper setting for Christian action, avoiding withdrawal from society and allowing the possibility of finding God in nature and, importantly, in other religious traditions.[119] For the purposes of this project, Niebuhr's work is especially helpful for framing our focus on communities. In particular, Niebuhr calls attention to the ways in which God is revealed within communities and how these communities shape us as moral agents. I am utilizing this framework to build an approach to ethics that focuses on how we can respond fittingly and responsibly within our specific communities and in full view of our relationship to the whole of creation and the One who created it. It is within the context of these multiple relationships, all centered ultimately by the relationship between God and God's creation, in which we respond to migration. Niebuhr further argues that the church, as a community, is grounded in its story about Jesus Christ and how we relate to God through Jesus.[120] We respond as Christian moral agents in relationship to our communities, the world, and God, and these relationships (and our understanding of them) are formed and shaped by our story, or stories, about Jesus.[121]

Curran's approach differs in a way that makes him a helpful conversation partner for Niebuhr's framework. As I highlighted above, he is much more robustly theological in his work. A post–Vatican II natural-law theorist, Curran considers his relationality-responsibility approach to capture the fundamental nature of Catholic theology. His point of departure, in contrast to Niebuhr's philosophic framework centered on the One, is the richness and specificity of the Catholic moral tradition.[122] The themes and values of Catholic social teaching are key grounding principles that inform Curran's work. While he largely takes

---

117. Gayle Gerber Koontz, "Confessional Theology in a Pluralistic Context: A Study of the Theological Ethics of H. Richard Niebuhr and John H. Yoder," *Mennonite Quarterly Review* 61, no. 4 (1987): 414.

118. Thomas James, "Responsibility Ethics and Postliberalism: Rereading H. Richard Niebuhr's *The Meaning of Revelation*," *Political Theology: The Journal of Christian Socialism* 13, no. 1 (2012): 39.

119. Koontz, "Confessional Theology," 414–17.

120. James, "Responsibility Ethics and Postliberalism," 41.

121. This will be addressed in more detail in chapters 4–5.

122. Hogan, "Formative and Transformative," 355–73.

Niebuhr's framework as his starting point, Curran fleshes this framework out with specifically (Catholic) Christian understandings of notions such as human dignity and the preferential option for the poor and oppressed. To do so is arguably to follow through on Niebuhr's understanding that our communities' stories shape us. Curran is shaped as a moral agent and theologian by the Catholic tradition's stories of who God is, how God has been revealed in Jesus, and what that means for us as people in relationship to God and to creation.

Chapter 5 will consider how some of this Catholic specificity informs Curran's understanding of the church. For now, it is simply helpful to acknowledge that although they have differing starting points and methodologies, Niebuhr and Curran complement each other's work in a way that is especially helpful for the present project.

Moving Forward Responsibly: Addressing the Limits of These Approaches

Because I am relying heavily on Niebuhr and Curran, it is also worth considering the limits of their approaches. In particular, any responsibility-based framework must be conscious of the potential pitfalls of relativism. Because "responsibility" is a term that "is very often used without any precise explanation of its meaning, and in some areas it tends to become a slogan which robs it of value and precision," Curran warns that "future theologians might have to adopt more specific models which flesh out the more generic approach of the model of responsibility."[123] Elsewhere he writes, "There remain some dangers in the use of the responsibility motif which should be noted. The adoption of such a model does not mean that moral theology no longer considers the good, the right, and the normative; but these must be understood in the context of the model of responsibility."[124] This is an important caution. A responsibility-ethics framework cannot exist on its own. Neither Niebuhr nor Curran is advocating for a relativistic approach. Rather, each grounds his responsibility approach in basic (normative) ideas about what is right.

Properly applied, a responsibility framework takes a universal standard of justice and applies it specifically, and in the case of migration explicitly works out what is owed because the United States has failed to live up to, for example, a Christian standard of just relationships. Further, Niebuhr's thoughts on other approaches to ethics, primarily deontological and teleological, are helpful for further grounding our responsibility framework. For Niebuhr, the goal is ultimately not to reject and replace deontological and teleological insights about

123. Curran, "Responsibility in Moral Theology," 118.

124. Niebuhr, *Responsible Self*, 132.

moral life. While he finds both approaches limited, he ultimately sees the responsibility approach as a way to avoid these pitfalls while "making room for the insights these methods have yielded."[125] In this way, Niebuhr roots his approach in insights of other ethical systems in order to keep it from being entirely contextually based.

Both Niebuhr and Curran also root their approaches in Scripture. Curran, as we have seen, finds extensive biblical evidence for a relational understanding of sin and salvation. This account of biblical values implies and relies on certain standards of just relationship—for example, Adam and Eve sinned and failed to be in right relationship with each other when they shifted away from their relationship of love and trust and turned on each other to protect their own individual interests. These biblical standards of justice can help direct and ground our responsibility framework. Similarly, Niebuhr sees responsibility to relationships as a recurring biblical theme. He writes,

> There is doubtless much about law, commandment, and obedience in the Scriptures. But the use of this pattern of interpretation does violence to what we find there. If now we approach the Scriptures with the idea of responsibility we shall find, I think, that the particular character of this ethics can be more fully if not wholly adequately interpreted. At the critical junctures in the history of Israel and of the early Christian community the decisive question men raised was not "What is the goal?" nor yet "What is the law?" but "What is happening?" and then "What is the fitting response to what is happening?"[126]

Again we see that Niebuhr is not denying the presence or importance of laws in Scripture, nor is he unaware that Scripture is often concerned with the proper and ultimate goals toward which humans ought to aim. These themes help shape biblical understandings of right behavior in relationships. What he argues is that woven within these notions of law and goal is a repeated theme of response, of acting fittingly based on the context and our responsibilities in that context. Laws and ultimate goals are included in that context but are not, for Niebuhr, the ultimate interpretive tool. Responsibility is.

Through this brief consideration, we can begin to see how a responsibility framework for migration must be grounded in secure theological foundations and a clear account of justice. This project looks especially to biblical notions of just relationships, identified with the help of a generally cosmopolitan worldview, in order to ground its responsibility framework. In chapter 5 we will also

125. Niebuhr, *Responsible Self*, 48–68, 136.

126. Niebuhr, *Responsible Self*, 66–67.

consider how Christology and ecclesiology might inform our understanding of responsible action.

Responsible Migration Ethics: Building a Framework

If we apply Niebuhr's and Curran's basic framework, along with the insights of third-way thinkers such as Hollenbach and Heyer, to what we have learned in chapters 1–2, we can begin to build a framework for responding to migration in the United States. Based on what we have learned here, a responsibility-based approach will include the following.

First, such an approach must consider history as fully as possible, conscious of whose point of view is being elevated and the dynamics of power and privilege that elevation entails. Niebuhr's core insight that humans respond interpretively, acting based on how we understand an action upon us, provides a lens for understanding the present state of immigration discourse and policy in the United States. In both policy and discourse, US citizens and lawmakers respond to migration into the United States based on interpretations of that act of migration. As Rajendra notes, we base our understanding on stories of who migrants are and why they are here. We can see, then, why it is important that we understand the history behind migration patterns more fully so that we can more correctly interpret migration into the United States and respond fittingly to it. The account of history provided in chapters 1–2 aims to participate in this work, highlighting dynamics of and perspectives on history that too often go unnoticed or are repressed. An adequate response to migration in the United States cannot be informed only by US history as it has been told by the victors, by those in power. When other perspectives are highlighted, certain realities come to light. We can see how US colonialist expansionism has both created systematic, global inequalities and influenced the paths of migration that lead back into the United States. In this way, migration can be more accurately interpreted, thus making it possible to respond more fittingly. By understanding that migration is in many cases a direct result of US action, we can establish specific US obligation to migrants due to US culpability in the situations that lead them to migrate in the first place. When the relationship between the United States and the migrants at and within US borders is more fully understood, it becomes clear that these relationships carry responsibilities up to which the United States is not living. For Niebuhr, an awareness of history helps moral agents make fitting choices as they consider their actions in relationship to the past, present, and future.[127] The importance of the reconstruction of US history is therefore apparent.

---

127. Niebuhr, *Responsible Self*, 107.

Furthermore, such an account of history can help us identify the ideologies and mythology informing US responses to migrants. These types of interpretations, Niebuhr finds, are culturally bound and include inherited ideas and learned, habitual responses. Constructing a fuller account of history helps us see the inadequacies of the interpretations we inherit, allowing us to reinterpret and respond better. "The just allocation of responsibility is possible only when we ask existing social narratives about how true they are to reality."[128] For example, when history is told from the mainstream US perspective, where the nation has a legitimate, possibly God-given, right and duty to protect the land it inhabits, the borders of that land become sacred spaces where the will of God is defended. The United States shaped itself over time through a series of responses to actions that were interpreted through the lenses of the doctrine of discovery, manifest destiny, and the frontier myth, as well as the white supremacy in which all three participate. That is, its responses have been shaped by sinful worldviews. Contemporary US discourse and policy is informed by these same sinful worldviews, as is evident in US interpretation of and response to migration.

We may consider, for example, commonly perceived links between migration and crime, and how this perception increases the likelihood that migration is interpreted as a threat to be defended against, leading to more militarized borders and a focus on deportation rather than paths to legalization or attempts to end visa backlogs and make legal migration more accessible. The Pew Research Center reports that nearly 40 percent of people in the United States consider immigration to increase the risk of terrorism. A smaller but not insignificant 19 percent consider immigrants more to blame for crime than citizens. Nearly half (47 percent) support the deportation of those living in the United States without legal documentation or with irregular status.[129] Rajendra argues that one popular way of viewing the relationship between undocumented migrants and citizens is to see citizens as lawmakers and undocumented migrants as lawbreakers.[130] This interpretation relies on several assumptions. First, it relies on an acceptance of the rule of law as just, at least to a degree. For nearly half of people to consider deportation the proper response to undocumented migration, there has to be a degree of acceptance that the law being broken is a good law, or at least an important one, and thus the breaking of that law is properly a punishable offense. Second,

---

128. Rajendra, *Migrants and Citizens*, 115.

129. Ana Gonzalez-Barbera and Phillip Conner, "Around the World, More Say Immigrants Are a Strength than a Burden," Pew Research Center, March 14, 2019, https://www.pewresearch.org/global/2019/03/14/around-the-world-more-say-immigrants-are-a-strength-than-a-burden/.

130. Rajendra, *Migrants and Citizens*, 130.

this interpretation is an acceptance of a global status quo in which membership, defined primarily as citizenship, allocates access to land and resources.

The account of history provided in chapters 1–2 contrasts these inherited interpretations and can therefore reform our response. For example, the lens of manifest destiny paints US land, as it now exists, as the nation's rightful territory. Migrants, as noncitizens, are understood to have little or no right to this land and its resources. The sovereignty of the nation's borders is assumed, and migrants must establish that their right to enter supersedes the nation's right to defend its borders. The burden of proof is on migrants. The account of history highlighted in chapters 1–2 shows the United States' claim to this land to be much more morally tenuous. The conquest of the land included bloody genocide, broken treaties, and a rampant disregard for human life. Understanding US history in this way unsettles US sovereignty, and the nation's right to dictate who does and does not have a right to the land and its resources becomes less evident. Sovereignty cannot, therefore, be the primary, unquestioned starting point against which all migrants' claims are measured. It is not that US sovereignty is unimportant, but rather that the United States' own repeated failures to respect the sovereignty of others properly requires us to take responsibility for those now at our borders.

Understanding the historical relationships US action has forged through history breaks open our conceptions of membership. If the way the United States has come to control this land is morally questionable, it cannot be said that only US citizens (or legal residents) have the right to the benefits of US membership. Furthermore, the United States, through its own actions, has forged relationships with people and nations beyond its borders. This establishes a form of membership current conceptions of citizenship and legal residence are unable to justly account for. Insofar as the United States has forged relationships with these nations and people, we become in a way members of a community that goes beyond citizenship. The worldview that has shaped US immigration policy thus begins to splinter, opening us up to a wider consideration of how to respond fittingly to migration. In this way, a fuller account of history that takes into account the perspectives and insights of those who have been systematically oppressed and marginalized helps break through the mythology that informs these communal interpretations.

Second, a responsibility approach will have to be properly flexible and open. When we begin to see the failings of the ideologies shaping our interpretations of the world to which we are responding, a wider spectrum of possible or conceivable responses become available. For Curran, it is important that we understand that all ideas are contextually rooted and can thus be changed.[131] We ought to take existing norms seriously but always understand that they

131. Curran, "Responsibility in Moral Theology," 133–38.

are contextual, human attempts at protecting moral goods. Conscious of historicity, a responsibility approach must understand the danger of applying a priori norms as if those norms could be cleanly separated from their historical context. Recognizing that treating historically rooted norms as ultimate has largely served the status quo, perpetuating injustice, Curran reminds us of the importance of being open to change. History is, of course, once again deeply important. Understanding the context current norms arose from allows us to consider whether these norms still fit or whether they are in need of adjustment to better fit the reality and needs of our current context (or to better help us uphold good moral values).

Furthermore, attention to the unprioritized perspectives of history can help us rethink our understanding of "universal" standards, such as justice. What insights about justice (or other moral values) have we been missing because we have focused too heavily on certain perspectives and too little on others? Understanding the realities of our relationship with those beyond US borders can help US citizens broaden and sharpen our understanding of what justice ought to entail in the contemporary world. Historicity calls us to flexibility and reflection. Our current understanding of and approach to borders, for example, is not and need not be permanent. It is possible to rethink both the way society is structured and the theology that has supported the current structure. Both Niebuhr and Curran therefore direct our attention to the importance of possibility and change.

Third, a responsibility ethics approach to migration will acknowledge and take seriously broad accountabilities. This broad accountability has several levels. It is to a degree related to the broader conception of membership and relationality established through our fuller account of history. If we have established relationships with people beyond our borders, we cannot only or even necessarily primarily think of our responsibilities to US citizens. These responsibilities are of course important, but they are not our only responsibilities. Both Niebuhr and Curran emphasize the ways in which we are called to accountability to relationships with those both near and far, on global and cosmic levels. Niebuhr reminds us that it is sinful to turn inwards, into ourselves or our communities, in a way that closes us off from the global human community and our responsibilities to that community. Similarly, Curran speaks of a people's fundamental option, their basic choice to affirm or deny their humanity through the lives they live. For Curran, living in affirmation of our humanity means affirmation of our inherent relationality. Such an affirmation of our humanity, made in the image of the triune God, who embodies just and mutual relationships, requires pursuing justice in our various relationships. A failure to be responsible to global relationships is a failure to live justly as relational people, a failure to live in affirmation of our humanity.

Taking responsibility in this way is especially relevant in the US context. Curran insists that individual freedom is constrained, or perhaps grounded, by the fact that people live in relationship with other people and communities and thus have responsibilities, so freedom is never absolute.[132] In the United States there exists a strong commitment to the liberal ideal of freedom. This fosters a resistance to anything that constrains these freedoms, making it difficult to pass laws or enact policies that are seen to impinge on individual freedom. In the United States, freedom is seen in individualistic, not communal, terms. It is about me having a largely unrestrained right to do what I choose.[133] In this context, it is especially important to situate any talk of freedom within the context of the responsibilities that properly limit or direct that freedom. Freedom, for Niebuhr and Curran, is communal. It is always in reference to our many relationships—with each other and with God—and the responsibilities we have to those relationships. From here, the work to dismantle an overattachment to state sovereignty can begin. Nations are free to self-determine and to self-govern, which sovereignty protects, but they also have responsibilities as members of the global community. It is necessary to decenter national sovereignty, as important as it can be, and bring responsibility to the fore in our discourse and policy.[134]

As this is an explicitly Christian ethic, this framework should also be aware of Niebuhr's reminder that we are always in conversation not only with each

132. Curran, "Responsibility in Moral Theology," 125.

133. We might think, for example, of the struggle to pass any sort of gun laws in the United States. Similarly, the 2020 Covid-19 pandemic has shown that many in the US have a difficult time giving up their right to do what and go wherever they want, even if that freedom endangers the lives of others. That we already have socially accepted laws that limit individual freedom for the good of the community (for example, laws regulating who is allowed to drive a vehicle under what circumstances) does not tend to factor into popular rhetoric about freedom in the US. The roots of this rampant individualism are related to some of the dynamics addressed in chapter 2, but a full consideration of this individualistic conception of freedom is beyond the scope of this project.

134. This is not to say that national sovereignty and the respect thereof is not deeply important to the fostering of just global relationships. The previous chapters outlined a history of US failures to respect the sovereignty of other nations and communities, highlighting the importance of sovereignty. My point is rather that the sovereignty of host nations such as the US has too often been a central guiding concern in immigration discourse and policy, to the detriment of global justice. We should instead center our focus on the creation of just relationships, which includes a general respect for one another's sovereignty but also acknowledges that the US may have specific responsibilities for the global inequalities it has helped create and the migration paths it has had a heavy hand in shaping. Sovereignty, while important, does not mean we are not responsible for the global community, especially given our history of imperialist expansion and continued penchant for interference in the affairs of others.

other but with a third, the One, that is, God. We have responsibilities to God. We are responding to God in every choice we make. Conscious of the dangers of ungrounded relativism, a Christian responsibility ethic will direct us to consider how our responses to migration honor (or do not honor) God. This, of course, requires further contextualization. What does honoring God look like in the concrete? As Christians, a helpful place to start is the life and ministry of Jesus. In the next chapter we will consider how Jesus's example of radical, concrete love can begin to guide our thinking on relationality. Chapters 5–6 will then consider how our christological commitments can ground our understanding of who we are called to be as Christians and direct us to respond to migrants in ways that honor God.

Further, Niebuhr's insistence that we are accountable for the possible responses to our action is also important in a context in which actions by the United States have in many ways directly contributed to the creation of the contemporary state of the world and of migration. Responsibility ethics holds that the United States has a responsibility to think through the potential responses to its actions and that it is culpable in those responses. The nation does not get to wash its hands and look the other way when, for example, the effects of NAFTA (foreseen, at least by some, and certainly not fully thought through in terms of global responsibility) bring migrants in dire need to US borders. It does not get to enact travel bans in order to limit refugees from nations in which it participated in wars that destabilized whole regions. A responsibility framework highlights these sorts of relationships in order to hold nations such as the United States responsible to the people and nations US actions directly affect and harm. In this way, Niebuhr's understanding of sin as a failure to act fittingly not only identifies the past sins of the United States for which the nation must take responsibility and atone but also shows that a continued refusal to respond well to the migrants at our borders and in our midst is sinful.

Broadening our understanding of accountability also requires a full understanding of individual and communal culpability. A responsibility framework has to establish not only US responsibility for and accountability to a broader spectrum of relationships than we are accustomed to but also the responsibility of individual US citizens. Taking US responsibility to those beyond our borders with whom we are in relationship seriously will mean changes that affect US citizens. In order to enact any change, people must believe in, call for, and participate in that change. This means individual people need to take their own culpability in the sins of the United States seriously. Niebuhr understands that sin can be structural, which allows this responsibility framework to name the dynamics of American imperialism as a structural, systematic sin for which American citizens are all culpable. His articulation of the responsible self who interprets actions and responds based on patterns of interpretation and response learned from society lends itself well to a social, structural understanding of sin, as articulated in chapter 1.

Further, social solidarity calls for us to be responsible to and for our communities and to work to direct those communities in good and just directions. As participants in and benefactors of the US systems that manifest these sins, individual US citizens are in some way responsible for the harms caused. Curran's understanding of sin as a failure to take responsibility for the world is helpful for further identifying US sin and culpability. Moral actors are meant to take responsibility for the world and their roles in it. Failing to acknowledge culpability in social and structural sin and take responsibility is one way in which we fail to take responsibility for the world.

Finally, a responsibility framework must include praxis, the intentional application of our beliefs and commitments through action. The application of responsibility ethics to migration in the United States is incomplete if it does not call us to action, informed by responsibility. Curran stresses that participation in salvation means working to change the world, economically, socially, and culturally. This final element requires significant fleshing out. This will be the task of the final three chapters of this book.

Concluding Thoughts

This chapter has called for a responsibility-ethics framework to help guide our responses to migration in the United States. I have outlined the tradition of third-way thinking on which this work is built and looked to H. Richard Niebuhr and Charles Curran to direct the building of such a framework. Such an approach upholds the important insights raised by communitarian and cosmopolitan approaches while moving beyond the too-narrow conversation this dichotomy has created. This framework does not claim to be exhaustive but seeks to offer something out of which fuller responses to migration may be built. While the focus of this book is the US context, the ideas put forth and the framework offered point to larger truths that should be of relevance in other contexts.

CHAPTER FOUR

Repair

So when you are offering your gift at the altar, if you remember that your brother or sister has something against you, leave your gift there before the altar and go; first be reconciled to your brother or sister, and then come and offer your gift.

—Matthew 5:23–24

Introduction

REPAIRING BROKEN RELATIONSHIPS is a central concern in Scripture. Sin breaks down our relationships with God, others, ourselves, and creation. Salvation entails restoring those relationships. A repeated theme in the Hebrew Bible is that God's people have failed to live up to the terms of their covenantal relationship with God and must therefore repent and act in some way to repair the relationship. Biblical scholar Bruce Birch highlights that "God's initiative is to restore relationships" and that this demands a response from Israel.[1] The New Testament continues this theme, and much soteriology throughout the tradition has been based on this basic idea that something is owed when a relationship has been broken, as has Christian thinking on conflict resolution.

The proper response to sin is generally framed as repentance. Repentance is not an empty apology. It is an honest and vulnerable reckoning with harm one has done and an effort to make the relationship right. Birch specifies that "the Hebrew verb for repent is šub," which translates to "to turn or return," meaning repentance involves moving "in a new direction."[2] We recognize that we have acted poorly, and we turn in a new, better direction. This understanding of repentance as concretely turning toward a new, better life influenced the thinking of the early church, for whom

> to become a Christian was to leave the realm of Satan and enter the community of the one true God, to renounce Satan and sin, to forsake idolatry and all the social customs and lifestyle that went with it. This

1. Bruce C. Birch, *Let Justice Roll Down: The Old Testament, Ethics, and Christian Life* (Louisville, KY: Westminster John Knox, 1991), 286–92.

2. Birch, *Let Justice Roll Down*, 290.

> repentance, or turning about, was essential, and was not something that could be simply assumed. It had to be practised, and it had to be demonstrated; Tertullian stressed, "it may not be exhibited in the conscience alone, but may likewise be carried out in some act."[3]

Repentance, we see, maintains this connotation of a turning about. It must be practiced, lived out in some tangible fashion. For the early church, repentance implied conversion from a life of sin to a new Christian life.[4] This carries an element of radical transformation that echoes through the tradition. John Wesley, for example, frames repentance "as a "self-knowledge" leading one to the conviction of sin," a "heavy burden" that causes one to "turn away from sinful behavior."[5] Here again, we see repentance framed as a turning away, rooted in the conviction that one has behaved wrongly, sinfully. For Wesley, repentance also necessarily includes some element of restitution or reparation when appropriate.[6] Christian repentance involves *doing* something, not simply apologizing for bad behavior.

As we consider what it might mean to respond fittingly to historically unjust relationships, Wesley's insight about reparation is helpful. A Christian responsibility-ethics framework can benefit greatly by rooting itself in the insights of reparative justice. This chapter will therefore offer a consideration of reparations, exploring how they can function to repair relationships and why a reparative lens can be a helpful one through which to understand praxis in light of migration and a history of US injustices.

Why Repair: Considering the Philosophical Case for Reparative Justice

In the contemporary United States, reparations are perhaps most commonly associated with slavery. Many have argued that Black people in the United States may be owed some form of reparation for the historical harms of slavery and for the ongoing injustices they face as a legacy of slavery.[7] Ta-Nehisi Coates, for

3. Ruth Sutcliffe, "Learning Not to Sin: Repentance in Tertullian and Cyprian," *Colloquium* 53, no. 1 (2021): 77. She cites Tertullian, *Paen.* 9.1 (CCSL 1:336).

4. Sutcliffe, "Learning Not to Sin," 77–78.

5. Kenneth W. Brewer, "Wesley, National Sins, and Repetance: Does True Repentance Mandate Reparations?," *Wesleyan Theological Journal* 56, no. 1 (Spring 2021): 25.

6. Brewer, "Wesley and National Sins," 24.

7. See, for example, John Torpey, *Making Whole What Has Been Smashed: On Reparation Politics* (Cambridge, MA: Harvard University Press, 2006); Roy L. Brooks, *Atonement and Forgiveness:*

example, argues that the United States owes a great debt that must be repaid. Coates compellingly outlines the history and present reality of systemic material disadvantages faced by Black people in the United States, as well as the ugly history of slavery, lynching, and other physical, moral, and emotional injuries perpetuated against them since 1619. Additionally, he highlights how deeply central chattel slavery was to the US economy. In the seven "cotton states, one-third of all white income was derived from slavery," and "by 1840, cotton produced by slave labor constituted 59 percent of the country's exports." The United States, Coates argues, "begins in Black plunder and white democracy, two features that are not contradictory but complementary."[8] His account of the founding of this nation and its entanglement with the systematic mistreatment of Black people aligns with the colonial history outlined in chapters 1–2 of this book. The United States has forged itself as a nation through its mistreatment and exploitation of those it has excluded from full membership. Coates writes,

> If we conclude that the conditions in North Lawndale and black America are not inexplicable but are instead precisely what you'd expect of a community that for centuries has lived in America's crosshairs, then what are we to make of the world's oldest democracy? One cannot escape the question by hand-waving at the past, disavowing the acts of one's ancestors, nor by citing a recent date of ancestral immigration. The last slaveholder has been dead for a very long time. The last soldier to endure Valley Forge has been dead much longer. To proudly claim the veteran and disown the slaveholder is patriotism à la carte. A nation outlives its generations. We were not there when Washington crossed the Delaware, but Emanuel Gottlieb Leutze's rendering has meaning to us. We were not there when Woodrow Wilson took us into World War I, but we are still paying out the pensions. If Thomas Jefferson's genius matters, then so does his taking of Sally Hemings's body. If George Washington crossing the Delaware matters, so must his ruthless pursuit of the runagate Oney Judge.[9]

A New Model for Black Reparations (Berkeley: University of California Press, 2004); Ana Lucia Araujo, *Reparations for Slavery and the Slave Trade: A Transnational and Comparative History* (New York: Bloomsbury Academic, 2017).

8. Coates, "Case for Reparations."

9. Coates, "Case for Reparations." North Lawndale is a neighborhood in Chicago that serves as one of Coates's examples in this article. He calls it "an extreme portrait of the trends that ail black Chicago."

If we take the history of this nation seriously, we see that the success and wealth of the nation was built on the backs of enslaved Black people. We see that democracy and a relatively stable peace between classes was preserved in part by pitting poor whites against their Black counterparts. This is a nation "built on the preferential treatment of white people."[10] With this in mind, it becomes hard to deny that the nation owes a debt.

Coates notes that from early on, there have indeed been recognitions of this debt. "Edward Coles, a protégé of Thomas Jefferson who became a slaveholder through inheritance, took many of his slaves north and granted them a plot of land in Illinois. John Randolph, a cousin of Jefferson's, willed that all his slaves be emancipated upon his death, and that all those older than 40 be given 10 acres of land." In New England, New York, and Baltimore, Quakers made it a requirement for membership that anyone who had previously enslaved people compensate them in some way. One Quaker wrote in 1796, "A heavy account lies against us as a civil society for oppressions committed against people who did not injure us, and that if the particular case of many individuals were fairly stated, it would appear that there was considerable due to them." In 1810 Timothy Dwight, the president of Yale, said, "We inherit our ample patrimony with all its incumbrances; and are bound to pay the debts of our ancestors. *This* debt, particularly, we are bound to discharge: and, when the righteous Judge of the Universe comes to reckon with his servants, he will rigidly exact the payment at our hands. To give them liberty, and stop here, is to entail upon them a curse." These attempts to reckon with a sense of debt represent an important through-line in US history: there have always been people who recognized the mistreatment of others as a serious wrong to be repaid. On a large scale, however, the United States has exhibited a persistent "inability to face up to the particular history of white-imposed black disadvantage."[11] The debt remains largely unpaid. Coates calls us forward, writing,

> We invoke the words of Jefferson and Lincoln because they say something about our legacy and our traditions. We do this because we recognize our links to the past—at least when they flatter us. But black history does not flatter American democracy; it chastens it. The popular mocking of reparations as a harebrained scheme authored by wild-eyed lefties and intellectually unserious black nationalists is fear masquerading as laughter. Black nationalists have always perceived something unmentionable about America that integrationists dare not acknowledge—that white supremacy is not merely the work of

10. Coates, "Case for Reparations."

11. Coates, "Case for Reparations."

hotheaded demagogues, or a matter of false consciousness, but a force so fundamental to America that it is difficult to imagine the country without it.

And so we must imagine a new country. Reparations—by which I mean the full acceptance of our collective biography and its consequences—is the price we must pay to see ourselves squarely. The recovering alcoholic may well have to live with his illness for the rest of his life. But at least he is not living a drunken lie. Reparations beckons us to reject the intoxication of hubris and see America as it is—the work of fallible humans.[12]

This call to take the whole of US history seriously, and to recognize that we owe debts that must be repaid in order for the nation to move forward toward something better, resonates with responsibility ethics. A responsibility framework calls us to respond fittingly, and a fitting response to historically unjust relationships may in fact require reparations.

In recent years, there has been a relatively small but promising development of research suggesting the merits of framing aid to migrants as a form of reparations. These arguments largely focus on forms of forced migration, types of migration in which there is a significant element of coercion. Migrants in these situations are on the move because of dire threats to their lives or livelihoods, either because of naturally occurring events (e.g., a natural disaster) or human action (e.g., war or persecution).[13] In such cases, the dominant framework has generally been to view global responses to these migrants as humanitarian aid. Humanitarian aid responds to generalized rights and duties. Migrants have human rights, and when they are forcibly displaced, we all have a general duty to do what we can to ensure those rights are met. Alternatively, a reparative approach highlights and seeks to respond to more contextual, historically rooted claims some forced migrants have. When the actions of specific parties have caused or contributed to the forced migration, more specific duties arise. Those who have caused or contributed to the displacement have a concrete duty precisely because they have caused the harm.[14]

This reparative approach can thus help responsible actors as they seek to move into praxis. Reparations are a type of praxis through which actors can respond to historic and ongoing failures to be in right relationship. In order to

12. Coates, "Case for Reparations."

13. "Forced Migrant," Migration and Home Affairs, European Commission, accessed August 7, 2023, https://tinyurl.com/bdezf79w.

14. Rebecca Buxton, "Reparative Justice for Climate Refugees," *Philosophy* 94, no. 2 (2019): 201.

better understand the promise of such an approach, it may be helpful to begin with an example. Philosopher Rebecca Buxton has worked to "build a preliminary account of reparative justice for climate refugees." She argues that "climate refugees are indeed owed reparations for their loss of land, and that these reparations should be paid by those outcome responsible for this wrong, namely, states who have not cut carbon emissions despite clear knowledge of their negative effects." This account hinges on two claims. First, we must accept that climate-caused displacement is a foreseeable consequence of the irresponsible or callous actions of states and corporations. States and corporations that have failed to appropriately limit emissions and other unsustainable and environmentally damaging practices are outcome responsible, that is, they are responsible for the foreseeable (and indeed, foreseen) consequences (outcomes) of these choices, such as the large-scale displacement of people. For example, because of climate change and rising sea levels, some states (e.g., the Maldives, Kiribati, French Polynesia, and Tuvalu) face the real possibility of becoming entirely submerged in the near future.[15] This is a predictable result of human actions, and so people and groups who have acted in such ways are outcome responsible.

Second, Buxton's account claims that forced displacement of this sort is inherently harmful. She identifies two specific and interrelated forms of concrete harm those forcibly displaced by climate change face: "loss of collective self-determination" and the loss of land that carries specific moral value or meaning.[16] The first, loss of self-determination, generally comes about due to loss of territory, as in the cases of island nations facing complete submersion. Buxton defines territory as "the area within which the state is usually assumed to be able to exercise legitimate force." In other words, a territory is the land over or within which a state exercises sovereignty and rights to self-determination. Relatedly, it is generally agreed that a state is "a geographically bounded territory over which a set of institutions hold jurisdiction and power."[17] Because the definition of a state usually centers on territory in this way, the loss of the territory puts the community in a position of particular and somewhat unique precarity. Are they still meaningfully a state, having lost the territory over which to govern and, in so losing, being deprived of the practical foundation for their self-governance and self-determination?

Without a territory, a state's rights become practically ineffective. Therefore, a complete loss of a territory as sea levels rise arguably constitutes a type of state death. Historically, state deaths have usually occurred due to invasion, annexation, or occupation by another state, meaning the land was still there but became

15. Buxton, "Reparative Justice for Climate Refugees," 193–94, 204–7.

16. Buxton, "Reparative Justice for Climate Refugees," 195, 197.

17. Buxton, "Reparative Justice for Climate Refugees," 196.

the territory of another political community. Climate-caused loss of land has the same effect as these invasions and annexations. The state is no longer able to exercise jurisdiction over the land in a meaningful way and therefore loses its effective control and rights as a state. However, climate-caused state death differs because it is not only the territory as such but also the land itself that disappears.[18] Under normal circumstances, the people of the "dead" state either stay where they are to be governed by a new state or are expelled (by means of removal or death). Those who lose their territory to sea-level rises do not become a part of the new state because there is no new state. The land is gone along with the territory. This loss is related to the types of loss other state deaths cause, but it is also particular and therefore raises new questions for these states and for the international community.

Additionally, Buxton highlights the fact that land cannot be thought of as "inherently undifferentiated." All land is not the same. Many communities have specific relationships to the land they inhabit. These relationships can be important religiously, spiritually, or culturally. The land might hold particular moral value or meaning to the community. The loss not only of one's territory but the land itself, preventing any hope that the land may be reclaimed, therefore causes a specific sort of harm Buxton argues must be attended to. She writes, "Therefore, discussions of justice for climate refugees must move beyond territorial claims and also highlight the importance of land. Although loss of self-determination is possibly a simpler harm to understand and therefore address, this loss of land as home must not be forgotten." It is the particular, subjective nature of this loss of place to which Buxton argues a reparative approach is best suited to respond.[19]

Often, justice for climate refugees has been understood primarily as compensation. Compensation offers money or goods with the purpose of placing the harmed person or community at the general level of advantage they would have had if the loss suffered had not taken place. Such compensation can be "means replacing," which would provide those harmed the means to pursue the ends they would have pursued had the loss not occurred, or "ends displacing," which allows those harmed to pursue a different end in which they are no less well off than they were prior to the loss. In the case of climate refugees, a means-replacing approach would involve a new territory not governed by another state. An ends-displacing approach might involve refugees being given land in another territory, where they would become members of a different state but retain some ability to self-determine as a community (and as members of a new community).[20]

18. Buxton, "Reparative Justice for Climate Refugees," 195–96.

19. Buxton, "Reparative Justice for Climate Refugees," 197, 211.

20. Buxton, "Reparative Justice for Climate Refugees," 198.

Despite the potential merits of either approach, Buxton finds compensation to be an inadequate lens through which to conceive of justice for climate refugees. She writes,

> This is because conceptualising justice for climate refugees as a matter of compensation misses a key feature of sea-level rise. Crucially, determining what climate refugees are owed demands an understanding of how this wrong came about. Climate change did not happen by accident. Instead, it is a result of the carelessness with which (largely) so-called "developed" states have polluted, through practices of burning fossil fuels, eliminating tropical rainforests, while ignoring basic emissions quotas. To put it simply, the plight of climate refugees is caused by the emissions of other states.[21]

Compensation is inadequate to respond to this type of injustice because, Buxton argues, compensation is primarily a response for accidental harms. We are compensated when, for example, a natural disaster destroys our home.[22] The harm done to climate refugees is different. It is the foreseeable result of states and corporations with resources and power failing to limit their emissions or move sufficiently away from other unsustainable practices, despite available data about the likely consequences. This is a failure to take sufficient care with a shared resource, the earth. It is a choice to put profit or comfort above the lives of others. This makes it an injustice. It is unjust because it stems from a failure to treat others as equals, worthy of consideration when one's actions will affect them. That those who contribute most to climate change currently face least of its impacts while those who contribute least face significant harm[23] highlights that this is an injustice, not an accidental or unavoidable harm. When seeking to rectify an injustice, reparations, not compensation, are needed.

This is to say, injustices of this nature are not only about the harmful outcomes but also about the relationship between those harmed and those who are responsible for that harm. When an accidental harm occurs, we might be compensated out of generosity or a sense that it is fair or good to help people who are in need. When we are harmed by an injustice, reparations declare that the harm should not have happened, that we should not have been treated in

21. Buxton, "Reparative Justice for Climate Refugees," 198.

22. With the growing awareness that there are connections between climate change and increasingly extreme weather and natural disasters, it is worth noting here that I mean naturally occurring natural disasters that are not the result of human action.

23. Justin Worland, "How Climate Change Unfairly Burdens Poorer Countries," *Time*, February 5, 2016, https://time.com/4209510/climate-change-poor-countries/.

this way. Reparations are about what is owed because wrongdoing took place (or is taking place). Reparations therefore necessarily involve a moral judgment about the harm that occurred. They serve "a strong moral function" of which compensation is conceptually incapable. The harm done to the relationships between people and communities by injustice cannot be addressed solely by compensation. Such compensation may address the most tangible losses and provide important resources to people and communities in need, which is important. It may even help level the playing field. However, compensation alone does not name the wrongdoing as injustice, and it cannot repair the relationship between those harmed and those who caused the harm.[24] We will continue to consider why this moral function is so essential later in the chapter.

Buxton's framework begins to highlight the benefits of a reparative approach for responding to the needs of migrants, especially migrants who are on the move as a result of historical and ongoing injustices. Reparations signal an acknowledgment that injustice has occurred, that relationships have not been as they ought to be. Because they serve this moral function and respond specifically to injustice, to human-caused harms that should not have occurred, reparations can be a helpful element of a fitting response to failures to be in right relationship. From this basic insight, we can begin to consider what it might mean to respond well to migrants who have been displaced by injustice.

What Does Reparative Justice Entail?

It will be beneficial to first consider in more depth what reparative justice is and what it requires. The work of philosopher Margaret Urban Walker is foundational for understanding contemporary approaches to reparative justice. To begin, she outlines two basic models through which we might think about reparative justice. These models shape how reparations are understood, the specific harms they are responding to, and what precisely we are aiming to repair. The first model is corrective justice. Generally, corrective-justice approaches argue that wronged groups or individuals may hold those who have wronged them accountable via some form of compensation or restitution.[25] This depends on a consensus "that there is a standard of moral acceptability for the impact we have on each other through our actions and interactions." In a community there exists, either in norms or in law, rules governing our interaction with one another and especially the ways our actions may affect those around us. Walker calls this a moral baseline. Corrective justice aims to correct the negative impact (harm)

24. Buxton, "Reparative Justice for Climate Refugees," 198.

25. Margaret Urban Walker, "Making Reparations Possible: Theorizing Reparative Justice," in *Theorizing Transitional Justice*, ed. Claudio Corradetti, Nir Eisikovits and Jack Volpe Rotondi (London: Ashgate, 2015), 217. Walker uses "compensation" slightly differently from Buxton here.

that occurs when people behave in ways that "fall outside of that standard" for morally acceptable behavior and interactions.[26] This corrective action is understood to restore, or attempt to restore, a just situation. Justice constitutes a return to the agreed-on norms or standards of behavior.

While this is a good idea in theory, the limits of this approach, according to Walker, hinge on the fact that it assumes an acceptable standard of justice exists within the community, as well as a level of accountability and reciprocity between parties. In practice, these often do not exist in a robust or acceptable fashion.[27] Corrective justice sees reparations as a way to return to the moral baseline, the agreed-on standard of behavior and interactions. The content of these approaches—what is owed, when, and by and to whom—depends on these standards, which may be just or unjust. Corrective justice, Walker asserts, "is only as morally legitimate as the baseline it treats as morally compelling." Under this model, what is corrected is the breach of acceptable conduct agreed on within a society. A corrective approach is therefore useful for returning to the status quo, returning parties to their position before the harm occurred. It is less useful if the status quo itself is unjust. Even as international agreements and laws evolve toward the hope of a universal standard or baseline of human rights, a standard of just behavior to which all people might be held, norms within local communities might not—and often do not—function in a just, mutual manner. A return to these norms, while perhaps helpful to keep society functioning, does not properly constitute justice.[28]

Walker notes in particular the problems of systemic injustices, situations in which the structures, laws, and norms of behavior within a society are themselves deeply unjust. In such communities, the social and structural dynamics of sin result in a situation of inequality in which all people do not have the same access to or protections of their human rights.[29] As we have seen, the rule of law has too often been shaped to support an unjust status quo. Many who may have need for some form of compensation or redress for wrongs done to them have little hope of finding that redress in the legal systems that have historically permitted and even ensured their oppression.[30] As we saw in chapters 1–2, Indigenous nations had little chance of gaining redress for the harms they suffered, specifically because the United States was committed to expansion over their territory, and the legal

26. Margaret Urban Walker, "Restorative Justice and Reparations," *Journal of Social Philosophy* 37, no. 3 (2006): 380.

27. Walker, "Making Reparations Possible," 217.

28. Walker, "Restorative Justice and Reparations," 380–82.

29. Walker, "Restorative Justice and Reparations," 381.

30. Walker, "Making Reparations Possible," 217.

systems within the nation reflected and protected that desire. Walker argues, "The framework of corrective justice strains, because it has never been meant to deal with either a massive scale of serious mayhem or a protracted and brutal subjugation and mutually ramifying indignities and atrocities that characterize oppressive and violently repressive systems."[31] When the status quo causes or allows for harm, a corrective model, which aims for a return to the status quo, cannot provide justice.

Additionally, when harm occurs interculturally or across borders, the lack of a shared moral baseline for behavior, as well as unequal power dynamics, can become a problem.[32] When human-rights abuses cross borders, the harm is often exacerbated because few reliable channels exist through which the citizens of one nation can reliably seek redress for harms caused by another nation. In fact, in many such cases where repair for harm might be sought, the harm has resulted from "a context where accountability and reciprocity themselves are at issue." In other words, it is precisely *because* relationships of accountability and reciprocity do not exist that many of these abuses have happened in the first place.[33] For example, an unequal relationship between Mexico and the United States is part of what allowed Mexican farmers to be deprived of their livelihoods by the impacts of NAFTA. Moreover, because Mexico agreed to NAFTA, these farmers have, in the view of the US legal system, little standing on which to lodge a complaint or claim for compensation. NAFTA established agreed-on norms of behavior. That status quo has not been breached, and so corrective justice has little to offer, even if the norms themselves are based on unjust dynamics of power.

Corrective justice aims to correct the behavior of actors when they fail to meet the moral baseline. The core question this approach is tasked with is whether these standards of behavior have been met and, if not, what forms of redress will correct this infraction. Reparations understood through the lens of corrective justice are ill equipped to respond when it is the systems themselves that are the problem. Because the norms, laws, and structures of society themselves can be unjust and are able to perpetuate harm, Walker suggests that reparations may be better thought of in terms of a restorative-justice model. The guiding norm of corrective justice is the standards of behavior within a particular society. Whether those standards are just or unjust, they dictate when reparations are needed and what the goal of those reparations is: a return to the status quo. Where corrective justice takes agreed-on standards of behavior as a baseline, "restorative justice begins from and defines itself in terms of the reality

31. Walker, "Restorative Justice and Reparations," 380.

32. Walker, "Restorative Justice and Reparations," 382.

33. Walker, "Making Reparations Possible," 217–18.

of violation, alienation, and disregard among human beings."[34] The point of departure is not the status quo or the standards of a community but an awareness that human beings have been wrongfully harmed through the actions of others. From this vantage point we can critique not only behavior that fails to meet community norms but also the community norms themselves if they are found to be causing, perpetuating, or allowing harm.

Where corrective justice may be described as a norms-centered approach to wrongdoing, concerned with whether a norm or a law has been breached, a restorative-justice approach is victim centered, concerned with whether someone has been violated or disregarded. To be clear, laws and norms can be extremely important ways through which we protect people from harm. A reparative approach simply shifts the focus away from whether a norm or law has been violated to the more important question of whether a *person* has been violated (whether or not the violation was a breach of laws or norms). Criminologist Howard Zehr asserts that when a crime occurs, what is most important, and most worthy of being responded to, is that a human being has been violated in some way. These violations create obligations, the most central of which is to right the wrongs done.[35] While the form of restorative justice Zehr describes primarily focuses on smaller-scale crimes and how reparative-justice approaches can augment the limits of the criminal justice system, other scholars have applied the principles of restorative (or transitional) justice to larger reconciliation projects, such as systematic violence in South Africa, the Balkans, and Argentina.[36]

Whether applied to small-scale criminal justice or large-scale reconciliation, restorative-and transitional-justice approaches involve a particular focus on relationships. When wrongdoing occurs,

> what demands repair is the state of the relationship between the victim and the wrongdoer, and among each and his or her community, that has been distorted, damaged, or destroyed. Serious harm to individuals creates a relationship charged with powerful negative feelings and burdened with losses that can continue to mar a victim's life. Restorative

---

34. Walker, "Restorative Justice and Reparations," 382.

35. Howard Zehr, *The Little Book of Restorative Justice* (Intercourse, PA: Good Books, 2002), 19.

36. See, for example, Robert J. Schreiter, *Reconciliation: Mission and Ministry in a Changing Social Order* (Maryknoll, NY: Orbis Books, 1992); Miroslav Volf, *Exclusion and Embrace: A Theological Exploration of Identity, Otherness, and Reconciliation* (Nashville: Abingdon, 1996); Desmond Tutu, *No Future without Forgiveness* (New York: Doubleday, 2000); Francesca Lessa, *Memory and Transitional Justice in Argentina and Uruguay: Against Impunity* (New York: Palgrave Macmillan, 2013); Martina Fischer and Olivera Simić, eds., *Transitional Justice and Reconciliation: Lessons from the Balkans* (New York: Routledge, 2016).

> justice targets a situation of negative connection or disconnection that might be an ongoing source of threat, insult, anger, fear, and grief. It is not always possible, nor is it always desirable, to restore relationship between those who have done or allowed harm and those who have suffered at their hands or by their indifference or carelessness. In some cases where restoration between victims and offending persons is possible, it can nevertheless mean only a wary coexistence. In any case, however, it is necessary to attempt to restore morally habitable conditions for those wronged within their supporting network of relationships and in their communities.[37]

Wrongdoing constitutes a way of treating one another that damages or destroys relationships. Serious wrongdoing not only harms the relationship between the wrongdoer(s) and the victim(s) but can also damage the victim's relationship with their community (as well as the perpetrator's relationship with the community). A restorative-justice process seeks ways to mend these relationships so that the victim might regain a sense of control, belonging, and safety, and ideally so that the perpetrator can also be reintegrated into society in a healthy and just manner.

Alongside the aim to repair harm and the centering of the needs of victims, Walker helpfully identifies four additional values that guide restorative justice. First, a restorative approach "insists on genuine accountability and responsibility-taking" on the part of the wrongdoer.[38] Second, those who have been wronged should be given ownership of the resolution. In other words, those harmed should have a substantial say in how that harm is addressed and repaired. Third, wrongdoers ought to be offered paths to take accountability and be reintegrated into the community. Finally, a restorative approach seeks to build the capacities of communities to work for justice rather than having to rely on outsourcing justice work to "experts." Here, restorative justice is in line with the principle of subsidiarity, which holds that larger bodies such as national governments "should not replace or destroy smaller communities and individual initiative" but should instead "help them contribute more effectively to social well-being and supplement their activity when the demands of justice exceed their capacities."[39] Local communities ought to be empowered to seek and create justice on their own terms.

37. Walker, "Restorative Justice and Reparations," 383.

38. Walker, "Restorative Justice and Reparations," 383.

39. United States Conference of Catholic Bishops, "Call to Family, Community, and Participation," accessed September 13, 2023, https://www.usccb.org/beliefs-and-teachings/what-we-believe/catholic-social-teaching/call-to-family-community-and-participation.

Within a restorative-justice model, reparations respond to the "affinity" or relationship created or shaped by the harm that has been done. It is specifically about the relationship between those who have been harmed and those who are responsible for the harm as well as the broader community or communities in which the harm took place. Reparation looks to repair these relationships, not simply address the most acute material effects of the injury. Injustice not only causes harm; it creates and/or perpetuates broken relationships.[40] Responding to injustice requires, among other things, work to foster better relationships going forward so that further harms are less likely in the future.

When speaking of restorative justice, the root word "restore" can be somewhat misleading. It may be the case that the relationship in question has never been sufficiently just, and so we are not so much restoring something as creating justice, mutuality, and accountability where it has previously been absent. In response to this concern, Walker proposes "that we understand 'restoration' in all contexts as normative: 'restoration' refers to repairs that move relationships in the direction of becoming morally adequate, without assuming a morally adequate status quo" existed previously.[41] She goes on to define a morally adequate relationship based on three themes: confidence, trust, and hope. Relationships should provide people with confidence in a standard of treatment they can share with others, the ability to trust others to follow those standards, and concrete hope that if they are treated in unacceptable ways, the behavior will not be ignored and they will not be abandoned by the community. A restorative model therefore offers a thicker account of what justice requires than a corrective model. It offers tools to question not only the morally inadequate behavior of the wrongdoer but also the morally inadequate structures in which that wrongdoing may have taken place. Walker argues that a restorative model offers "a more adequate framing ideal for reparative practice where there is a need to establish a governing understanding of 'right relationship' and to approach its realization, rather than to intervene episodically to correct deviations from an existing standard."[42]

In focusing on harm to people rather than on violations of existing norms, a restorative approach is able to ask more relevant questions about the nature of the harm, why it took place, and how those involved might move forward in a fitting manner. Within this model, reparations function to explicitly highlight the need for tangible means of repair in order to build just relationships where unjust ones (temporary or long-standing) currently exist. The forward-looking nature of restorative justice can result in a desire to move on too quickly. We might prioritize reconciliation, for example, without adequately addressing the

40. Buxton, "Reparative Justice for Climate Refugees," 199.

41. Walker, "Restorative Justice and Reparations," 384.

42. Walker, "Restorative Justice and Reparations," 379.

harms victims endured or the social and structural realities that allowed those harms take place. Doing so not only inadequately responds to the needs of victims but also undermines the work to build a better future. The language of reparative justice is therefore intended to draw attention to the vital role tangible reparations play in the process of establishing relationships of accountability and reciprocity where they have previously not existed.[43]

Recall Buxton's differentiation between compensation and reparations. Compensation makes up for a loss sustained by a person or group. Reparations serve a moral function, acknowledging that harm resulted from a failure to take the rights, needs, or dignity of another person or community into sufficient consideration when undertaking an action or actions that would foreseeably, negatively affect them. In other words, it is an acknowledgment that what happened was an injustice. For Walker,

> [reparations] are about demonstrating (rather than establishing) relations of accountability and reciprocity that no process or program of reparations can itself guarantee. Reparations are a medium for the contentious yet hopeful negotiation in the present of proper recognition of the past and proper terms of relation for the future. As such they require mutually reinforcing commitments in multiple registers of relationship: money, acknowledgment, public ritual, social change.[44]

Negotiating a better relationship going forward requires recognition and acknowledgment of past wrongdoings. These wrongdoings took place precisely because the wrongdoer(s) did not treat the victim(s) as equal. The relationship lacked mutuality and accountability. Reparations serve as a tangible acknowledgment that harm was done and that responsibility for that harm is being taken. They are an acknowledgment that a person or community that should have been treated as an equal was not. As such, reparations signal a real commitment to developing accountability and reciprocity where these have previously not existed. Wrongdoers who will not take responsibility in this way signal an unwillingness or inability to be accountable in the future. Those who have been harmed are offered little reason to believe the relationship will be different moving forward. If past injustices are not meaningfully addressed, why should the victim(s) expect better behavior in the future? Because reparations respond to relationships that have lacked mutuality and accountability, they can offer victims of injustice reason to believe that new relationships are possible by signaling in tangible

43. Walker, "Making Reparations Possible," 215–19.

44. Walker, "Making Reparations Possible," 217.

ways that others are committed to understanding historical injustices, taking responsibility, and working toward new ways of relating and organizing society.

Reparations aim at a rearranging of the material, social, and structural conditions of a society so that those who have been harmed precisely because they have not been treated as worthy of consideration or redress may begin to be brought into the circle of rights bearers in a tangible way. The goal, then, is not a maintenance of status quo but rather the affirmation of "a new baseline for moral and political engagement going forward."[45] With this understanding of reparations in mind, the next question becomes: What form should reparations take? How might a commitment to accountability and reciprocity be properly signaled?

What Forms Might Reparations Take?

Often, reparations are spoken of in monetary terms. While material compensation often cannot be substituted, Walker insists that what is most important is that the reparative action serves to empower victims, acknowledge the dignity that has been denied to them, and signify real commitment to ensure the injustice is not repeated. Reparation may therefore take a variety of forms, including symbolic action, acknowledgment of past wrongs, and policy or other structural changes, as well as monetary or other material forms of redress.[46] The restorative-justice model centers the needs of victims. This focus suggests that perhaps first and foremost, "we must listen to the views of those seeking reparations."[47] Reparations serve as acknowledgments that the dignity, rights, or well-being of individuals or communities were insufficiently respected. To try to do this without taking seriously the expressed needs and desires of those to whom reparations are owed repeats the same relationship dynamics that led to a need for repair in the first place. Reparative justice looks simultaneously backward and forward. The process is backward-facing insofar as it looks to respond to past (and ongoing) harms. It is forward-facing because it seeks to make a different, better future possible. Reparations are first steps toward a future in which people who have been harmed precisely because others have failed to treat them as worthy of consideration are now treated with respect. This absolutely necessitates their robust participation in shaping that future. Therefore, when considering the form reparations might take, we must first and foremost consider the wishes of those seeking reparations.

Because reparations seek to shape a better future, they are inherently about progress. Progress, however, can be a fraught concept. People in the Global

45. Walker, "Making Reparations Possible," 217–18.

46. Walker, "Making Reparations Possible," 217–19.

47. Buxton, "Reparative Justice for Climate Refugees," 213.

North often speaks in terms of progress, taking for granted that it is an ideal goal without considering what definition of progress is operating behind progressive efforts, who is benefited by this progress, and whether our notions of progress are tied up in patterns of thinking that are at their core colonialist. It is worth remembering that some of the actions that dispossessed Indigenous nations of significant portions of their land base, such as the Dawes Act, came under the guise of help by self-professed friends. While the Dawes Act was not reparations, it is a helpful illustration of the problem. If input from Indigenous people had been sought and taken seriously, further harm might have been avoided or at least mitigated. Instead, plans for the future were imposed on them. They were not treated as equals who ought to have a say in a shared future.

In conversations with people living on the border between the United States and Mexico, I have been struck by how pervasive these questions of progress, power, and self-determination are, especially among community organizers within the most marginalized communities there. Reparative justice responds to situations in which people's rights and dignity have been ignored. As reparations seek to build toward a better future, they must do so in ways that honor these communities' wisdom, their hope of defining what is good for their communities themselves, and their desire to lead their own liberative projects. To do this, we must be conscious of how we think about progress and work to disentangle our vision of how the world ought to be from the settler-colonial worldview.

Alongside a robust inclusion of those seeking reparations in the process of determining what form those reparations might take, philosopher Laura Santi Amantini offers three principles that might guide the determination of proper reparations. Amanti's principles are intended specifically to offer guidance on reparations as a response to forced migration. This makes her principles especially apt for our project of responding well to migrants. However, I argue that these principles are helpful for reparations in general and need not be thought of solely in terms of forced migration.

The first principle Amantini offers is the specificity principle. This principle requires that reparations address "specific needs, and not just survival needs or general human rights."[48] Individuals and communities seeking reparation are not simply vulnerable people in need, to whom we respond out of a generalized duty to meet their human rights. They are people who have been harmed in specific ways, which gives rise to specific needs. This once again emphasizes the necessity of listening to and taking seriously the perspectives of those seeking reparations, as they are usually in the best position to understand their specific needs. In the case of forced migrants, Amantini notes that displaced people have suffered specific losses that require unique responses. This, she argues, "implies

48. Laura Santi Amantini, "Reparative Responsibility for the Harms of Forced Migration," *Journal of Social Philosophy* (2022): 9, https://doi.org/10.1111/josp.12493.

recognizing forced migrants as people who have been forcibly displaced, instead of subsuming them into a generic category of 'vulnerable' people in need of humanitarian concern until they eventually access a 'durable solution' and become indistinguishable from the nondisplaced population, with whom they share the same claims to human rights protection."[49] By this, she means that the specific harms displaced people face (loss of home, loss of community, loss of livelihood, etc.) call for specific reparations that go beyond the more immediate response of resettlement.

Amantini's attention to the long-lasting needs of displaced people draws us to her second principle: continuity. Continuity requires that needs are addressed until they no longer exist. In the case of forced migrants, she argues that this principle "prescribes overcoming a rigid temporal separation between a displacement phase and a postdisplacement phase in which a 'durable solution' such as resettlement, repatriation, or local integration has been reached.[50] Among policy makers, theorists, and activists, there has tended to be a consensus that displaced people who have not achieved a durable solution (resettlement, etc.) are in a temporary assistance phase in which they require emergency aid. Once the durable solution has been implemented, they enter a more stable situation in which their needs are more or less similar to any other person. Amantini pushes back against this sharp division between the pre- and postdurable solution phase, noting that displaced people have specific prolonged needs that must be addressed even after they have access to a durable solution. Because these needs persist, "outcome-responsible actors continue to bear reparative duties even when forced migrants are repatriated or locally integrated elsewhere."[51] The specific harms of forced displacement (loss of community, livelihood, security, etc.) continue after resettlement. Reparative responsibility therefore also continues.

This example helps illuminate the importance of the continuity principle. Reparations are not compensation. They are not meant to make up for a loss and bring a person or community back to where they were or would have been before the loss. Rather, they aim to address harms as an acknowledgment that those harms should not have happened and that they happened specifically because not enough care was taken to avoid negatively affecting other people (or because certain actors behaved maliciously due to a failure to see the other as an equal deserving of dignity). Responding to this type of harm requires a commitment to the relationship, which in turn requires a willingness to address harm even when it is long lasting.

49. Amantini, "Reparative Responsibility," 9–10.

50. Amantini, "Reparative Responsibility," 9–10.

51. Amantini, "Reparative Responsibility," 10.

Finally, Amantini suggests the principle of expressivity. This principle is about acknowledgment. Specifically, Amantini suggests reparations must involve two acknowledgments: recognition of specific needs and recognition of reparative responsibility. We have already discussed the importance of taking the specific, expressed needs of those seeking reparations seriously. Expressivity requires that this be acknowledged explicitly. It also requires an explicit recognition of responsibility for causing harm and a responsibility to repair that harm. Whatever form reparations take, whether financial, targeted social services, policy changes, or something else, Amantini insists that it is important that public language around and justification of these measures be explicit about the responsibility being taken. For example, policies that aim to assist forced migrants in gaining or regaining economic independence ought to be explicitly implemented "based on the recognition that forced migrants were harmed (economically, but also socially and psychologically) when forced to abandon their source of livelihood and thus should be redressed" by those responsible for their displacement.[52] Walker argues that a restorative model insists that, "at a minimum, others must acknowledge the wrong and harm done to victims and accept the legitimacy of victims' demands for recognition and redress." Failure to do so communicates to those harmed that they do not matter and that the wrongs done to them are unimportant, undercutting any efforts to build a better relationship going forward.[53] We must be clear when making reparations that they are in fact reparations.

Walker notes that in many cases, the meaning of reparative measures is "powerfully shaped by the larger frame: other gestures of recognition, acknowledgment, atonement, memorializing, social support and guarantees of prevention determine" whether reparative measures such as financial compensation send "an acceptable and dignifying message to victims and perpetrators, as well as to society generally."[54] The public recognition of the truth, of the fact that individuals or communities were harmed, that they should not have been, and that other individuals or communities bear responsibility for causing that harm, is important. This truth telling allows those who have been harmed to move forward in their lives and to recover important "social and epistemic status." Victims of injustice are often harmed not only by the wrongdoing itself (slavery, genocide, forced displacement, etc.) but also by the fact that they have been treated as if they do not matter, a "morally annihilating insult" that must be addressed alongside more concrete material harms.[55] Having been treated in

52. Amantini, "Reparative Responsibility," 10.

53. Walker, "Restorative Justice and Reparations," 383–84.

54. Walker, "Restorative Justice and Reparations," 380.

55. Amantini, "Reparative Responsibility," 13.

this way, they are owed truth telling, by which they are elevated to the status of a recognized rights bearer, deserving of consideration and respect and capable of credibly giving an account of their own experience and needs. Truth telling is therefore "both a reparation measure in itself and a precondition to all other reparations."[56] It aids victims in recovering self-esteem and overcoming feelings of humiliation that can result from being treated as unworthy of respect, and it establishes the social recognition that forms the basis of other reparative efforts.

Robust input from victims of harm, alongside the principles of specificity, continuity, and expressivity, offer us a helpful guide as we consider what form reparations ought to take in any concrete context. Buxton also offers a helpful, practical caveat to consider. While still upholding the vital importance of needs and preferences of victims of harm, she notes that "some reparations may still be more appropriate than others from the perspective of fairness."[57] It may be necessary, she highlights, to allow for "reasonable refusal" of requested reparative measures. As an example of what this might look like in practice, Buxton notes that while climate refugees might be owed land as reparations, should they request land vastly larger than what was lost, outcome-responsible parties might reasonably refuse such a request. This does not mean that these parties do not continue to have a responsibility, simply that they do have a valid say in determining what reasonable reparations entail. "We should move forward with clear consideration of the desires of climate refugees," she writes, "but tread carefully with the idea of 'reasonableness' in mind."[58] Walker similarly holds that "reparations policies must be politically feasible" but also helpfully maintains that they must not "add further moral insult to moral and material injury" by appearing to be "cheap buyouts" and failing to adequately address the needs of victims.[59]

Whatever form of reparations is determined to be fitting, what is important is that they make real, measurable steps toward better ways of relating. For example, changes to the US immigration system that honor the history of aggressive and unjust action in Mexico on the part of the United States could

56. Amantini, "Reparative Responsibility," 13.

57. Buxton, "Reparative Justice for Climate Refugees," 211.

58. Buxton, "Reparative Justice for Climate Refugees," 211. Reasonableness is also a helpful caveat as we distinguish legitimate reparative claims. Not every person or community that believes themselves to be unjustly harmed is necessarily a victim of injustice (although we might say their experience of harm is always worth responding to in some way). Nor are communities always accurate about who is to blame, especially when scapegoating can be so emotionally persuasive. Claims that one is owed reparations are open to standards of reasonableness, just as specific reparative preferences are. Buxton's criteria of reasonably foreseeable impacts can be helpful here.

59. Walker, "Restorative Justice and Reparations," 380.

be one form of reparations aimed at creating accountability where there has been none. Such changes would tangibly signal US commitment to treating the people outside its borders as worthy of respect and consideration, and to reframing its understanding of membership to include the relationships it has forged with Mexico. A reparative focus can help bring about more reciprocity in the relationship.

A Note about Collective Responsibility

A potential difficulty with the reparative approach this chapter is proposing is that the global dynamics that drive migration are often complicated, and it is not always easy to determine responsibility in a direct, mathematical sort of a way (e.g., the United States is *x* percent responsible for migration from El Salvador and therefore ought to provide *x* percent of reparative justice). Often, global structures are at play, over which individual state actors have some but not complete control. Structures, such as political, social, and economic realities, "serve as background conditions for individual actions by presenting actors with options; they provide 'channels ' that both enable action and constrain it"[60] This complicates matters. For example, Buxton highlights that "climate change is often described as a 'perfect moral storm', comprised of problems of collective action failure, diffused responsibility, and intergenerational justice." This makes it difficult to allocate responsibility and determine who specifically owes reparations. For Buxton, "the difficulty lies in linking certain agents to the harm of climate displacement."[61] If we wish to employ a reparative approach in order to respond to the harms of climate change, such as island nation's losing its territory, we must be able to meaningfully identify who is responsible for sea level rise. When global structures cause or contribute to forced migration (climate-caused or otherwise), we have to consider how we accurately (and convincingly) establish responsibility for harm.

Amantini proposes a structural account of harm that may enable us to work through this difficulty. Citing philosopher and political theorist Iris Marion Young, who argues that all who participate in these global structures "bear responsibility for structural injustice because they contribute by their actions to the processes that produce unjust outcomes,"[62] Amantini moves to consider how collective responsibility might be differentiated. While all who contribute to global structures that cause displacement bear responsibility, they do not bear

60. Iris Marion Young, "Responsibility and Global Justice: A Social Connection Model," *Social Philosophy and Policy* 23, no. 1 (2006): 112, https://doi.org/10.1017/S0265052506060043.

61. Buxton, "Reparative Justice for Climate Refugees," 206, 201.

62. Young, "Responsibility and Global Justice," 119.

it equally. Additionally, she notes that those who benefit the most from the status quo of these global structures tend also to be those who have contributed most directly to those structures and also those who have the most ability to remedy them. Buxton similarly highlights the importance of paying attention to who benefits from harmful global dynamics such as climate change and proposes that benefit might "[trigger] a secondary duty of repayment."[63] Amantini offers power as a proxy category for naming these dynamics of contribution, benefit, and ability to repair. A state's relative power can help determine that state's responsibility for reparative justice. She argues, "Using power as a proxy highlights the frequent alignment of (historical) contribution to structural injustices, benefit and capacity to remedy."[64] Those with the most capacity to remedy harmful global systems and dynamics such as climate change most often also benefit most from and contribute most to these systems. Power can indicate a responsibility for repair.

Amantini concedes that there may be cases where these dynamics (contribution, benefit, and capacity) do not align. A nation may have contributed significantly to the creation or sustaining of an unjust system historically but currently have limited capacity to remedy that situation.[65] We will do well to keep this possibility in mind when analyzing specific cases. However, as a general rule, power is a helpful indicator of responsibility. Generally speaking, "the [Global] North does more to cause forced migration than to stop it, through enforcing an international economic and political order that causes underdevelopment and conflict."[66] The point of the power-proxy model for considering responsibility for global dynamics is "to underline how external states can be connected to forced migrants not only through particular acts and omissions but also through global processes and structures in which they participate."[67] Amantini's account can be aligned with responsibility ethics and especially Niebuhr's account of social solidarity. We are responsible to and for our societies and communities. We have a responsibility to try to move those societies in good, just directions. Participation in harmful global dynamics goes against this responsibility. Therefore, when we have participated in these harmful dynamics, we have a responsibility to participate in the work of robust repair.

63. Buxton, "Reparative Justice for Climate Refugees," 205–6.

64. Amantini, "Reparative Responsibility," 8.

65. Amantini, "Reparative Responsibility," 8.

66. Stephen Castles, "Towards a Sociology of Forced Migration and Social Transformation," *Sociology* 37, no. 1 (2003): 18, https://doi.org/10.1177/0038038503037001384.

67. Amantini, "Reparative Responsibility," 9.

Responsibility and Repair

A reparative-justice approach pairs well with a responsibility framework as outlined by Niebuhr and Curran. In particular, we can identify five elements of this reparative approach that align with the tenets of responsibility ethics.

First, Buxton notes that an obligation-based reparative approach emphasizes the moral responsibility of those responsible for the harm done. While other approaches primarily hinge on the rights of the claimant, obligation-based "reparative claims depend on the existence of a duty-bearer." In other words, we are looking not for a rights-bearer, which all people are and should be treated as, but someone who is responsible for violating, ignoring, or neglecting the rights of others. "In focusing on obligation bearers, this approach centres on the responsible agent," the person who has acted unjustly.[68] Heyer's shifting of moral focus from the survival choices of migrants to the systems that push them to migrate in the first place[69] pairs well with Buxton's account. Additionally, a reparative model hinges on the idea that moral actors are responsible for not causing avoidable harm, and that when they cause such harm, they have obligations. These "are not obligations generated on the grounds of equity, but the grounds of responsibility."[70] The moral center of this approach is our responsibility to treat one another well, as worthy of consideration and respect. Failure to do this creates a responsibility to repair the damage. Similarly, responsibility ethics frames the moral agent as responsible to various relationships. Failure to be adequately responsible in the past demands an adequate response in the present.[71]

This leads to the second reason reparative justice is well suited for a responsibility framework: repair is fundamentally time-full in nature. The historicity emphasized in responsibility ethics is echoed in the way these reparative accounts move away from a synchronic approach, which focuses on a particular moment in time, to a diachronic approach, which emphasizes and takes seriously the historical developments that have led to, for example, the production of refugees.[72] In other words, attention to history calls us to look beyond what

68. Buxton, "Reparative Justice for Climate Refugees," 200–201.

69. Heyer, *Kinship across Borders*, 156–57.

70. Buxton, "Reparative Justice for Climate Refugees," 201.

71. It may be worth explicitly aligning this centering of the duty bearer with Walker's victim-centered restorative justice model for framing reparations. Restorative justice begins with a recognition that someone has been harmed, violated, or treated as undeserving of consideration (as oppose to corrective justice, which begins from a violation of a law or standard of behavior). A call for reparations recognizes that there is someone who caused that harm or violation, someone who failed to be responsible to and for others, and who therefore has a duty to repair the harm.

72. Buxton, "Reparative Justice for Climate Refugees," 201.

is happening in the present moment to ask important questions about how we got here. Buxton's approach to climate refugees is a helpful example. "Under our current normative framework," she writes, "refugees have ongoing humanitarian claims which generate general duties. However, some refugees have an important historical element to their claim, namely, their displacement results from the actions of a specific party."[73] Niebuhr holds that we act responsibly when we have an adequate understanding of what we are responding to. We cannot respond well or responsibly to harm if we do not know how and why the harm took place.

Buxton identifies three central questions for reparative justice: "Who (if anyone) is owed reparations, who (if anyone) should pay, and in what form (if any) should payments be made?" To the first question, she responds, "The answer to this question largely depends on what reparations are owed for."[74] Responsibility ethics frames moral behavior as primarily a question of acting fittingly, based on a cosmic understanding of responsibility in which all of our actions ultimately respond to God. Failure to respond fittingly to one another and to God constitutes sin. To respond fittingly in the face of our sin requires repairing the harm that our unfitting actions caused. Therefore, to act well, or fittingly, when we have been responsible for injustice requires responding in a way that addresses the specific injustice and those who were harmed by it. The question of who is owed reparations is largely a question of who has been harmed by past or ongoing unfitting actions, the injustice to which we are responding. Who owes and what they owe can then be based on this analysis. This is a time-full analysis of harm. Attention to history is essential for responsibility ethics and for reparative justice.

Third, reparative justice, understood through the lens of restorative justice, responds to interconnecting webs of relationship in which we are all situated, as described by Niebuhr and affirmed by Curran. The foundation of reparative justice is the notion that our choices have the ability to affect other people and that we have a responsibility to consider those impacts and avoid harm. This is what it means to live in a web of relationships. Our choices affect one another, and so we must be considerate. When we do not sufficiently consider other people and, because of this lack of consideration or concern, cause harm, we owe something to those people precisely because we were not behaving as responsible moral actors. Additionally, attention to the global dynamics in which we participate, which Amantini and others call us to, is attention to the webs of relationship in which we are situated as moral agents. Responsibility ethics and reparative justice

73. Buxton, "Reparative Justice for Climate Refugees," 201.

74. Buxton, "Reparative Justice for Climate Refugees," 202–3.

both draw us to concern for the impact our choices have not only on those most directly close to us but all people, because in an increasingly globalized world our choices have the capacity to harm those far beyond our immediate circle or community.

Fourth, a reparative approach can help us be accountable for anticipating (or failing to anticipate) the likely responses to (or outcomes of) our actions.[75] This is outcome responsibility, responsibility for the consequences of our actions. Buxton writes,

> Reliance on outcome responsibility when determining whether reparations are owed is meant to accommodate the intuition that reparations are owed even when agents are "morally innocent." Consider the case of a "just war" whereby a state may be justified in invading a foreign country, for instance, to stop genocide. This state could be held outcome responsible for any displacement caused, but perhaps not morally responsible.[76]

While reparations have a specifically moral function, responding to and naming situations that are unjust, agents need not have intended harm to be properly outcome responsible.

Recall that reparative claims require a duty bearer, someone who is responsible for harm. That duty bearer may very well have acted with good intentions, but responsibility ethics tells us that we are responsible for both considering the potential repercussions of our choices and for following through on our choices. Concretely, this may mean repairing harm that we have caused, whether or not that harm was intended. The outcome-responsible standard Buxton highlights allocates responsibility based on foreseeable consequences. Sea-level-rise flooding island nations is a clearly foreseeable consequence of high carbon emissions warming the earth. Nations and corporations that have contributed to this sea-level rise had a duty to consider this outcome before they acted and continue to have a duty to follow their choices through now, potentially by offering reparations to those harmed.

Finally, a reparative framework offers a productive challenge to present language and legal categories. In doing so, this framework helps us better understand and interpret that to which we seek to respond fittingly. In particular, a reparative-justice framework for migration can push to expand the language of "refugee." Legally speaking, a migrant must meet certain criteria

75. Niebuhr, *Responsible Self*, 63–64.

76. Buxton, "Reparative Justice for Climate Refugees," 204.

to be properly called a refugee and to therefore have access to the rights, protection, and aid national and international law provides for refugees. Buxton writes,

> Notably, the existing legal definition of a "refugee" places great emphasis on persecution based upon race, religion, nationality, social membership or political opinion. However, from a moral perspective, it is not clear that those fulfilling this definition should have exclusive access to protection; persecution may be a sufficient but not necessary condition of refugeehood. Instead, our legal definition neglects the central normative issue of refugeehood, namely, that refugees have lost the protection of their state.[77]

Persecution names some but not all of the reasons a person might be forced to migrate. Take, for example, Buxton's conversation about those forced to migrate because of climate change. As it currently stands, international law does not protect these migrants.[78] Their reasons for fleeing, however, are clearly as dire as those who flee explicit persecution. Because a reparative framework, rooted in restorative justice, allocates responsibility based on "the reality of violation, alienation, and disregard among human beings,"[79] it highlights the ways all forced migrants are wrongfully displaced. Whether forced to move because of persecution, climate change, economic instability, or for other reasons, the central factor linking all of these migrants is that they are unable to stay where they are precisely because they have not been or are not being sufficiently treated as worthy of consideration. Centering the loss (or absence) of a stable citizen-state relationship, rather than persecution, allows Buxton to propose treating climate refugees as true refugees, owed protections similar to those fleeing persecution. I contend that centering violation or disregard—the recognition that a person or group of people acted in a wrongful manner by not meaningfully seeking to avoid a predictable, harmful outcome and therefore treating others as if they are not worthy of consideration—even more helpfully directs considerations of how the definition of a refugee might be expanded.

The present definition of a refugee as someone fleeing persecution provides important protection that should be upheld, but it does not respond fully to the reality of forced migration. A responsibility-ethics framework prioritizes

77. Buxton, "Reparative Justice for Climate Refugees," 194.

78. Sumudu Atapattu, "'Climate Refugees' and the Role of International Law," Oxford Research Group, September 12, 2018, https://tinyurl.com/ytwbrsj4.

79. Walker, "Restorative Justice and Reparations," 382.

a robust understanding of that to which we seek to respond. Without a full understanding, we cannot respond fittingly. A reparative framework, with its emphasis on violation and disregard, helps us better encapsulate the reality of forced migration and could help national and international law respond more fittingly to forced migration in all its forms.

It is clear that a relationality-responsibility framework for responding to migration in the United States will benefit greatly from a consideration of the role reparations must play in creating accountability and reciprocity in international relationships and leveling out gross global inequality. I contend that this focus on tangible repair is also consistent with Jesus's focus on building community based on just relationships and with the deeply relational nature of the universe, created in the image of a triune God. Thus far, we have explored reparations primarily from a secular vantage point. It is worth now considering what Christian theology brings to the table to deepen our understanding of reparative justice.

Radical Love and Reparative Justice: Sin, Salvation, and Repair

Reparative justice is a tall order. The United States has failed repeatedly to be in just relationships with other countries. There is arguably little hope that the nation, on its current path, will not only stop acting unjustly but also actively pursue real justice. Here, Christianity has something to add: radical, transformative love.

Drawing on Audra Lorde, M. Shawn Copeland suggests that the love Jesus exhibited for humanity is best defined as "eros." Eros, she says, involves deep emotional connections between people. It "validates our refusal of docility and submission in the face of oppression" and "steadies us as we reach out to other bodies in reverence, passion, and compassion, resisting every temptation to use and assimilate the other" as the world has taught us to do. To say that Jesus had an eros for others is to say that he loved others passionately, that he gave freely of himself because of a deep, concrete love, a radical type of love that led ultimately to his death on a Roman cross.[80] This is a love that seeks to include others, to build communities of care and compassion, especially with those most often rejected by society.[81] This love

80. Copeland, "Marking the Body of Jesus," 64–65.

81. Copeland, "Marking the Body of Jesus," 61. Here we begin also to see the standards on which we might base inclusivity. Inclusivity modeled after Jesus begins with and centers the inclusion of the marginalized and oppressed. It is the inclusion of those most often rejected by society that is foregrounded in Jesus's ministry. Of course, Jesus also seeks to include everyone. God's love, incarnate in Jesus, is directed toward the whole of creation. But the prioritization

Jesus modeled is precisely the type of love we are called to in service of the kin-dom of God.[82]

Moving toward reparative justice will require this radical form of love. The radical love of Jesus was a tangible, practical love. It healed physical ailments. It fed hungry bellies. Jesus was God's love for the world so passionately tangible that it incarnated in a fully embodied human life. Radical love cares for the concrete realities of human beings so much it became one. William O'Neill calls us to understand the neighbor as someone with concrete and specific needs. Looking at the parable of the good Samaritan, we further see that, biblically, being a neighbor is something we do actively. The Samaritan was a neighbor to the man in need because he acted as one. He took responsibility for him, got him medical attention, and committed long term to providing more if it was needed. This is how Jesus defines being a neighbor (Luke 10:25–37). Within the broader context of his work of radical love and community building, Jesus tells his followers this story about a Samaritan being a good neighbor by establishing a new relationship with someone in need, a relationship that models the concrete, tangible love Jesus lived and preached. This is precisely the type of love that calls us to reparative justice, to tangible actions that establish accountability and justice where there has been injustice. Radical love empowers just relationships and the building of community. It invites us to conversion and renewal, renewal that can reshape relationships that have been broken. As a verb, radical love participates in this work of repair, interrupting injustice and oppressive social structures with a prophetic vision of God's reign.[83]

Moreover, Copeland argues that Jesus's eros for humanity, his radical love, was deeply contagious. Radical love calls people toward it. Jesus attracted the outcasts, the arrogant, the timid, and the suspicious to him because his eros was so compelling.[84] In other words, it sparked conversion or at least curiosity about other ways humans might live together. In chapter 6 we will consider the role churches and Christians can play in pursuing justice for migrants.

---

of those society has marginalized remains the guiding principle of this inclusion. Jesus says that the first will be last and the last will be first (Matt 20:16). He calls his followers to provide care for those who are homeless, incarcerated, hungry, sick (Matt 25:31–46) and to invite those who are poor and disabled to their feasts (Luke 14:12–14). The rich young man is asked to sell all of his possessions and give to the poor (Matt 19:16–22). Based on this example, inclusivity ought to prioritize those who have been marginalized, and the inclusion of those who have not been must never come at the expense of the marginalized. Christian communities ought to model their community building on this.

82. Copeland, "Marking the Body of Jesus," 65.

83. Copeland, "Marking the Body of Jesus," 83–84.

84. Copeland, "Marking the Body of Jesus," 65.

The power of the radical love Jesus modeled will have an important role to play in helping Christians begin to build just, responsible communities that show the world what is possible and call others to join in. Embodying this love can call others to participation and conversion, moving us toward justice one heart at a time.

The understanding of social sin and individual culpability outlined by Niebuhr and Curran can also be a helpful conversation partner for reparative justice. Social sin firmly establishes that those who do not understand themselves to be culpable in, for example, the ongoing sins of the United States remain responsible regardless. This resonates with the biblical account of justice, which Tisha Rajendra argues suggests "that our unchosen national identities may give us inherited responsibilities."[85] Part of what it means to be a member of a community is that we inherit the legacy of that community, good and bad, including the legacy of social sin. Justice calls us to take responsibility for the communities we are members of, whether by choice or by birth. For US citizens, this means taking some responsibility for the harms the United States has caused. The United States would not exist as it does today without the harmful actions and ideologies that drove and sustained its founding and expansion. This means that as citizens we benefit in a basic sense from those harmful actions. The dynamics of social sin highlights that participation in (and benefit from) systems and ideologies that cause or have caused harm does not require active malicious intent nor indeed even a conscious awareness of one's participation in sin. We are responsible by virtue of our participation and benefit, regardless of intent.

A reparative-justice framework can help us take this seriously. Reparations, in that they aim at establishing relationships of mutuality and accountability, are concerned with all sides of a conflict. An explicit goal is to help those responsible for harm take responsibility and move forward toward better relationships and reintegration into the community. Participating in discussions regarding appropriate reparations and the building of accountability can provide an opportunity for those who have not yet recognized themselves as culpable to experience a form of conversion through listening to the stories of victims. For example, we may consider the ongoing discussions of reparations for slavery in the United States highlighted above. Participation in these discussions, when undertaken in good faith, might provide white US citizens with a deeper understanding of the systemic injustices Black people face in the United States and of the often unseen ways in which white people benefit from structural privileges that can be traced back to the impacts of slavery on the nation. This can help white people understand why they, as individuals, have a stake in building more just and responsible relationships moving forward. We can begin to encounter our own

85. Rajendra, *Migrants and Citizens*, 98.

responsibility, not because we caused the situation but because we benefit from (and at times participate in) it.

Discussions of reparations, in that they seek to establish what has been wrong in relationships and how to build better relationships going forward, provide space for the types of encounters that can open minds and help people grapple with their own culpability and responsibility in productive ways.[86] This is part of the role Amantini's expressivity principle plays. When we are explicit about reparative responsibility, we can be called to acknowledge our own culpability. US citizens may be invited, through discussions of reparative justice on large and small scales, to more fully consider their own culpability in US sins against migrants.

Finally, a theological lens, in which we view reparations as an outgrowth of the radical love Jesus calls us to embody, can move us from practical questions of who most rightfully owes those who have been wronged to questions of what might I/we do to repair relationships, even if we are not the primary responsible party or only benefit from rather than directly cause harm. Existing literature considering reparations as a response to forced migration often includes a consideration of how to determine who is most responsible for harm and therefore primarily responsible for offering reparations. These practical questions of who ought to pay are important. From a Christian perspective, however, we can understand reparative justice as calling us to the work of repair even if someone else can and should take on responsibility for reparations. We are called to repair broken relationships, and so we should participate in that work however we can.

Jesus encouraged his followers to go and reconcile with those who had something against them before offering gifts at the altar (Matt 5:23–24). In other words, reconciliation and the repair of broken relationships is a prerequisite for worship. We can and should understand the church to be called to this work of repair. This is one facet of embodying the radical love Jesus offered and exemplified.

Concluding Thoughts

This chapter has proposed a reparative justice–focused responsibility framework that can help us move out of unjust patterns of relating and toward justice. Reparations are a vital way we can respond to the practical requirements of the responsibility approach outlined in chapter 3. The recognition that a debt might be owed to migrants is of great importance to the argument I am making in this book. The United States should strive to treat all people in a way that befits their dignity and respects their human rights. Our immigration policies and practices could certainly do this better. More specifically, however, the

86. It is important that these methods for grappling with culpability are productive rather than simply shame-based, for both victims of injustice and the beneficiaries of privilege.

nation has a reparative duty to many of the migrants at and within our borders specifically because it is our failures to treat them as worthy of consideration that have led to their need to migrate. This is a particular claim that is worth naming and responding to in a robust fashion. The central question for migration ethics is not "How do we balance the rights and needs of states with the rights and needs of migrants?" but "How can we take responsibility for the harm that we have caused and that has forced millions of people to uproot their lives and leave their homes behind?"

Given the concrete structural inequalities that US imperialism has created and the United States' ongoing failures to live in just, reciprocal relationship with other countries, tangible reparations that establish accountability must be a nonnegotiable component of justice for migrants. This project focuses on reparative justice in order to emphasize the need to repair the harm that has been done in tangible ways that address inequality. The United States has through its actions participated in the creation of severe global inequality. This is to say nothing of the complete failure on the part of the United States to create or implement immigration policies that adequately address its role in the creation of migratory patterns or its history of colonial sins. Taking responsibility for this requires both repentance and reparations in order to show real commitment to building a more just and accountable world order.

Buxton concedes, "The task of reparations is a great one, demanding far more collective action than the political reality has made possible thus far." Robust reparations for forced migration (and the global dynamics that contribute to it) will require significant global cooperation, the likes of which we have yet to see in practice. Despite the difficulties of implementing a reparative approach to migration, Buxton contends that justice demands we try, that we "shoot the arrow as close to the target as we can."[87] For citizens of the United States, this requires something from each of us. With Rajendra, we can come to understand that we inherit a responsibility to respond to the harms our nation has caused, to do what we can, even if that is only on a small scale. Walker argues, "Restorative justice accommodates and perhaps requires bottom-up and incremental attempts at repair as a social and political process."[88] With or without participation from national governments, people and communities can and should consider what we can do at the local, grassroots level to begin the work of repair. With this in mind, the final chapter of this book considers the question of what individuals and churches can and should do in the face of the United States' reparative responsibility to migrants. First, however, it is important to establish a basic foundation for how we understand the role of Christians and the church in the world. To that end, we turn in chapter 5 to an exploration of Christology and ecclesiology.

---

87. Buxton, "Reparative Justice for Climate Refugees," 219.

88. Walker, "Restorative Justice and Reparations," 279.

CHAPTER FIVE

Discipleship

BEFORE MOVING INTO a discussion of the practical implications of a responsibility-based approach to migration, the present chapter seeks to ground our conversation in a discussion of who and what the church is called to be. This chapter provides a bridge between the conceptual work of the first four chapters and the practical proposals of the final chapter. It considers how what Christians say about Jesus relates to who and what the church is meant to be and how its mission in the world is understood. In other words, it fleshes out the content of the radical love proposed in chapters 3–4. In order to do so, the chapter begins by identifying helpful christological and ecclesiological insights in Niebuhr and Curran. Beginning with Niebuhr and Curran in this way allows this chapter's theological account to remain firmly grounded in the responsibility framework of chapter 3. This chapter retrieves from Niebuhr and Curran an account of responsible discipleship defined as a radical commitment to opposing the sinful forces that crucified Jesus, especially through focus on just relationships and open dialogue.

Such a discipleship ought naturally to draw Christians (especially those with privilege) into dialogue with those against whom these sinful forces of empire still rage. As highlighted by the historical account offered in chapters 1–2, this means especially engaging in dialogue with Indigenous and Latine people. It is in light of this that this chapter turns to consider the perspectives of several Indigenous and Latine theologians, connecting these back to Niebuhr and Curran and allowing them to shape an understanding of responsible discipleship that will inform chapter 6. Such a dialogue is consistent with the aims of an immigration ethic rooted in responsibility in that it is an integral part of the establishment of accountability and the formation of more just ways of relating.

Niebuhr and Curran: Christological and Ecclesiological Perspectives Rooted in Responsibility

Christology

Chapter 3 established that, for Niebuhr, all of our choices are responses to God, and they are responses specifically shaped by the story of God as mediated through Jesus (and through our community's telling of the story of Jesus). Niebuhr's own understanding of Jesus can therefore help us create a basic foundation on which to build an understanding of how Christology shapes or ought to shape us as moral agents who respond ultimately to God in all things that we do.

Despite his more philosophical bent, Niebuhr still remains very much a Christian theologian who does engage Christian themes and sources, if sometimes to a lesser degree than others.[1] In his work, Jesus is both a model for our lives and a person and event through which Christians should view the world. As a model, Jesus represents the human person par excellence. Niebuhr writes, "Christ was the perfect man, the moral emergent, the revealer in word and conduct of the ideal, the proclaimer and realizer of the Kingdom of God or of the realm of ends."[2] What this means, for Niebuhr, is that Jesus, in all he does, models the human person as perfectly responsible. He argues that in all of Jesus's responsive actions, he interpreted the actions upon him within the context of the universal action of God, that is, as signs of God's divine action. He acts in concert with God's will and in anticipation of the eschatological future, God's vision for the fulfillment of the world. Jesus's responsive action, then, is completely fitting. Christians attempting to live out a Christian ethos do so by attempting to conform their lives to Christ's. In this way, he is a model. It is important to Niebuhr, however, to establish that Jesus's responsiveness to God's will is not a mechanical obedience or resignation to God's will. Rather, Jesus responds in the context of a loving relationship with God, interpreting everything from acts of nature to the actions of religious and political authorities within a context of God's initial creative action and power.[3] In the context of chapter 3, we might say that Jesus perfectly models a relationship to the world based on radical love and grounded in his relationship with God.

Niebuhr describes God's action not as evidence of fatalistic determinism but as being more like the action "of a great wise leader who uses even the meanness of [their] subjects to promote the public welfare." That is, belief in God's will and power, for Niebuhr, does not mean that Judas's betrayal or global wars were predetermined or foreordained. Rather, God is present in these events and works to produce good. Jesus, as a model of responsibility, interprets events such as these as within God's power to transform, and he therefore responds to them accordingly. For Niebuhr, this is not only how Jesus interpreted and acted in the world but also how Christians today are meant to view the world and respond accordingly. Jesus models the proper posture for encountering the world as a

1. Koontz, "Confessional Theology," 417.

2. Niebuhr, *Responsible Self*, 174.

3. Niebuhr, *Responsible Self*, 164–72.

responsible moral agent. Through Jesus's example, humanity's proper end "as seer of God, as contemplator of the eternal," comes into view.[4]

Jesus is, however, more than a model for Niebuhr. He is also savior, the rescuer of humanity. Not only does he show us our proper end; he is our way to it. That is, Jesus is not simply someone whose model we ought to follow in order to live as responsible selves; he is someone Christians encounter as "the one who lived and died and rose again for this cause of bringing God to [people] and [people] to God and so also of reconciling people to each other in their world." M. Shawn Copeland highlights the compelling nature of Jesus's radical love. Encountering Jesus transforms us so that we too may love radically. For Niebuhr, Jesus's saving action rescued humanity by healing the human spirit from death. Recall that Niebuhr describes humanity's state of sin as one in which God is encountered as enemy. As people respond out of distrust of God, he argues, they become closed off to the world, operating out of an ethics of self-defense, which is ultimately an ethics of death. Salvation entails a reorientation, a turn to respond to God out of trust, which restores our vision of the world to that of God's.[5]

For Niebuhr, then, Jesus is the one who accomplished in history humanity's ultimate goal, fully taking on an ethos of responding to God in complete trust. More than this, he is also the one with whom an encounter can begin to turn us from our suspicion of God and help move us toward trust. Christians know, according to Niebuhr, that more often than not they fall short of the goal of complete trust, returning instead to interpreting the word and responding to it through the ethics of death. Yet, we have hope in Christ, he argues, because Jesus has accomplished exactly this goal in history. Moreover, Jesus is the one who actualizes us as children of God, able to trust God because of our encounter with Jesus and Jesus's salvific life, death, and resurrection. Human movement toward reconciliation with God is "inaugurated and maintained in [them] by Jesus Christ," who empowers them.[6]

Jesus is more than a moral exemplar. He is the one who, particularly through his passion, made our salvific transformation possible, who invites us to radical change. Niebuhr writes, "Through Jesus Christ, through his life, death, resurrection, and reign of power, we have been led and are being led to *metanoia*, to the reinterpretation of all our interpretations of life and death."[7] Niebuhr understands the cross and Jesus's death on it to be "a revelation of the order of reality." The cross can illuminate our situation, making the reality of the world clear. It is

4. Niebuhr, *Responsible Self*, 165–74.

5. Niebuhr, *Responsible Self*, 174, 43, 99–100, 133.

6. Niebuhr, *Responsible Self*, 175–77.

7. Niebuhr, *Responsible Self*, 143.

important that in articulating this notion, Niebuhr explicitly links Jesus's death to unjust suffering and to the notion that such suffering might be made fruitful. Niebuhr understands the cross and resurrection as events that teach important truths about the powers of the world that cause unjust and unnecessary suffering, and about God's promises to transform that suffering. Furthermore, our earthly situations can reveal new insights into the cross. Niebuhr explicitly links the suffering of the innocent Jesus on the cross with the suffering of innocent people in his own time, noting that such modern crucifixion should call people to repentance.[8] For example, we might understand migrants as people unjustly crucified by the United States and respond with a radical love for them that calls us to repent of our complicity in those crucifixions and change the material circumstances that lead to those crucifixions.

Like Niebuhr, Curran highlights aspects of Jesus's life that he finds especially exemplary. Jesus, he argues, did not come to force his kingdom on humanity. Rather, he comes to invite us to respond freely to his call. For Curran, Jesus's death on the cross exemplifies God's radical love for creation and God's commitment to preserving human freedom. Furthermore, his resurrection bears witness to the new life to which God raises humanity.[9] He writes,

> Jesus came into the world to free us from sin and evil. Redemption involves the successful struggle of Jesus against the power of sin and evil. The cross and the resurrection show forth the reality of redemption. The cross is at once the victory of sin, evil, and death, and the redeeming love of Jesus. The resurrection represents the triumph of Jesus over all enemies, primarily evil, sin, and death. The triune God offers us salvation and reconciliation through the redemptive love of Jesus. However, resurrection as destiny—as the fullness of the triumph of Jesus—has not yet taken place. The fullness of the reign of God is not yet here.[10]

This passage contains the core of Curran's christological perspective. Jesus is the savior whose victory over the powers of death and evil opens humans up to the possibility of redemption and reconciliation. This victory takes place in and directly affects human history, although its fulfillment will take place outside history. Jesus, as the person in whom the divine and the human become perfectly joined, strengthens the fundamental goodness inherent in all people.[11]

---

8. H. Richard Niebuhr, "War as Crucifixion," *The Christian Century*, April 28, 1943, 514–15.

9. Curran, *Christian Morality Today*, 33.

10. Curran, *Catholic Moral Tradition Today*, 34.

11. Curran, *Catholic Moral Tradition Today*, 33.

He makes radical love possible. Curran goes on to argue that Christians are saved insofar as they enter "into the mystery of redemption and transformation from death to life." This salvation, evidenced through Jesus, is God's primary work. In response to this understanding of Jesus's person and work, Christians are called to "conform our ways to his" and to participate in the paschal mystery.[12] In other words, we are called to love as Jesus did, concretely and radically.

Curran notes that suffering will at times be part of every Christian life. The cross shows us that God is revealed even in the midst of suffering and human death. The cross and the resurrection also make clear the human need for transformation. Curran argues that through Jesus's death and resurrection, human suffering is imbued with meaning, becoming a part of how we die to ourselves and rise instead to new life in God. Importantly, this does not mean that all human suffering will be redemptive. Recall that the fulfillment of Jesus's victory remains beyond history. Further, not everyone will grow because of suffering they experience. Curran is very clear that suffering is a mystery, and the redemption in suffering enacted through the cross is paradoxical and ultimately beyond our full comprehension. However, he argues that Christians are able to "see suffering in light of the cross and resurrection of Jesus." This "indicates the proper Christian approach to suffering," which is not to seek suffering out in order to be redeemed but to bear suffering that does come "in light of the suffering and transforming love of Jesus."[13]

This concern with the call to participate in the life and work of Jesus leads Curran to a discussion of discipleship. While the four Gospels portray

---

12. Curran, *Christian Morality Today*, 9, 33, 38.

13. Curran, *Christian Morality Today*, 9, 43–44. While it is to Curran's credit that he nuances his articulation of redemptive suffering in this way, this understanding of suffering remains potentially problematic. As various liberationist theologians (feminist, Black, Latin American) have argued, theologies of redemptive suffering have too often been detrimental for oppressed people, used to convince them that their suffering is proper to the Christian life, that it serves a higher purpose, or that at the very least it will be worth it when they are rewarded in the next life. For example, Shawn Copeland highlights the ways in which "the Christianity of the plantation" manipulated Christian virtues in order to bind and pacify enslaved people by teaching them that long-suffering patience was godly. See M. Shawn Copeland, "Wading through Many Sorrows: Toward a Theology of Suffering in Womanist Perspective," in *A Troubling in My Soul: Womanist Perspectives on Evil and Suffering*, ed. Emilie M. Townes (Maryknoll, NY: Orbis, 1999), 122.

Elizabeth Johnson argues that theologies of redemptive suffering belie the immensity of human suffering, especially in the face of something like the Shoah. See Johnson, *Quest for the Living God: Mapping Frontiers in the Theology of God* (New York: Continuum, 2011), 52. The potential for suffering to be redeemed by God is theologically important, as is the reality that the Christian life may come with a cost, but Copeland and Johnson show that the notion that the cross imbues human suffering with meaning remains dangerous, especially to those who are oppressed.

discipleship in distinct ways consistent with their broader themes and goals, Curran identifies four unifying features out of which he builds a framework of what it means to be a disciple of Christ. This model of discipleship can help us flesh out what it means to participate in the radical love of Jesus. First, Curran argues, God makes the first step. Discipleship is possible because of a gracious call and gift from God, incarnate in the person of Jesus. Second, discipleship is never simply about an individual relationship with Jesus but always takes place within and involves a wider community. Moreover, discipleship is meant to transform our various relationships. Through discipleship, Curran argues, we are called to treat others as God has treated us, with love and mercy. In particular, discipleship is meant to transform our relationship to the most vulnerable, those marginalized, oppressed, and cast out by society. This means we will see and relate to the most vulnerable in the way Jesus would. Third, Curran argues that discipleship is characterized by totality and radicality. That is, discipleship affects and transforms the entire person, and it comes at a cost. Jesus's radical love for the world, after all, led to his death. As a basic commitment, discipleship is meant to direct every aspect of our lives, forming us in the image of Jesus, and this might come at a cost. Finally, this radical and total commitment forms the foundation of Christian growth. The radical goals of discipleship, including the transformation of relationships with self, neighbor, and world, are the ground on which the work of Christians (and of the church) is built.

Two important aspects of this final feature warrant closer consideration. First, Curran is clear that the radical nature of the Christian life is a call into the world, not out of it. While the Christian life is deeply eschatological, this eschatology urges transformative work in the world. Jesus loved the world concretely, entering into human life and repeatedly showing concern for people's material circumstances. Second, it is worth highlighting that Curran's account of discipleship centers on the transformation of relationships. This is consistent with his anthropology and his understanding of the moral life (as explored in chap. 3). Centering relationships will continue to be key as we move into the practical proposals of the next chapter, and thus Curran's understanding of discipleship is especially helpful for this project.

Curran's understanding of the link between Christology and the transformation of relationships can be fleshed out further. Jesus, he argues, is a unifying and equalizing figure. Curran cites Galatians 3:28, noting that in Jesus, all the human identities that produce power imbalances (slave and free, male and female, etc.) become irrelevant.[14] This becomes especially important for Curran's ecclesiology, which will be discussed in the following section. It is also, however, indicative of his overall Christology. His emphasis on catholic inclusiveness, rooted in

14. Curran, *Catholic Moral Tradition Today*, 7.

the Galatians passage, highlights his understanding of who Jesus was and is and how he affects the lives of Christians to this day. For example, with liberation theologians, Curran sees Jesus as a victim of empire, put to death unjustly by the reigning powers of his time and thus in intimate solidarity with those who are victims of empire and oppression throughout time. This interprets Jesus's salvific work as explicitly political and concrete. By taking the actual human life of Jesus as his christological point of departure (Christology from below) rather than focusing on questions of metaphysics that emphasize Jesus's preexistence (Christology from above), Curran (borrowing from liberation theologies) draws attention to the content of Jesus's life as theologically and ethically significant.[15] Attention to how Jesus lived provides a model for what radical love might look like and the types of concrete action it ought to include.

Curran argues that Jesus's humanity precludes the "dualistic opposition" of the material world and the spiritual.[16] This highlights the importance of material well-being as relevant to salvation and keeps theology firmly grounded. The incarnation prevents purely spiritual, eschatologically future understandings of salvation. Salvation is also liberation, and it works on three levels: political, historical, and liberation from sin. We may also conclude that because Jesus creates a community in which the power imbalances of the world have no weight, in which all are welcome, especially those most oppressed and despised by the world, this is theologically and morally relevant. Further, because of Jesus's specific solidarity with those on the margins, even to the point of death, it becomes clear that Jesus's radical inclusiveness is not equivalent to neutrality, and thus his followers ought not to aim for neutrality either. While the ideal community Jesus envisions is one in which socioeconomic status has no bearing on inclusion, the world in which Jesus incarnates is one in which these imbalances carry an immense weight. In that context, Jesus very clearly takes a side. We can say, therefore, that while inclusion in the kin-dom is open to all, inclusion may mean a reckoning with those identities through which we participate in the oppression of others.[17] Christology from below makes implications such as these evident in a way that a Christology too focused on Jesus as preexistent can miss or downplay.

15. Curran, *Catholic Moral Tradition Today*, 21–22, 92.

16. Curran, *Catholic Moral Tradition Today*, 33–34, 44.

17. Consider, for example, the situation of social sin in the US as it has been articulated in the preceding chapters. Participation in the kin-dom of God may call those of us who are US citizens, especially those of us who are white, to consider how those identities make us complicit in harm to migrants and what our responsibilities for ending and repairing that harm may be. This is not, per se, a requirement for admission into Christ's community, but it is the call of that community, the way of living Jesus exemplifies and invites us to.

Thus the importance of Christology for this project becomes clear. Understanding who Jesus is and how he brings salvation has direct implications for the moral life. Christians gain insight into who they are called to be and how they are called to radically love the world by exploring what they believe about Jesus Christ. What we believe about Jesus can therefore help guide our responses to migration. With Niebuhr, we can begin to model our responsible action after Jesus's by aligning our will with God's and interpreting migration within the larger context of God's vision for a more just world (one in which relationships are just and accountable, not colonial and oppressive). Encountering Jesus draws us into radical transformation, away from the ethics of death and suspicion that supports US colonialism and fear-based immigration policy, and toward an ethic of life and trust that interrupts US mythology and opens us up to more just relationships. Curran similarly highlights how Jesus's victory over death opens up the possibility of human reconciliation, which we can participate in through radical, communal discipleship. This discipleship calls us to side with oppressed people in radical solidarity, like Jesus did, and to oppose the systems that harm them. In summary, then, Christians are called to solidarity with migrants and to join in the work of dismantling the systems that crucify them.

Christians do not, however, engage in this work alone. Jesus gathered communities around himself, in his life and after the resurrection. Discipleship is meant to be done in community. It is therefore necessary to turn to ecclesiology in order to further uncover how the insights of Niebuhr and Curran can direct our understanding of the proper role and work of the church so that we might begin to envision what the role of churches and Christians may be in responding to migration in the United States.

Ecclesiology

Niebuhr insists that community is a central factor in shaping a person's point of view. This puts him in contrast with certain modern views of the person as a decision-maker "largely abstracted from history and tradition." In other words, ethics needs to focus on how moral agents acquire identities based on their communities.[18] While Niebuhr's ecclesiology is perhaps underdeveloped, he does offer helpful insights on the topic that can be built on to form a fuller account of the role Christian communities play or ought to play in shaping people into responsible moral agents.

Niebuhr's Christology leads directly into his view of the proper Christian life, especially as lived in community. Through Jesus, he argues, the church is called to humanitarian work, radical compassion (love), and to a deep reverence

18. James, "Responsibility Ethics and Postliberalism," 53.

for all life.[19] In a general sense, then, we can say that caring for and about the needs of migrants is proper to the church. Second, he argues that the church is called to the work of reconciliation. Because Niebuhr understands the moral life to be so centered on responsibility to relationships, and because his account of sin is a breaking of relationships among people and between people and God, the proper work of the church is therefore to reconcile its own relationships and to promote and aid in the reconciliation of relationships everywhere.[20] Radical love actively pursues just relationships, which requires repairing past harms.

We may say, then, that the work of reparative justice, in that it contributes to the overall project of reconciliation and the creation of a just community, is the proper work of the church. This is an especially important point in our consideration of how Christology and ecclesiology shape an understanding of discipleship that can inform a response to migration rooted in a responsibility framework. Chapter 4 established that reparative justice focuses on the harm caused in relationships that lack accountability, reciprocity, and mutuality. A church that understands sin as a force that breaks relationships ought to be especially concerned with repairing this sort of harm by creating, supporting, or calling for accountability where it has not existed previously. Reparations are the proper work of the church. This will mean finding ways to establish accountability to those the church has harmed, such as Indigenous people, citizens of countries the United States has colonized, and migrants, whom Christian theology has historically helped to cast as a threat. It also means walking with marginalized people, supporting them as they work for liberation from the forces that harm them and deny them the reparative justice they are due.

Third, for Niebuhr, the church is meant to disrupt the harmful narratives of the world. The world is gripped by the ethos of death and survival, by inaccurate narratives and harmful myths. Christianity, he insists, has a better story, one it is meant to share with the world.[21] Chapter 3 links the ethics of death and survival to manifest destiny and the frontier myth. These mythologies view anything that is "other" as a potential threat, and they have led to colonial foreign policy and approaches to immigration rooted in fear. The church has a perspective on the world that can interrupt these narratives, and Niebuhr insists that we are called to share that story with the world. In other words, this interruption of harmful narratives of death is the work of the church. This will become especially important below, as Indigenous and Latine theologians call the church to the work of truth telling and the interruption of harmful narratives.

---

19. Niebuhr, *Responsible Self*, 168.

20. Niebuhr, *Responsible Self*, 144.

21. Niebuhr, *Responsible Self*, 107.

Niebuhr argues that the church knows how it and people in general ought to live as responsible agents. We can see in this that there is something about the insights the church finds through reason and in Jesus that is applicable beyond the church community. It can be inferred from this that part of who the church is called to be, part of the work it is called to engage in, draws it outside itself in order to share its wisdom with the broader community. As will become apparent below, Curran provides a more explicit account of the church as called beyond itself. The church is a community that has wisdom worth sharing with the world in general. This need not be a call to proselytization but is perhaps more helpfully understood as a call to participate in the public sphere in whatever ways may be helpful to the common good.

Finally, Niebuhr insists that the church is a community that is aware of human limitations. The church, he writes, knows that the work it undertakes is ultimately beyond its ability. Yet, the community is compelled to aim at that which it cannot achieve on its own, hope against hope, because it is empowered to work and hope in and through Christ.[22] This is important in that it establishes Jesus as a source not just of our insights into the proper way of living as responsible agents but also as the very hope on which that work hinges. The church does not undertake its work through its own power. A posture of humility and surrender to the will and power of God is appropriate in all that the church does. This is antithetical to the colonial mindset. Further, awareness that the work of the church will be a steep uphill battle, that it calls us beyond our own abilities and will only find full completion in Christ,[23] stands as an important protection against widespread temptations to burnout or despair.

For Curran, "the Christian and the Church continue through their actions the redeeming work of Christ." The inclusive community Jesus created around himself is part of the saving work of his life, death, and resurrection, and therefore becomes the proper work of the church, called to continue Jesus's work in the world. To this end, Curran identifies four characteristics of the Catholic Church's catholicity through which Jesus's inclusive mission can be lived out. First, churches are to be inclusive in membership. Rooted in the Galatians passage, Curran insists that the catholicity of the church means that there is no standard of holiness that must be met in order to gain access into the community. He warns that this must not mean the church fails to be light and salt to the earth, that is, that it lose its prophetic edge. Rather, the church must find a balance between heeding "the call to holiness and the recognition that sinners belong in the church." Second, a truly catholic understanding of the church calls the

22. Niebuhr, *Responsible Self*, 163.

23. I do not think it inconsistent with Niebuhr's thinking to infer that this is an eschatological fulfillment that takes place beyond history.

church to be concerned with all aspects of the world. Just as Jesus's incarnation into full humanity draws us away from purely spiritual theologies, so too is the church called to live fully in the world.[24]

Third, the church must be inclusive of realities other than its own. That is to say, the church must recognize that its members belong to a variety of communities, social groups, and institutions, all of which make legitimate claims on them. He argues that while faith certainly enters into these other domains with these believers, the church must maintain an understanding that these groups have their own systems of meaning and operating that are not derived from faith. More importantly, this must be understood as a positive, not negative, reality.[25] The church should know its lane and respect the proper domain and autonomy of other institutions. Finally, the church is inclusive of various levels of society. By this Curran means that the church's universal calling cannot distract from the importance of the local, especially local embodiments of the church. In some ways, this is about subsidiarity. The church must allow local levels of church, community organizing, and government to do what they can for themselves and their communities, in their own ways, as much as possible. Further, this respect for the local also translates into an awareness of and respect for the traditions of local church communities.[26]

Curran's focus on catholic inclusivity paves a path into the following section and into the practical proposals of chapter 6. A church that takes seriously the belief that it is meant to be open to all will not and cannot abide the cultural boundaries reinforced by white supremacy and the frontier myth. Curran highlights the importance of historicity and the role context plays in shaping theology and moral norms, and calls the church to be more open to collaboration with the laity.[27] Together this focus on context and collaboration is a helpful reminder that God is always revealed and mediated in culturally specific ways. The trappings

24. Curran, *Catholic Moral Tradition Today*, 12, 4–7. Curran highlights the 1986 US bishops letter on the economy, which addresses itself to members of the church *and* the broader public in order to show how this inclusive approach is different from a sectarian approach in which the church is primarily concerned with the moral and religious life of its members. For Curran, catholicity properly draws the church outward, into the world and into the public fray.

25. Curran, *Catholic Moral Tradition Today*, 7–9. Curran contrasts this with the past, in which the church sought to subsume these institutions into and beneath itself. The contemporary church does not seek such a position of dominance.

26. Curran, *Catholic Moral Tradition Today*, 7–9. This respect for local incarnations of the church is important also in that it helps nuance the notion that "there is no Jew or Greek" in Jesus. This passage is not a rejection of culture or identity but rather a prophetic equalization of power imbalances, a vision of a just world in which sex, race, and socioeconomic status need not have a bearing on people's quality of life or their participation in community.

27. Hogan, "Formative and Transformative," 365, 367.

of Euro-American culture cannot serve as a barometer of Christian piety or commitment. This begins to break through the mythology that casts those outside our physical and conceptual borders as threats and requires migrants to conform to a set of imposed norms in order to be included in churches and in US society.

Furthermore, the notion that the church must be inclusive in its concerns, that it exists in the world and is properly concerned with all that happens in that world, explicitly religious or not, establishes the exploration of US history and its relationship to contemporary migration as the proper concern of the church. Curran understands work toward a just world to be a fundamental part of the church's mission.[28] The church cannot do this work without allowing itself to be drawn outside church walls, into the world. This means the church has to learn about the world, learn about the history of how the world came to look the way it does, how structures of injustice have been created and how they continue to be perpetuated.

Inclusivity also establishes that while justice for migrants is firmly within the proper realm of concern and mission for the church, the church must not engage in this work in a way that recreates patterns of colonial domination. This means that the church must be respectful of the space of others: other organizations, grassroots efforts, activists, and so on. The church is called to partner with marginalized people in this work and must do so with humility, by learning, by letting others lead. This will be an especially important standard for the proposals made in chapter 6. In order for the church to participate in justice work, Curran argues, the church must also utilize its power responsibly. Change, he argues, does not happen without the exercise of power. Therefore the church must use what power it has well and in the service of the kin-dom. Even so, he cautions that institutional power needs to be checked in order to protect against abuses.[29] In other words, the church must be aware of the power it has, use that power well, and ensure that checks are in place so that the church's power is not wielded in harmful ways. This is especially important considering the history of Christian complicity with and outright participation in the very injustice Christians are called to dismantle. The church must understand its own historical role in systems of injustice so that it might begin to do better.

Curran's call for inclusivity and respect for institutions beyond the church is an important part of this careful use of power. In order to engage in the work of justice, the church will need to know when and where to properly use its power, when and how to support (and not try to control) other groups' work, and where its involvement may not be welcome or appropriate. In a related way, the church's inclusive respect for local communities will be necessary for ensuring

28. Curran, "Responsibility in Moral Theology," 136.

29. Curran, "Responsibility in Moral Theology," 136, 138–39.

that those on the ground are given the space and support to lead their own fight for justice. Furthermore, Curran calls the church to be inclusive of local traditions and practices. This injunction brings to mind the controversy over the 2019 Amazon Synod and the desecration of Pachamama statues, one recent example of a history of Euro-American rejection of inculturated Christian practices. The not inconsiderable outcry that such inculturated practices were somehow lesser than Euro-American forms of inculturation, or that they were idolatrous or inherently pagan, represents a failure on the part of churches to foster respect for local incarnations of church.[30] In Curran's words, for too long "a false universalism too readily identified the church with western culture."[31] Work toward justice for migrants will thus require careful consideration of what trappings of Euro-American culture and colonial impulses have become embedded in church culture in unhelpful ways. Doing so will provide space for the culturally specific traditions of migrants and aid the church in ridding itself of the theologies and practices that have supported and benefited from US colonialism.[32]

Curran also insists that the responsible church will be flexible, be able to work with "the various elements in the society as they struggle to bring about a more just society," and be willing to listen to insights from new voices and relinquish control.[33] The responsible church must not be too set in its established way of doing things. Rather, the church must be willing to try something new, to think on faith and the world in new ways, to listen and change. As we turn to listen to the insights of Indigenous and Latine theologians in the following section, this flexibility and openness will be especially vital, both because they, too, emphasize the importance of flexibility and because turning to them with an open posture is in line with Curran's call for flexible inclusivity.

---

30. Elise Harris, "Central American Bishops Defend Francis over Amazon Synod, 'Pachamama,'" Crux, December 2, 2019, https://cruxnow.com/church-in-the-americas/2019/12/central-american-bishops-defend-francis-over-amazon-synod-pachamama/.

31. Curran, *Catholic Moral Tradition Today*, 10–11.

32. This is not, of course, to suggest that the church ought to embrace relativism. Take as an example Roger Haight's work, which establishes the Trinity as a narrative doctrine that opens Christians up to pluralism that is not relativistic. Haight insists that religions are noncompetitive and that the God revealed in Jesus Christ is a God who wishes to be present with and to all people. He writes, "If Jesus reveals the very nature of God, there is no intrinsic reason for limiting God's action in Jesus to the person of Jesus," and therefore, based on Christian doctrine, we ought to anticipate God's revelatory action in other religions and be openly in dialogue with them. This not only means making space for culturally specific incarnations of Christianity but also calls Christians to respect other traditions as potential bearers of truth, diminishing the drive to convert at any cost that so underpinned Euro-American colonization. See Haight, "Trinity and Religious Pluralism," *JES* 44, no. 4 (2009): 539–40.

33. Curran, "Responsibility in Moral Theology," 137–38.

Finally, the formation of its members as people of faith and moral agents is a primary focus of the church. Curran insists that the entire church must participate in both learning and teaching. While in the past there has been separation between those meant to teach and those meant to learn, a post–Vatican II church, he argues, recognizes that both teaching and learning take many forms and are required of all members in various ways. This means that the whole church must be aware of the main sources of moral wisdom: Scripture, tradition, reason, and experience. Moreover, it means that we must learn to listen to each other and respect the various forms of knowledge and individual experience each member brings to the whole.[34] This type of listening, this practice of honoring experiences and forms of wisdom that have not always been seen as valid in church communities or the wider society, will be vital for responding to migrants (and all those affected by US colonialism) and working toward justice with them. In other words, it is a vital component of radical love. In the spirit of Curran's learning church, we turn now to the insights of Indigenous and Latine theologians in order to continue contextualizing what Christian theology can teach us about how to love radically.

New and Ancient Perspectives: Expanding beyond Eurocentric Theology

Decisions regarding how to move forward in acknowledgment of the past and the complex web of relationships within which the United States operates cannot be done without significant leadership and input from those with whom the nation continues to be in particularly unjust relationships. Radical love calls us to reorient these relationships so that they will be built on justice, and part of this requires allowing those who have been treated unjustly to lead.[35] As this project intentionally works against the imperial dynamics identified in chapter 2, it draws especially from communities affected by the US immigration system and US imperialism. This requires, in particular, the lifting up of Latine and Indigenous perspectives on Jesus Christ and the church in order to decenter Euro-American perspectives and see how the insights of these thinkers challenge dominant US theologies. In doing so, this section intends not to imply that there are definitive, homogenous Indigenous or Latine perspectives. Rather, the intent is to profile a variety of perspectives while highlighting common themes that recur across the diversity.

---

34. Curran, *Catholic Moral Tradition Today*, 197–98.

35. This type of flipping relationships on their head is characteristic of Jesus's "the last shall be first" approach to community building.

It is important that this turn to Indigenous and Latine theological insights strives not to simply recreate colonial relationships, plundering these theologies and extracting what can be made useful for white Christianity. This chapter aims to engage and learn from Indigenous and Latine thinkers in a manner that is respectful and collaborative, not appropriative or violent. It does so by seeking to provide comprehensive accounts of each thinker's work and by allowing these thinkers space to speak for themselves as much as possible, relying heavily on direct quotations. Furthermore, wherever possible, this chapter will consult these thinkers' own articulation of the broader significance of their theological insights in order to ascertain how they intend for their work to be read and applied. This project aims to be in conversation with these thinkers, considering how white churches and theologians can learn and adjust based on their work, not what we can take as our own.

Christology

Wazhazhe Theologian George "Tink" Tinker writes that "amer-european cultural proclamation[s] of the gospel did as much as the U.S. Army to change the political landscape of each Indian nation."[36] A result of this is that much existing language for understanding Jesus is largely inappropriate in Native American contexts, both because of the harm it has caused and because of the ways this language was imposed. The question of who Jesus is has therefore become a question with which all Indigenous theologies must grapple. Fresh, culturally appropriate language must be found to replace colonial imagery.[37]

Tinker's christological account is helpful for understanding the role of churches and Christians in responding to migration and working to dismantle US colonialist systems for several reasons. First, his insights will underscore the importance of listening to the communities most affected by US colonialism. As a member of the Wazhazhe Nation, he can provide unique wisdom and insights from his culture. The harm caused by imposed Christianity makes it more important than ever that Indigenous people be determiners of their own theologies and relationships to church and to Christianity. The fight for justice for migrants, and for all those most harmed by US imperialism and Euro-American missionary Christianity, must be led by migrants and by those who are Black, Indigenous, and people of color. They must be given space to self-determine

36. George E. "Tink" Tinker, *American Indian Liberation: A Theology of Sovereignty* (Maryknoll, NY: Orbis Books, 2008), 89. Tinker finds, however, that the reality of violent colonialism means that the appropriateness of even this project is ultimately always in question. Tinker does not shy away from this tension. Rather, he engages in his christological account with this fundamental question at the forefront of his mind.

37. Tinker, *American Indian Liberation*, 84.

their own liberation. Tinker's work highlights why this is vital. As a member of a community that has been systematically oppressed by the United States, Tinker can provide specific insights into the nation's sins. He has a particular, intimate understanding of the harm Christianity and US colonialism has caused and can thus help white Christianity reckon with its failures to be in just relationships.

For Tinker, there are Christian beliefs with which many Native communities have a natural affinity. For instance, he argues that basically every Indigenous culture in North America understands the notion of vicarious suffering, such as that of Jesus on the cross, as there are widespread Indigenous ceremonies through which members of the community might take on discipline for the sake of their community. This, Tinker writes,

> gives Indian people an inherent understanding of the Christian concept of grace, an understanding that predates the arrival of the missionaries. We could even go so far as to insist that we already knew the gospel! We were taught differently by the missionaries, of course. They had a vested interest in separating Indian people from their ancient ceremonial structures and consistently taught that those ceremonies fell short of the Christian ideal.[38]

Tinker goes on to call this "a self-serving lie," perpetuated by missionaries in order to further colonial interests and reshape Indigenous belief systems.[39] To the missionaries, these ceremonies were little more than blasphemous, pagan idolatry. This sentiment was echoed in the outcry against Pachamama during the 2019 Amazon Synod. Against this mischaracterization, Tinker argues that these ceremonies are better understood as signs of what might be called grace. The history of missionaries disregarding the validity of these cultural insights and signs, part of a systematic effort to erase Indigeneity from the continent, highlights for Tinker the importance for Indigenous people "to hang on to the good news wako^{n}da originally gave us rather than blindly consume the good news that the missionaries would impose on us at the cost of losing our own set of cultural values and losing our inculturated sense of community and individual self

38. Tinker, *American Indian Liberation*, 85–86. Tinker does not specify the definition or understanding of grace he is referencing here. Given that he is connecting it to themes of vicarious suffering, it is perhaps likely he has in mind the notion of grace as made available by Jesus's self-sacrifice rather than the Rahnerian notion of grace as God's gift of self-presence. Regardless of his exact definition, Tinker's point is that there are resonances between Indigenous belief systems and Christian beliefs that were completely disregarded by missionaries looking to convert Indigenous people to Christianity.

39. Tinker, *American Indian Liberation*, 86.

esteem."[40] Tinker is identifying the same anti-Indigenous systems that chapters 1–2 outlined, systems that must be toppled in order to achieve any semblance of justice for migrants and for Indigenous people. Curran calls the church to be flexible and to respect local incarnations of faith. Allowing marginalized people to reclaim their own inculturated religious practices and beliefs rather than forcing Euro-American cultural trappings on them is one way to begin the work of dismantling US mythology and building just relationships.

For Tinker, it is vital that Indigenous people have the space and freedom to look to their own cultural wisdom, to assert that their ancestors received spiritual insights that remain relevant and life giving. In the US context, where Euro-American colonialism has sought to systematically strip Indigenous people of their culture as it stole their land and murdered their people, this becomes especially important to Tinker as an act of resistance. He writes, "Given the particularity of our history of oppression and particularly of the role of missionization in the conquest of our territories and our indigenous nations, it is important to begin the process of sorting out what the function of Christianity and Christology is and might be for us as we continue our struggle and resistance against ongoing colonization."[41] Because of the immense harm caused by the church to Indigenous communities, the relationship between these communities and the church is deeply fractured. Niebuhr insists that the work of reconciliation is proper to the church. The church ought then to be concerned with various forms of reparation that can be offered in order to establish accountability with Indigenous peoples. One part of repairing that relationship is to allow these communities the space to recover and uplift their own traditional forms of wisdom and to set the terms of their relationship to Christianity and to Jesus themselves.

For Tinker, this sorting out the function of Christology has three levels. First, he offers a political and cultural analysis. In particular, he looks to the insights of Latin American liberation theologies, noting their role in making clear that theology is always necessarily and inherently political. He writes, "How one identifies the Christ and understands the functions of Christology determines much of one's political reality and how one deals with it."[42] Christologies can teach us to be comfortable with systems of oppression, or they can illuminate the injustice of those systems and call us to the work of liberation. Likewise, Tinker turns to African and Asian theologies in order to stress the importance of a cultural analysis of Christology. With these thinkers, he asserts the importance of affirming "who we are . . . in terms of our traditional cultures and value systems." This affirmation is a radical act in a nation that has systematically

40. Tinker, *American Indian Liberation*, 86–87.

41. Tinker, *American Indian Liberation*, 87.

42. Tinker, *American Indian Liberation*, 88.

erased Indigenous culture and criminalized Black and Asian people. In particular, Tinker argues, it is important for Indigenous theologies to find ways of understanding Jesus in terms that are culturally compatible, that are rooted in the traditional wisdom and insights gifted to them by wako^{n}da. Indigenous Christologies "must begin with and continually be in touch with the analysis of the political" and cultural contexts in which they take place, especially as these contexts are related to the realities of past and ongoing colonization.[43]

Second, in the spirit of this political and cultural analysis, Tinker outlines some of the specific ways in which Euro-American Christologies have been harmful to Native people. For example, he explores the "destructiveness caused by the varieties of the typical fall-and-redemption evangelism proclaimed in Indian mission contexts." Native American cultures, he writes, do not have the sense of human depravity that pervades European culture and theology. This sense of sinful depravity therefore had to be forced onto Indigenous communities in order for the missionaries to then offer them the gospel in Euro-American terms. Tinker argues that the destructive impact of this forced internalization of a sense of deep depravity, through which Native people were taught to hate themselves and venerate whiteness, is still felt today. As a rejection of this harm, "any proclamation of the gospel among Indian peoples must begin with some sort of affirmation of Indian people as Indian and as human beings," and emphasize their inherent goodness and creation in God's image. This is part of the process of decolonization.[44]

Chapters 1–2 traced the development of highly racialized notions of belonging that undergirded Euro-American colonialism, demonized those who did not (or could not) conform, and provided the conceptual building blocks for modern US immigration and foreign policy. Furthermore, it established the role of Christian theology in the development of the United States' founding mythologies. Tinker's articulation of the harms caused by fall-and-redemption represents part of this colonial process of forced conformity to Euro-American ideas and culture. Decolonization includes the process of breaking down these harmful, imposed patterns of thinking. It then necessarily involves the articulation of theologies that are rooted in marginalized peoples' own traditions and are liberative rather than harmful.

Third, Tinker argues that it is necessary to understand and respect traditional Indigenous spiritualities and ceremonies on their own merits outside any affinity with Christian concepts. Because Christianity has been forced onto Indigenous people and because there are now many Indigenous people with legitimate commitments to Christian faith, however, it is also necessary

43. Tinker, *American Indian Liberation*, 89–91.

44. Tinker, *American Indian Liberation*, 91.

to "demonstrate the plausibility of Indian religious traditions on the basis of an interpretation of the colonizer's own texts."[45]

With these considerations in mind, Tinker considers what comparisons may be made between traditional Indigenous stories and the Christian gospel. The fundamental question, he argues, is whether there is salvation to be found in traditional Indigenous beliefs and practices. Tinker looks to the traditional stories of Corn Mother as an example of an Indigenous story that functions in a christological fashion. In all variations of this central story, Corn Mother undertakes a "willing self-sacrifice (vicarious suffering) . . . on behalf of her children." Tinker writes, "In all these retellings the self-sacrifice of the woman is emphatically consistent and results in the enduring fecundity of the earth and the production of vegetable foods."[46] That is, the death of Corn Mother, undertaken in an act of radical love, provides life and flourishing to the people.

This story results in several important theological insights. First, all life, even that which Euro-American forms of science might consider not to be life at all, is understood as being a relative. Corn Mother became one with the earth, and so all parts of the earth—people, plants, animals, rocks, water, and so on—are deeply interrelated. Second, as the first experience of death, this story teaches that death is in fact simply a changing of realities. Death and transformation become linked. Those who have died, then, are understood to continue to live in the people, especially as the people eat from the earth to which their ancestors have returned. This deeply relational interpretation of reality is in keeping with Niebuhr's articulation of the moral life, aimed at understanding ever broader circles of responsibility and relationality. Third, Tinker highlights the ethical content of these Corn Mother stories. He writes,

> in those variants of the story in which Corn Mother is killed by male off-spring, there is an implicit warning to men about the potential for male violence in society. Men are to pay attention to the results of immature male decision making, especially when it leaves women out of the decision-making process. . . . Moreover, we are to pay attention to the inherent valuing of female gifts and wisdom in our communities. We are to forever remember that healing in the form of both food and spiritual sustenance have come to us traditionally not through men but through a woman. . . . This wisdom is a constant tempering of male dominance, aggression, and assertiveness in our communities.[47]

45. Tinker, *American Indian Liberation*, 98–99.

46. Tinker, *American Indian Liberation*, 99, 107–8.

47. Tinker, *American Indian Liberation*, 109–10.

This analysis of the Corn Mother story is reminiscent of the ways in which the gospel is a constant reminder against the dangers and sin of empire. Just as many variants of the Corn Mother story include male aggression as the vehicle of her death, Curran argues that the Gospels tell the story of Jesus as killed unjustly by the forces of empire, to which he is a threat. Again, then, we are being called to notice and oppose systems of death that unjustly oppress people.[48]

Tinker asserts that this story, in all its variations, is "God's unique self-disclosure" to Indigenous communities. It is his hope that this christological analysis of the Corn Mother story "will make it possible to understand the notion of Christ with much greater inclusivity and parity of power between colonizer and colonized."[49] While Indigenous Christologies[50] may differ considerably from those of the missionaries and colonizers (Christologies that are still prominent in many churches today), Tinker makes it clear that there are natural affinities between Christian understandings of Jesus and traditional Indigenous spiritual wisdom.

Tinker intends his work to "speak somehow to both colonizer and colonized, to Amer-European and American Indian." Specifically, he writes, "it would seem that the colonizer churches themselves will necessarily have to rethink their notion of Christian exclusivity and make room for American Indian religious traditions as being potentially powerful and salvific as the best vision well-intentioned people have for Christianity." Tinker's Christology and his indictment of the colonialist missionary machine's weaponization of Euro-American theology, it seems, is precisely why Curran's insistence on inclusivity is so important. In particular, the need for churches to respect local incarnations of church leads in the direction of accepting Tinker's terms. Asserting that God can and does speak

48. In both cases, the suffering in question was caused by human action, not willed by God. This is an important distinction to uphold.

49. Tinker, *American Indian Liberation*, 111.

50. Other Indigenous theologians have similarly proposed culturally specific models for understanding Jesus today. For example, Martin Brokenleg draws on his Lakota traditions and centering of family in order to articulate an intimate understanding of Jesus as relative. See Brokenleg, "Church—Wocekiye Okolakiciye: A Lakota Experience of the Church," in *Coming Full Circle: Constructing Native Christian Theology*, ed. Steven Charleston and Elaine A. Robinson (Minneapolis: Augsburg Fortress, 2015), 133–49. Marcus Briggs-Cloud emphasizes Jesus's healing and transformative qualities by calling him a "Maker of Medicine." See Briggs-Cloud, "Creation—The New Creation: A Maskoke Postcolonial Perspective," in Charleston and Robinson, *Coming Full Circle*, 90. Kaitlin Curtice insists that Jesus is someone meant to be encountered and known, not someone to know about. See Curtice, "Have We Missed Who Jesus Is Altogether?," *Sojourners*, June 27, 2017, https://sojo.net/articles/have-we-missed-who-jesus-altogether. From these and other Indigenous perspectives, we can not only learn the importance of inculturated, authentic understandings of and encounters with Jesus. We can also find our own understandings both challenged and expanded.

specifically to local communities in ways that are culturally appropriate highlights the need for all Christians to respect these local incarnations of wisdom and enter into dialogue with them, even if they look vastly different from each other. Moreover, the harm caused by overly universal applications of culturally specific theologies cannot be overstated.[51] Euro-American culture cannot be the barometer for determining whether spiritual insights are sufficiently Christian or salvific.

Christians, then, must provide space that allows, for example, Indigenous peoples to find (or retrieve) language and symbols that make sense to and for them by drawing on their own traditions of divine self-disclosure. In doing so, we stand in opposition to the homogenizing forces of colonialism that chapters 1–2 identified and condemned. Moreover, we might consider how these perspectives can broaden our own understanding of Jesus and salvation. Tinker's caution about the harms of fall-and-redemption Christologies, for example, might teach white Christians that sin is multidimensional. Tinker's point here is likely not that Indigenous peoples are somehow without what Christians call sin. His understanding of the story of Corn Mother as a caution against male aggression and arrogance proves that traditional Indigenous cultures are not without a conception of sinful behaviors to which humans might be prone. Rather, not unlike Valerie Saiving's critique of Reinhold Niebuhr's account of sin,[52] Tinker is drawing attention to the reality that Euro-American understanding of human sin and salvation may not be universally applicable and may in fact cause harm.

Potawatomi author and poet Kaitlin Curtice encourages Christians who wish to do the work of justice to decenter whiteness in their faith by reading and listening to the perspectives of people who are Black, Indigenous, or people of color, both Christian and non-Christian, in order to gain a better understanding of the history of colonization and break Christianity's ongoing commitments to the powers of empire.[53] This engagement with perspectives from society's margins can help white Christians gain historical perspective, illuminating the harms that have been caused by the US empire and the ongoing needs of those most harmed by colonialism. In other words, it can help Christians respond more justly by

51. Tinker, *American Indian Liberation*, 84, 111, 91.

52. Valerie Saiving, "The Human Situation: A Feminine Viewpoint," *Pastoral Psychology* 17, no. 3 (1966): 29–42. Saiving argues that the traditional definition of sin as pride does not speak to the situations of people who have historically not been in situations of power (specifically, for Saiving, women). People whose dignity and flourishing is threatened are harmed by theologies that equate sin with pride and self-centeredness because these theologies can discourage self-care, self-assertion, and self-value.

53. Kaitlin Curtice, "Decolonize Your Faith This Lent: A Reading List," *Sojourners*, March 6, 2019, https://sojo.net/articles/decolonize-your-faith-lent-reading-list.

providing a better understanding of the history that has led to migration and to Indigenous resistance in the United States. Any Christian response to migration in this context that does not center the perspectives of those most harmed by the sins of the United States will fall short of true reparative justice.

As the church engages in this work of listening, the next step will be, Curtice argues, to actively decolonize Christianity. This work is undertaken in the spirit of Curran's inclusive church, which is respectful of the domains of others. Further, a responsibility ethic suggests that the church must be accountable for the harms it has caused. That is, as we learn to see the harm caused by Christian colonialism, we will need to begin the work of actively disentangling our faith from harmful patterns of thinking, speaking, and believing. For example, Tinker highlights the way fall-and-redemption Christology has forced Indigenous peoples to internalize a sense of worthlessness or of being less than whiteness. Understanding this encourages Christians to be less universal in their articulations of salvation and to make space for God's revelation to come from a variety of cultures and take a number of forms.[54] Decolonization calls us to be sensitive to the specific needs of a community and how theology meets or exacerbates these needs. It may be the case that white US Christians have a great need for a deeper sense of our own sinfulness and need for redemption in the form of conversion from a state of participation in social sin. Fall-and-redemption Christology might be one helpful vehicle for white conversion, one way in which encounter with Jesus can, as Niebuhr argues, draw us to conversion from death to life. This does not, however, mean that this Christology can or ought to be universally imposed. Other, culturally appropriate ways of understanding Jesus's salvific action, such as traditional ceremonies and beliefs about Corn Mother, ought to be encouraged. We can decolonize by de-universalizing Euro-American ways of believing.[55]

---

54. This is not an argument against the universal nature of Jesus's salvific work but rather a call to humility. We ought to let go of the notion that any one tradition has a monopoly on understanding how this salvation operates and has been offered or revealed to the world in history. In other words, we must remember that God's love and God's offer of salvation are far more expansive than anything we can comprehend or articulate. Niebuhr is helpful here. Aware of the limits of human knowledge, his theocentrism leads him to insist on openness to the presence of significant insight about God and the divine nature outside Christianity. Trusting in the sovereignty of the One God ought to lead to an openness to dialogue, not defensiveness. Moreover, this approach leads him to assert that responsibility to God, who is over all things and who created all things, draws us into responsibility to the whole world. See Koontz, "Confessional Theology," 414–17.

55. Other theologies, however, might call Christians to more radical decolonization. Both Tinker and Curtice call out the destructive impact of Euro-American Christology in which Jesus's lordship has implicitly and explicitly sanctioned colonial conquest and the subjugation of peoples. The harm it has caused might mean its use has expired. Black and Indigenous theologians as well as other marginalized theologians can help white Christians identify theology that is or

Tinker insists that Christology has direct consequences for our political engagement. Indeed, the connection between theological commitments and political engagement is, in varying degrees, prominent in all the thinkers profiled throughout this book. In general, the entire project of Christian ethics depends to some degree on the notion that Christian beliefs can and should be brought to bear on the way people live in the world.[56] Some, like Tinker and Curran, make this more explicit in their work and outline their understanding of what this means. For others this connection is more implicit. Either way, what we believe about Jesus influences how we engage with the world. This means that in order to work for justice (for example, justice for migrants), we must turn to Christologies that promote just living and away from those that have supported injustice. Curtice likens this work to pruning a garden, cutting away decay in order to make room for new life to grow. Pruning keeps plants healthy. Likewise, we must prune back harmful or fruitless theologies in order to keep the church healthy. She writes,

> The hard work of pruning off the fruitless parts of American Christianity to make way for something new is our current task. It may be our history of racism, our patriarchal power plays, or our blind eye toward the least of these—the poor, widowed, orphaned. Maybe it's lack of care for the earth and creatures on it, or the constant support of companies that take advantage of the earth's resources and the poor communities that have what the rich want. If we are to pave a new way forward for the church, we must make room for the painful work of deadheading. It is messy and uncomfortable, and it takes time for new fruit to be born. Nevertheless, it is necessary for a beautiful plant to grow, for new fruit to make its way into the world.[57]

We must begin to leave behind Christologies that perpetuate or mask harmful political and social action. This will be long, sometimes painful work. Our attachments to ways of thinking we are used to may be challenged. We will need

has been too harmful to warrant keeping. If we are to partner with migrants in encouraging US accountability and reshaping the nation's relationships to those it has systematically harmed, we must be willing to stop engaging with theologies that have caused that harm and to find more fruitful ways of understanding who Jesus is and what he calls us to do.

56. Here, "political" is defined broadly, encompassing the functioning of the polis. In other words, "political" signifies anything having to do with the ways in which people negotiate living in community.

57. Kaitlin Curtice, "It's Time to Prune Back the Unfruitful Parts of American Christianity," *Sojourners*, May 8, 2017, https://sojo.net/articles/it-s-time-prune-back-unfruitful-parts-american-christianity.

to practice humility as we listen to the perspectives of the people our theology has harmed and do so without resorting to defensiveness. This work is necessary because our ability to grow new fruit, to do the work of justice Jesus calls us to and to transform our relationships with those Christianity has helped to harm, depends on our willingness to prune what has been harmful.

As I have drawn heavily from Niebuhr and Curran in this chapter and the last, it is worth considering their complicity in the harms Christianity has perpetuated. In general, this book takes the position that all white Christians are in some ways complicit in the harms of white-centric theology. Curran himself acknowledges the omnipresence of white privilege in theology and its effect on his own work.[58] White supremacy and privilege center white experiences, casting them as normative and superior. As such, white privilege has a deep impact on the way theology is/has been approached and understood as a discipline, especially in the West. It has shaped the field's biases, how we have evaluated and granted authority to people and ideas, and what we have understood to be common sense. For example, Curran notes how for years he unconsciously cast his colleagues and students of color as objects to be helped and himself as the helping subject, and how his "white theology [operated as] the theological standpoint from which all others were to be judged."[59] This is often insidious and pervasive, and Curran highlights how easy it is to participate in it without being aware. It is in fact a facet of white privilege that the prevalence of white supremacy goes unnoticed, particularly by those it benefits. It is a privilege of whiteness that theologians such as Curran can, as he admits, spend a lengthy career writing about social ethics while barely referencing racism or noticing its impact on the church and theology.[60] While Niebuhr does not take up this topic explicitly, it is consistent with Curran's account of the omnipresence of white privilege to find Niebuhr guilty of this sort of participation as well.

Specifically, theological positions that are related to those Tinker and Curtice might identify as problematic can be identified in the work of both Niebuhr and Curran. Curran's use of the notion of redemptive suffering for example, while nuanced, still participates in patterns of thinking that have been used to coerce and/or mollify oppressed people by teaching them that their suffering was proper to Christians and that they would be rewarded in the next life.[61] Similarly, Niebuhr's articulation of sin as a distrustful response to God

58. Charles Curran, "White Privilege," *Horizons* 32, no. 2 (2005): 363.

59. Curran, "White Privilege," 364.

60. Curran, "White Privilege," 361–62.

61. See, for example, James H. Cone, *The Cross and the Lynching Tree* (Maryknoll, NY: Orbis Books, 2011), 155.

that causes a selfish turn inward, while very helpful for naming the sins of the United States, still fails to avoid the problems of fall-and-redemption soteriology Tinker names as harmful to Indigenous people.

It is due to the consuming prevalence of white privilege in (especially Western) Christian theological study, and to the lack of awareness of many who—like Niebuhr and Curran—benefit from it, that it is especially important to turn to perspectives such as that of Tinker and Curtice. Curran cites the work and influence of theologians such as Shawn Copeland and Bryan Massingale as central to his process of becoming aware of his own limitations.[62] Similarly, the Indigenous and Latine thinkers profiled in this chapter can help draw awareness to and indict the failings of white theology,[63] as Curtice and Tinker make the problems with Curran's account of suffering and Niebuhr's theology of sin evident. It is, however, also worth noting that Niebuhr and Curran each also begin to push against some of the Christian tradition's more harmful beliefs and practices. In this way, the Indigenous and Latine thinkers profiled in this chapter complement and expand on Niebuhr and Curran, helping identify what is worth keeping and how their thoughts may be carried forward.

For example, Niebuhr prefaces *The Responsible Self* by explicitly de-universalizing Christian experiences and understandings. His own life, he argues, has been conditioned and influenced by his Christian relationship with and understanding of God, but this is "simply part of [his] fate." He does not place his culturally rooted, Christian experience of God above, for example, a Muslim or Jewish experience.[64] This fundamental openness and humility represents an awareness of his own biases, allows Niebuhr to position himself in a less oppressive way, and helps him avoid the recreation of colonialist dynamics. Curran, in his centering of inclusivity and flexibility, intends to be open to and respectful of great cultural diversity within the church, as well as in the world outside of Christianity. These moves position Niebuhr and Curran in opposition to colonialist Christianity, which universalizes and oppresses, even as they fail to completely disentangle themselves from it. Responsibility ethics, as a framework, is helpful precisely because it provides space for adapting, for nuancing, or for rejecting that which is harmful. By framing moral action as response, and the trajectory of ethical action as a process of learning in order to respond more fittingly, responsibility ethics invites precisely the process of reflection, repentance, and change that Tinker and Curtice are suggesting.

62. Curran, "White Privilege," 362–63.

63. By "white theology" I do not mean any theology that happens to be done by white people but more specifically theology that upholds white supremacy, centers the experiences of white people as normatively human, or otherwise fails to be reflective of its biases.

64. Niebuhr, *Responsible Self*, 42–45.

Moreover, responsibility ethics proposes a two-way-street of evangelization. Niebuhr characterizes responsible action as participation in an ongoing conversation. This conversation is meant to be responsible, accountable, and mutual. Both Niebuhr and Curran remain helpful, then, even as their approaches are open to critique. We can carry forward their commitment to openness and dialogue, centering of relationships, linking of Christian salvation to tangible human liberation, and understanding of discipleship as a radical, communal commitment to participating in the work of God by opposing the ethics of death and the powers of empire that killed Jesus on the cross.

Along with Indigenous theologians, Christians must also learn from Latine approaches to Christology. Argentinian theologian Marcella Althaus-Reid emphasizes the communal nature of Jesus's development as Messiah. Jesus's own understanding of who he was as Messiah and what that role and identity meant was shaped over the course of his life in the context of his sociopolitical location and often in conversation with women on the margins. Althaus-Reid writes, "Jesus became a messiah walking with poor women, in a dialogical process of popular conscientization." Jesus was born of a woman, in whose womb he was formed and at whose breast he was fed. Additionally, Althaus-Reid argues, his mother was herself nurtured by a community of women. Biblically, for example, she spent time with Elizabeth while both were pregnant, but Althaus-Reid also imagines the community of women in Mary's life who "received the news of future birth in the village; especially in the collective work of preparing clothes and sharing their humble food with the future mother." From the beginning, then, Jesus's life was shaped by a marginalized community and especially by the women of this community. Moreover, the adult Jesus's ministry includes an ongoing process of becoming, in continued dialogue with oppressed and outcast people.[65] Consider, for example, Jesus's conversation about his identity with the Samaritan woman at the well (John 4:4–26) or the Syrophoenician woman, who convinces him to expand his understanding of his own mission (Matt 15:21–28). Throughout the Gospels, marginalized people are Jesus's partners in conversation as he works out his own understanding of his role and mission.

Althaus-Reid argues that this process of messianic becoming continues today as Christ is in dialogue with women (and all marginalized people) for whom he becomes savior in concrete and specific ways. This dialogue centers on Jesus's question "Who do you say that I am?" (Matt 16:13–20)?[66] As oppressed people answer this question of who Jesus is as Messiah, rooting their answer in the concrete realities of their lives and their struggles for liberation, they

65. Marcella Althaus-Reid, *From Feminist Theology to Indecent Theology: Readings on Poverty, Sexual Identity and God* (London: SCM, 2004), 25–26.

66. This connects back to Tinker, who saw the question of who Jesus was to and for Indigenous people as central.

dismantle harmful and closed understandings of Christology, notions that have supported their oppression and barred them from authentic and culturally rooted participation in theological dialogue.[67] Rejecting such a limited and harmful Christology, they "reclaim the freedom of Latin American women to enter into this process too, recreating a new dialogue with Jesus,"[68] one that speaks to their present realities.

Latin American women also turn the question back on Jesus. Althaus-Reid writes, "The basis of [a] feminist and Latina Christological proposal is given by the question that women are now asking Christ," a question that "seeks to initiate a dialogue and not to find a normative reply."[69] In other words, Latina women are asking Jesus who *he* says *they* are too. In this way the process is truly a conversation. Althaus-Reid articulates Jesus's identity as something continually forged in an ongoing process of dialogue with the needs and hopes of marginalized people. This ought to shape our understanding of what it means to be a disciple of Jesus. Christians must ask ourselves what it might look like to have our discipleship molded with and by a Christ whose identity as savior is continually shaped in dialogue with the needs of those for whom he is savior, for example, in dialogue with migrants. We must understand our own salvation and our participation in God's salvific work as linked to and fundamentally directed by their liberative hopes, because who Jesus is as savior is affected by the specific contexts in which he is encountered.

According to José Rodríguez, Latine Christians do not separate Christology and soteriology. Who Jesus was (and is) is tied up in what he did. This is not dissimilar from Niebuhr's account, which characterizes Jesus as the one in whom we encounter transformative salvation and the one who models a new way of being. In other words, Niebuhr understands Jesus through his work. Rodríguez's approach is similar. He summarizes Jesus's work as the bringing forth of God's salvation for the whole of human existence and for all of creation. This salvation Jesus brings is multidimensional, and "for Latino/a theologians in the United States, the Christian message of salvation is fundamentally related to the praxis of liberation and human fulfillment in the various dimensions of daily life."[70]

67. Althaus-Reid, *From Feminist Theology*, 57–59. This is tied to Tinker's critiques of Euro-American missionary colonialism and its denial of Indigenous people's experiences of divine self-disclosure, and his insistence on the importance of communities reclaiming their own understandings of Jesus (such as his Corn Mother Christology).

68. Althaus-Reid, *From Feminist Theology*, 26.

69. Althaus-Reid, *From Feminist Theology*, 59.

70. José Rodríguez, "Shaping Soteriology a la latina," in *Building Bridges, Doing Justice: Constructing a Latino/a Ecumenical Theology*, ed. Orlando Espín (Maryknoll, NY: Orbis Books, 2009), 112–13.

Building on the work of Latin American, Black, and Asian liberation theologies, Rodríguez outlines a Latine soteriology that "emerges and is contextually conditioned as an effort to articulate the witness of faith of Hispanic/Latino/a people in their history of struggle and experience of discrimination in North America." Rodríguez identifies several distinctive themes that make Latine christological work unique. These themes include paying close attention to the popular religious practices of the people (through which their beliefs about Jesus can be seen), the identification of "ghetto crosses"—ways in which Latine people are "torn by the scorn and deceit of evil forces" in their own communities—and a strong emphasis on the need to radically transform sinful institutions, including the church, in order to anticipate the eschatological reign of God.[71] This identification of Jesus's suffering with the suffering of oppressed people in history, not dissimilar from both Niebuhr's and Curran's accounts, links the suffering of migrants to Jesus's death. Jesus's radical solidarity with migrants and other oppressed people calls the church to radical solidarity with them as well. Moreover, Rodríguez makes especially clear that the sinful institutions that have crucified people include the church. In order to be in solidarity with oppressed people, churches must acknowledge this, repent, and commit to doing better before they can begin to dismantle structural sin elsewhere. This will be explored more fully in the ecclesiological discussion below and made concrete in the proposals of chapter 6.

For Rodríguez, the primary way Jesus's redemptive action is engaged in the world is through inclusion in the story. That is, people are led to salvation through finding in the story of Jesus the story of their own redemption, redemption that involves the confrontation of evil that systematically deprives people of their dignity. For example, Rodríguez argues that Jesus's identity as a Galilean man allows those who are mestizo to see themselves reflected in the story, because Jesus's Galilean identity "mirrors the experience of social and cultural discrimination of Mexican Americans and Latino/as from other cultural backgrounds in the United States."[72]

As was highlighted in chapters 1–2, Roberto Goizueta focuses on the border as a mythical frontier in the US imagination. His Christology similarly centers on Jesus's identity as a Galilean border-dweller. He argues that Jesus's identity establishes borderlands as the privileged locus of God's revelation[73] and insists that Jesus's distinctiveness is central to the gospel and to the implications of the gospel in the modern world. Jesus was a concrete human person from a historical

---

71. Rodríguez, "Shaping Soteriology a la latina," 123–31.

72. Rodríguez, "Shaping Soteriology a la latina," 115.

73. Roberto Goizueta, "Corpus Verum: Toward a Borderland Ecclesiology," in Espin, *Building Bridges, Doing Justice*, 154.

borderland, a place of mixed identities, and so "this social, political, religious, and geographical reality takes on soteriological significance as the place that defines the character of the Christian revelation, for the Good News is incarnated in the person of Jesus Christ, Jesus the *Galilean Jew*."[74] God's revelation and salvific action in the person of Jesus took place in the midst of outcasts, on the margins, in the borderlands. Jesus's historical existence as a marginalized Galilean border-dweller draws Christian attention to the world's most vulnerable people, to modern borderland people and marginalized groups. There is therefore a direct connection between the crucifixion of Jesus the Galilean Jew and the suffering of migrants as modern borderland people.

Moreover, the resurrected Christ is encountered, Goizueta argues, among those same marginalized people.[75] Linking Jesus's life and saving work to the struggles of marginalized people, such as migrants fleeing violence and scarcity for which the US is co-responsible, makes clear how a contextual Christology can influence our understanding of how what we say about Jesus leads into how we understand the role and work of Christians. In this way, what was conceptual in Niebuhr and Curran becomes concrete in the experiences of Latine people. If God incarnated in the midst of the marginalized, in a borderland, and if the resurrected Jesus is found amongst those on the margins today, then that is where Christians are called. The question becomes, How do we, too, join in radical solidarity with those on the margins, that is, with migrants, with undocumented people, with Indigenous communities still struggling under the imperial thumb of the United States?

Cuban-American theologian Miguel Díaz offers an account of soteriology rooted in anthropology. Díaz writes,

> Salvation cannot be understood in "merely" religious terms, as a divine promise that concerns the world to come, bearing no relationship to the survival of and transformation of the present one. God's radical activity in the world, *especially God's presence in Jesus,* where human reality is not destroyed by rather "assumed," "raised," "perfected," and "transformed," underscores the theological referent of all created and historical reality, as Rahner rightly noted, *from this Christological perspective, anthropology is for all eternity theology.*[76]

74. Goizueta, "Corpus Verum," 153.

75. Goizueta, "Corpus Verum," 152–55.

76. Miguel Díaz, "Outside the Survival of Community There Is No Salvation," in Espin, *Building Bridges, Doing Justice,* 105 (emphasis added).

For Díaz, God's incarnation into full humanity implies something about God's deep care for human life. More specifically, God's incarnation as a Galilean, as a marginalized person of the borderlands, illuminates God's specific care for those most marginalized by society. This notion links back to Curran's insistence that Jesus's full humanity rejects hierarchical dualism between the spiritual and the material. For Díaz, salvation cannot be understood as exclusively religious or spiritual. Rather, it happens within the context of human communities. In fact, he argues that without historical liberation, salvation cannot exist. This is related to Althaus-Reid's articulation of Jesus's ongoing messianic becoming, done in conversation with the needs of marginalized people. Díaz insists that the "the survival of particular communities, and all that this implies with respect to social, cultural, gender, political, economic, and religious factors that contribute to or hinder this survival, provides a starting point for envisioning a US Hispanic Catholic soteriology."[77] Salvation begins in the liberation of oppressed communities.

This communal element is central for Díaz. Jesus's incarnation as a Galilean was an incarnation into a marginalized *community*. Latine soteriology, for Díaz, does not conceive of salvation outside the work of liberation. This uplifts the struggle of Latine communities. Díaz writes, "Any struggle in favor of the survival of our communities . . . must be seen as more than just a human struggle—it is also an ethical struggle to preserve historical links to the life of God." Survival, defined as a fullness of being encompassing both physical and cultural survival and as something that "depends to a large extent on self determination and self-identity," becomes "the key anthropological piece" in the construction of a Latine soteriology.[78] Specifically, Díaz argues that this links salvation directly to the survival of Latine identity in the United States in the same way Latin American liberation theologies link salvation to the liberation of oppressed peoples.

In this way, Latine soteriology, as articulated by Díaz, takes up not only a preferential option for the poor but also a preferential option for culture. Díaz explicitly names the US deportation machine as a threat to survival so conceived, especially as it is a threat to the stability of the communities and families that make physical and cultural survival possible and that are often one of the most fundamental means by which human beings encounter God's salvation.[79] The US deportation system, then, is a threat to God's salvific work and is something with which all Christians should be concerned. As we turn to practical proposals

77. Díaz, "Outside the Survival," 97, 99, 92.

78. Díaz, "Outside the Survival," 106, 100.

79. Díaz, "Outside the Survival," 100.

in chapter 6, it is important to keep in mind that the protection of migrant communities is participation in God's salvific work.

In this way, Díaz's articulation of salvation helps to direct how Christians ought to be shaped by our own encounters with Jesus's person and saving action, as others above have also done. This ought to influence our posture, thinking, and praxis related to migration in the United States. Díaz argues that Latine popular Catholicism, with its culturally specific symbols pointing to God's grace in the form of an "intention to preserve and save particular human communities," serves as a reminder that the preservation of particular communities absolutely requires "the transformation of unjust social, economic, political, cultural, racial, and gender experiences."[80] If salvation includes the preservation and liberation of communities, then participation in Jesus's saving work includes work to support the preservation and liberation of Latine communities in the United States. This is the proper work of all those who follow Jesus. This work, while firmly grounded in the real struggles and successes of communities in the here and now, also necessarily has an eschatological bent. Díaz writes,

> What *is* essential is whether or not Latino/a Catholics and Protestants come to a consensus with respect to the *theologal* nature of our earthly citizenship. Or, to be more precise, can we see our earthly communal citizenship as an embodiment of our heavenly communal citizenship? Can we understand our temporal efforts to preserve community as being consistent with the eternal plan and life of God? Could we agree that the survival of our particular communal identities is essential because what is at risk is the encounter with God? How we represent that accompaniment is secondary and particular to our distinct religious histories.[81]

To support the survival and liberation of Latine communities, in other words, is to participate now in the world to come. The Christologies and soteriologies of Díaz, Goizueta, and Rodríguez make clear that justice for migrants, for mestizo people, for all Latine communities, is something that is deeply consistent with the heart and work of Jesus and is therefore something with which all Christians should be concerned.

---

80. Díaz, "Outside the Survival," 102.

81. Díaz, "Outside the Survival," 104. The term "theologal" refers to "the dimension in which a person, because he is connected to reality, is more than himself [*sic*]." It has to do with our ability to encounter the divine. See Ignacio Ellacuría, "Zubiri, filosofo teologal," *Vida Nueva*, no. 1249 (1980), as cited and translated in Kevin F. Burke, *The Ground beneath the Cross: the Theology of Ignacio Ellacuría* (Washington, DC: Georgetown University Press, 2000), 31.

From the Indigenous and Latine perspectives on Christology outlined above, along with the earlier insights from Niebuhr and Curran, a clear picture emerges of the ways in which our beliefs about Jesus can inform our engagement with the world and our responses to migrants. From the particularity of Jesus's life and work, in radical solidarity with marginalized people, several insights can be carried forward into our analysis of ecclesiology. First, the insights of Indigenous thinkers highlight the immense harm overly universalized articulations of Jesus have caused. They offer an indictment of Christianity's failings and a path forward. With Curran, they call Christians to inclusivity, to openness, and especially to respect of local cultures, traditions, and wisdom. This informs the posture with which we will approach partnership with migrants and Indigenous people. This care for the local is further underscored by Latine theologians, who connect Jesus's incarnation into a specific, marginalized human life to the realities faced by specific, marginalized people throughout history. Just as Jesus's salvific work took place within the concrete realities of a specific people, so too does our participation in that work involve concrete human liberation. Justice for migrants is the saving work of Christ. Finally, Jesus was formed in and by a community, and so salvation cannot be understood outside community. This reaffirms the importance of theology that is authentic to and consistent with specific communities, and the need for an openness to plurality. Niebuhr argues that Jesus acts in concert with God's will for the world. This will is not a universal, homogenous Euro-American Christendom. Justice begins in the specific lives of communities, and so Christians are called to protect the dignity and specificity of communities. This must inform our response to migrants, who come with all their particularities and cultural traditions, to a nation that too often looks on particularity and diversity with derision and fear.

Further, Jesus's formation in community indicates the importance of community for shaping individuals as disciples. If Jesus's salvific work came out of his formation in a specific community, so too is our discipleship meant to be formed in community. This final point makes clear that in order to more fully discern what practical proposals might be made from these insights, we must turn to a consideration of ecclesiology. The following section outlines Indigenous and Latine perspectives on ecclesiology in order to build on the christological insights and develop a fuller understanding of the role of the church as an institution called to radically love the world and model what community based in love looks like.

Ecclesiology

As Jesus became Messiah within and through his community, so too are Christians meant to develop in faith together. As we aim to live out the implications of the contextual Christologies outlined above, we do so as members of various communities and especially as members of church communities. It is therefore necessary to consider how Indigenous and Latine theologians understand the function and role of church communities to better understand what the role of the church is in forming disciples who love radically and in partnering with oppressed people in their struggles for justice. This section will consider four themes that are common in both Indigenous and Latine accounts of the church: the centrality of community, the church as storytellers, church in solidarity, and the importance of flexibility.

1. Model Communities

For Lakota theologian Martin Brokenleg, church is a community we become. He writes, "The original understanding of the ekklesia, the church, is that of the community gathered together." Growing up as a Lakota Christian, Brokenleg's experience of church was that it was indistinguishable from family. In the Lakota culture, family is understood as tio'spaye, which refers to much more than the nuclear family unit. Rather, tio'spaye refers to about 250 people across a five-generation span of relatives. Brokenleg's relatives were all members of the same congregation; his tio'spaye was his church community. Moreover, for Brokenleg and his family, the church was a *Lakota church*.[82] Tinker outlines ways in which Euro-American culture has been falsely universalized under the veil of Christianity. Brokenleg is similarly aware and critical of this dynamic. While his Lakota church community originally took on the trappings of English culture, as given to them by the missionaries who planted the church, he reports that in recent decades it has begun to reclaim its authentic Lakota identity, putting "on Lakota clothing and concepts, to become incarnate among the People."[83]

Like Brokenleg, Latino theologian Gary Riebe-Estrella understands church primarily in terms of familial relationships. Drawing on the notion of pueblo, which can refer to both people and town, he conceives of church as a community rooted in a network of relationships that form individual identities. Thus, as with families, church emerges quite naturally out of the relationships of people striving to live as people of God together. Moreover, like families, church communities consist of networks of relationships that form us and make claims on us. For Riebe-Estrella, a church is not something a person becomes a part of voluntarily and can depart from whenever convenient but rather a given reality, something that shapes and is shaped by relationships. He insists that the church's identity as a people of God is therefore rooted in the concrete lives of specific communities.[84]

---

82. Brokenleg, "Church—Wocekiye Okolakiciye," 133, 135–37.

83. Charleston, "Articulating a Native American Theological Theory," 1–5.

84. Gary Riebe-Estrella, "Pueblo and Church," in *From the Heart of Our People*, ed. Orlando O. Espín and Miguel H. Díaz (Maryknoll, NY: Orbis Books, 1999), 173–82.

Choctaw Episcopal Bishop Steven Charleston also emphasizes how central community is to Indigenous thinking and conceptions of church. Native theory, he argues, is inherently communal in nature. Within this emphasis on personal relationality, Charleston identifies three criteria for Indigenous communication: "accessibility, adaptability, accountability."[85] Native forms of communication and analysis create space for everyone to participate, and remain highly flexible and open to a variety of interpretations and applications. Perhaps most importantly, though, Charleston argues that Native communication is grounded by a strong sense of being accountable to the community. Thus, being consistent with the responsibility framework proposed in chapter 3, the criteria Charleston provides give shape to an Indigenous understanding of right relationships from which the church can learn. The church community ought to mirror "the call of Christ to relationships that do not allow some to 'lord it over' others but asks all to be responsible for one another (Mark 10:42–45)."[86] That is, the church community is meant to be one that engages in and models just and mutual forms of relationship. The work of repairing both Christianity's relationship with the survivors of US imperialism (in whose suffering the church is complicit), and on a broader scale the United States' relationship with these communities, is the proper work of the church.

Niebuhr and Curran both understand the church to have a specifically public role, interrupting sin and offering the world a better way of living (Niebuhr) and participating in God's saving action through working for justice (Curran). The above insights on what it might look like for the church to live as community further concretize these understandings. Centering relationships and understanding human identity as fundamentally communal is a direct contradiction to and rejection of US individualism, which suggests that everyone is primarily responsible for themselves and that justice is best understood as the protection of individual rights.[87] Such individualism leads to overly simplified understandings of migration that miss the deeper issues of unjust and broken relationships. A more relational understanding of humanity can help shift the discourse on immigration toward a consideration of responsibility to

85. Riebe-Estrella, "Pueblo and Church," 5.

86. Riebe-Estrella, "Pueblo and Church," 16.

87. This point also illustrates the limits of a reliance on human-rights language for sufficiently defining justice. While human-rights language can be a helpful framework for articulating that which each person may be owed solely by virtue of their humanity, the focus on individual rights is epistemologically limiting and has tended to focus attention inward (*my* Second Amendment right must be protected). The strength of a responsibility approach is that it draws focus instead to the ways in which justice ought to be framed relationally rather than individually (we are responsible for keeping each other safe from gun violence, even if that places constraints on our individual freedoms).

these relationships. The church, insofar as it is able to center relational self-understanding and focus itself on just relationships, can model a more relationship-focused practice to the wider United States (and beyond). In other words, it can model radical love. Charleston insists that Indigenous ways of relating offer a better way forward to the world. By focusing on its own (varied, culturally rooted) resources for relationality, the church can similarly promote a more just way of being, especially within a hyperindividualized context such as the United States. While this ultimately goes beyond Curran's own work, it is consistent with his vision for the church.

2. Storytellers

The establishment of this communal understanding of church identity raises the question of how exactly communal identity becomes known and transmitted and how it forms people. For Cuban-American theologian Natalia Imperatori-Lee, the church's communal identity is known through narrative, forged through a combination of history, theology, biblical study, and social science, which articulates "what it means to be the people of God." This narrative is not some grand and universal metanarrative but rather something rooted in the everyday lives of God's people and concerned with the functioning of the church in their lives. The church is a community of people seeking to know and love God together. We can only understand the identity of the church by taking into account the stories of the people who make up the community. The church, then, is a community of storytellers.[88]

Latine theology, Imperatori-Lee argues, is especially suited to a shift to narrative ecclesiology, a way of doing ecclesiology that centers narrative. Latine theology is concerned with the story of salvation history as it is encountered in the lives of communities and individuals, not as it can be understood through doctrine alone. This is inherently narrative in form. Moreover, Latine theology is intentionally collaborative, focusing especially on mutuality and respectful dialogue. In particular, it is committed to making space for the voices of those

88. Natalia Imperatori-Lee, *Cuéntame: Narrative in the Ecclesial Present* (Maryknoll, NY: Orbis Books, 2018), 72 Imperatori-Lee's turn to narrative helpfully grounds Niebuhr's work on responsibility, which has at times been accused of failing to adequately include the categories of narrative and community in his account of ethics, thus abstracting moral subjects from their social context. Thomas A. James argues that the implicit social theory behind *The Responsible Self*, as well as Niebuhr's more explicit work in *The Meaning of Revelation*, does in fact ground his insights in narrative and community, but he does not deny that ecclesiology plays less of a role in Niebuhr's work than in the work of some of his critics. This more explicit turn to consider the role of narrative and how the church can or ought to shape responsible agents, seen here in Imperatori-Lee but also present in the other thinkers profiled in this chapter, strengthens an underdeveloped theme in Niebuhr's work. See James, "Responsibility Ethics and Postliberalism," 38–40, 52–54.

who are marginalized and have often been left out of theological discussions, particularly in academic spaces. It is, Imperatori-Lee writes, an intentionally and necessarily multicultural endeavor. Ecclesiology, especially understood as a narrative project, will need these skills, particularly if it is to engage justly with a diverse and plural world rather than attempt to homogenize. This is especially true if ecclesiology is to offer a helpful framing of justice for migrants, who are, of course, diverse and multicultural. Finally, Latine theology is especially suited to a narrative approach to ecclesiology in that it commits itself to the importance of the everyday—lo cotidiano—and to popular religious practices of everyday practitioners. Understanding both as important sites in which grace is encountered, Latine theology is intentional about uplifting everyday stories, especially stories of laywomen, as important loci of theological reflection.[89]

Latine theology takes seriously the belief that revelation occurs in everyday life. As such, there is no other place in which to encounter, welcome, and respond to God's living word. Because of this, people's faith happens primarily in the context of everyday life, expressed in a variety of popular religious practices.[90] For Imperatori-Lee, popular Latine religious practice and the everyday experiences of Latine religious people reveal "with particular poignancy the universal truth of God's engagement with a particular set of communities in history—and what is ecclesiology if not the story of that engagement? What is the church if not the community that responds to that engagement?" In particular, we might consider how inclusion of these stories, these everyday experiences of God as articulated in the religious practices of migrants, might influence our process of becoming disciples, how they might shape our participation in God's work. As an important caveat, Imperatori-Lee cautions that Latine communities are certainly not the only communities in which inculturated popular religious practices play a central role in church life. Rather, it is the identification of these practices as vital for theological study, pioneered by Latine theologians such as Orlando Espín, that she understands to be a central and unique contribution from Latine theologies to the church as a whole.[91]

When Jesus sat down at the Last Supper, he told his followers to "do this in remembrance of me" (Luke 22:19). According to Charleston, Native theory frames this request as evidence of Jesus's understanding that his words would become part of his story, through which his followers would find a sense of identity. He insists that communal identity "originates in memory" and that Indigenous theology, as with other forms of Indigenous wisdom, has been

89. Imperatori-Lee, *Cuéntame*, 17–18.

90. María Pilar Aquino, "Theological Method in U.S. Latino/a Theology," in Espín and Díaz, *From the Heart of Our People*, 39.

91. Imperatori-Lee, *Cuéntame*, 21, 38–39.

"undertaken through the medium of story." Memory, especially communal forms of memory shared most often through storytelling, shapes a community's understanding of its origins, identity, and vocation. Charleston insists that for the survival and thriving of a community, "it is crucial to reenact the story, to bring the old words alive over and over, so that we can remember who we are, live into that memory again, and most importantly, forward the memory into the future, because if we do not, there will be no future."[92]

The tragic truth, however, is that for many Indigenous communities, these stories have been obscured by centuries of calculated efforts to "civilize" the continent, erasing as many traces of Indigeneity as possible. This was achieved through overt means, such as in boarding schools where Indigenous children were punished for speaking their native languages or dressing in traditional clothing, or in subtler ways, such as the internalization of a sense of sinfulness and the emulation of Euro-American culture Tinker describes. Such intentional distortion or denial of the collective memory of oppressed peoples is a strategy of oppression that causes deep harms to the oppressed community. The legacy of such colonialist oppression is "the fracturing of particular communities into pockets of amnesia, the dividing of people into broken fragments of what had once been a cohesive community." Native theory and theology, as a retrieval of traditional stories, wisdoms, and ways of being, becomes for Charleston "a methodology of repair," and "a project of restoration."[93]

In highlighting the importance of storytelling for shaping community identity, especially in response to such efforts to rob communities of their traditional stories, Rodríguez and Imperatori-Lee both lift up literature as a proper source for theology. For Rodríguez, literature is significant "as the focal expression of Latin American existential drama in all of its manifold complexities." Literature is especially important in that it can be a space for expression for "lowercase people," that is, people who are often not identified as sources of knowledge due to a lack of formal education.[94] In other words, it can lift up stories that have been systematically repressed or erased, like Indigenous stories and traditions have been and as the realities of migrants often are. For Imperatori-Lee, literature "brings to light divergent strains of popular religious practices, attitudinal shifts

---

92. Charleston, "Articulating a Native American Theological Theory," 4, 10. This notion of community identity as formed through narratives resonates with other theological insights. In particular, Johann Baptist Metz's articulation of dangerous memories that cry out from history to disrupt harmful ideologies and call systems into question certainly resonates with the ways in which the history of US colonialism, especially as told from the perspective of those most harmed, calls current US structures and policies into question. See Metz, *Faith in History and Society.*

93. Charleston, "Articulating a Native American Theological Theory," 10–11, 14.

94. Rodríguez, "Shaping Soteriology a la latina," 124–25.

in people's understandings of doctrine, and the reality that all doctrinal expressions, prayers, practices, political stances are culturally bound even as the God that grounds the church and the Spirit that enlivens it are not."[95] In other words, literature provides a window into the sensus fidelium.[96] The church is better able to know God and to understand God's salvific work by coming to know the stories of God's people, all of which create a piece of the whole story of the church and of God's salvation. Imperatori-Lee understands this total story to be like a mosaic, made up of smaller stories of individuals and communities encountering God in their everyday lives. Moreover, literature contains important insights beyond, but absolutely pertaining to, religious practice. These insights into the inner workings of communities, people's understanding of identity, and the realities of human relationships can, she argues, help the field of ecclesiology and the church better understand both global and local realities. Importantly, as with the Christologies surveyed above, this work is best conducted "from below," starting with people, their experiences, and their stories, rather than beginning from above with doctrine and theory.[97]

Taking the stories of people and communities seriously, Imperatori-Lee writes, allows Latine theologians to "retell the story of the people of God, not in a definitive way but in a way that attempts to draw together, to synchronize and harmonize" all the pieces of the mosaic into a messy, authentic whole.[98] By centering the stories of particular communities of faith, Indigenous and Latine theologies draw attention to the particular lives and faiths of migrants as an intrinsic part of the Christian story and to the importance of these stories for shaping Christian identity. That the stories of people oppressed by US colonialism are part of the Christian story, part of the identity of the church, ought to inform the relationship of Christians to the United States and put us in opposition to its forces of empire.

Althaus-Reid calls for a methodology of reading texts (defined broadly as written texts, art, culture, tradition, social structures, community stories, etc.) with, rather than for, oppressed people. The way we read can either legitimize existing power structures or interrupt them. Reading with oppressed people helps to sharpen our understanding of and opposition to oppressive structures. Althaus-Reid draws on Paul Ricoeur's notion of reading as "rupture,"

95. Imperatori-Lee, *Cuéntame*, 52.

96. Sensus fidelium translates as "the sense of the faithful" and refers to the way in which the Catholic "faithful together understand and live the faith." Maria C. Morrow, "'Sensus fidelium': The Sense of the Faithful," Catholic News Service, 2018, https://catholiccourier.com/articles/sensus-fidelium-the-sense-of-the-faithful.

97. Imperatori-Lee, *Cuéntame*, 52–53.

98. Imperatori-Lee, *Cuéntame*, 53.

arguing that this method of reading harnesses the "imagination of a community, in an ongoing process of interpretation of their own faith and everyday reality."[99] Stories, especially those stories that constitute lowercase literature, emerging from the margins, can aid in this interruptive, rupturing reading of society, history, and religion. In other words, reading society and history with migrants can aid the church in confirming that US history and policy is sinful and can therefore draw attention to particular injustices in need of repair. In order to partner with migrants, we need to listen to their stories and read with them.

Niebuhr's understanding of responsible moral action highlights the importance of history and calls us not to amnesia but to the task of remembering well.[100] For Anglo-American Christians committed to engaging in more just forms of relationship, awareness of the importance of memory for establishing community identity and of the ways US colonialist action has robbed communities of this important connection to memory means we must take stock of our own story, our full history in all its ugliness. Becoming aware of this history leads to rupture, to the interruption of dominant narratives of Christian and US history. Althaus-Reid highlights the historical mistreatment of women, especially Indigenous women, in Latin American countries, asking, "How have we interpreted Scriptures for the last 500 years, for these women to be reduced to this appalling condition?"[101] Faced with the ongoing harms caused by the historical patterns of colonialism outlined in chapters 1–2, churches must ask themselves precisely this question. How have we been reading Scripture, tradition, theology? How is it that Christian theology and witness have so often supported rather than opposed systems that cause so much harm, and what does it look like to take responsibility for that harm now? The church is especially called to consider the role Christianity has played in depriving others of their own histories. Healing of any kind requires looking at the wound in question.[102] The church must also consider what it could look like to support the efforts of these communities whose histories and communal stories we helped to squash to reclaim their traditional stories.

Charleston argues that Native theory turns to storytelling in order to engage in a process of truth telling. This builds on the notion of stories as interruptive of oppressive structures. It is a direct response to the theft of the communities' collective memories, part of the restorative project with which he understands

---

99. Althaus-Reid, *From Feminist Theology*, 17–18.

100. Niebuhr, *Responsible Self*, 102.

101. Althaus-Reid, *From Feminist Theology*, 20.

102. Charleston, "Articulating a Native American Theological Theory," 12.

Native theory to be tasked. Truth telling seeks to challenge (rupture) the dominant narratives of oppressive victors by retrieving and telling the too often untold stories, "the uncomfortable and even chilling historical reality of the Native experience of conquest, war, and genocide." These truths are told "not as an end in themselves, a source for blame, but as a transformative catalyst, a vision of truth that can be brought back into the story of the people, reinterpreted and then used as that memory moves into the future."[103] For Charleston, truth provides a path to be followed. Living out of shared traditions and collective memory connects past traditions with present experiences in a way that reveals a path forward that is consistent with whom the community has been and intends to be. It illuminates the way toward liberation and seeks to restore "people to the ongoing story of salvation." Truth telling, he writes, "announces a new vision of cooperation and justice that has ancient resonance in the memory of not only Native America, but of all societies that have known oppression. In this way, it embraces the vision of Christ for an open and caring community (John 13:34–35)."[104]

In other words, truth telling is participation in God's salvific work. It strives to do what Jesus requested of his disciples: to remember in order that the people might have a future.[105] It strives to remember key stories of who the community has been so that they might move forward grounded in that history and identity. Charleston argues that the conquest of people and continent that robbed so many of their traditional stories and land also created artificial lines and borders between people. The forced movements and separations of Indigenous peoples and the creation of US borders that slice right through traditional Indigenous land was, he writes, a denial of traditional commonalities and shared stories.[106] Recall, for example, how the US action such as the Allotment Act of 1887 divided up land that had been collectively held by communities and turned it into private property to be bought and sold, attempting to force an artificial sense of individualism and selfishness onto the community.[107] Telling the truth of what was lost sets a path forward toward justice. It reminds us that the lines colonialist capitalism has drawn between people are not natural and therefore need not be permanent. The church can envision more radically inclusive ways of being in the world. It is not bound to the categories and patterns of the world, especially not the ones that are harmful and oppressive. This is especially important to

103.Charleston, "Articulating a Native American Theological Theory," 12. Also see Metz, *Faith in History and Society*, on dangerous memory.

104. Charleston, "Articulating a Native American Theological Theory," 13, 10, 14, 17.

105. Charleston, "Articulating a Native American Theological Theory," 14.

106. Charleston, "Articulating a Native American Theological Theory," 14.

107. Dunbar-Ortiz, *Indigenous Peoples' History*, 157–59.

understand if the church is going to work alongside migrants and Indigenous people toward a more just and inclusive world.

In this way, Native theory "affirms the claim of Christ that the process of truth will ultimately set us free (John 8:32)."[108] In doing so, this project centers the hopes of specific peoples. For Charleston, this means that Native theory is specifically concerned with the particular hopes of Indigenous communities. This book, of course, is concerned with the concrete hopes of migrants. Justice for migrants, however, is intrinsically linked to justice for Indigenous peoples. The development of patterns of Euro-American colonialism, which sought to remove all vestiges of indigeneity from the continent by means of forced assimilation and violent conquest, directly lead to US foreign policy, which destabilizes other nations for US gain, and to US immigration policy, which fails to take responsibility and instead exacerbates harm. Furthermore, many migrants are Indigenous people, driven to migrate to the United States by the same colonialism that stole the Indigenous land that would become the United States. Any attempt to reckon with these patterns of harm and to work for reparative justice will therefore necessarily require the involvement and leadership of Indigenous people as well as migrants.

This project has also concerned itself with Indigenous history and Euro-American injustices against Native nations and communities in order to problematize the very conceptual basis from which is built the right of the US government to dictate who may inhabit this land and under what conditions. Any argument for the rights of nations to control their borders must contend with the reality that those nations have often gained control of their land through incredibly violent and unjust means. The building of a more just world in which past and ongoing harms are repaired through the creation of tangible accountability is a project that includes but extends beyond specific consideration for just and humane migration policy. Justice requires a complete reimagining of global relationships. This means understanding the many links between systems of injustice (chapter 2 also briefly considered, for example, how the history of chattel slavery, anti-Blackness, and the continued exclusion of Asian people from US society connects to the same colonialism that harms Latin American nations, migrants, and Indigenous peoples).[109] While this book seeks specifically to outline a response to migration in the United States, it does so in the awareness that this project must always be tied to concrete, reparative justice for Indigenous

---

108. Charleston, "Articulating a Native American Theological Theory," 15.

109. This chapter, and indeed the entire book, is unable to contend fully with all of these interrelated forms of systematic harm. The focus on migrants and Indigenous peoples is meant to provide a workable scope for this project, not imply that the harms done to other groups by the US are any less real, important, or related. Indeed, migrants and Indigenous people can be and are Black, Asian, queer, etc. These intersections are vital to keep in view.

peoples. Therefore, while the proposal of specific reparations for Indigenous communities is beyond the scope of this project, the insights, wisdom, and specific liberative hopes of Indigenous peoples remain relevant.

Ecclesiologically, this means that the salvific hope in which the church believes and participates cannot be understood outside the specific hopes of marginalized peoples. Charleston insists that hope becomes particular and concrete in these specific liberative hopes of marginalized and oppressed communities.[110] For the US church, this includes the hopes of migrants and of Indigenous communities. This is consistent with the account of Christology outlined above. Jesus's life, ministry, and salvific work began within a specific marginal community and was rooted in that community's particular struggles and hopes. The work of the church to participate in salvation, then, must be rooted in the specific hopes of communities seeking liberation. This means that the church can fulfill its call to participate in God's saving action by supporting and partnering with these communities in their work for justice.

Native theory, in its retrieval of Indigenous memories, centers the "we," rather than the "I," in its analysis of all matters social, economic, and spiritual.[111] Furthermore, it does so, as we have seen, with a particular emphasis on just communal relationships by striving for accessibility, adaptability, and accountability. In its resistance to artificial divisions, vision of just communities, and commitment to leaning into ambiguity, Native theory offers another option to a world broken apart into "hostile bunkers of religious intolerance, all competing for dwindling resources with no plan for peace other than preparing for war." This option is a "vision of global community" rooted in the "pragmatic experience of liberation from conformity." This, Charleston insists, "is a vision for what the Christian community can be."[112] That is, it offers to the church and to the world a new way of living, a vision for community and relationships that is not the dominant vision provided by US capitalism. In this way, it offers concrete insight into what radical love looks like. Native theory calls the church to embrace "the mysterious ways of God" that have always moved beyond the boxes human beings have tried to place around God. Living into this reality encourages humility and flexibility, and calls the church to embrace diversity rather than encourage conformity, all of which will be vital if the church is to engage in work for justice and the dismantling of empire.[113]

This reemphasizes the importance of understanding justice as an inclusive, multidimensional project and underscores why reparations for Indigenous

110. Charleston, "Articulating a Native American Theological Theory," 17.

111. Charleston, "Articulating a Native American Theological Theory," 15.

112. Charleston, "Articulating a Native American Theological Theory," 24–25.

113. Charleston, "Articulating a Native American Theological Theory," 23–24.

communities (and for people who are Black, Asian, queer, etc.) is directly tied to justice for migrants. The vision Native theory offers to the church is inclusive and plural. It rejects the separations of people into the categories and boxes imposed by Euro-American colonialism and unites people in interrelated projects of liberation. Offering a similarly inclusive vision of justice, Imperatori-Lee argues that Latine theology is "simultaneously a narrative of liberation (of oppressed and marginalized Hispanic persons in the United States) and one of resistance to the brute forces of assimilation and the erasure of difference that tend to dominate U.S. culture." This is resistance to and liberation from the colonialist patterns of erasure and assimilation outlined in chapters 1–2. Imperatori-Lee suggests, "The church should be a place where our individual and communal stories are heard, retold, celebrated in the telling and retelling of the story of Christ's Incarnation."[114]

This draws us back to truth telling as a primary task of the church.[115] Historical narratives, especially those that interrupt harmful ideologies and dominant narratives, can "help ecclesiologists shape a vision of what is possible in the church in light of what has taken place in the past. History can preserve dangerous memories and thereby foster alternative tomorrows for the church."[116] Moreover, this brings to light another dimension of this characteristic: a truth-telling church must always also be a listening church. Recall Curran's conciliar insistence that the whole church is always both a teaching and a learning church. Imperatori-Lee argues that listening to stories, especially the stories of those most often forgotten and marginalized, allows the church to gain a better, more nuanced understanding of the identity and history of the whole church rather than the narrow narrative that results from universalizing certain experiences.[117]

Similarly, Curtice cautions against our often too-quick impulses to action. In our effort to provide answers and do the work of justice, we too often forget that some of the most important, as well as the hardest, work we can do

> is the act of listening, of learning, of walking beside instead of charging ahead. . . . We can learn a lot from listening. We can learn a lot from quiet prayer. We can learn a lot by becoming people who walk alongside those we say we are working so hard to care for. And while we walk beside them, we can practice respectful silence, so that as we move

114. Imperatori-Lee, *Cuéntame*, 20–21, 72.

115. To call the church to the task of truth telling is, importantly, not to establish the church as arbiter of or final authority on truth. This is why listening is key.

116. Imperatori-Lee, *Cuéntame*, 56.

117. Imperatori-Lee, *Cuéntame*, 39.

> forward we might better know how to care for them. We might better know what it was like for Jesus to care for people.[118]

In conversations with Latine and migrant community activists and in listening to the voices of Indigenous people, a common theme arises: progress ought not to be undertaken for its own sake. Rather, we must ask whose progress we are fighting for. The specifics of the vision of the future toward which the church aims matter, as do the origins of that vision. Too often US visions of progress, driven by a capitalist, neocolonial quest for dominance and profit, have come at the expense of marginalized people, even when they have been well intentioned.[119] The church must consider how we can make space for oppressed communities to envision their own liberation and support them in that work, rather than try to lead or impose our own visions of progress onto them.

For Charleston, it is important to highlight that this work can and "must be undertaken by both Native and non-Native people together." Moreover, he insists that "Christianity in the Native story is not consigned to being part of the problem, but that it can actively become part of the solution." He argues that Native theory offers a vision for the world that aligns with and embraces the vision of an open and loving community that Jesus taught and lived. Native theory calls people to "take responsibility for their actions, not in theory but in practice."[120] If this is taken seriously, it provides direction to the church. The church is called to take responsibility for its history of colonialism and its continued participation in ongoing harm. This responsibility is not simply words or internal reckoning but necessarily includes reparative action. Chapter 6 will consider what forms such action might take.

It is important to emphasize that this responsible action, the proper work of the church, puts churches in direct contradiction to the dominant narratives of both the United States and much of the world. The church is not meant to conform to the ways of the world. Goizueta argues that the church, insofar as it is working for God's kin-dom, will regularly find itself in conflict with the world, particularly with modern empires.[121] In a nation where the partnership of church and state has supported colonialism and caused such widespread harm, this insight is especially vital. The church must be prepared to be in conflict with the world.

---

118. Kaitlin Curtice, "Dear Church, It's Time to Listen," *Sojourners*, May 25, 2017, https://sojo.net/articles/dear-church-it-s-time-listen.

119. Consider, for example, Senator Henry Dawes's concern that Native people were not "selfish enough" and were therefore unable to progress as they "should" (see chap. 1).

120. Charleston, "Articulating a Native American Theological Theory," 13, 17–18.

121. Goizueta, "Corpus Verum," 143–66.

3. Solidarity

Further highlighting the importance of stories, Goizueta argues that the lived faith of Latine people helps to make ecclesiology more historically rooted "through a retrieval of the intrinsic connection between Christology and ecclesiology."[122] His Christology, as articulated above, pays particular attention to the incarnate Christ as a person who lived a historically marginalized, borderland human life. For Goizueta, the character of God's historical incarnation into the margins also means that the people of God are called to fundamentally identify with those who are oppressed. Recall that Jesus's incarnation is part of his radical love; he loved the world so much he entered fully into it. Such solidarity with oppressed peoples is therefore the third vital ecclesiological theme.

Latine experiences of oppression can help to concretize the idea that the church is a relational people called to be in the image of a relational God through the work of radical love. The people of God, so conceived, will always understand and "[constitute] itself over against a dominant other." Moreover, this will call the church into "conflict and confrontation" as it resists the forces of sin in the world.[123]

Althaus-Reid calls the church to a task she calls "walking with women serpents." This language is rooted in two methodological shifts that call for theologians to take seriously women's caminata (literally "walk"; this word here is used to signify women's "style of 'doing' theology in a community process or 'walk'") and to understand theology as "a creative path of acting and reflecting about the presence of God in our lives." It is further a reference to the Mexica goddess Cihuacóatl (the serpent woman). In this tradition, women held official roles in the temple, and the serpent was a symbol of union with God and of wisdom. The language Althaus-Reid uses is therefore an homage to Latin American women, meant to signal a fundamental siding with them. It is a move of solidarity, and Althaus-Reid calls the whole church to this walk. Walking with women serpents means letting "Otherness take the lead for a while, to teach us something new, and . . . to share with us the experience of . . . losses suffered at the hands of the

122. Goizueta, "Corpus Verum," 145.

123. Goizueta, "Corpus Verum," 145–46. It is important that this is not understood as conflict for conflict's sake. The idea that Christian faith calls us into some form of conflict with the world has been taken to sanction all manner of harmful behavior, such as resistance to "worldly norms" such as the affirmation of LGBTQ people. The exaggerated sense of Christian persecution in the US that exists in some circles of Christianity is also an example of this problem. To avoid these pitfalls, the call to resistance to the anti-kingdom must be rooted in Jesus's identification with those on society's margins and his deep concern for the material realities of people's lives. In other words, it must be rooted in Christology from below. Goizueta further clarifies this point by arguing that the church becomes a crucified people, suffering in and with Christ, by placing itself on the side of the oppressed, that is, by standing (and possibly suffering) with those the world crucifies.

European conquistadores."[124] Walking in solidarity, then, is deeply tied to the call to be a listening and learning church.

To be in solidarity with Latin American women, Althaus-Reid argues, we must listen to their stories, to their experiences, to the uncomfortable truths of history.[125] This means listening to migrants, hearing their stories, taking seriously their reasons for coming to the United States and what those reasons indicate about this country. This is especially true of listening to the reasons some migrants cross the border undocumented, which can illuminate ongoing failures in the US immigration system, to which we must respond from a place of solidarity with them rather than with the powers that oppose them. Neutrality, Althaus-Reid insists, is a myth in service of the status quo.[126] Walking in solidarity means choosing a side. We cannot claim to be in solidarity with someone and not oppose that which harms them. While Christians ought to respect the humanity of every person—migrant, border patrol, ICE agent, politician, concerned citizen—we are called not to neutrality but to solidarity with migrants, with whom Jesus lived, died, and resurrected in radical solidarity.

Above, we considered how Curran's Christology, while fundamentally inclusive, still conceives of Jesus as a victim of empire, put to death by the same systems of sin that oppress and crucify people to this day.[127] Curran argues that this radical act of solidarity on the part of Jesus calls us to solidarity with the victims of this oppression throughout history. Althaus-Reid's Christology calls us to a discipleship of becoming, in which participation in God's salvific work requires a process of joining Christ in dialogue with oppressed people, whose struggle for liberation can direct our understanding of salvation and therefore our understanding of what it means to participate in God's work of salvation. Listening to the stories of migrants and entering into radical, nonneutral solidarity with them is part of what this discipleship looks like, and it is what the church is called to do.

Thus the role of the church, as it positions itself on the side of the oppressed and in opposition to dominant and sinful forces, will be to stand in contradiction to the United States' history of unjust relationships and its continued failure to take responsibility for its actions. The church, Goizueta argues, is a sacrament

124. Althaus-Reid, *From Feminist Theology*, 18, 12 (with n1), 19.

125. Althaus-Reid, *From Feminist Theology*, 16.

126. Althaus-Reid, *From Feminist Theology*, 16.

127. Chapter 3 noted that Jesus's inclusivity still prioritizes the inclusion of marginalized people and the meeting of their needs. This, then, is a radical inclusivity that still has criteria. Or, perhaps more to the point, Jesus's inclusivity comes with responsibility for the creation of just relationships by prioritizing the needs and interests of those who have been marginalized and oppressed.

of the reign of God. It is called to signal *and mediate* God's coming reign. This "demands a practical commitment to *be* what we already *are* by virtue of God's creative-salvific activity in history," that is, God's radical act of love that took the form of an incarnation directly into the margins. To "be what we already are" is to be the body of Christ, which means living into the connection between God's people and Jesus's crucifixion by seeking out "the crucified peoples of our world" and living in active solidarity with them, just as Jesus did in his life and his death at the hands of his oppressors.[128]

Just as Jesus's incarnate body fully sided with the oppressed, even unto death, so too must his body as the church. This is what it means to constitute ourselves as people of God in contradiction and opposition to dominant and sinful forces and in solidarity with those who are oppressed, to live true radical love. The church's very identity is meant to be forged in solidarity with crucified people, in radical opposition to the forces that oppress them. The following chapter will consider what this contradictory stance might entail.

4. Flexibility

Imperatori-Lee argues that by focusing on the everyday stories of encounters with God and practices of faith and discipleship, Latine theology "challenges the church to broaden its notions of holiness, the role of the laity, and particularly the importance of women in the interpretation and transmission of the faith."[129] Consistent with Curran's vision for the church, this challenge to broaden our understandings leads directly to our fourth and final ecclesiological theme: flexibility. Goizueta's insight about Jesus's borderland particularity calls the church away from the rigidity of US Christianity and into new ways of being, particularly influenced and led by the popular religion of those who inhabit borderlands. The church, he argues, is being increasingly shaped by grassroots communities of faith, found especially in society's margins. Jesus's historical particularity can "ground an ecclesiology racially and culturally in the experience of those marginalized people."[130] The hybrid, mestizo culture of this land is precisely where God's self-disclosure takes place in the person of Jesus, a Galilean Jew. Moreover, according to the Gospel of Matthew, it is where the disciples gather in the wake of his death and resurrection. In other words, this marginal borderland, among oppressed and crucified people, is where the ekklēsia begins.[131] For Goizueta, this

128. Goizueta, "Corpus Verum," 147, 150.

129. Imperatori-Lee, *Cuéntame*, 39.

130. Goizueta, "Corpus Verum," 153.

131. Goizueta, "Corpus Verum," 154.

means that the church is "intrinsically a borderland church, born in the midst of multiple cultural, racial, and religious influences."[132]

Galilee, as a mixed and plural borderland and home to marginalized people, defines the identity and self-understanding of the church. Drawing a connection between the hybrid religious practices of the people of Galilee and the popular religion of Latine people of faith, Goizueta concludes that popular religion is therefore at the heart of what it means to be church. This form of lived religiosity is deeply flexible and hybrid. It is primarily lived out in the everyday lives of people who are often less concerned with doctrinal continuity and strict adherence to creeds, people whose very reality and identity is often mixed and liminal—mestizo. In fact, Goizueta argues that an accurate account of Christian history shows "a fluid, dynamic panoply of religious practices that include but go beyond the 'official' practices of the church." All of this highlights an inherent openness as proper to the church. Latine cultures, in which more porous understandings of boundaries and comfort with hybridity are prominent, therefore have much to offer the wider church to help it embrace flexibility, plurality, and openness.[133]

Goizueta concludes that "the church will remain a vital, credible sacrament of the reign of God to the extent that the church identifies itself with women, children, and men who are the privileged witness to the crucified and risen Christ"—that is, people of the borderlands. Migrants, then, have much to offer not only the United States but the church specifically, and they are those with whom the church is called to identify. Moreover, Goizueta's articulation of the "borderlands as privileged ecclesial location, a privileged place for being church,"[134] offers vital tools for moving forward as a church committed to justice for migrants. Churches committed to building mutual, just relationships with migrants (and with Indigenous people) will need to make space for a diversity of culturally rooted religious practices and beliefs, even when they differ from (or contradict) those more common in US churches. True communion with those who US imperialism has shoved aside and exploited will be messy and vibrant and mixed. It will be hybrid.

Goizueta identifies a certain rigidity in US church culture, a rigidity that is evident in the history of US colonialism and the need to conquer and Christianize the world. Anglo-American US churches, then, will need to learn and embrace a more flexible way of doing and being church in order fully engage in this communion. Furthermore, as Tinker articulates, the United States has a

132. Goizueta, "Corpus Verum," 39, 153–55.

133. Goizueta, "Corpus Verum," 155–58, 161–63.

134. Goizueta, "Corpus Verum," 163.

long history of separating people from their traditions and denying the validity of their cultural wisdom and expressions of faith. Any attempt to establish accountability and mutuality in these relationships going forward will require not only repentance for this history but also a change in behavior going forward. This means respecting and learning from the unique insights of migrants as well as other marginalized Christians and non-Christians.

An open, hybrid church comfortable with a multiplicity of faith expressions lives in direct contradiction to the colonialist interests and behaviors of the United States. This does not mean there are no limits to such multiplicity. Complete relativism is a threat to justice. As an extreme example, expressions of faith that align with white supremacy should not be something to which churches are open. Rather, in contrast to the Christianity of colonialism, which takes Euro-American cultural expressions of faith as its normative criteria, a more open, hybrid church will find normative criteria that make space for a variety of cultural realities. Such criteria will be rooted in the (biblically based) relational understanding of justice outlined in chapters 3–4 and in contextual accounts of Jesus's life and ministry such as those profiled above, not in any particular cultural trappings. The contours of Christian faith, by which we can claim commonality amid diversity, will be shaped by biblical justice and the example of Christ, not colonialist expressions of civility. Flexibility, so conceived, is therefore the proper posture for a church called to form itself in contrast to dominant powers of sin.

Goizueta is not alone in highlighting the need for flexibility. In calling for ecumenical consensus on understanding "earthly communal citizenship as an embodiment of heavenly citizenship" in which we strive to live into the eschatological future we proclaim, Díaz cautions that such work will raise "ancient questions" on which we have long disagreed. Latine hybridity, he argues, can help teach churches to live in the ambiguity of our disagreements and foster new approaches to living as communities of faith.[135] Imperatori-Lee argues that all "epistemological presuppositions, like any knowledge, are culturally bound."[136] Similarly, Althaus-Reid insists, "Any attempt to produce a liberating theology needs to consider how knowledge is invented, and why and how certain ideas become paradigms, while others do not."[137] Such an examination of the roots of theological knowledge, of how ideas about Jesus, God, and the church come to be considered canon, is a fundamentally destabilizing project. It requires asking

---

135. Díaz, "Outside the Survival," 104.

136. Imperatori-Lee, *Cuéntame*, 22.

137. Althaus-Reid, *From Feminist Theology*, 16.

uncomfortable questions about our own assumptions and commitments, theological and epistemological.

Further, Althaus-Reid names subversion as an important tool for walking with Otherness. We have explored above some of the ways this subversive interruption of status quo and established epistemological paradigms is vital to being church, especially in the United States, where Christianity has too often supported systems of sin. Althaus-Reid cautions that this methodology of subversion will "make our theology vulnerable" by moving it beyond the language and concepts that are familiar and comfortable.[138] Flexibility can help us weather this vulnerability and embrace it as a strength, not a weakness. Such vulnerability is what will allow us to grow, to change, to do better. Subverting the mythology of the United States through truth telling, for example, may make us vulnerable as we reckon with unlearning what we have been taught. Deconstructing harmful theology and mythology may lead, for a time, to instability. This reckoning is, however, also what allows for more just, responsible action. The subversion of false myths allows truths to break free—truths, for example, about why people migrate. By responding to these truths rather than to the mythologies that cast immigrants as threats, we can therefore begin to respond better. In other words, subversion is a necessary element of the responsibility ethics framework outlined in chapter 3, and fostering flexibility in our communities can prepare us for this work.

Curtice also calls the church to flexibility and to learning from those who have been marginalized, oppressed, and left out by US imperialism and US Christianity. She calls us to learn from the insights of Native thinkers and to follow their lead in deconstructing the doctrines, teachings, and practices in our churches that perpetuate injustice.[139] In doing so, Curtice warns, we must be willing to ask difficult questions about what we have been taught by both the church and the United States.[140] For Charleston, adaptability is a tenet of Native theory he offers for helping the church envision a better future. He insists that in ambiguity, we encounter the edge of imagination. Leaning into the discomfort of the ambiguous helps us imagine what is possible, not based on what the world has told us but based on the vision and promises of God. Native theory emphasizes a lack of certainty as being proper to humanity and especially to

138. Althaus-Reid, *From Feminist Theology*, 20.

139. Kaitlin Curtice, "Is The Work of Deconstruction Violent or Fruitful?," *Sojourners*, March 6, 2019, https://sojo.net/articles/work-deconstruction-violent-or-fruitful; Curtice, "Decolonize Your Faith This Lent."

140. Curtice, "It's Time to Prune Back."

Christianity.[141] This serves an important function in breaking down US myths of certainty and control that undergird US colonialism and contribute to anti-immigrant sentiments. Moreover, learning to lean into ambiguity in this way is consistent with Niebuhr's articulation of salvation as "deliverance from deep distrust of" God.[142] Similarly, Curran highlights that it is God who makes the first salvific step toward humans and that discipleship is only possible because of God's gracious call. Discipleship, then, requires trust. Leaning into profound trust in this way can help Christians let go of the myth of certainty and learn instead to be flexible.

The perspectives outlined above highlight the importance of the locus theologicus. Because these thinkers explicitly do theology from their particular contexts and sociopolitical locations, their theological accounts are particularly thick. As such, they are able to provide accounts of what it means to be church that expand beyond Niebuhr and Curran, and they have helpfully fleshed out what radical love might entail. This sort of rich, contextual ecclesiology can help us break through the homogeneity of colonialist, Euro-American Christianity and move us toward a more just world.

Conclusion

Imperatori-Lee argues that Latine theology invites readers out of their own experiences and into the world, allowing the stories of others to spark insights that shape and reshape our understanding of church.[143] Similarly, Indigenous theologians such as Tinker offer perspectives on Christian history and theology that often go unnoticed and with which all Christians must contend. Drawing especially from Indigenous and Latine thinkers, this chapter has outlined how Christologies that take seriously the particulars of Jesus's earthly life can begin to shape an understanding of discipleship that draws Christians into transformative relationships with those on the margins, based in radical love. This reflects the accounts of responsible discipleship provided by Niebuhr and Curran. These contributions extend beyond Niebuhr's and Curran's foci, however. Grounded in specific contexts of marginalization, they are able to provide insights into Jesus and discipleship that are beyond the more theoretical accounts of Niebuhr and Curran. These thinkers challenge the limits of white theological approaches and move Christian discipleship closer to the lived experience of Jesus, the marginalized Galilean border-dweller.

---

141. Charleston, "Articulating a Native American Theological Theory," 23.

142. Niebuhr, *Responsible Self*, 142.

143. Imperatori-Lee, *Cuéntame*, 72.

The chapter has also considered how Indigenous and Latine ecclesiology can inform our understanding of how that discipleship is best lived out (and formed) in the church, outlining the themes of community, truth telling, solidarity, and flexibility. These accounts were similarly thick and rooted in particular contexts of oppression at the hands of US colonialism, and as such provide a path toward accountability, reparations, and just relationships. These insights into the proper role of Christians and the church provide a theological basis that directs the practical proposals of the final chapter.

CHAPTER SIX

Friendship

FROM APRIL 2016 through February 2017, several camps that had been constructed north of the Standing Rock Indian Reservation in order to halt the construction of the Dakota Access Pipeline became the site of the largest movement of Indigenous resistance in the twenty-first century. In *Our History Is the Future,* Oceti Sakowin scholar Nick Estes highlights the historical roots and future-oriented nature of this movement. The events at Standing Rock, Estes argues, were "the most recent iteration of an Indian War that never ends."[1] The building of a pipeline that endangers Indigenous lives and denies Indigenous sovereignty, the location of which was intended specifically to avoid interrupting white neighborhoods, can be viewed as an outgrowth of manifest destiny and the frontier myth. The highly militarized and violent responses of the Dakota Access Pipeline and of the South Dakota government to the Water Protectors at Standing Rock fit into the patterns of US colonialism outlined in chapters 1–2.

The connections Estes draws between history and this movement do not, however, revolve solely around patterns of colonial aggression. Rather, he connects the work of the Standing Rock Water Protectors to the long-standing history of Indigenous resistance to US colonialism. Chapters 1–2 gestured toward this history of resistance, which Roxanne Dunbar-Ortiz credits with making possible the continuation of Indigenous existence and ways of life to this day. Estes agrees, arguing that "Indigenous resistance draws from a long history, projecting itself backward and forward in time."[2] He elaborates, writing,

> Karl Marx explained the nature of revolutions through the figure of the mole, which burrows through history, making elaborate tunnels and preparing to surface again. The more dramatic moments come when the mole breaks the surface: revolution. But revolution is a mere moment within the longer movement of history. The mole is easily defeated on the surface by counterrevolutionary forces if she hasn't adequately prepared her subterranean spaces, which provide shelter and safety; even when pushed back underground, the mole doesn't stop her work. In

1. Nick Estes, *Our History Is the Future: Standing Rock versus the Dakota Access Pipeline, and the Long Tradition of Indigenous Resistance* (London: Verso Colophon, 2019), 10.

2. Estes, *Our History Is the Future,* 18.

> song and ceremony, Lakotas revere the mole for her hard work collecting medicines from the roots underfoot. During his campaign against US military invasion, to protect himself Crazy Horse collected fresh dirt from mole mounds. Because he knew it to contain medicines, he washed his body with the dirt. Hidden from view of outsiders, this constant tunneling, plotting, planning, harvesting, remembering, and conspiring for freedom—the collective faith that another world is possible—is the most important aspect of revolutionary work. It is from everyday life that the collective confidence to change reality grows, giving rise to extraordinary events.[3]

While direct actions such as demonstrations and legal action against the Dakota Access Pipeline brought the most media attention to the fight taking place at Standing Rock, there was another side of the work being done at the camps, less visible but just as important. Every day, people in the camps undertook the vital tasks of caring for one another. Estes reports that camp members provided nourishment, encouragement, friendship, songs and stories, and love. This, he says, is the primary work of the mole, the work of Indigenous resistance tunneling through history and sustaining Indigenous communities.[4]

Estes's articulation of the Standing Rock Water Protectors and of Indigenous history more broadly focuses on a history of relationships, highlighting in particular relationships among Indigenous people and between Indigenous people and the United States. By focusing on these relationships, he argues, "we can see that Indigenous history is not a narrow subfield of US history" but rather that "Indigenous people are central subjects of modern world history." This in itself is a radical way to frame US history, especially in a society that has historically centered the stories of Euro-American "victory." Decentering these Anglo stories and perspectives offers a more complete picture of the history of this continent. It also allows Estes to center the patterns of continual Indigenous resistance to colonization. The history of the United States becomes not simply a story of US expansion and domination of the continent but a story of the people with another, older claim to that continent, the story of their resistance to colonization, even in the face of near annihilation.[5] Focusing on this history of relationships also resonates with a responsibility-ethics framework. Niebuhr and Curran articulate a deeply relational view of the moral life, in which good moral choices require acting fittingly in all our relationships. Viewing history with a

3. Estes, *Our History Is the Future*, 18–19.

4. Estes, *Our History Is the Future*, 19.

5. Estes, *Our History Is the Future*, 21.

focus on relationships can help us view the moral dynamics of our history and so can help us respond fittingly in our relationships today.

By centering these relational stories, and especially the stories of Indigenous resistance, Estes is able to show how the movement that came up from beneath the ground at Standing Rock in 2016 was one that looked backward and forward. It looked backward to find strength, identity, and vision, and it looked forward with that vision to see what the world could be if Indigenous liberation were won. Estes's work can help direct the practical proposals of this chapter, which ought to similarly look backward and forward. People have been fighting against US colonialism and the US immigration system since the beginning of the United States. Most of these resistors have been marginalized people most harmed by these systems. Recognizing that this fight is not new, honoring those who have come before, and drawing on their vision for liberation to guide us into the future will help ground our work for justice going forward.

The findings of the preceding chapters have suggested the need for a significant conceptual shift regarding US history and migration in churches as well as in the broader nation. There is simply no way to create stable change without changing the narratives we tell in order to undercut the national myths that have generated and upheld harmful policies. Like Estes and Dunbar-Ortiz, law professor and immigration lawyer César Cuauhtémoc García Hernández highlights the importance of understanding history in order to forge a better path forward. In his book *Migrating to Prison*, he acknowledges the difficulty of imagining a US immigration system not dependent on detention. Justice, however, demands that we do imagine such a future and that this reimagining be grounded in a fuller understanding of the history of immigration detention and its impacts on migrants.[6] Change of this nature will, however, take time, and the people who have migrated or who need to migrate cannot afford to wait. This chapter therefore primarily considers the types of actions that can be taken now to disrupt harmful, dehumanizing policies. How can Christians begin to take responsibility and offer reparations for the ways the United States, aided by Christian theology, has contributed to the causes of migration?

This chapter proposes three areas of application: conceptual shifts, practice, and policies. At the level of conceptual shift, there is a broader need to reframe the way US citizens think about immigration and about the people who cross the US border. This conceptual shift will necessarily include (or bring about) changes in policy or in policy advocacy. This chapter ends by outlining some basic contours of what more just immigration policies should look like in order to guide Christians as they consider what sorts of policies to advocate for in the public sphere. These policy proposals highlight the need for concrete reparations.

6. García Hernández, *Migrating to Prison*.

This chapter's main focus, however, is an exploration of what churches, Christian organizations, and individual Christians[7] ought to be doing day to day if migration is approached and understood through a responsibility framework.

It is important to make a few points with regard to posture and method at the outset. First, this book is intentionally ecumenical. Therefore, the word "church" is used in its broadest sense, to signify the people of God. Second, whatever churches and individual Christians do, it must be done always in partnership with migrants, letting them lead and dictate the terms. Estes's articulation of resistance movements highlights that the people most affected by US colonialism have been resisting from the beginning, whether or not that work has always been visible on the surface. We cannot partake in work to build justice without acknowledging this history. Any work done in the service of those who migrate must be undertaken with a clear understanding of migrants as capable agents navigating and often intentionally standing in defiance of a system that has largely failed them. Churches and Christians may walk with migrants in this fight, but US citizens, especially white US citizens, must remember our place in it is not primarily as leaders.[8]

Third, churches can and should work to interrupt sinful and unjust laws. This is proper work for Christians in an unjust world. Christians, especially white Christians who benefit from a certain amount of privilege, ought to disrupt injustices that go against the values of our faith. A responsibility framework establishes such disruption of harm as *owed* because US citizens have benefited from the systems that have necessitated migration, because the US immigration system has failed to protect or promote the dignity of those who migrate, and perhaps especially because Christianity has played such a role in creating and/or sustaining the myths and ideologies that have created injustice. Christians are responsible for the legacy of manifest destiny and the lasting effects of the frontier myth. We are responsible for the ways in which the upholding of law and order in the name of Christian values has protected the interests of some at the expense of others. Additionally, we are responsible for the ways in which the ongoing legacy of manifest destiny and the frontier myth has contributed and continues to contribute to push and pull factors driving migration.[9] Using our

7. We might also include people of goodwill, who may also find the proposals offered in this book compelling or helpful.

8. This is not to say the church has no role in sharing insights or resources with the world but that we must do so from a posture of humility, especially given the harms Christianity has caused or been complicit in throughout history.

9. For example, consider Roberto Goizueta's argument linking the frontier myth to economic and political expansion into Latin America, which chapter 2 showed to be directly related to the formation of migration patterns into the US.

privilege to interrupt injustice is one of the ways in which Christians, especially white, US citizen Christians, can take responsibility.

Finally, churches ought to offer better narratives related to the founding of this nation, US actions abroad, and the reasons people migrate. For example, there have been movements in some denominations to denounce the doctrine of discovery and Christian participation in manifest destiny. Churches need to provide better (truer) narratives to interrupt the myths of the nation. This is not necessarily about churches offering history lessons, although there are many ways that the stories of US history are shared in churches. Rather, by better narratives, I have in mind the deeper types of stories we tell about the way the world is or should be. Manifest destiny offers a story of how the world ought to be and makes claims about what is fundamentally true (the US is destined by God to conquer the continent). Christianity has better, truer stories to tell about God, the world, and the powers of empire that can undercut harmful US narratives. We have a responsibility to tell these stories, even (perhaps especially) if it puts us in conflict with US interests. Chapter 5 highlighted Roberto Goizueta's argument that the church will often be in conflict with empire. Insofar as the United States is and has been imperialistic in nature and to the degree that its actions and beliefs have been counter to God's kin-dom, there should be a difference between what the United States projects as its doctrine and what the church teaches, something that can help Christians begin to question history as it has been told to us and the future toward which we might direct ourselves.

Chapter 5 outlined a vision of ecclesiology in which the church is called to repentance and conversion in the face of social sin. This is done out of solidarity to those most harmed by it in order to build inclusive, just communities that offer glimpses of a better way of being together. The following case studies are offered as examples of what this might look like on the ground.

Practical Proposals for Christian Communities

In order to consider what practical actions Christian communities might take in response to migration in the United States, this section examines four case studies that spotlight situations in which action is being taken that exemplifies the principles of the moral framework established throughout this book. The hope is that they can help guide Christian communities as they consider the types of praxis in which they themselves might engage. In outlining these exemplars, this section will also highlight how their actions fit the four ecclesiological themes established in the previous chapter as well as what further proposals their insights warrant.

This chapter's particular focus on grassroots community action, rather than solely on policy change, is intentional. Tejana theologian Neomi De Anda cautions that a focus on policy change alone is not sufficient. To foster real change, Christians must begin by considering what she calls "the logic of domination." In Christian terms, a tendency toward domination is often rooted in a particular understanding of God's granting of dominion over the natural world to Adam and Eve (Gen 1:26–28), which has at times shaped Christian relationships with land and often with other people. De Anda specifically highlights how this logic of rightful dominance fed into the violent US acquisition of the Americas, which can be linked to this book's discussion of manifest destiny and the frontier myth. What De Anda is articulating, therefore, is a harmful pattern of relating to people and land as things to be dominated rather than subjects with whom to foster right relationships. It is because this logic of dominance is so deeply embedded in the US psyche, as chapter 2 argued, that policy is not the sole nor even necessarily the first thing that needs radical transformation in order to provide justice for migrants. De Anda calls instead for a more comprehensive transformation of our hearts and minds as well as our ways of thinking and acting. She calls Christians to consider the ways the logic of domination shapes our ways of relating to other people, to the land, and to God, so that we may begin to shift away from these habits and holistically commit ourselves to more just patterns of relating.[10]

The following case studies represent examples of how we might begin to reshape our ways of relating to one another. In addition, they each highlight particular Christian values explored in chapter 5, showing what it can look like to live out these ideas in concrete reality.

El Gran Paro Estadounidense

On May 1, 2006, Latine workers, activists, and others "initiated the largest general strike in the history of the Americas."[11] El Gran Paro Estadounidense, also called the Great American Strike or A Day Without Immigrants, was organized and attended by "immigrants' rights groups, undocumented and documented migrants, school children, workers in industries dominated by immigrants—notably agriculture, construction, catering—plus anti-war protesters and others."[12] Organizers encouraged people to take to the streets, to boycott shops, and to skip school. The goal was to make a statement about the contribution immigrants make to the US economy, explicitly including the millions of

10. "El Paso: One Year Later," *The Commonweal Podcast*, July 31, 2020, https://tinyurl.com/nhft6t6j. The logic of domination is one of the stories Christianity might counter with better stories about how we ought to relate to one another (and to the land) in light of God.

11. Ortiz, *African American and Latinx History*, 163.

12. Dan Glaister and Ewen MacAskill, "US Counts Cost of Day without Immigrants," *Guardian*, May 1, 2006, https://www.theguardian.com/world/2006/may/02/usa.topstories3.

undocumented migrants working and living in the United States. This movement represented a public melding of two deeply related causes: workers' rights and justice for migrants. It was also heralded as "the emergence of a powerful Latino political voice angry at a system which they say judges them good enough to work in the US but not good enough to be citizens." Protests took place in over fifty US cities, some boasting crowds of up to four hundred thousand participants.[13]

This strike had a wide-reaching impact. Students walked out of school, and "meatpacking, garment manufacturing, port transportation, trucking, and food service in many parts of the country" were forced to shut down and turn away customers. Paul Ortiz notes that this initial action launched a new movement that took seriously the concerns and needs of workers and everyday people.[14] This movement was rooted in an understanding that neoliberalism (an outgrowth of manifest destiny and the frontier myth) is a threat to the lives and flourishing of not only Latine workers but also immigrants of all sorts, Black people, and others who are marginalized in the United States. The organizers intentionally formed alliances across race and class lines, realizing that promoting the rights of immigrants was an issue that spanned beyond the Latine community. Partnerships were built between Palestinians and Mexicans, undocumented students and workers, those fighting against unequal educational access and those fighting for better wages, and among various countries experiencing aggressive US foreign policy. Leaders insisted that the movement's longevity and success hinged on its commitment to diversity and its ability to connect people with a wide spectrum of experiences and needs together to work for common purposes. This commitment to intersectionality seems to have been productive. Ortiz writes, "Less than a decade after the big strike, workers chanting 'fight for fifteen [dollars] and a union!' had joined forces with a reinvigorated Black freedom movement to demand an end to labor exploitation, police violence, and US imperialism."[15] Because of the commitment to diversity and understanding the interconnected nature of injustices, the movement has been able to address a wide range of related concerns since the initial strike.

Workers' rights have naturally been at the forefront. The movement sought to build networks of leaders and supporters who could be rallied to put pressure on corporations and elected officials to promote and protect workers' rights. In the aftermath of the strike there was increased participation in unions as the potential power of these groups became evident. Furthermore, some organizers and participants focused on enhancing recognition of unseen workers,

13. Glaister and MacAskill, "US Counts Cost."

14. Ortiz, *African American and Latinx History*, 163, 173–74.

15. Ortiz, *African American and Latinx History*, 175, 163.

the "ghosts" who clean buildings and prepare food, hoping the visibility of their humanity would aid their fight for better wages and working conditions.[16]

Immigration reform has also been a key issue. The initial strike was planned in the context of organizing in opposition to Congressman Jim Sensenbrenner's 2005 Border Protection, Anti-Terrorism, and Illegal Immigration Act, which sought to make undocumented migration and the aid of undocumented migrants a felony. While this act ultimately failed, it highlighted the extreme vulnerability of immigrant workers and further solidified the link between the fight for workers' rights and the fight for just immigration reform. Additionally, the movement leaders recognized that rampant voter disenfranchisement, particularly in communities of color, paved the way for the implementation of policies that disproportionately affected Black people, Indigenous people, and other people of color as well as people experiencing poverty. To combat this, organizations such as We Are America Alliance "launched naturalization and voter registration drives."[17] The intentional intersectionality of the movement's origins has allowed it to evolve in this way.

Ortiz argues that the "larger currents of protest" this movement encapsulated may point the way to a more just future built on a "tide of grassroots freedom movements and the ability of people throughout the hemisphere to draw inspiration from each other's struggles." Ortiz's vision of the future, linked as it is to the concrete struggles of marginalized people fighting for justice, can help direct Christian communities aiming to work for justice and right relationships. The 2006 strike built explicitly on a history of resistance that has existed long before the strike began. For example, its formation was indebted to a 2001 coalition of Black and Brown activists in North Carolina who organized a Juneteenth event celebrating "the unity of Black and Latino workers in the new movement for justice in the south." The event focused on issues of common concern such as an end to unjust economic policies that forced workers to migrate, the rights of workers to form unions, a living wage, reparations, and an end to racial profiling. Ortiz notes that "African American and Latinx organizers are drawing on the lessons of history to build momentum for social justice movements."[18] This method of building on history, understood as both a history of interlinking

16. Ortiz, *African American and Latinx History*, 175–76, 172.

17. Ortiz, *African American and Latinx History*, 170–72, 164–65, 174. This organizing around voter engagement and turnout can be linked to President Barack Obama's election. In 2008, 67 percent of Latine voters chose Obama over Senator John McCain, and in 2012 Latine voters favored Obama over Mitt Romney by a margin of 71 percent. This was achieved in the face of reports that speculated that Latine communities would never vote for a Black man, highlighting the importance of the movement's commitment to uniting people under common causes. Ortiz, *African American and Latinx History*, 177.

18. Ortiz, *African American and Latinx History*, 181–84, 171.

oppressions and ongoing patterns of resistance, is closely related to what Estes understands the Standing Rock Water Protectors to have done. Furthermore, both Estes and Ortiz see these movements as a way of living out the future that is hoped for. This connects well with a Christian eschatological commitment to living into the hope of the kin-dom of God.

For Ortiz, the movement born of El Gran Paro Estadounidense intentionally built coalitions that resisted the ways society attempts to divide and conquer marginalized people. The May Day strike represented a movement that transcends borders, growing out of the diverse but often connected experiences of marginalized people throughout the Western Hemisphere and around the globe. These movements "represent the potential future promise of the Americas," precisely in their commitment to diversity as a strength. Furthermore, the flexibility of this movement, its ability to expand to encompass broadening understandings of what justice requires, pushes society toward a brighter future. As an example, Ortiz points to the partnerships forged between the outgrowths of the strike and movements such as Black Lives Matter. He writes, "Initially focused on police homicides of African Americans, Black Lives Matter quickly connected anti-black violence to other forms of oppression," openly criticizing US imperialism in Latin and Central America and the war on terror in the Middle East, both large drivers of migration.[19]

Ortiz's repeated use of "the Americas" rather than referencing just the United States is also important. Both Ortiz and the movement he is reporting on conceive of justice as a project that includes cross-border imagining and collaboration. The violation of human dignity is just as unjust when it is perpetuated outside US borders and beyond the jurisdiction of US laws. Moreover, US laws cannot be fully just if the community they take into account is solely made up of US citizens. Rather, our sphere of consideration must be broad, recognizing and accounting for relationships beyond US borders. When deciding whether a law or policy is sufficiently just, consideration of its impact only on US citizens is too narrow a lens.

The intentional inclusivity of this movement is in a way echoed in Estes's articulation of the Standing Rock movement. Estes argues that despite historical efforts to pit poor whites and Indigenous people against each other in a battle for limited resources (and despite the existence of long-standing animosities between these groups), Standing Rock saw these groups collaborate toward a shared good. By transforming relationships in this manner, the movement defied societal expectations and in doing so proclaimed future possibilities.[20] While neither El Gran Paro Estadounidense nor Standing Rock

---

19. Ortiz, *African American and Latinx History*, 173, 182–83.

20. Estes, *Our History Is the Future*, 7.

was an explicitly Christian movement, this attention to inclusivity and to redefining relationships offers an example of what it might look like to live out the Christian commitment to community explored in chapter 5. Resisting the patterns of relating into which we have been conditioned by dominant US society, rooted in colonialism and domination, we can instead forge relationships across the lines meant to divide us, recognize shared interests, and take responsibility for one another by joining in each other's struggles and fights. We can do this in particular through participation in movements like El Gran Paro Estadounidense and Standing Rock. This is a fundamentally Christian thing to do.

Both movements were also organized and led by the communities most affected by the injustices they were fighting against, another important connection that can guide church communities working for justice. Ortiz writes, "An African American and Latinx history of the United States teaches us that the self-activity of the most oppressed is key to liberty in the future of the Americas."[21] Churches, especially congregations and parishes that are predominantly white citizens, ought to be careful to take our cues and direction from those already leading in the movement and to work for liberation as it is defined by the communities in need of liberation. Maintaining such a posture keeps us from recreating colonial dynamics of domination by allowing oppressed communities to define the terms of their own liberation. In this way, we can live into more Christian models of human relationality, grounded in humility and a radical love that makes space for the most excluded. Thus, El Gran Paro Estadounidense, while not a Christian movement as such, is a helpful example of one form Christian reparative action can take.

El Paso, Texas

In the late 1970s, Ruben Garcia and a group of other young Catholics in El Paso, Texas, were looking for ways to live meaningful lives of faith in solidarity with poor and marginalized people. During their discernment, they encountered a young man experiencing homelessness who had been turned away from a homeless shelter because he lacked immigration papers. Garcia explains, "Of the two shelters that existed, neither accepted undocumented people. So, in 1978 in El Paso, we asked ourselves: 'What are the groups of people that God would identify with?' The answer was, probably, the undocumented."[22] Out of that realization, the group founded Annunciation House, a shelter for migrants in El Paso, in 1978.

21. Ortiz, *African American and Latinx History*, 184.

22. Gus Bova, "Shelter Director Ruben Garcia on How Struggling Nonprofits Carry the Load of the Migrant 'Crisis,'" *Texas Observer*, June 24, 2019, https://www.texasobserver.org/crisis-management-el-paso-interview-annunciation-house/.

The shelter's service to migrants has shifted over time. Initially, they provided shelter and services to undocumented migrants in the community. Since 2014, when the border was redefined by increased numbers of Central American asylum seekers who turn themselves in rather than attempting to evade Border Patrol agents, the shelter has come to primarily aid these asylum seekers after their release from ICE custody. Once at Annunciation House, they receive clothing, a shower, food, and aid contacting relatives and organizing travel to their intended destination within the United States to await their court dates.[23] In addition, the organization also participates in various education and advocacy projects. All of these efforts are explicitly rooted in faith, specifically the tenets of Catholic social teaching, such as solidarity and the preferential option for the poor.[24]

For decades, Annunciation House sheltered undocumented migrants and asylum seekers, sometimes by the hundreds, expanding from three central buildings to a network consisting of twenty-five hospitality sites, including hotels and church buildings. In April 2019, the organization purchased a 125,000-foot warehouse in order to keep up with the rising need, having taken in a record 825 people in one day in late March. That same year, however, the Trump administration began rolling out a series of policies aimed at constraining asylum policy and drastically reducing asylum seekers' access to US land and the rights afforded to them once on it. On January 25, 2019, the Department of Homeland Security introduced "Migrant Protection Protocols" (MPP), also known as the Remain in Mexico Policy. Under MPP, border patrol was allowed to send non-Mexican asylum seekers to Mexico to await their court dates. This policy, touted as a way to ensure resources were funneled to "legitimate" asylees, resulted in a full-blown crisis on the Mexican side of the border. Those turned away by this policy were forced to attempt to find shelter in a country they did not know, often ending up in very dangerous neighborhoods, where they faced assault, robbery, kidnapping, and other dangers. Furthermore, they were cut off from access to legal counsel or protection, afforded little transparency into their US immigration proceedings, and denied any "meaningful access to due process in the United States."[25] Between January 2019 and February 2021 (when the Biden administration initially announced the end of the program), at least sixty thousand people were subject to this program.[26]

---

23. Bova, "Shelter Director Ruben Garcia."

24. Annunciation House homepage, last updated August 6, 2020, https://annunciationhouse.org/.

25. "Q&A: Trump Administration's 'Remain in Mexico' Program," Human Rights Watch, January 29, 2020, https://www.hrw.org/news/2020/01/29/qa-trump-administrations-remain-mexico-program.

26. Kelsey Ables, "U.S. Judge Halts Biden Attempt to End 'Remain in Mexico' Policy, *Washington Post*, December 15, 2022, https://www.washingtonpost.com/nation/2022/12/15/remain-in-mexico-policy-immigration-texas-judge/.

In the wake of MPP's implementation, the number of asylum seekers entering the United States slowed to a trickle. In July 2019, Annunciation House was taking in 100–150 a day, significantly fewer people than they had been serving a few months prior. That their recently acquired warehouse, stocked with food, medicine, and cots for sleeping, now sat nearly empty while thousands struggled to survive mere miles away in Ciudad Juarez[27] underscores the extreme cruelty of the policy, cutting off people in need from those willing and able to assist.

It is worth pausing here briefly to consider the legal battle over the ending of MPP. The Biden administration announced the end of MPP in February 2021. On June 1 of that year, a memo officially ending the program was issued by the secretary of homeland security. However, both Texas and Missouri filed lawsuits against the program ending, and in August 2021 Matthew Kacsmaryk, a Fifth Circuit federal judge in Texas, ordered MPP to be reinstated, arguing that its ending was a violation of the Immigration and Nationality Act. The Department of Justice appealed this decision, and on June 30, 2022, the US Supreme Court ruled that the termination of MPP was not a violation of the Immigration and Nationality Act and that Kacsmaryk did not have the authority to block the termination of the program. The Biden administration moved forward with ending the program in August 2022.[28] However, in December 2022, Kacsmaryk issued a stay on the termination, arguing that the policy had been improperly terminated and that the federal government had not sufficiently considered the impacts of undocumented border crossing.[29] As of September 2023, the ultimate fate of the program remains in a state of limbo. That this legal battle has spanned years while vulnerable people are left waiting, often in dangerous

27. Nick Miroff, "Momentary Border Reprieve Rests on a Rickety Foundation, as U.S. Immigration Policies Are Put to the Test," *Washington Post*, July 13, 2019, https://tinyurl.com/2vm8atf2.

28. Elizabeth Carlson, Luis Guerra, and Tania Guerrero, "Supreme Court Holds That Biden Administration's Termination of the Migrant Protection Protocols Did Not Violate the Immigration and Nationality Act Authors," CLINIC, August 24, 2022, https://tinyurl.com/wz7z96vk; "Biden Administration in the Clear to End MPP," American Immigration Council, last modified August 9, 2022, https://www.americanimmigrationcouncil.org/news/biden-administration-clear-end-mpp.

29. Kacsmaryk used the term "illegal border crossing." However, asylum law holds that seekers have a right to cross the border without documentation in pursuit of asylum. I contest Kacsmaryk's casting of asylum seekers as illegal border crossers. The nature of asylum is that those seeking it are or understand themselves to be in acute danger and may not be able to wait in line at an official port of entry. They therefore need only be on US land and request asylum, whether they entered through official channels or not. International Rescue Committee, "Is It Legal to Cross the U.S. Border to seek Asylum?," last modified May 10, 2023, https://tinyurl.com/5n6vx6bk.

situations, highlights the persistent inability of US policy to create just situations for migrants and indicates why more comprehensive change is needed in order to ensure justice.

The impact of MPP was also in some ways exacerbated by the Covid-19 pandemic, especially Title 42. Invoking the Public Health Service act of 1944, the Trump administration began in March 2020 to place significant limits on migrants' access to the United States. In the name of public health, Title 42 allowed "immigration authorities to quickly expel migrants and [deny] entry to asylum seekers," without a hearing.[30] Though it was a Trump-era policy, Title 42 continued and was expanded under Joe Biden.[31] The Center for Disease Control and Prevention announced intentions to end the program in May 2022, and it was scheduled to end in December of that same year. However, some lawmakers were resistant to the end of the program, and a legal battle ensued. It was not until May 2023, when the Supreme Court dismissed the case, that the policy was actually ended.[32] The impact of these laws on migrants, and on organizations such as Annunciation House that seek to partner with them, has been immense. Under Title 42, at least 2.4 million migrants were expelled. Additionally, we can once again see the way the US legal and political system can leave vulnerable people waiting while politicians fight legal battles over these policies.

After Title 42 ended, the Biden administration replaced it with the "Circumvention of Lawful Pathways" rule. Like MPP, this rule presumes most migrants who travel through a third country before arriving in Mexico to be ineligible for asylum. Opportunities to overcome this presumption of ineligibility are limited. The rule also penalizes asylum seekers who do not enter the country at an official port of entry. Before its implementation, it was predicted that this policy would push migrants who are most vulnerable into dangerous situations. Indeed, the percentage of migrants whose asylum claims are rejected

---

30. Deepa Shivaram, "What to Know about Title 42, the Trump-Era Policy Now Central to the Border Debate," NPR, April 24, 2022, https://www.npr.org/2022/04/24/1094070784/title-42-policy-meaning; Brett Samuels, "Here's What the Supreme Court's Decision on Title 42 Means," The Hill, December 28, 2022, https://thehill.com/homenews/administration/3791054-heres-what-the-supreme-courts-decision-on-title-42-means/.

31. This expansion was due to an agreement with Mexico. While Venezuelan asylum seekers were initially excluded from the Title 42, they were added to the policy in October 2022 when Mexico agreed to accept them into their own asylum programs. Priscilla Totiyapungprasert, "Annunciation House Helps Undocumented Immigrants Apply for Asylum," El Paso Matters, January 20, 2023, https://elpasomatters.org/2023/01/20/el-paso-migrants-apply-for-asylum-with-annunciation-house/.

32. Shivaram, "What to Know"; Vanessa Romo, Joel Rose, and Marisa Peñaloza, "Title 42, a COVID-Era Halt on Asylum Applications, Has Ended. Here's What to Expect," NPR, May 12, 2023, https://www.npr.org/2023/05/11/1175378000/title-42-expires-asylum-us-border-texas.

has more than doubled under the new rule, increasing the chances that some will be returned to extremely dangerous situations.[33] While rhetoric around immigration and asylum often differs, lawmakers on the left have often been just as guilty of unjust and harmful immigration policy as those on the right.

Annunciation House provides an example for Christian communities to follow, especially given the continued failures of US policy. First, the project arose out of a specific, local need that presented itself: the lack of resources such as homeless shelters for undocumented people in the city. Organizing around this specific need as it presented itself allowed Annunciation House to make a concrete impact on the El Paso community. Church communities interested in building just communities would do well to follow Garcia's example of presenting himself as open and available to live out his faith and responding flexibly to concrete needs that present themselves to him. Furthermore, Garcia's ability to know and respond to this need was dependent on his presence in and relationships with the El Paso community. Without building relationships in our local communities, especially relationships with those who may be marginalized, it becomes difficult to be available in the way Garcia was. Church communities ought to commit themselves to building real relationships by being present in their communities, seeking humbly to make connections with those who might be vulnerable, plugging into existing networks of care and support, and being open to any needs that may present themselves.

Annunciation House's commitment to sustaining relationships continues in their methods of providing aid. Volunteers live at the hospitality sites with the guests, providing accompaniment and companionship that helps build relationships. Providing aid in the absence of such relationship building fails to foster real solidarity, which chapter 5 established as a main tenet of Christian relationality. Furthermore, being in close relationship with the community being served allows the organization to adjust as new needs arise. Initially, they served largely undocumented people turned away from homeless shelters. More recently, need has shifted as the population crossing the border has become primarily asylum seekers. Asylum seekers need different resources from undocumented migrants, including different forms of legal aid and help getting transportation to their final destination. In working with asylum seekers, Annunciation House has also

33. Alexandra Villarreal, "The US Asylum Rule Replacing Title 42 Is Strict—Here's What We Know," *Guardian*, May 15, 2023, https://www.theguardian.com/us-news/2023/may/15/explainer-strict-asylum-rules-replacing-title-42; Nick Miroff, "Biden Toughened Asylum Screening. It Won't Contain a New Border Surge," *Washington Post*, March 17, 2024, https://www.washingtonpost.com/immigration/2024/03/17/biden-migrants-asylum-new-restrictions/. The American Civil Liberties Union sued the administration, arguing that the new restrictions are unlawful. Their suit was supported by the union representing asylum officers, which also argues that the restrictions violate US law as well as the professional ethics of asylum officers. As of March 2024, litigation on this case was paused in the interest of negotiating a settlement.

developed a working relationship with ICE, which brings migrants to hospitality sites after they are processed. They continued to undergo changes as the Trump administration halted the flow of asylum seekers into the country with MPP and Title 42, and in the shifting legal landscape of recent years.

These changes also represent a practice of solidarity. Initially, Annunciation House had a poor relationship with ICE as they housed and stood with undocumented people. As the needs of the community shifted, solidarity with asylum seekers meant a shift to more cooperation with immigration officials. Additionally, as policies such as MPP, Title 42, and the Circumvention of Lawful Pathways rule have limited migrants' access to the United States and to many of the services Annunciation House offered, the organization had to be flexible and find different ways to serve. Relationship building helps to make that possible. Commitment to building relationships and the ability to be flexible as needs change has allowed Annunciation House to provide for migrants' actual needs, highlighting the relationship between building solidarity and remaining flexible. Both will be necessary for Christian communities to be able to meet the needs of migrants in their own communities.

Annunciation House is far from the only organization in El Paso serving migrants and fighting for justice for border communities. The city boasts many such organizations, often interconnected in a network of support and collaboration. La Mujer Obrera, a community-organizing and activist group led by Latina and Indigenous women, is one such organization. Their mission "is to develop and use our creative capacity to express the dignity and diversity of our Mexican heritage, from indigenous Mesoamerican roots to contemporary expressions, and to develop and celebrate our community through economic development, community building, community health and civic engagement."[34] In other words, La Mujer Obrera connects liberation, which in Christian terms we might call salvation, to the survival and thriving of specific communities.

La Mujer Obrera has initiated a number of projects and initiatives aimed at fulfilling this purpose. A core tenet of their approach to activism and political action entails the right and ability of Latine and Indigenous communities to define the terms of their own liberation. To this end, one of their main objectives is to empower low-income women workers, fostering their capacity to self-advocate. This includes ensuring that all organizing is done in a way that is well thought through and intentionally participatory. La Mujer Obrera is also committed to (re)connecting communities to their cultural heritage and to building a vision for the future that is rooted in that heritage. For decades they have hosted "cultural festivals featuring the cuisine and culture of different regions of Mexico," along with "various film screenings, poetry and book readings, and

34. "Our Mission," La Mujer Obrera, accessed December 12, 2020, http://www.mujerobrera.org/.

cultural events featuring local, national, and international artists working in the intersection of art and resistance." On a one-acre piece of land, they maintain a community farm on which they "reclaim ancestral food growing practices."[35] They also run a daycare and learning center committed to preparing children for kindergarten while also fostering their creativity, curiosity, and sense of connection to and respect for the natural world.

Efforts such as the daycare center intentionally provide "meaningful employment for NAFTA-displaced garment workers based on community needs."[36] La Mujer Obrera takes seriously the creation of economic opportunities for Latine and Indigenous communities affected and often displaced by colonialism and capitalist expansionism. In 2001 they opened Café Mayapán, a restaurant that provides employment and training to members of the community and traditional Mexican food to the people of El Paso. Café Mayapán focuses especially on celebrating Mexican heritage by serving unique dishes not found in other restaurants. Alongside the restaurant, the organization also runs a fair-trade import company, selling goods made by Indigenous women from all across Mexico. They established a related network, called Nui Matat Napawika, which links and assists women with small business efforts. Both efforts are intended to support "the right of people to remain in their communities if they choose, to not be displaced from their lands by forced migration," through the fostering of alternative sources of income and stability.[37]

La Mujer Obrera is a clear example of grassroots, community-led organizing. It is envisioned, organized, and implemented by Latina and Indigenous women. Their methodology provides clear examples of what it might look like to center community building, supporting the survival and flourishing of particular cultures and building relationships in spite of the ways the empire tries to divide us. Given commitments to the concrete survival of communities and cultures outlined in chapter 5, Christian communities can learn from such an example. Additionally, they ought to respect and support such efforts and to refrain from imposing Euro-American ideals of progress onto them (inadvertently perpetuating colonial patterns). Churches need to make space for grassroots, migrant-led justice efforts. Ideally, they would build relationships and partnerships with such groups, joining in their community building, and thus be in positions that would allow them to offer any support that is wanted. Less formally, Christians might consider how their purchasing decisions support or compete with these sorts

35. "Social Enterprises," La Mujer Obrera, accessed December 12, 2020, http://www.mujerobrera.org/.

36. "Social Enterprises."

37. "Social Enterprises."

of grassroots efforts. Dining at Café Mayapán, for example, supports La Mujer Obrera's work in a concrete and noninvasive way.

The focus of La Mujer Obrera's work can also guide church communities. The organization works for the survival, liberation, and flourishing of Latine and Indigenous communities through political activism, education, and celebration. In chapter 5, we underscored Miguel Díaz's insistence that such activity, aimed at the liberation and preservation of communities and their specific cultures, is the work of salvation. How can church communities support this salvific work? How can pastors frame salvation in such a way as to make this connection evident? These are some of the questions the work of La Mujer Obrera calls Christian communities to consider.

One final program worth exploring in El Paso is the Encuentro Project. The product of a collaboration between the Central and Southern US Province of Jesuits, the US and Mexican Marist Brothers, and the Hope Border Institute, the Encuentro Project offers what it calls a "ministry of encounter." The program fosters encounter by offering housing and programming to students and church parishes that wish to better understand the realities of the US-Mexico border. This form of ministry was the vision of Father Rafael Garcia, SJ, the program's director, in response to Pope Francis's call to create a culture that overcomes fear and indifference through encounters with migrants. The hope is that this weeklong immersion experience in the El Paso/Ciudad Juárez community gives participants "a greater understanding of the complex history and present reality of migration" and "inspire[s] participants to challenge the borders in their own communities that push immigrants to the margins."[38] In doing so, the Encuentro Project participates in truth telling, introducing participants to the often untold truths of US actions and their impacts on border communities and people in Central and Latin America. Moreover, the Encuentro Project does this by providing space for migrants themselves to tell their own experiences of the impact of US policies on their home countries and their experiences with the US immigration system. This is very much in line with the role of churches as truth-telling communities.

Pope Francis has called for the cultivation of a "culture of encounter" in which people reach out to one another across barriers and divides in order to create dialogue and friendship. In particular, the pope encourages us to

38. Mary Baudouin, "The Encuentro Project: Encountering the Other on the El Paso/Juarez Border," Jesuits Central and Southern, accessed January 20, 2021, https://www.jesuitscentralsouthern.org/stories/the-encuentro-project-encountering-the-other-on-the-el-paso-juarez-border/. Immersion experiences such as Encuentro differ from service trips in that they aim not at a paternalistic goal of fixing or helping but rather at fostering new relationships and learning. These programs are still open to the pitfalls of more traditional service or mission-style trips but can offer a helpful reframing.

encounter those who are most marginalized.[39] At a 2013 Vigil of Pentecost, the pope said,

> Ask yourselves this question: how often is Jesus inside and knocking at the door to be let out, to come out? And we do not let him out because of our own need for security, because so often we are locked into ephemeral structures that serve solely to make us slaves and not free children of God. In this "stepping out" it is important to be ready for encounter. For me this word is very important. Encounter with others. Why? Because faith is an encounter with Jesus, and we must do what Jesus does: encounter others. We live in a culture of conflict, a culture of fragmentation, a culture in which I throw away what is of no use to me, a culture of waste . . . and with our faith we must create a "culture of encounter", a culture of friendship, a culture in which we find brothers and sisters, in which we can also speak with those who think differently, as well as those who hold other beliefs, who do not have the same faith.[40]

Francis draws on a well-established Christian tradition of connecting encounters with marginalized people to encountering Jesus, and his call for fostering a theologically rooted culture of encounter fits well with the ecclesiological vision of chapter 5. Encounters that aim at authentic dialogue and friendship promote stronger communities. Dialogue allows for truth telling that breaks through the myths we believe about each other and the ideologies that help perpetuate oppression. Encounter across division creates community that rejects the divisions a sinful society strives to impose, the culture of fragmentation Francis cites. True solidarity requires actual relationships, a culture of friendship. Peruvian liberation theologian Gustavo Gutiérrez argues that true work for liberation, true solidarity with the poor and oppressed, requires establishing actual, lasting friendship with them.[41] Solidarity happens when

39. John L. Allen Jr., "Francis and the 'Culture of Encounter,'" National Catholic Reporter, December 20, 2013, https://www.ncronline.org/blogs/ncr-today/francis-and-culture-encounter.

40. Pope Francis, "Vigil of Pentecost with the Ecclesial Movements: Address of the Holy Father," Vatican, May 18, 2013, http://www.vatican.va/content/francesco/en/speeches/2013/may/documents/papa-francesco_20130518_veglia-pentecoste.html.

41. Gustavo Gutiérrez, "Expanding the View," in *Expanding the View: Gustavo Gutiérrez and the Future of Liberation Theology*, ed. Marc H. Ellis and Otto Maduro (Maryknoll, NY: Orbis Books, 1990), 18. Gutiérrez's work, while not explicitly drawn on elsewhere in this book, represents an important moment for Euro-American theology's encounter with the theological and religious reflections of Latin Americans specifically and marginalized communities more broadly. It is therefore a helpful touchpoint for our consideration of encounter and solidarity.

we truly share our lives with each other. This is what Francis calls the world to, and all of the efforts in El Paso highlighted in this section aim at authentic solidarity of this sort.

Encuentro Project programming includes some form of direct encounter with migrants, asylum seekers, or refugees, often through work in a shelter. Various site visits throughout El Paso and Juarez are offered to provide immersion into the realities of the El Paso–Juarez border community. Its focus on education highlights the factors that contribute to migration, especially as those factors are related to US action, and the tenets of Catholic social teaching that are especially relevant to a faith-based response to migration. The Encuentro Project depends on and participates in a vast existing network of migrants and allies in the El Paso area. By inviting faith groups to encounter this network, Encuentro actively expands it, building community that spans the whole of the United States. This work of inviting people into encounters with migrants also creates the possibility for people to develop relationships of solidarity. Solidarity requires first that we know in some real sense those with whom we aim at being in solidarity. Encuentro provides opportunities for faith communities to begin to know migrants, opening up the possibility of true friendship and solidarity that has the power to transform hearts and influence behavior. Moreover, Encuentro does this work in a way that aims at partnering with (or accompanying) and respecting border communities rather than exploiting their stories or invading their spaces. Christian communities ought to take part in such opportunities to encounter migrants.

El Paso and Juarez present a particularly helpful context in which to consider the makeup of borders. Standing high above the city at the Scenic Drive Overlook park, it becomes hard to tell where one city ends and the other begins, especially at night, when the cities are just seas of lights. Being in either city, "one gets a sense of being in two worlds, two cultures, two realities at the same time and in the same place."[42] Through their very existence, El Paso and Juarez unsettle the legitimacy of US borders. The networks of solidarity, care, and community building, driven by the needs and visions of these cities' most marginalized people, build on this to actively reject that legitimacy. They offer a vision for what inclusive, just, cross-border community building modeled after the radical love of Jesus might look like.

Churches committed to participating in the creation of responsible and reparative justice for migrants would do well to start with a humble posture of openness and availability, ready for and actively seeking out encounters with migrants and others who continue to be harmed by US colonialism. These experiences, both as encounters with marginalized people and as encounters with Jesus,

42. Baudouin, "Encuentro Project."

have the capacity to open our hearts and spark conversion, pulling us out of the logic of domination and colonialism and into the kin-dom of God.

Sanctuary Communities

In the 1970s and 1980s, US-funded "dirty wars" wreaked havoc in Central America, causing a large number of migrants to seek asylum and refuge in the United States. Chapter 2 outlined how US intervention and exploitation drove migrants north, where those who did not fit the agenda of the nation's anticommunist foreign policy were largely denied asylum, considered deportable after failing their "credible fear" screening.[43] By 1980, five hundred to one thousand asylum seekers from Guatemala and El Salvador were being deported each month. As the dirty wars raged on, US involvement with them began gaining notice among US citizens. Religious communities became especially aware of the human-rights abuses taking place after the death of Salvadoran archbishop Oscar Romero.

In the wake of this growing awareness and driven by scriptural injunctions to welcome the stranger, church communities in the United States and Central America founded a sanctuary movement. Christians from the United States "crossed the border to help undocumented Central Americans enter" and "traveled to observe conditions in refugee camps in Honduras and El Salvador."[44] Congregations became places of shelter for those to whom the US government had denied asylum. A network made up of more than 160 houses of worship and community organizers, aided at times by journalists, facilitated the movement of several thousand undocumented asylum seekers around the United States, supporting them with housing and necessities and helping them gain a platform from which to raise awareness of their plight. Historian Rachel Ida Buff writes,

> An anonymous article in the professional journal *Social Work* described the "early days" of the sanctuary movement, when advocates focused on raising monies to release migrants from prison. Gradually, sanctuary workers and migrants realized that even when they were successful in freeing prisoners, Central American migrants were still considered undocumented, with few rights or economic prospects. This realization led to bolder actions, like a "freedom train" in which undocumented

43. Rachel Ida Buff, "Sanctuary Everywhere," *Radical History Review* 2019, no. 135 (2019): 25, https://doi.org/10.1215/01636545-7607809. Buff also notes that policy discrimination based on nationality and/or race also "corresponds with the long history of white supremacist immigration policy that originates in late nineteenth-century Asian exclusion, evolving into national-origin quotas and restrictive border policies throughout the twentieth century" (26).

44. Buff, "Sanctuary Everywhere," 27.

> Central Americans traveled from city to city, publicizing their situations. As the anonymous attribution suggests, advocates recognized the threat they faced by aiding undocumented migrants. Section 274 of the McCarran-Walter Act criminalized transporting "illegal aliens" across the border or within the country, as well as "concealing, harboring, sheltering," or even "encouraging" undocumented individuals. Sanctuary workers faced penalties: fines of $2,000 and up to five years of incarceration for each individual assisted.[45]

Sanctuary workers understood that they were putting themselves in potentially costly opposition to US foreign policy and US legal systems. The movement became a target for FBI surveillance as it subverted federal law in order to be in solidarity with those fleeing US-sanctioned violence. In 1985–1986, eleven workers, many of them clergy, were put on trial. Eight were convicted.[46] Solidarity can come at a cost.

The sanctuary movement embodies many of the ecclesiological themes identified in chapter 5. In particular, it represents a form of radical solidarity. Buff reports, "Sanctuary workers invoked Archbishop Romero's invocation that 'accompanying' the struggles of the poor constituted holy work, asserting the moral necessity of international solidarity across borders of nation, race, and class."[47] Sanctuary volunteers consciously enter into a space of shared vulnerability with undocumented immigrants, placing themselves on the side of the oppressed and in direct, concrete opposition to a US immigration system they consider unjust. The eleven workers put on trial are evidence that solidarity with migrants requires a willingness to become vulnerable, to take real risks. To a degree, sanctuary workers extend a bit of their privilege as US citizens (especially white citizens) to help protect undocumented people. But even as they utilize their privilege in this way, they also make themselves vulnerable by opposing the systems that harm migrants. They make an active choice to oppose systems of power in the United States, putting themselves at risk. Christian communities committed to justice must consider how they can be in concrete solidarity in this way. It may mean offering physical sanctuary but should always be led by the professed needs of migrants in their communities and achieved through the establishment of real relationships.

Furthermore, sanctuary efforts consciously build community in an intentionally cross-border way. Citizens of the United States and of Central American

45. Buff, "Sanctuary Everywhere," 28.

46. Buff, "Sanctuary Everywhere," 29.

47. Buff, "Sanctuary Everywhere," 27.

countries worked together to establish lines of communication, to spread information about abuses taking place in Central America, and to create safe ways to get migrants into the United States and in contact with the legal counsel they needed. The creation of such a community represents a vision of how the world could be if we honored our relationships of responsibility. Sanctuary efforts present society with the question, "What might it look like if the United States began behaving as though it had relatives?" In this way, sanctuary churches become model communities, showing the world what is possible.[48]

Sanctuary movements both relied on and intentionally centered the importance of truth telling. Indeed, truth telling formed the movement, which gained momentum as more churches encountered the stories of those fleeing violence, stories that "exposed the falsity of [the] official line" that depicted asylum seekers as "a menacing coalition of Sandinistas and Soviet apparatchiks."[49] Some North American members of the movement traveled to Central America in order to confirm the accounts of asylum seekers from the region, bringing back affirmative testimony and pressuring media outlets to provide more accurate, extensive, and equitable coverage of the conflicts driving people north. Moreover, the trial of the eleven sanctuary workers highlighted the importance of narrative. The prosecution depicted the actions of the sanctuary workers as "alien smuggling" and referred to the Central Americans involved in the movement as "alien co-conspirators." This language fits a particular narrative the US government was invested in maintaining, one that foisted all responsibility for undocumented migration on to migrants and those who aided them and portrayed the United States as a victim of subterfuge and invasion. That these narrative choices were intentional and calculated is supported by the fact that the prosecution attempted to ban use of the word "refugee" from the trial. In this context, the choice to participate in sanctuary becomes a public rejection of dominant narratives. Catholic theologian Leo Guardado calls sanctuary efforts and the protection of migrants "a form of diplomacy that communicates the truth about persons seeking refuge in

48. Take, for example, Scott Warren, a young man in Arizona whose humanitarian aid to migrants at the border got him arrested and tried for harboring and conspiracy. That the simple act of caring for the blisters on another human's feet is seen as a threat to US security is a sharp indictment of the US immigration system. Warren's humanity and his insistence on caring for others regardless of what empire might say offers a glimpse at how the world could be. See Ryan Devereaux, "Humanitarian Volunteer Scott Warren Reflects on the Borderlands and Two Years of Government Persecution," The Intercept, November 23, 2019, https://theintercept.com/2019/11/23/scott-warren-verdict-immigration-border/. See also Rose Cuison-Villazor and Ulrich Schmiedel, "'No More Deaths.' Religious Liberty as a Defense for Providing Sanctuary for Immigrants," in *Christianity and the Law of Migration*, ed. Silas W. Allard, Kristin E. Heyer, and Raj Nadella (New York: Routledge, 2022), 212–29.

49. Buff, "Sanctuary Everywhere," 29.

the United States."[50] To participate in sanctuary is to enter into dialogue with an unjust US immigration system and propose a better way forward, one that acknowledges the dangers migrants face and aims to protect them.

The sanctuary movement's ability to interrupt false and self-serving US narratives was also rooted in its popularization of sanctuary as a concept. Bringing sanctuary into the public consciousness also brought "the shortcomings of human rights law" into broader consciousness and presented the public with one answer to those shortcomings, an answer that imagined a world beyond the status quo handed down from generations past. That US foreign policy and the US legal system created a need for sanctuary served as an indictment of the nation. Sanctuary in this context is a "moral, political, and legal decision—an act to communicate to legislative bodies their [i.e., participants'] dissatisfaction with current United States Central American policies."[51]

The eight convicted sanctuary workers used their subsequent Supreme Court appeal as an opportunity to articulate their motivations on a public stage, arguing that the rights of asylum seekers, protected by the 1980 Refugee Act, were being violated by US policy. As with the case studies above, this movement explicitly drew on a history of resistance to imperialism that exists in US history. The movement was emboldened to do so from a position of Christian faith by liberation theologians such as Ignacio Ellacuría and Jon Sobrino. The movement was furthermore explicitly and intentionally international in nature, forging cross-border partnerships and envisioning justice in a way that called the international status quo, as well as US-first rhetoric, into question. Even within US borders, the sanctuary movement was diverse. In Chicago, for example, six hundred Black organizers worked to declare sanctuary in the city, and further east the Akwesasne Nation declared sanctuary on its land, which encompasses the border between New York and Canada, working especially to provide legal counsel to Guatemalan Mayans.[52] Both of these examples highlight the interconnected nature of injustice as outlined above in the movement that grew out of the May Day Strike. Justice for immigrants, for Black people, and for Indigenous people are all related because the same systems of white supremacy cause the oppression of these groups.[53]

---

50. Leo Guardado, "Just Peace, Just Sanctuary," in *A Just Peace Ethic Primer: Building Sustainable Peace and Breaking Cycles of Violence*, ed. Eli Sasaran McCarthy (Washington, DC: Georgetown University Press, 2020), 83.

51. Buff, "Sanctuary Everywhere," 29–30, 28.

52. Buff, "Sanctuary Everywhere," 29.

53. Moreover, there are overlaps between these groups. Some migrants are Black, Indigenous, or both. The recognition of the intertwined nature of oppression is also a recognition of shared realities and identities.

Guardado frames sanctuary work as work for just peace. Just peace responds to conflict by looking to root causes, considering how that conflict might (and ought to) be transformed, and commits to actively breaking cycles of violence in order to foster a situation of true peace. Guardado analyzes the realities migrants face—the reasons they leave, the trials they face on their journey, and the reception they receive in the United States (detention and deportation)—and concludes that "unauthorized" migrants face a situation of warfare. Christians, he argues, ought to see this situation as an opportunity for the conversion of violent and unjust circumstances, understanding the church's "task as one of *transforming* the conflict by *protecting* those most affected by the violence of the conflict."[54]

Within a situation in which the warfare and violence migrants face is perpetuated, at least in part, through the legal actions of the state, sanctuary work "is a creative nonviolent response to legalized violence in society." Sanctuary as an activity of just peacebuilding also reimagines what is possible. Guardado writes, "Sanctuary actions are a positive force that begins to imaging and enflesh a more human community in the present."[55] That is, sanctuary is one way of living into the belief that we can and ought to create more just patterns of relationship. This is not simply picturing a more just future but intentionally enfleshing that future, living into it by creating just communities. Sanctuary builds cross-cultural and cross-border communities that explicitly reject the models of relationship promoted by the United States. This is an embodiment of the Christian eschatological vision of inclusive community.

While the original sanctuary movement largely died out in the 1990s, the vision of the movement lived on in the imaginations of those who sought a more just world. In 2007 a New Sanctuary Movement was founded in response to post-9/11 immigration enforcement packaged as national security initiatives. The New Sanctuary Movement draws on the lessons and strategies of the 1980s movement but in a "radically transformed" contemporary context. Sanctuary in the twenty-first century therefore looks considerably different.[56] It is, however, centered on the same basic practice of providing safe spaces for migrants under threat of deportation. In some cases, this has meant housing migrants in church buildings. The practice, which had dwindled with the rest of the original sanctuary movement, saw an expansion "in the waning years of the Obama administration as thousands of largely Central American immigrants

54. Guardado, "Just Peace, Just Sanctuary," 78–83.

55. Guardado, "Just Peace, Just Sanctuary," 78, 87.

56. Buff, "Sanctuary Everywhere," 30.

were deported after having crossed the border" without documentation.[57] The nativist, anti-immigrant attitude and policies of the Trump administration only exacerbated a situation that was already tenuous for the millions of people living undocumented in the nation. In particular, the Trump administration began pursuing a more indiscriminate deportation policy than the Obama administration, which had largely prioritized migrants who had committed crimes (beyond the initial undocumented border crossing).[58]

In response, as of 2018, at least fifty different houses of worship were providing physical sanctuary to migrants facing deportation. One such woman was forty-year old Rosa Gutiérrez Lopez. Originally from El Salvador, Gutiérrez Lopez came to the United States in 2005 and was detained at the border. She was supposed to appear in immigration court but was not aware she needed to confirm her hearing date and missed the court appearance, resulting in a deportation order. Learning of her mistake years later, she contacted ICE and has appeared for regular check-ins since. In October 2018, she was told by ICE to buy herself a plane ticket back to El Salvador and to be out of the country by December 10. Gutiérrez Lopez purchased a ticket but dreaded returning to a country in which she feared for her life. Moreover, she had three children, ages eleven, nine, and six, whom she would either have to leave behind or bring to a country she considered highly dangerous. Her youngest also had Down syndrome, requiring medical care that is difficult to obtain in El Salvador. So instead of getting on the plane, Rosa made the choice to enter sanctuary at Cedar Lane Unitarian Universalist Church in Bethesda, Maryland.[59]

This choice was undertaken in an effort to buy time while her legal counsel worked to get her a stay of deportation. The ability to buy this time by entering sanctuary hinges on a current ICE policy under which entrance into "sensitive" spaces, such as houses of worship, is not encouraged (although, importantly, it is not prohibited).[60] Gutiérrez Lopez's legal team also used this time to work to get her case moved from Texas to Baltimore or Arlington. Where an immigration case is heard can be a strong predictor of whether someone will get a favorable verdict, and so many migrants work with their legal teams to try to

---

57. Arelis R. Hernández, "She Was Supposed to Be Deported, Leaving 3 Children. Instead, She Hid in a Church," *Washington Post*, December 12, 2018, https://tinyurl.com/tbwt3uyx.

58. Miriam Jordan, "Court Widens Scope of Deportations," *New York Times*, June 25, 2022, https://www.nytimes.com/2022/06/25/us/immigration-enforcement-priorities-court.html.

59. Hernández, "She Was Supposed to Be Deported."

60. U.S. Immigration and Customs Enforcement, "FAQ on Sensitive Location and Courthouse Arrests," last updated September 25, 2018, https://www.ice.gov/ero/enforcement/sensitive-loc#wcm-survey-target-id.

move their cases away from where they first entered or were apprehended to a court nearer where they live. Gutiérrez Lopez believed that the Fourth Circuit Court of Appeals in the Baltimore area "has better case law for cases involving gang violence," which could be a benefit to her.[61] Having cases moved closer to where they currently reside also helps ensure that migrants have communities of support with them throughout their trials, which can also influence outcome. For its part, the Cedar Lane community has chosen to act in opposition to what "they deem an amoral U.S. immigration system." They also consider this choice to be an outgrowth of values they have long held, a living out their faith in the concrete. Logistically, along with providing the physical space, volunteers at Cedar Lane also help provide Gutiérrez Lopez with food, supplies and necessities, and protection. They pledged to do so for "as long as it takes."[62] As long as it takes, as it turns out, is no small undertaking. Gutiérrez Lopez was in sanctuary for eighteen months before she was granted a stay of deportation that allows her to move freely around the DC area.[63]

Rosa Sabido, a fifty-three-year-old woman from Mexico, lived in the Mancos United Methodist Church from 2017 until sometime in early 2023.[64] Like Gutierrez Lopez, Sabido has been regularly checking in with ICE when, all of a sudden, they stopped granting her stays of deportation. Her lawyer told her that if she appeared for her next check-in, she would likely be deported, so instead she took refuge at a church. Like the Cedar Lane community, the Mancos community banded together to provide for Sabido's needs. In addition to food, supplies, and shelter, the community also worked to help her maintain emotional and mental health, providing yoga classes, spiritual guidance, and opportunities to teach cooking classes or provide meals for others in the community.[65] Still, Sabido reports that the experience was draining and difficult. Journalist Stephanie McCrummen writes,

61. Leigh Giangreci, "After 18 Months in Sanctuary at a Bethesda Church, This Undocumented Mother Has Been Granted a Stay of Removal," DCist, June 5, 2020, https://dcist.com/story/20/06/05/rosa-gutierrez-lopez-cedar-lane-ice-pandemic/.

62. Hernández, "She Was Supposed to Be Deported."

63. Giangreci, "After 18 Months."

64. As of March 2023, Sabado had been granted a stay of deportation and had left sanctuary. She and members of the church continued to work together to help her gain more permanent status. Chris Clements, "KSJD Local Newscast—March 22, 2023," KSDJ, March 22, 2023, https://www.ksjd.org/podcast/ksjd-local-newscasts/2023-03-22/ksjd-local-newscast-march-22-2023.

65. Stephanie McCrummen, "A Sanctuary of One," *Washington Post*, March 31 2018, https://www.washingtonpost.com/news/national/wp/2018/03/31/feature/after-30-years-in-america-she-was-about-to-be-deported-then-a-tiny-colorado-church-offered-her-sanctuary/.

> She felt most like herself when she was awake in the middle of the night. She could think in Spanish without translating. She could remember who she was. "Yes, I am Rosa," she would say to herself. "Yes, I feel lonely. Yes, I'm in sanctuary." She could think about whatever she wanted, about how at times she felt "like a pet, like the bear of the zoo everyone wants to come and see," or "like the excuse" people needed to vent their anger about where the country was headed. She could wonder why one person had brought her a can of soup that was expired and why another had brought her a traditional Mexican blouse. She could feel guilty for questioning all the good will. She could feel selfish for being a burden to Pastor Craig, to Roberto and to her sick mother. She could remember all the things she loved. Like reading a biography of Edgar Allan Poe. Like her dogs, or driving from Cortez to Mancos with music blaring. Most of all, she could remember how she loved living in her blue house with all the possibilities of America outside her doorstep. She had always loved that feeling, ever since she was a little girl in Mexico City who told her teacher that what she wanted to be was not a doctor or a lawyer but a person who lived in America. She kept reminding herself that was why she was here.[66]

Sabido's struggles highlight the importance of seeing and treating migrants as whole people. Having physical shelter from ICE and basic necessities provided for her did not make being stuck on the church grounds any less difficult. Well-meaning people inadvertently made her feel less than human, like a means to an end or an interesting attraction to visit. She describes multiple times she was outside near the border of the church property and people passing by shouted to remind her to stay where it was safe.[67] This was well intended, and this critique is not meant as an indictment of the Mancos community, who have responded with love and human imperfection to a person in need. Rather, it is a reminder to Christians wishing to work with migrants that our good intentions are not always enough. Efforts must be taken to center the agency of migrants, to encounter them in their full humanity and not as a project or an opportunity to do good.

Another consideration that must be undertaken by any community considering offering any form of sanctuary to people under threat of deportation is the proper balancing of publicity versus privacy. Some sanctuary communities make their actions very public, making a statement against an unjust system.

66. McCrummen, "Sanctuary of One."

67. McCrummen, "Sanctuary of One."

In other cases, people taking sanctuary might decide that it is in their best interests to be less public, to protect the details of their story that they would rather not share or that could put them in danger if spread widely. People who enter sanctuary are choosing to fight against a system that would see them deported. They fight to stay with their communities, to keep their lives and livelihoods, to stay with their families somewhere they consider safe (or safer). That fight first and foremost belongs to them. They know their own needs and vision of liberation, and they have the most to lose. Church communities that provide sanctuary (or other forms of aid and partnership) are invited to participate in that fight but must always remember to decenter themselves and to let the sanctuary guest lead. Especially for those of us who are white Christians, learning to decenter ourselves in a world that has often centered our needs will require a commitment to flexibility, a willingness to unlearn socially ingrained habits and to try new things. White Christians must be willing to make ourselves uncomfortable.

The modern sanctuary movement has also expanded the notion of sanctuary beyond church buildings and communities to encompass, for example, cities and campuses. This expansion has required an imaginative set of new tools and practices. For example, Harvard University Law Clinic has partnered with immigrant rights organization Cosecha to produce "extensive legal resources for campus organizations seeking to protect foreign-born students, faculty, and staff." Like the original movement, modern sanctuary efforts on campuses are encouraged to build explicitly on histories of resistance. The lawyers and activists who created these legal resources argue that colleges and universities have historically been made into spaces of resistance and protection of the most vulnerable, and so are capable of providing that same resistance and protection now for those under threat from increasingly punitive and indiscriminate US immigration policy.[68]

Other efforts have included courtroom solidarity, in which teams of volunteers accompany migrants to their court hearings. This provides visible support to migrants themselves and also demonstrates their deep ties to the community, which can influence court decisions. Additionally, Estes describes Indigenous activism around immigration justice, which often centers on a "refusal to cede moral authority over who belongs and who doesn't to a settler nation."[69] This activism is itself a form of sanctuary. It unsettles the United States' right to implement an immigration system at all, offering a form of conceptual, narrative sanctuary that reimagines what belonging means and who has access to it. The

68. Buff, "Sanctuary Everywhere," 32.

69. Nick Estes, "Go Back Where You Came From," Open Space SFMOMA, November 4, 2019, https://openspace.sfmoma.org/2019/11/go-back-to-where-you-came-from/.

US government might say undocumented immigrants are in the United States illegally, but that is not the only narrative.[70] Indigenous communities offer an alternative story about the land and who belongs on it (and who has actually come to inhabit it illegally).

Undocumented youth activists, many of whom are DREAMers, have also emerged as a powerful political force. Activists have "worked against federal as well as state and local anti-immigration policies," organizing "civil disobediences and [infiltrating] detention centers to monitor conditions there."[71] Such actions can be seen as the extension of an expansive form of sanctuary, one that refuses to let detained migrants disappear into the shadows of the deportation machine. Instead of offering detained migrants shelter in their communities, these activists bring their communities to detainees, a sort of sanctuary on the go.

Sanctuary efforts often also include marches, protests, and other similar actions. At times, specific aspects of the United States' unjust approach to immigration gain attention and come under broad public criticism. For example, in spring 2018, photos of the conditions faced by children separated from their parents under the Trump administration's zero-tolerance policy caught widespread attention, sparking nationwide protests. While this widespread attention can aid the fight against unjust policy, it can also narrow the focus of people of goodwill too much. Immigrant rights activists insist that a much broader understanding of the unjust nature of immigration policy is needed and that this broader view should ground political action and demands. One recent focus of pro-immigrant activism that has developed with this sort of broader lens has been the social media–based movement #abolishICE. Becoming popular in 2018, #abolishICE challenges the narrative that ICE is necessary for the safety and security of US citizens, recognizing both its very recent founding (2003) and its ongoing record of human-rights abuses that endanger rather than protect communities. #abolishICE envisions a world beyond the status quo.

As a movement with broader focus, many proponents of #abolishICE have a wide-reaching vision for a more just world, acknowledging "the depredations of walls within as well as between sovereign nations," linking activism around immigrants' rights to other justice issues, such as the occupation of Palestine, recognizing "that to work against such walls is to work against a global system of empire, which includes the brutal legacies that have created the contemporary map of nations as well as ongoing imperial practices."[72] In other words, this movement recognizes that justice requires the dismantling

70. For example, chapter 2 offered a more nuanced articulation of some of the push and pull factors that cause migration and calls US immigration laws into question.

71. Buff, "Sanctuary Everywhere," 32.

72. Buff, "Sanctuary Everywhere," 33.

of global systems that have been made to seem necessary and inevitable but actually only protect the interests of the few at the expense of the people these systems make vulnerable.

The status quo maintains itself by appearing inevitable.[73] When the status quo is unjust, churches, called to truth telling and solidarity with oppressed people, ought therefore to find themselves in opposition to these systems. Christian communities must participate in undermining that sense of inevitability by imagining new ways of being in the world. One way the sanctuary movement reimagines what is possible and challenges the status quo is by divorcing its understanding of moral goodness from legality. The Mancos United Methodist Church, when accused of promoting lawlessness by offering sanctuary to Rosa Sabido, answered by pointing out the long history of unjust laws in the United States, among which they include present immigration policy.[74] While communitarians insist that the rule of law is worth upholding because strong systems of law protect human rights, people within the sanctuary movement highlight the human-rights abuses the system of law has itself perpetuated and upheld. Laws, they argue, do not earn the right to respect and compliance simply by being laws. Rather, laws must be just in order to warrant following. Those within the sanctuary movement encourage others to interrogate the purpose of law. How has the law functioned historically? Whom has it served?

The dominant narrative, rooted in the frontier myth's casting of anything outside the boundaries of Anglo civility as a threat, is that the rule of law has and continues to serve US citizens and keep us safe. Chapters 1–2 showed how the rule of law has in fact often served the needs of the few at the expense of many. US immigration policy, in many ways an outgrowth of manifest destiny and the frontier myth, similarly protects some with little regard for who is harmed as a result. Moreover, the few that this system serves does not even encompass all US citizens. Mass detention and deportation does not demonstrably make the general US population safer. For example, many immigrants, especially undocumented immigrants, fear reporting crimes because it may lead to scrutiny and deportation.[75] A system that discourages the reporting of crimes does not make communities safer.

Rather, to a large degree the current system primarily profits the owners and stockholders of for-profit detention centers as well as politicians who use the threat of dangerous migrants as a tool to gain support and get elected. García

73. Estes, "Our History Is the Future," 149.

74. McCrummen, "Sanctuary of One."

75. American Civil Liberties Union, "New ACLU Report Shows Fear of Deportation Is Deterring Immigrants from Reporting Crimes," May 3, 2018, https://www.aclu.org/press-releases/new-aclu-report-shows-fear-deportation-deterring-immigrants-reporting-crimes.

Hernández outlines how the practice of detaining migrants developed and became tied to the economic interests of the US elite. While the mid-twentieth century saw positive views of incarceration drop dramatically, García Hernández reports that in the wake of the civil rights movement interest in incarceration swung back up. The so-called war on drugs is by now well known for jump-starting mass incarceration, particularly of Black men.[76] At the same time, however, immigration detention also began to rise dramatically. García Hernández links this rise in immigration detention to "a broader securitization regime" in which the US government demonstrates that it remains in control by use of brute force against perceived threats. Detention allows the government to give the impression that it is keeping its citizens safe, even when the data shows that such draconian immigration tactics do little to enhance anyone's security or quality of life. While ineffective and often inhumane, detention has proven itself to be "a sharp-edged political tool" that remains "remarkably effective means of dividing workplaces, friendships, families, and communities."[77] Such division helps elites maintain power by distracting average people from the real source of their problems and providing scapegoats toward which to channel anger and mistrust.

Moreover, García Hernández finds that of all forms of incarceration, the detention of migrants has proven most profitable. He reports that "with eye-catching dollar amounts moving from Washington to small towns" with immigration detention centers (which also provide needed jobs for these communities), "it is no surprise elected officials fight to keep federally financed prisoners in their communities." In reality, detention centers are far less reliable as sources of jobs and money and can often leave communities, taxpayers, and local governments footing the bill. The real beneficiaries of the expanded use of detention are private prison corporations. García Hernández reports that the private prison industry receives $3.2 million a day from ICE, a huge incentive for them to increase detention and keep their prisons full of migrants.[78] Following the example of the sanctuary movement, Christians ought to question whom current systems serve and be ready to oppose those systems, such as mass detention, which fail to establish any recognizable justice.[79]

Furthermore, Christians must consider how we currently collaborate with these systems and how we can divest from this entanglement. The previous

76. See Alexander, *New Jim Crow*.

77. García Hernández, *Migrating to Prison*, 93; see 55–73.

78. García Hernández, *Migrating to Prison*, 126–28, 130.

79. See also Tanya Golash-Boza, "The Immigration Industrial Complex: Why We Enforce Immigration Policies Destined to Fail," *Sociology Compass* 3, no. 2 (February 2009): 295–309.

chapters have outlined some of the ways in which Christian theology, particularly white, Euro-American Christian theology, has helped create and perpetuate harmful ideologies and systems throughout US history. Churches wishing to build a more just world ought to come to understand this entanglement and actively work to dismantle it. As discussed in chapter 5, this may mean abandoning harmful theologies or expanding to accept a more pluralistic (not relativistic)[80] view of theology. Churches ought also to consider what gets explicitly and tacitly supported in Christian services and our methodologies. Does the way we talk about history collaborate with the harmful ideologies of manifest destiny and the frontier myth, or do we offer a different story? Do we talk about justice and morality as if they were totally tied to positive human laws, or are we able to articulate a deeper source of justice? What types of authority do we give weight to, implicitly and explicitly? Might we be upholding colonialist standards of knowledge? How might even our activism perpetuate the ideologies or practices of colonialism? This is one of the reasons it becomes so important to allow space for marginalized communities to lead. White US citizens imposing ideas about justice onto the lives of immigrants just repeats the intrusive dynamics of colonialism. Our ways of seeking justice need to inhabit new ways of relating.

Consider, for example, how our language participates in or undermines dominant US narratives. One common way this occurs is when well-meaning allies use language that implies "good" versus "bad" immigrants. Often this is done to point out the arbitrary nature of the immigration system. How could the system hurt someone like this, someone who implicitly is good enough to not deserve that treatment. Richard Morales, director of the Faith in Action national immigration campaign, said of Rosa Gutiérrez Lopez, "We don't see why she is a priority for deportation. There is no reason to separate this woman from her children."[81] Morales's point is clear. The system is so unjust and arbitrary it would deport someone who poses no definable threat to US communities. But the implication, however unintentional, is that others might be less good and therefore less worthy of care or more deserving of draconian immigration enforcement policies. Working for justice requires that we question the necessity, effectiveness, and morality of punitive and aggressive immigration policies, full stop, no matter whom they are harming or how well that person fits into a "good immigrant" narrative.[82]

80. See, for example, Haight, "Trinity and Religious Pluralism," 539–40.

81. As quoted by García Hernández, *Migrating to Prison*.

82. See also García Hernández's exploration of "good" and "bad" immigrants and how this plays into the US propensity for detaining migrants (*Migrating to Prison*, 95–117). Another example of how well-meaning people play into harmful narratives can be seen in conversations around DREAMers. Insistence that DREAMers came to the US illegally "through no fault of

Sanctuary efforts, in whatever form they take, provide a way for church communities to be sacramental, to proclaim God's vision for the world and God's presence in the midst of suffering and evil. The world that sanctuary churches invite us to envision is a world in which relationships of care and responsibility extend beyond borders, one in which we, as humans, understand ourselves to belong to each other in a very real sense, regardless of borders or national origin. It is the world implied in responsibility ethics, in which we are meant to respond justly to and be in right relationships with all people, not to put our nation first at the expense of others.

As the previous chapters have shown, this vision for the world aligns well with Christian values. Communities committed to living out these values and working for justice must be willing to think beyond the legal and criminal justice systems of this nation and to abandon legality as a measure of moral rightness. This is not to imply that human law has no role to play in the creation of justice and the protection of human rights. Rather, I am drawing on the long tradition of a Christian separation of human law from the law of God, perhaps best exemplified by Martin Luther King Jr., who, drawing on Aquinas, wrote, "There are two types of laws: just and unjust. . . . One has a moral responsibility to disobey unjust laws."[83] In line with this tradition, this book argues that just laws ought to be obeyed on the grounds that they are just, not by virtue of being laws. Christians will only be able to work toward true justice for migrants insofar as we take this seriously.

St. Cloud, Minnesota

In recent decades, Minnesota has become home to a large population of Somali refugees and immigrants. This final case study explores the experiences of these newcomers, their trials and triumphs, and the community actions that seem to have best served them. Before doing so, it is worth acknowledging that up until this point, this book has focused almost entirely on migration from Latin and Central America. Despite this narrower focus, this turn to Somali migration is helpful for two reasons. First, the situation in central Minnesota offers unique insight for Christian communities considering what praxis aimed at justice for migrants might look like and is therefore a valuable resource despite the deviation from this project's scope. That the situation in Minnesota is different from the other cases explored above is especially helpful in that it highlights how praxis

their own" because they were too young to make that decision implies that their parents are at fault and might therefore not be due the same protections as their children. We must be careful, in defending particular migrants from an unjust system, not to imply some migrants are more deserving of rights than others.

83. Martin Luther King Jr., *Why We Can't Wait* (Boston: Beacon, 2010), 93.

can and should look different in different contexts. Díaz's link between salvation and concrete cultures and Marcella Althaus-Reid's conception of Jesus's messianic becoming in conversation with marginalized communities drew our attention to the importance of shaping liberative praxis to the needs and circumstances of specific contexts. Christian communities should tailor their approaches to their specific context. The differences in this case study can help us consider what that looks like. Second, by ending with an example of a different type of migrant experience, this final case study highlights how the framework outlined in this book has broader relevance and is applicable beyond the specific relationships highlighted thus far.

The situations Muslim refugees and migrants face in the United States are influenced by modern Islamophobia and xenophobia, fueled by the rhetoric of the war on terror and an increasingly security-focused view of immigration policy. Roxanne Dunbar-Ortiz linked the contemporary war on terror to the Indian Wars and the tactics used to tame the frontier. Chapters 1–2 outlined how these practices and attitudes came to shape US foreign and immigration policy. It is no surprise, then, to see increasingly aggressive foreign action against "terrorism" coincide with increasingly militaristic immigration policy. Recent history shows that,

> After 9/11, an emergent grammar of Homeland Security drew on residual nativism and Islamophobia to conflate Muslim and Arab Americans with both terrorism and out-of-control migration. This discourse deployed the Cold War semantic division between deserving refugees and threatening migrants during almost two decades of refugee-generating conflicts waged by US forces, allies, munitions, and drones in Iraq, Afghanistan, Pakistan, Israel/Palestine, Yemen, and more. At this moment of increased US international engagement, a nationalist language of borders and securitization that perceived refugees as potential terrorists gained traction. As refugees became associated in this discourse with "terror," it eroded the post-1951 distinction between "deserving" refugees and suspect migrants. This rhetoric of counterterrorism advanced further in the Trump administration's rapid implementation of Executive Order 13769, a controversial ban on travelers, refugees, and migrants from seven mostly Muslim nations.[84]

This increased conflation of migration with terrorism has had a wide-reaching impact on migrants from around the world, and it has fueled increasingly exclusionist rhetoric and policy proposals. Most migrants are negatively affected by

84. Buff, "Sanctuary Everywhere," 31.

this shift, facing increasingly difficult hurdles to gaining entry into the United States and new forms of fear and mistrust from some US residents once they do arrive. Muslim immigrants, however, are especially affected, often linked to terrorism regardless of any evidence or lack thereof.

It was in this context of fear and securitization that Somali Refugee Hudda Ibrihim wrote *From Somalia to Snow: How Central Minnesota Became Home to Somalis*. Ibrahim's work is an exercise in truth telling. She is aware of the false narratives that exist about why Muslim immigrants come to the United States and why so many Somali refugees have come to central Minnesota. Her response is an attempt to counter these false narratives with a fuller depiction of reality. In doing so, her narrative causes a rupture, as defined by Althaus-Reid, by interrupting dominant US narratives about Muslim migrants and inviting people to read history with the Somali community. To create this rupture, Ibrahim offers a brief, accessible history of Somalia, outlining its colonization, independence, and internal conflicts and showing how this has led to many fleeing violence and persecution.[85]

She then outlines how Somali refugees came to congregate so heavily in central Minnesota and in the St. Cloud area specifically. In the late 1980s and early 1990s violence and unrest forced many Somalis to flee to Kenya and Ethiopia. While most anticipated an end to the violence would come soon and make it safe to return home, instead the violence persisted, and many ended up in refugee camps. Many were eventually resettled in the United States, with waves of refugees being resettled in the 1990s, 2006, and between 2010 and 2015. Those who arrived in the 1990s had no choice about where they were resettled. Many ended up in Minnesota because of the active network of resettlement agencies working there. Initially, many refugees were resettled in Rochester and Marshal, Minnesota, but when the factories in those areas began to close, groups of single Somali men began moving to St. Cloud, where several businesses such as Jennie-O and Golden Plump offered jobs that did not necessitate English proficiency. As numbers in St. Cloud grew, nonprofits were established to aid new arrivals. Word spread among Somali communities, and many more moved to St. Cloud seeking work and community. Being somewhere with a large, relatively established Somali community provides access to many forms of concrete material and cultural support, and guarantees the existence of places to worship, procure cultural goods, and participate in traditional customs. More recently, relatives of those who moved to St. Cloud have also traveled to join them, contributing to the development of a large and vibrant Somali community in the St. Cloud area.[86]

85. Hudda Ibrahim, *From Somalia to Snow: How Central Minnesota Became Home to Somalis* (St. Paul, MN: Beaver's Pond, 2017), 1–14.

86. Ibrahim, *From Somalia to Snow*, 26–52.

Ibrahim's book can be a helpful starting point for local church communities that want to work for justice in central Minnesota or places like it. Groups can begin by simply reading the book. Works such as this provide a basic opportunity to begin to learn about local migrant communities. Becoming educated in this way not only helps diminish fear and distrust but can also begin to open pathways to relationship building. Furthermore, Ibrahim outlines many of the concrete realities of Somalis in the area, relying on her own experience and on extensive interviews. While it is no substitute for actual relationships with Somali neighbors, the book (or works like it[87]) can be an entry point for those considering what needs might exist in their communities and how they may be positioned to partner with existing networks to get those needs met. In this way, the book becomes a first step toward reading with marginalized communities, as Althaus-Reid calls Christians to do. Churches must work to educate themselves and to promote education in their broader communities.

Chapter 5 discussed the importance of stories for interrupting dominant narratives and forging community identity. Rodríguez and Althaus-Reid highlight that reading "lowercase" literature that emerges from society's margins can create rupture out of which we can work for justice. Engaging and promoting the stories of migrants and refugees, stories that counter the misinformation that surrounds them and the US-centered narratives that harm them, can begin to expand our understanding of who we are (or ought to be) in community with. This is an important task churches can undertake in service of these goals. This might mean starting book clubs, hiring speakers, or using a broader range of stories and examples in sermons and other church events. Althaus-Reid's presents the idea of Jesus's messianic becoming, a process of becoming savior in conversation with marginalized people and their concrete needs. If the church is called to participate in Jesus's work, Christians in places like St. Cloud ought to consider how they too might conceive of the work of liberation as necessarily developed in conversation with the needs of Somali communities and how this might shape their understanding and presentation of the gospel. Christian communities that respectfully engage the stories of Muslim migrants in particular can help counter the notion that to be Christian is to be anti-Muslim. This breaks through the narrative that religions must compete and that religious differences fundamentally divide. Churches can in this way intentionally foster a community that once again proclaims to the world what is possible. They can model what right, responsible relationships can look like.

87. See, for example Hasme Warfa, *America Here I Come: A Somali Refugee's Quest for Hope* (Makati City, Philippines: Sunshine, 2014); Abdi Nor Iftin, *Call Me American: A Memoir* (New York: Vintage, 2019); Ilhan Omar and Rebecca Paley, *This Is What America Looks Like: My Journey from Refugee to Congresswoman* (New York: Dey St., 2020).

Pro-immigrant activism in the St. Cloud area has focused largely on education and encounter. #UniteCloud, a nonprofit organization founded in 2015 by Natalie Ringsmuth for the purpose of reducing "racial, religious, and cultural tensions in Central MN,"[88] provides a helpful example. At the time of its founding, 73 percent of non-Somali St. Cloud residents reported trusting their Somali neighbors. This was already a significant increase from 56 percent in 2010. However, this number was still well below trust of other racial groups in the area, all of whom were trusted by over 90 percent of residents.[89] Groups such as #UniteCloud work to continue closing that gap. Speakers from #UniteCloud provide programs such as "Stepping Out of Your Comfort Zone . . . in Faith" and "Empathy, Refugees, and Immigrants" to businesses, church groups, and other meetings. They also provide various trainings, such as "know your rights" programs and workshops about Islam, Somali culture, and forms of activism. Much of the speaking team is made up of Somali residents, providing an opportunity for people to encounter members of this new population and build relationships instead of relying on stereotypes.[90]

Ringsmuth reports that myths about Somalis fuel fear and resentment and lead to divisions in the St. Cloud community. These falsehoods include the belief that Somali refugees are in the country illegally or that they have increased crime rates in the area when in fact the opposite is true. Prominent myths in St. Cloud's white communities also link high unemployment and low wages in the area to the increased Somali population, and suggest that Somali residents rely heavily on aid from social services, draining community resources. In reality, neither concern is founded, and both Ibrahim's research and local reports show that the Somali community has established a vast network of support through which they are able to take care of each other and support new arrivals. A small amount of the county's tax levy money goes to supporting refugees in the area. The majority of social-services resources in the area go to white residents born in the area.[91] Rumors such as these, while often easily disproved, cause fear and animosity, and have led some to call for an end or halt to resettlement in

---

88. #UniteCloud, "#UC Leadership," accessed December 12, 2020, https://unitecloud.org/staff/.

89. Austen Macalus, "Conversations Lead to Acceptance of Somali Refugees," Associated Press, November 2, 2019, https://apnews.com/f6621f7f15d048098c3779bcad75c947.

90. #UniteCloud, "Education and Speaking," accessed December 12, 2020, https://unitecloud.org/education-speaking/.

91. While countering these falsehoods is indeed important, it is also worth noting that such narratives can play into harmful ideas about who is worthy of aid and what the cost of community ought to be. This book argues that the US has a responsibility toward migrants, regardless of their ability to establish their own internal networks of support or their potential "drain" on US resources.

St. Cloud. In the fall of 2017, city council member Jeff Johnson called for a moratorium on resettlement while a study of the impacts of immigrants on the city could be studied.[92] While this resolution ultimately failed and in fact an alternative resolution was passed to declare St. Cloud "a welcoming community for refugees," Johnson's call highlights the persistence of negative myths about refugees and immigrants.[93]

Ibrahim's book is one helpful resource for countering these harmful myths. It is, however, not the only method she has used to counter harmful narratives and misunderstandings. She also hosts regular "Dine and Dialogue with a Muslim Neighbor" events, in which guests have an opportunity to learn about each other in an informal setting. The goal of these dinners is to "help foster better understanding of immigrants and refugees" in order to diminish prejudice rooted in misunderstandings.[94] In addition, these community-building dinners provide opportunities for participants to "read" with each other, as Althaus-Reid calls us to, by engaging in conversation about each other's traditions and about the shared community of St. Cloud. Local Somali teacher Ekram Elmoge has undertaken a similar effort to educate and build relationships, committing to frequent conversations over coffee with people who are "skeptical" or "outright opposed" to refugees. Elmoge is also "working to start a group that teaches young Somali women how to share their stories" so that they might be empowered to have these bridge-building conversations.[95] St. Cloud's Somali residents lead the way on these conversational approaches to increasing tolerance and respect. Some of the area's white residents have also followed suit, not only engaging in these conversations but beginning to initiate them as well. St. Cloud mayor Dave Kleis "holds chili feeds at his house to bridge cultural gaps among different races and religions."[96] In 2017, #Unite Cloud held a panel titled "I Don't Mean to Offend You, But . . ." which provided a safe opportunity for St. Cloud's non-Somali residents to ask questions they may otherwise have left unsaid and that, when unanswered, can foster resentment and fear.

---

92. Jon Telvin, "Untruths Fan Flames of Fear in St. Cloud," *Star Tribune*, October 23, 2017, https://www.startribune.com/jon-tevlin-untruths-fan-flames-of-fear-in-st-cloud/452139823/?refresh=true.

93. Melissa Marolf, "The $63 Billion Dollar Reality Check," #UniteCloud, accessed January 20, 2021, https://unitecloud.org/the-63-billion-dollar-reality-check/.

94. Telvin, "Untruths Fan Flames."

95. "Tech High School Expands World Language Opportunities," BARR, January 24, 2022, https://barrcenter.org/2022/01/24/tech-high-school-expands-world-language-opportunities/.

96. Telvin, "Untruths Fan Flames."

Linda Thielen, a white lifetime St. Cloud resident, found that speaking with her Somali neighbors began to shift her perspective on their presence in the community. At first, as Thielen began to notice the growing Somali population in St. Cloud, she was nervous, angry, and confused. She did not understand why they were coming, and she reports that in the back of her mind she connected them to the 9/11 terrorist attacks. She worried the increased presence of Muslim people in St. Cloud might lead to another attack, this time in her own backyard. Thielen's concerns caused tensions between her and her daughter, who works at a nonprofit that aids in the resettlement of refugees. After a particularly heated argument, she was challenged to get to know a Somali neighbor. She began tutoring Somali students and baking cookies for the Muslim family who had recently moved in down the street. Because of these efforts, she learned about their culture and got to know them as people. Over time, she realized that her prejudices against Somali people were in contradiction with her Christian faith. She knew, she says, how Jesus wants people to treat one another, and she came to acknowledge that the biblical injunction to love one's neighbor included the Somali and Muslim residents of St. Cloud. Thielen has come a long way from her initial fear, and now she is trying to bring others in her life along with her, encouraging them to get to know their new neighbors like she did. She reports that some are making steps toward acceptance and respect, though the process is slow.[97] Natalia Imperatori-Lee highlights the importance of revelation in the everyday. Thielen's encounters with her Somali neighbors became such occasions for everyday grace, through which she was able to encounter God in the other and be transformed by love.

Although social scientists often predict that increased diversity will lead to a decrease of overall trust in a community, St. Cloud demonstrates the reverse: between 2010 and 2015, both diversity and trust increased. This included both overall trust and trust between non-Somali and Somali residents. Local peace studies professor Ron Pagnucco hypothesizes that "the increase of the number of Somalis led to an increase in likelihood that members of the broader community would get to know Somalis (as fellow students, as coworkers, as fellow shoppers, as neighbors, etc.) and that getting to know a Somali person in these contexts increases the likelihood of developing trust and a more positive view of Somalis" in general. This hypothesis is supported by Pew Research, which suggests knowing someone who is Muslim increases a person's likelihood of having a positive overall view of Muslims. Importantly, in the period between the 2010 survey and the 2015 survey, Pagnucco reports that bridge-building efforts were undertaken by individuals and groups such as church communities and nonprofits. These efforts, he suggests, positively directed the impact of the

97. "Tech High School Expands World Language Opportunities."

overall increase in diversity in the area, enabling that diversity to generate greater rather than lesser trust.[98]

#UniteCloud's efforts to provide educational resources and opportunities for encounter build on this work. Furthermore, the organization also works to bring the knowledge and experience it has gained from working in the St. Cloud area to other communities around Minnesota and beyond in order to help build relationships across divisive tensions elsewhere. Speakers from the organization help other communities create "honest and useful discussion in a safe and familiar environment," in which the speakers aim to talk with participants rather than at them.[99] This highlights that the organization understands the connections between the division in central Minnesota and divisiveness around the United States. Like the organizers of El Gran Paro Estadounidense, #UniteCloud recognizes that building a more just world is a project that may begin with a small, specific focus but that must grow to encompass a broad set of interconnected liberative projects.

The efforts taking place in St. Cloud and the surrounding area offer examples for how churches and Christian communities might participate in opening lines of communication that help dispel harmful myths about migrants and create a basis for more inclusive communities and networks of care that exemplify to US society how taking responsibility for each other can work. In other words, St. Cloud provides an example for how truth telling can build bridges and create expansive communities of solidarity. These communities proclaim to the world what is possible. The focus on building community exemplified in St. Cloud is held in common by all four of the case studies explored in this section. At its core, the ecclesiological vision of chapter 5 aims at and can only be lived out in an ever increasingly inclusive and just pattern of community building.

Chapter 5 lifted up four ecclesiological themes that give theological flesh to responsible, reparative action and radical love: model communities, truth telling, solidarity, and flexibility. The cases outlined above illuminate how these themes might inform concrete action. For example, El Gran Paro Estadounidense shows the importance of solidarity through the various partnerships forged in the movement that became integral to its project. Sanctuary movements provide model communities that offer a vision of how the world could be, of what it might look like to live as though we are truly responsible for one another. The organizing and activism in El Paso exemplifies flexibility, continually adjusting and readjusting as new needs arise. In St. Cloud, we can see the great importance of truth telling

98. Ron Pagnucco, "Editorial Counterpoint: There's More to the Other Side of the St. Cloud Story," *Star Tribune*, July 8, 2019, https://www.startribune.com/editorial-counterpoint-there-s-more-to-the-other-side-of-the-st-cloud-story/512438282/?refresh=true.

99. "Education and Speaking."

and view several models for how individuals and communities might go about disrupting harmful narratives. These examples have been intentionally diverse. They highlight a variety of tactics that might be taken in different contexts and based on particular needs, strengths, and resources. Christian communities are encouraged not to mimic these cases but to allow them to inspire and direct their own particular, contextual work of radical love in service of the kin-dom of God.

Broadening the Scope

The case studies profiled above provide a variety of examples for how Christians might live out the ecclesiological vision outlined in chapter 5. They vary in overall approach, particular focuses, and the specific tactics used. Some are very public, such as the El Gran Paro Estadounidense and #UniteCloud. Other approaches are much more interpersonal, such as the Encuentro Project's ministry of encounter or Ekram Elmoge's conversations with people suspicious of Somali migrants. Some require explicit resistance to the laws and powers of the United States, such as Annunciation House's earliest work and the sanctuary movement of the 1980s. At other times, some cooperation with the system becomes prudent, as when Garcia coordinates with ICE in order to provide shelter and services to asylum seekers, or the modern sanctuary movement's reliance on ICE's policy of not entering certain locations. A flexible, contextual approach will need all of these tactics and more. Pursuing justice will look different in each context, and a variety of actions will be necessary to build a more equitable world.

Our exploration of these responses to migration began with De Anda's call to holistic transformation away from the logic of domination and toward right relationships. These case studies have highlighted that this turn to right relationships requires Christians to take sides. Truly turning away from the logic of domination means actively opposing systems of domination. Failure to do so implicitly supports the status quo. In all of its diverse embodiments, the ecclesiological vision of this book maintains that political neutrality is not an option for people of faith. In line with this vision, researcher and activist Ibram X. Kendi compellingly argues against the illusion of neutrality in his book, *How to Be an Antiracist.*

Kendi defines racism as "a marriage of racist policies and racist ideas that produces and normalizes racial inequities."[100] This normalization of inequalities is key. Social sin makes systems of injustice and inequality seem natural. In such a situation, neutrality is not possible. Either we work to actively dismantle social sin within and around us, or we contribute to its normalization through efforts to remain neutral. Social sin has to be actively rejected. Kendi can help elucidate this point. He argues that because racist policies and "racist ideas have defined

100. Ibram X. Kendi, *How to Be an Antiracist* (New York: One World, 2019), 17.

[US] society since its beginning," they often "feel so natural and obvious as to be banal," and so "antiracist ideas remain difficult to comprehend, in part because they go against the flow of this country's history."[101]

In a context such as this, with pervasive systems of racism in our thoughts and our laws, each person must decide how to proceed, which side of history to place oneself.[102] Choosing the side aiming to dismantle racism and racially-based injustices means abandoning a "race-neutral" approach. Similarly, choosing solidarity with the victims of US colonialism and unjust immigration policy means neutrality is not an option.[103] As Christians, of course, we hold a certain commitment to all people, even those to whom we are opposed. An insistence on taking sides is not an insistence that we abandon those on the opposing side. Rather, I am reminded of the two hands of nonviolence. One hand is raised, palm out, in a firm insistence that mistreatment stop. The other is extended, palm up, in recognition of the humanity of the other and in invitation to change.[104] In a similar way, we can stand in opposition to systems of sin without being closed off to the humanity of those with whom this position calls us into confrontation.

Kendi describes antiracism as a set of choices made in each moment.[105] We must all continuously choose to be antiracist, in whatever form that may take in each context. When it comes to responding to migration in the United States, whichever types of action Christian communities deem most appropriate in their contexts, these actions must also be guided by a rejection of attempts at neutrality and a commitment to actively dismantling social sin in whatever form it takes. The case studies presented above provide examples of what some practical actions to oppose social sin might look like, particularly as this relates to the reception and protection of migrants in the United States.

Kendi also looks closely at policy. In particular, he criticizes approaches that aim solely at equal treatment, approaches characterized by insistences that one "does not see race" and that this is the correct model for how we should proceed. Instead of equal treatment that ignores racial difference, Kendi argues that the United States needs equity. Equity discriminates, but while discrimination has

---

101. Kendi, *How to Be an Antiracist*, 22.

102. Kendi, *How to Be an Antiracist*, 21.

103. Guardado condemns what he calls "futile attempt[s] at neutrality that merely [condone] sinful structures and [idolize] security," insisting that the church is already deeply "embedded within the broader sociopolitical conflict surrounding immigration" ("Just Peace, Just Sanctuary," 82–83).

104. Ryan Hall, "The Two Hands of Yes and No," Campaign Nonviolence, October, 8, 2019, https://paceebene.org/blog/2019/10/8/the-two-hands-of-yes-and-no.

105. Kendi, *How to Be an Antiracist*, 13–22.

often been identified solely with racism (or other unjust forms of bias), antiracist discrimination results not in inequality but in equity.[106] To explain this, Kendi quotes Lyndon B. Johnson, who once said, "You do not take a person who, for years, has been hobbled by chains and liberate him, bring him up to the starting line of a race and then say, 'You are free to compete with all the others,' and still justly believe that you have been completely fair."[107] In order to compete fairly with the other runners in this analogy, the formerly chained runner would need extra help, "discrimination"[108] that will get him onto equal footing with his fellow runners. So too, then, with dismantling racism in the United States. What is needed are not neutral attitudes and policies that operate as if everyone begins life on equal footing when in reality a history of systematic racism has created deep inequalities that set people of color at a disadvantage. The goal, therefore, is not purely equal treatment but discrimination aimed at righting the wrongs of history and establishing equal footing for all.

To return to immigration, Christians must take a serious look at the policies they support and oppose and then reevaluate. For policies to be just, they must work not to preserve neutrality but instead to promote just discrimination, or equity. We need policies that pay attention to historical and ongoing disadvantages so that these policies are able to address those disadvantages and move toward justice. In Christian terms, we might call this a policy-focused preferential option for the poor.

Contours of Just Immigration Policy

Taking seriously the ecclesiological vision of chapter 5 means letting it shape not only church community action but also the types of policy we support or advocate for. However, this book does not aim to offer a detailed proposal for immigration policy in the United States. Rather, it has concerned itself primarily with proposals for Christian action and advocacy. Still, it is worth briefly considering what the contours of a just, responsible approach to immigration policy might entail. To that end, this final section considers policies proposed or supported by several pastoral bodies, both Catholic and Protestant. In doing so, this section suggests guidelines for the types of policies Christians informed by this book's ecclesiological vision ought to support, through voting, advocacy, public discourse, and other forms of direct political action.

106. Kendi, *How to Be an Antiracist*, 19, 18.

107. Lyndon B. Johnson, "Howard University Commencement Address, June 4, 1965," quoted in Kendi, *How to Be an Antiracist*, 19.

108. This is Kendi's language. His use of it can be related to the preferential option for the poor and the idea that preferential treatment or focus is required to reach justice and equity.

In order to propose some basic contours for just immigration reform, we must first consider the relationship between policy and justice. This book has outlined an understanding of justice as relational, rooted in responsibility and an accurate understanding of history. It has also insisted that laws must be just in order to warrant obedience, contrary to perspectives that seek to protect the rule of law as a good in itself. What the project has not yet considered is what the formation of just laws might entail. What follows is not intended to be an exhaustive consideration of this question but rather a brief outline of how Kendi's articulation of antiracist policies shapes this book's view of just policymaking.

In line with his rejection of neutrality, Kendi argues that policies must work not simply to mitigate or end harm but to actively dismantle the inequalities forged in history. Kendi writes,

> A racist policy is any measure that produces or sustains racial inequity between racial groups. An antiracist policy is any measure that produces or sustains racial equity between racial groups. By policy, I mean written and unwritten laws, rules, procedures, processes, regulations, and guidelines that govern people. There is no such thing as a nonracist or race-neutral policy. Every policy in every institution in every community in every nation is producing or sustaining either racial inequity or equity between racial groups.[109]

In a US society so wracked with deep-seated social sin, just policy proposals will often need to seek not to build on the established status quo but rather to actively dismantle and replace it. A weakness of both communitarian and cosmopolitan approaches to immigration is that they both require a certain degree of acceptance of the world as it is. They do not require actively breaking down or questioning the status quo, instead taking the present world order too much for granted and seeking reforms that will push it in more humane directions. With Kendi, this book supports a more radical approach, recognizing the sin that exists deep in the roots of the United States, sins that cannot be sufficiently eradicated through reforming what exists. Instead, we must build something new.

Antiracism and responsibility-based immigration ethics are both committed to historicity, to recognizing patterns of injustice across history and the way those patterns shape our lives to this day. Both approaches aim to actively undo these ongoing harms, to heal the damage and establish equity, accountability, and justice where it has not existed. Kendi writes, "To be an antiracist is a radical choice in the face of this history, requiring a radical

109. Kendi, *How to Be an Antiracist*, 18.

reorientation of our consciousness."[110] Similarly, responsibility ethics, rooted in reparative justice, requires the radical reimagining and reforming of unjust historical relationships.

The policy contours proposed below are driven by this radical reimagining. They are organized into three themes: *responsible*, *relational*, and *creatively comprehensive*. Chapters 3–4 outlined the appropriateness of a responsibility-ethics framework for understanding migration. This framework calls first for immigration policy that takes stock of the realities of history and the relationships the United States has forged with nations and people beyond its borders. Our policy must be responsible and acknowledge those relationships of responsibility in tangible ways. Second, in keeping with the spirit of responsibility, just immigration policy must also achieve sufficient recognition of a wider variety of human relationships and commit to greater protection of these relationships. The responsibility-ethics framework outlined in this book places relationships at the center of our work for justice. It has also called us to consider a broader network of relationships than we have been accustomed to. Considering how policy might better reflect the centrality of these relationships is therefore a vital step toward justice. Finally, chapter 4 highlighted the importance of reparative justice for grounding immigration ethics. In practice, a focus on repair will necessitate creative approaches to establishing accountability where it has not existed. A first step in establishing accountability will be an overhaul and expansion of current legal paths to membership in the United States in acknowledgment of US failure to be in just relationship with the people now migrating to and through US borders. However, accountability ought also to expand beyond direct migration policy, reshaping international relationships on a broader scale in order to address past injustice and prevent injustice in the future.

In *Strangers No Longer: Together on the Journey of Hope*, the United States Conference of Catholic Bishops and the Conferencia del Episcopado Mexicano insist that all migrants, regardless of documentation status, possess inherent dignity and value and must be treated in ways that respect this dignity. The church is called to defend this dignity and to proclaim and promote the basic unity of all humanity. The unity of the church is an image of the broader vision God has for humanity. Migration presents the church with the opportunity to fulfill the call to all followers of Jesus to cultivate hospitality by making migrants feel welcome in parish spaces. No one is to be a stranger in the church.[111] The document calls for immigration policy that expands legal pathways to citizenship, allows

110. Kendi, *How to Be an Antiracist*, 23.

111. United States Conference of Catholic Bishops and Conferencia del Episcopado Mexicano, *Strangers No Longer: Together on the Journey of Hope* (Washington, DC: United States Conference of Catholic Bishops, 2003), 38–39, 103, 41.

more families to stay together, and grants legal status to migrant workers.[112] Just immigration policy will include all of these concerns. They seek to protect and promote human relationships through keeping families together.

Furthermore, in highlighting the relationship between the United States and the undocumented migrants on whom the nation relies for labor, the bishops push to expand understandings of membership so that US policy might honor existing relationships in new ways. Legally recognized or not, undocumented workers participate in the US economy and are members of various US communities. Creating paths to legal membership, by which they might achieve a greater sense of stability and safety as well as access to important resources for self-advocacy, is one way of honoring these existing relationships. Additionally, the cross-border collaboration the bishops engaged in, which led to the proposals found in *Strangers No Longer*, provides an example of how we might reenvision the process of creating policy proposals.[113] Collaborating across borders is a first step. Chapter 5 offered an ecclesiological vision that invites us to consider how we might create inclusive communities that center the needs and desires of those who are most marginalized. This work does not end with cross-border coalitions of clergy, but the bishops' collaboration moves us in a helpful direction.

More recently, Bishop Mark Seitz of El Paso, Texas, has offered what is perhaps the Catholic Church's most expansive ecclesial response to migration. In the wake of the "matanza en El Paso," a mass shooting explicitly motivated by white supremacy and anti-immigrant fear that left twenty-three people dead and many more wounded, Seitz dedicated an entire pastoral letter to calling out the pervasive situation of racism present in the United States. Anti-immigrant and anti-Latine sentiments, he argues, are "ancient demons" that have "reawakened" and "old wounds" that have been "reopened." In response to this, Seitz calls the church to reckon with this country's racist heritage and the church's own complicity. He then calls the church to help "write a new chapter in our history of solidarity and friendship" that anticipates the kin-dom of God.[114] By doing so, we can take responsibility for history. With the humility to name the US legacy of white supremacy and his prophetic call for inclusive bridge building to create a more just future, Seitz is an exemplar for how Christians ought to think about

---

112. Ten years after *Strangers No Longer* was published, a compilation of reflections on its themes was released. The contributors to this volume offer perspectives that affirm what the bishops do well while pushing the church toward a more expansive response to migration. Todd Scribner and J. Kevin Appleby, *On Strangers No Longer: Perspectives on the Historic U.S.-Mexican Catholic Bishops' Pastoral Letter on Migration* (New York: Paulist Press, 2013).

113. United States Conference of Catholic Bishops and Conferencia del Episcopado Mexicano, *Strangers No Longer*, no. 40.

114. Mark Seitz, "Night Will Be No More," Hope Border, October 13, 2019, https://www.hopeborder.org/nightwillbenomore-eng.

policy advocacy. Are we advocating for imaginative policies that build bridges and live into the justice of God's kin-dom, or are we accepting the status quo as it has been given?

Moreover, Seitz is calling readers to an encounter of sorts: an encounter with our own history and its victims. Encounter, in many forms, is perhaps the best method for sparking conversion, especially in those who support (or are supported by) the status quo. Chapters 1–2 highlighted Roberto Goizueta's insistence that the dark side of Euro-American progress, the harms it has caused, have largely gone unnoticed, buried beneath a story of victory. We believe in the status quo because we have been taught to. Encountering fuller narratives of US history, narratives that highlight the perspectives of those who have been trampled over in the name of progress, are in a way encounters with the victims of history. These encounters, along with encounters with those who are still so harmed by US colonialism, actively unsettle belief in the status quo. They therefore can and should be a part of the widespread conversion needed to bring about a new, more just future.[115] It is boldness of vision, as exemplified in Seitz's prophetic voice, that will call people to conversion, not tepid attempts at "bothsidesism."[116]

Seitz is not alone in reimagining what is possible. Insisting that both family detention and family separation are contrary to Catholic values, the United States Conference of Catholic Bishops Committee on Migration rejects the false binary between detention and family separation and advocates for alternatives to detention that allow families to stay together without detaining them. In refusing to accept this false choice presented by the US government, the committee highlights the importance of imagining beyond the status quo. Responsible, relational, and comprehensive immigration policy will need such imagination and creativity. The bishops also call for attention to the root causes of migration, an important step in the direction of comprehensive, responsibility-based immigration policy.[117] Churches ought to continue promoting such responsibility and

115. Certainly those who support the status quo appear most obviously in need of conversion. However, wherever we might be politically and theologically situated, we are all in need of continual conversion away from the mentalities and habits that social sin has ingrained in us and toward more full participation in the radical love of Jesus.

116. This is not to say that we ought not to take seriously the concerns of those with whom we disagree on the issue of migration. It is rather to say that taking these concerns seriously need not mean a dulling of the church's prophetic voice. Encounter is fundamentally about relationships. When we encounter each other (or when we encounter history), we are building relationships, relationships in which we might acknowledge the deeply held concerns of those we disagree with, even as we continue to boldly call out social sin and injustice.

117. United States Conference of Catholic Bishops, "Binary Choice: Separation or Indefinite Detention," accessed December 12, 2020, https://justiceforimmigrants.org/wp-content/uploads/2020/05/Binary-Choice-QA.pdf.

indeed expand their consideration of how US policy might take responsibility and establish accountability. Beyond policies aimed at reshaping US immigration policy, all US foreign and domestic policy that affects those beyond US borders ought to be reviewed and reconsidered with the goal of ending harm, repairing past harms, and establishing just, accountable international relationships.

The Committee on Migration joins other Catholic leaders in insisting that international laws protecting migrants, refugees, and asylum seekers be followed by all governments.[118] Here, unlike with the question of family separation, the committee appears content with existing laws. At the very least, it does not actively challenge the law or seek to expand it. Certainly, current protections ought to be upheld. However, as many activists and scholars note, current international law does not offer sufficient protections to all who are forced to leave their homes. One clear example is climate refugees, people forced to flee their homelands because the effects of global climate change have made them unlivable. As it currently stands, international law does not protect these migrants.[119] Their reasons for fleeing, however, are clearly as dire as those who flee explicit persecution or war. Moreover, the United States, which contributes greatly to the climate crisis, is certainly as responsible for these migrants as for those who flee wars in which the United States has contributed or participated.

Responsible, comprehensive immigration policy ought to expand to offer firm protections for those who, like climate refugees, are not presently sufficiently protected under current laws. A long-term response to climate refugees would include the implementation of laws and practices that sufficiently address global climate change and mitigate or reverse the negative impact of climate change on the countries and populations already experiencing its most devastating effects. Creative and comprehensive policy will aim to limit the reasons people are forced to migrate in the first place. A smaller step, however, would be to expand international and US protections to include more categories of forced migrants in order to establish accountability for the role the United States plays in causing vast numbers of people to flee.[120]

President Biden's pre-inauguration promise to raise the United States' refugee admissions cap to 125,000, coupled with a starkly different rhetorical approach

---

118. United States Conference of Catholic Bishops, "Asylum," accessed December 12, 2020, https://tinyurl.com/h49mthpk.

119. Atapattu, "'Climate Refugees' and the Role."

120. We might also push for US law to take more seriously the role the US plays in causing economic migration. It is no accident that nations whose economies the US has destabilized to forward its own interests are also the nations sending large numbers of migrants to US borders. Responsible immigration policy would create paths to membership for a wider variety of migrants, including climate refugees and economic migrants, in order to establish accountability where it has not existed and to take responsibility for US actions at home and abroad.

from that of his predecessor,[121] is one step. However, much more remains needed in order to create truly responsible immigration policies, especially given the reality that as of early 2023 only about 20 percent of that number had been admitted. Experts warn that meeting these goals will take years, "leaving thousands of people in danger waiting in line" and "tens of thousands of unfilled slots for people fleeing perilous conditions." This delay, which was expected, is caused both by Trump-era cuts to refugee resettlement infrastructure and limits inherent to the programs and the US legal system, highlighting the need for substantial structural change.[122]

Additionally, as noted above, the Biden administration's own Circumvention of Lawful Pathways rule places limits on a significant number of migrants seeking asylum in the United States. Policies such as these go against the very heart of asylum, which is an understanding that people who are in acute danger should be allowed to get to safety by any means necessary before beginning their legal battle to be granted asylum. The entire point is to allow people the flexibility to get out of harm's way first and then to access legal channels for official recognition. Policies that hinder this belie the notion that the United States is "a nation of immigrants" or that it is "committed to fairly and efficiently considering asylum claims."[123]

In keeping with a tradition in Catholic social teaching, the bishops uphold the rights of sovereign states to control their borders. This book has intentionally unsettled the conceptual groundwork on which that right rests. State sovereignty and the rule of law have repeatedly failed to protect the rights and dignity of all people. In particular, chapters 1–2 showed that a consistent failure on the part of the United States to respect the sovereignty of Indigenous and Latin American nations has characterized US actions at home and abroad and has led directly to the failing immigration system we see today. What rights the United

121. Deborah Amos, "Biden Plans to Reopen America to Refugees after Trump Slashed Admissions," National Public Radio, November 11, 2020, https://www.npr.org/2020/11/11/933500132/biden-plans-to-reopen-america-to-refugees-after-trump-slashed-admissions.

122. Rebecca Morin and Dan Keemahill, "Biden Pledged to Fix a Broken US Refugee Program. Two Years Later He's Nowhere near His Goal," *USA Today*, March 2, 2023, https://www.usatoday.com/story/news/politics/2023/02/27/biden-us-refugee-cap-not-met-2022/11112116002/.

123. "Fact Sheet: President Biden Sends Immigration Bill to Congress as Part of His Commitment to Modernize Our Immigration System," The White House, January 20, 2021, https://www.whitehouse.gov/briefing-room/statements-releases/2021/01/20/fact-sheet-president-biden-sends-immigration-bill-to-congress-as-part-of-his-commitment-to-modernize-our-immigration-system/; "FACT SHEET: The Biden Administration Blueprint for a Fair, Orderly and Humane Immigration System," The White House, July 27, 2021, https://www.whitehouse.gov/briefing-room/statements-releases/2021/07/27/fact-sheet-the-biden-administration-blueprint-for-a-fair-orderly-and-humane-immigration-system/.

States has to control its borders under these circumstances is open for substantial debate.[124] In particular, the church would do well to question how well the current world order lives up to a relational understanding of justice as it further develops its migration ethic and related policy priorities. Christians ought to feel emboldened to radically reenvision how the world might be ordered and to offer that vision in official documents as well as in action and on-the-ground community building.

Protestant pastoral approaches to migration are varied. The Evangelical Lutheran Church in America (ELCA) calls for laws that promote the common good by taking our responsibility to those who migrate seriously.[125] This insistence on responsibility is the right direction for churches to push policy. In addition, the ELCA has advocated against travel bans enacted by the Trump administration barring migrants from predominantly Muslim countries and actively opposed family separation at the border.[126] Family separation represents a clear threat to human relationships. Just, relational immigration policy will reject such threats. Family reunification, a long-standing priority of US policy, must be protected and expanded, especially as so-called chain migration has come under increased attack.[127]

Furthermore, current US policy defines family in very Western, Euro-American terms: the nuclear family. Pastoral advocacy from many denominations also tends to foreground the nuclear ideal. This fails to account for the family structures of cultures that differ from (heterosexual) Euro-American norms. Immigration policy can only be just if it finds ways to acknowledge and account for a broader set of familial relationships than it currently protects. Nonheterosexual relationships, extended family, nonblood relatives, and other

---

124. It is beyond the scope of this project to propose a full answer to the question of state sovereignty. Certainly some nations (Latin American, Indigenous) need their sovereignty to be upheld in a far greater way than it has been. Nations such as the US, which have protected their own sovereignty while disregarding that of others, may have less of a right to sovereignty when faced with the need to take responsibility for the harms they have caused.

125. Evangelical Lutheran Church in America, "Social Statement on the Church in Society," September 1991, https://tinyurl.com/4mptfecz.

126. Evangelical Lutheran Church in America, "Support the NO BAN Act," accessed December 12, 2020, https://support.elca.org/site/Advocacy?cmd=display&page=UserAction&id=1211; Evangelical Lutheran Church in America, "Family Separation," September 2018, https://tinyurl.com/yc75xm3r.

127. For more on family reunification, see Migration Policy Institute, "Legalization for DREAMers Would Result in Chain Migration of an Average of 1 Person or Less over a Lifetime—Far Fewer than Critics Suggest, MPI Estimates," November 30, 2017, https://www.migrationpolicy.org/news/legalization-dreamers-would-result-chain-migration-average-1-person-or-less-over-lifetime; Heyer, *Kinship across Borders*, 61–98.

types of family need greater access to reunification and protection. Doing this well will require a more imaginative approach as well as collaboration with and input from migrant communities, who know best which types of relationships need greater protection.

This book does not aim to propose a concrete plan for precisely how such an expanded program of protections would be implemented. Rather, the goal is to encourage Christians to imagine beyond present laws, to truly dig into the resources within our traditions to consider what is at stake, and to defend a bold understanding of human dignity, even when that might include the promotion of policies that are a harder sell in the public sphere. A commitment to pragmatism is certainly vital, but so too is our willingness and ability to be a prophetic voice urging the nation toward radical justice. The US immigration system must reimagine how membership is understood and defined to better encompass these broader forms of relationship and belonging, whether historical, familial, or communal.

In response to an influx of unaccompanied child migrants crossing the US border in 2014, the ELCA provided resources for church members interested in traveling to Mexico and Central America. These resources focus on translating these experiences into advocacy through gaining and spreading fuller narratives about the realities in countries people often migrate from. These ELCA resources stress the importance of connecting with local decision makers and organizers in Central America, actively listening to communities on the ground, and accompanying communities with their permission in ways that are intentionally inclusive, sustainable, empowering, and mutually vulnerable. Participants are then encouraged to allow these experiences to shape their political engagement with the assistance of ELCA Advocacy network. Contacting elected officials is especially prioritized.[128] After an ELCA staff visit to Central America in 2015, the church affirmed,

> The ELCA is called to bear witness to the conditions affecting so many communities and work to find solutions that will acknowledge the humanity in all of God's children. ELCA Advocacy continues to lift up and amplify the voices of ELCA congregants, partners, children and families, and Lutheran churches in Central America with a goal of ensuring the safety and protection of all our brothers and sisters.[129]

128. Evangelical Lutheran Church in America, "From Ministry to Advocacy: A Guide to Advocacy after Visiting Lutheran Churches in Central America and Mexico," accessed September 20, 2023, https://tinyurl.com/bdn4666f.

129. Evangelical Lutheran Church in America, "Addressing Forced Displacement in Central America through Advocacy," accessed December 12, 2020, http://download.elca.org/ELCA%20Resource%20Repository/Factsheet_Addressing_Forced_Displacement_2016.pdf.

By grounding its public advocacy in intentional cross-border relationship building, the ELCA offers a potential model for how churches might conceive of their roles in political activism and policy advocacy: done always in true solidarity with those most affected, grounded in actual relationships. Churches ought also to consider what relationships might be built not only across national borders but within their own cities and towns. Building relationships with migrants and others who are under the thumb of US empire must be the foundation of our political action and policy work.[130]

The creative establishment of relationships of accountability will require changes to foreign policy, especially insofar as US foreign action has so often been imperialist in nature. This will be best achieved if it includes partnering with other nations in new ways and rethinking (in partnership with other nations) what foreign aid looks like. It will require creative collaboration with migrants, Indigenous people, citizens of other countries, and more. The ELCA advocates for international and local laws that protect people fleeing persecution and for "policies that honor the humanity and voices of our Central American" siblings.[131]

As with the Catholic advocacy explored above, the ELCA is on the right path but could also significantly expand the policy vision for which it advocates. For example, the call for laws protecting those who flee persecution is good, but it does little to challenge or expand current US law. Current US asylum policy, for example, provides protections for any foreign national within US borders who fits the international definition of a refugee.[132] According to the testimonies of migrants and advocates familiar with the system, this leaves the vast majority of people who come to the US fleeing violence and seeking asylum with nothing. Based on chapter 2's articulation of US responsibility for much of the instability and violence that causes migrants to flee their homes, a more responsible immigration system would need to expand paths to citizenship (or other forms of membership[133]) to those to whom the nation is responsible. That is to say,

130. The dynamics of these sorts of visits can be tricky, as is relationship building more generally. Too often, well-meaning Christians enter the spaces of marginalized people in ways that are invasive, echoing colonial relationships. There is no easy solution for how to establish relationships without being invasive, but a focus on listening, accompaniment, and solidarity is a good start.

131. "Addressing Forced Displacement in Central America."

132. "Asylum in the United States," American Immigration Council, June 11, 2020, https://www.americanimmigrationcouncil.org/research/asylum-united-states.

133. By other forms of membership, I mean to challenge the system in which access to rights is so based on citizenship. In the present world order, paths to citizenship provide the best way to ensure migrants have access to protections and self-advocacy. Expanded and clear paths to citizenship are therefore an important thing to advocate for. However, the kin-dom of God

the United States must account for the way its own actions have formed migration paths and incorporate this understanding to create more humane policies. Policy that honors the voices and experiences of migrants demands nothing less. This may include explicitly including categories into US immigration policy for refugees fleeing wars or conflicts the US has supported, funded, or participated in; economic migrants driven from their lands and livelihoods by US foreign policy, especially expansionist capitalism; and migrants fleeing gang violence influenced by US presence or action. For example, many migrants flee gang violence that has arisen out of instability caused by US intervention in Latin and Central America.

Both the ELCA and the Catholic Church have generally cosmopolitan approaches to migration, foregrounding human dignity and kinship. The Evangelical Immigration Table (EIT), a group of evangelical Christian leaders "committed to learning more about what the Bible says about 'welcoming the stranger,' and living out these biblical principles in our churches, our communities and our nation,"[134] offers a different approach. They aim at a humane, pastoral approach to policy rooted in a more communitarian commitment to protecting the rule of law. At the heart of their approach is a "restitution-based" plan for immigration reform that would aim to uphold the rule of law without unduly separating mixed-status families. It would do so by providing a path to legal residence that includes "among other appropriate requirements" that undocumented immigrants pay a "significant fine as a penalty for having overstayed their visas or crossed into the U.S. unlawfully."[135] Asserting that God has created each person in God's own image and that the role of civil governments has been ordained by God, they call for an approach that upholds the rule of law while protecting human rights. In particular, they insist that the family unit, created by God, must not be violated "except in the rarest of circumstances." The EIT also insists that because "God delights in redemption," those who violate U.S. laws ought to be "restored."[136] In order for this restoration to take place, the EIT proposes a process of restitution which they explicitly separate from any form of amnesty, in which undocumented or irregular visa status immigrants pay

---

provides Christians with the creative capacity to envision a world in which membership in communities and access to rights might not require citizenship as it is presently conceived. This book intentionally leaves categories of membership open in order to encourage creative reimagining.

134. "Welcome to the Table," Evangelical Immigration Table, accessed November 12, 2019, http://evangelicalimmigrationtable.com.

135. "Restitution-Based Immigration Reform."

136. "Evangelical Call for Restitution-Based Immigration Reform," Evangelical Immigration Table, accessed December 12, 2020, https://evangelicalimmigrationtable.com/evangelical-call-for-restitution-based-immigration-reform/.

"significant fines/penalties" to make up for their violation of US law. Migrants who came as children would, in this proposal, have a separate path to legal residency. The proposal furthermore "encourage[s] fairness to taxpayers by requiring that all immigrants be self-sufficient, work, pay taxes, and be productive, or be in families and households that are doing so."[137]

The final aspect of the EIT proposal is an encouragement for the US government to establish an orderly immigration system and a secure border. This desire for security and order illuminates the communitarian bent of the EIT. It takes for granted the United States' right to its borders and errs toward faith in the status quo. The proposals it makes are moderate and practical. Most strikingly, the EIT encourages responsibility for past harms but in doing so locates the majority of responsibility with migrants themselves, who are depicted as wrongdoers who owe the United States, and especially US taxpayers, restitution, productivity, and self-sufficiency. The primary wrong with which the EIT is concerned is the alleged harm of violating US immigration law, for which they insist undocumented migrants owe the United States a debt.

Furthermore, the EIT proposal implies that membership in US communities requires productivity, self-sufficiency, and some form of payment for the failures of a system in which migrants have little say. This book has foregrounded the importance of relationships and community and encourages an expansion of how community membership is understood. Another important way immigration policy can be reshaped is through the formal acknowledgment of existing community membership. In particular, people who are undocumented or who have an irregular visa status are, in concrete and vital ways, already members of US communities. They are neighbors, parishioners, employees, business owners, friends, classmates. They have deep ties in this country, ties immigration policy fails to adequately acknowledge. This has been exacerbated in recent years as deportations have become increasingly indiscriminate. Just immigration policy must honor existing relationships undocumented people have with their various US communities. Our legal and personal conceptions of membership must expand beyond citizenship and legal residence to include those who do not meet those standards but are no less part of our communities, and legal pathways must be created to acknowledge and honor this expanded understanding of membership.

Center for Migration Studies executive director Donald M. Kerwin argues that a person's immigration status has wide-reaching impacts. For migrants themselves, the stakes may be obvious. Legal status and residency come with better access to housing, health care, employment, benefits, and political participation. With legal status comes the ability to more effectively and safely

137. "Evangelical Call for Restitution-Based Immigration Reform."

self-advocate, because in the United States the vast majority of structural and legal protections for individuals and families are tied to citizenship or legal residency. Furthermore, migrants with permanent, legal residency are statistically more able to integrate fully into their communities. These benefits, however, are not solely for migrants. Migrants' families and wider communities also benefit, as does the nation. Kerwin argues that it is for the good of both migrants and the United States as a whole that pathways to legal status and naturalization be made more accessible to all migrants.[138]

In light of the centrality of just, inclusive, accountable communities highlighted in chapter 5, the broad benefits of a more inclusive conception of membership are unsurprising. The entire community benefits when we move toward equity and justice. The EIT recognizes that the best path forward will include paths to legal residency for those who are undocumented, but in putting requirements such as fees, self-sufficiency, and productivity on migrants, they hinder the process to the detriment not only of migrants themselves but of the communities these migrants are already a part of and therefore to the detriment of the nation as a whole.

The EIT argues that while many undocumented migrants are fleeing difficult circumstances, with a few exceptions "they still did knowingly break U.S. law."[139] They go on to say, "This is why amnesty is wrong: Amnesty communicates that the law doesn't matter. Even when laws don't work well, they shouldn't simply be ignored—participants in a democratic society should work to change them." The problem with this argument is that noncitizens have few options for such work. The US legal system does not meaningfully consider undocumented migrants (or would-be migrants) participants in US democratic society. When the United States has contributed to the reasons people migrate and has offered little to no tangible accountability or acknowledgment of that responsibility, it is unclear what precisely migrants are supposed to do to challenge these laws aside from breaking them or waiting for a critical mass of US citizens and lawmakers to make necessary changes. Political theologian and ethicist Ulrich Schmiedel notes that migrants are people about whom laws are made, often without their input. The theopolitical figure of the migrant therefore offers a challenge to democratic systems that rely on the idea that those the law affects ought to have a say in the

138. Donald M. Kerwin and Robert Warren, "Putting America First: A Statistical Case for Encouraging Rather than Impeding and Devaluing U.S. Citizenship," *Journal on Migration and Human Security* 7, no. 4 (2019): 109–17.

139. They note specifically "those brought as minors or trafficked to the U.S. against their will" as exceptions. "Respecting the Rule of Law," Evangelical Immigration Table, December 3, 2019, https://evangelicalimmigrationtable.com/respecting-the-rule-of-law/.

creation of that law.[140] The idea that "the citizens who are affected by the law are also its authors and that the citizens who are its authors are also affected by the law"[141] appears to underpin the EIT's insistence that bad or inefficient laws be challenged and changed by participants in democratic society. The problem is that those who the EIT wishes to hold accountable for breaking immigration law are by and large not citizens and have therefore not had the opportunity to participate in shaping the laws that nonetheless affect them immensely.

The reality that laws are made about migrants without their input disrupts the sharp distinction between citizen and noncitizen and raises the question: "Whose laws should apply to whom?"[142] This challenges us to expand our understanding of membership and the rights and responsibilities that go with it. Migrants are part of our communities, because they are already here participating in them in a number of ways and, perhaps more fundamentally, because the United States has created relationships with them by virtue of ignoring the sovereignty of other nations. Until US immigration law reflects this reality in a substantial way, we can and should expect undocumented migration to continue. Migrants, as people with whom the United States has a relationship and about whom the United States makes laws, challenge the democratic system in which it is assumed that those who are affected by the law are also given an opportunity to shape it. Responsible immigration policy will need to seriously consider how those about whom laws are made (migrants) might have a more meaningful say in the shaping of those laws. This is how we begin to acknowledge that we are (and have been) in relationship with those beyond our borders and therefore move toward responsible, relational, and creatively comprehensive policy.

This points to a difficulty with the EIT's approach overall: they fail to sufficiently recognize the role the United States itself has played in creating mass migration. Their proposals therefore do not aim to hold the United States accountable other than through the tepid encouragement of an "orderly" system. This is, at its core, a failure to recognize where the power lies in the relationship between the United States and migrants. Just, responsible immigration policy grounded in the ecclesiological vision of chapter 5, while acknowledging the agency of migrants, will recognize that the United States has consistently been in a position of power and has failed to hold itself accountable. The primary responsibility for broken immigration laws rests on the United States, not on migrants making often impossible choices for survival.

---

140. Ulrich Schmiedel, "The Theopolitics of the Migrant: Toward a Coalitional and Comparative Political Theology," in Allard, Heyer, and Nadella, *Christianity and the Law of Migration*, 212–29.

141. Schmiedel, "Theopolitics of the Migrant," 212.

142. Schmiedel, "Theopolitics of the Migrant," 224.

While the EIT approach is perhaps most starkly opposed to the responsible, relational, and creative approach outlined in this chapter, all three pastoral approaches to policy advocacy profiled in this section fail to fully live up to the vision of this book. The ultimate weakness of these approaches is a lack of comprehensive vision. Certainly these pastoral bodies highlight important failings in the US immigration system, raise up key Christian values that ought to be upheld, and seek to protect human dignity in many ways. It is evident that they are genuine in their desire for justice. Most include sharp indictments of the present situation. I contend that they simply have not looked far enough beyond what currently exists to see what could be. Too often the way we think and talk about immigration—especially when "we" are white US citizens for whom the status quo more or less works—is bound by the way things are or have been. We need to think beyond this, to recognize how systematically the status quo fails people, and to imagine new ways of being in relationship with one another. Justice will be built by creative reimagining, not stubborn adherence to the way things presently work.

After outlining the history of immigration detention in the United States and establishing it as a flawed, inhumane system that serves the political and economic interests of a few elite US citizens while failing to respect the human dignity of migrants (as well as failing to actually make US citizens safer), García Hernández calls us to dream about what could be. It is time, he argues, for people to "push back against the decades-old bipartisan politics of fear with a politics of creative, impassioned courage: courage to discard what we in the United States do *for what we should do*."[143] This is the proper work for Christians. Chapter 5 highlighted resources in the Christian tradition for thinking beyond the status quo and imagining a more just world. Christians would do well, in their policy proposals and advocacy, to aim for more, for a world rooted in God's, rather than empire's, justice. In doing so, we move toward abolishing all that hinders true, relational justice.

This overview of the policy-related work of three pastoral bodies has illuminated some proposed policy contours intended to help Christians engage in public conversation about reform and aid them in being informed voters. Paired with the earlier proposals for steps Christian communities can take in order to foster the sort of holistic conversion that will help foster a more just situation for migrants, these reflections on policy offer Christian communities a foundation on which to begin, reimagine, or shift their responses to migration in the United States.

---

143. García Hernández, *Migrating to Prison*, 165–66. García Hernández speaks specifically with a vision for prison and detention abolition. This abolitionist lens, which dares to imagine what could be if we let go of what is, is well suited for the task of creating a more just future for migrants.

Conclusion

The proposals in this chapter and throughout this book aim at encouraging Christians to work tangibly for justice through the work of relationship building in their communities. Based on the christological and ecclesiological proposals of chapter 5, I have argued that such work is the proper work of the people of God. Additionally, to aim to establish greater justice for migrants is also to aim at greater justice for citizens of the United States, many of whom do not see the majority of the benefits of US imperialism. While it is beyond the scope of this book to fully attend to this dynamic, it is worth noting that the nation's racist colonialism has always benefited and continues to benefit the elite few while leaving most behind. Strategically, tying colonialist interests to whiteness, patriotism, and Christianity keeps US citizens aligned with the elite rather than with migrants, with whom their interests are in truth more linked. Moreover, with Kerwin, this book asserts that true justice and equity benefits all. The kin-dom of God puts the needs of the most vulnerable first in order to establish true, expansive justice for all.

Conclusion

When the United States withdrew from Afghanistan and left thousands of translators and others who had aided US efforts behind, there was widespread public concern. This was a recognition on some level that we had a duty to these people because of the specific relationships we had pursued with them. Many people saw the failure to provide adequate, long-term safety to those who put themselves in danger by engaging in a working relationship with the US military as an injustice. In Tisha Rajendra's terms, the United States failed to be faithful to the demands of these relationships. This is an important insight and one that we do not always recognize in the United States, where the language of individual freedoms often reigns supreme and where "America first" has too often been our operative moral framework.

We live in a deeply relational universe. Christian theology has long held this to be the case, emphasizing our unity in Christ and as people created in the image of God. That the God whose image we bear is triune, a mutually indwelling relationship, suggests that we are fundamentally social, meant to be in relationship with one another by our very creation. Science can also offer us a picture of a relational cosmos. Ecologist Robert E. Ulanowicsz argues that mutualism is a fundamental element of the evolutionary process. "The root and drive of all evolution, and even of competition itself, is seen to be mutual beneficence," he writes, "as if the Creator placed the divine signature on nature as a pale reflection of the love shared by the Holy Trinity."[1] Ethicist Dennis Edwards highlights the work of recent scientists who suggest that humans share an evolutionary basis for morality with other primates, such as bonobos and chimpanzees. Additionally, those specific characteristics that make humanity unique, our particular moral, emotional, and intellectual capacities that differ more sharply from our evolutionary cousins, appear to have developed as adaptations from our common ancestry. In other words, our shared capacities enabled humans to develop into the unique creatures we are today.[2]

---

1. Robert E. Ulanowicz, "Mutualism in the Darwinian Scenario," Washington Theological Consortium Conference, April 14, 2012, 6, 10, https://washtheocon.org/wp-content/uploads/2013/12/Mutualism-Darwinian.pdf.

2. Denis Edwards, *The Natural World and God: Theological Explorations* (Adelaide, Australia: ATF, 2017), esp. 55–77.

Similarly, scientists working on the Human Microbiome Project, which aims to identify and classify the various microbes inhabiting the human body, found that the nonhuman microbes within human bodies outnumber our genetically human somatic and germ cells by a ratio of 10 to 1.9. Because these nonhuman biota are both extremely prevalent and very necessary for our bodies to function, these scientists conclude that the human body can be thought of as "a composite of microbial and human species."[3] That is, whenever we talk about the human person, we are talking about some sort of "collaborative effort between some mysterious emergent 'self' and trillions of microbes representing over 10,000 species composed of elements passed along through ages of planetary and biological evolutionary development as well as that 'self's' formative interaction with his or her physical and social environment! [The] 'I' is a dynamic ecosystem—indeed, a collection of them."[4] The Human Microbiome Project offers a vision of the human person as the product of relationships both with other people and creatures but also with the very particles that make up the cosmos.

Like Ulanowicsz, ethicists Jacob Kohlhaas and Ryan McLaughlin put these scientific findings in conversation with trinitarian theology, looking in particular at the Trinity understood as mutual indwelling, which suggests that the oneness of God is constituted in and by the intimate relationships of the three persons. The center of God's God-ness, what unifies the diversity of the Trinity and makes the three persons equally God, is the loving, mutual, equitable relationship they share. From here, we can see that human selfhood, something constituted by relationships not only on the social level but on the cellular, microbial level, is precisely how we image the triune God. They argue that "the interconnectedness of beings is a consequence of existence within a universe that images the Triune God."[5] The mutual character of the cosmos reflects the mutual character of God. The universe is relational because God is.

This reality carries moral weight. Emphasizing the relational nature of justice, viewing just action not as adherence to a series of abstract norms but as a dynamic process of being faithful (responsible) to our various relationships,[6] can help us respond to the deeply relational universe in which we live. By defining

3. Jacob M. Kohlhaas and Ryan Patrick McLaughlin, "Loving the World We Are: Anthropology and Relationalioty in *Laudato Si*," *JRE* 47, no. 3 (2019): 508; Peter J. Turnbaugh, Ruth E. Ley, Micah Hamady, Claire Fraser-Liggett, Rob Knight, and Jeffrey I. Gordon, "The Human Microbiome Project: Exploring the Microbial Part of Ourselves in a Changing World," *Nature* 449, no. 7164 (October 18, 2007): 804–10.

4. Kohlhaas and McLaughlin, "Loving the World We Are," 509.

5. Kohlhaas and McLaughlin, "Loving the World We Are," 513.

6. Rajendra, *Migrants and Citizens*, 93–141.

right moral action as action that responds fittingly to our specific circumstances and the people we are in relationship with, a responsibility-ethics framework can provide important tools for attending to our relational reality.

This book has offered a consideration of US history that focuses especially on the voices and perspectives of those who have been ignored or silenced. Rajendra highlights the necessity of such a retrieval, arguing that justice, understood relationally, "incorporates the option for the poor not as a universal directive to care for the poor," although of course we continue to take this call as central to Christian ethics, "but as a reminder that those whose voices are ignored or forgotten are those whose perspectives are most often left out of social narratives." Responsibility ethics highlights the central role these social narratives play in shaping our understanding of right (fitting) moral choices. Justice demands accurate narratives,[7] and that necessitates a full consideration of the perspectives of those who have been left out, silenced, and harmed.

Attention to history, and especially to the unjust relationships the United States has forged with the people most often left out of our founding stories, highlights the need for a responsibility ethic that takes seriously the ways in which US actions have shaped migration patterns and thus obligate the United States to make reparations for the inequalities it has caused. I have argued for a conceptual shift in Christian dialogue in order to more adequately respond to the historical and relational realities of migration and to foster conversion, and have offered some practical steps for resisting continued US imperialism. These practical proposals are grounded in the christological and ecclesiological contributions of Latine and Indigenous theologians, which help thicken and contextualize radical Christian love.

This book's focus has largely been North American, looking particularly at US history and at the realities faced by those who migrate to the United States. More broadly, however, the findings of this project suggest a methodology that might be applied to a variety of contexts. Nations other than the United States are currently struggling with how best to handle migration. Many, like the United States, have some history of imperialistic or colonial action that has affected migration flows and shaped migration policy. They too would do well to consider how this history might make them specifically responsible to migrants and how that responsibility can be best addressed in concrete actions. More broadly, this book has argued that justice requires taking responsibility for relationships that have been unjust and working to create justice through the establishment of accountability, mutuality, and equity. Reframing questions of migration ethics and policy to foreground relationality in this way can lead not only to more humane treatment of migrants but also to more creative actions

7. Rajendra, *Migrants and Citizens*, 115, 109.

and policies that build toward a just future, especially when we let the visions of those who are most vulnerable lead the way.

Additionally, while space and scope have not allowed for a robust consideration of the many ways in which harm to migrants and harm to the environment are connected, I believe a robustly relational approach to ethics is well suited to attend to these connections. More than almost any other issue we face today, climate change makes abundantly clear that the world is deeply relational. The choices individual nations make affect the whole climate and can have drastic consequences for people and nations to whom we do not always think of ourselves as connected. We need moral frameworks that can help us take this seriously and take responsibility for the relationships we have not always seen or acknowledged. More basically, a responsibility framework highlights unjust patterns of relating that undergird not only our harmful treatment of other people but our harmful treatment of the earth. Science and theology both highlight that we are in relationship with all of creation. Do our social narratives sufficiently acknowledge this? How might we be more responsible, respond more fittingly to these relationships? Might Earth be owed some reparative justice alongside migrants?

It is not the intention of this book to argue that a turn to relationality and responsibility will be an easy fix or will solve all problems and disagreements. Human relationships are difficult and messy. Vulnerable and marginalized people will not all want or need the same forms of reparative action. Disentangling immigration policy and discourse from deeply entrenched and harmful ideologies so that it might function in a more just manner will be a massive undertaking. What a turn to relationships and responsibility does do, however, is shift focus away from debates between human rights and state sovereignty. Framing migration ethics instead in terms of human relationality, asking questions about how we have harmed each other and how we might move forward, keeps space open to consider the important commitments of communitarians and cosmopolitans while opening up a more dialogic method of proceeding out of which we might begin to build a more just future. It is my hope that this book may contribute in some way to that goal.

BIBLIOGRAPHY

Ablavsky, Gregory. “The Savage Constitution.” *Duke Law Journal* 63, no. 5 (February 2014): 999–1089. link.gale.com/apps/doc/A360474541/AONE?u=txshracd2799&sid=bookmark-AONE&xid=f2013f83.

Ables, Kelsey. “U.S. Judge Halts Biden Attempt to End ‘Remain in Mexico’ Policy.” *Washington Post*, December 15, 2022. https://www.washingtonpost.com/nation/2022/12/15/remain-in-mexico-policy-immigration-texas-judge/.

Aguilera, Jasmine. “Here’s What to Know about the Status of Family Separation at the U.S. Border, Which Isn’t Nearly Over.” *Time*, September 20, 2019. https://time.com/5678313/trump-administration-family-separation-lawsuits/.

Aizenman, Nurith. “Trump Wishes We Had More Immigrants from Norway. Turns Out We Once Did.” National Public Radio, January 12, 2018. https://www.npr.org/sections/goatsandsoda/2018/01/12/577673191/trump-wishes-we-had-more-immigrants-from-norway-turns-out-we-once-did.

Alexander, Michelle. *The New Jim Crow: Mass Incarceration in the Age of Colorblindness.* New York: New Press, 2012.

Allen, John L., Jr. “Francis and the ‘Culture of Encounter.’” National Catholic Reporter, December 20, 2013. https://www.ncronline.org/blogs/ncr-today/francis-and-culture-encounter.

Althaus Reid, Marcella. *From Feminist Theology to Indecent Theology: Readings on Poverty, Sexual Identity and God.* London: SCM, 2004.

Amantini, Laura Santi. “Reparative Responsibility for the Harms of Forced Migration.” *Journal of Social Philosophy* (2022): 1–19. https://doi.org/10.1111/josp.12493.

American Civil Liberties Union. “New ACLU Report Shows Fear of Deportation Is Deterring Immigrants from Reporting Crimes.” May 3, 2018. https://www.aclu.org/press-releases/new-aclu-report-shows-fear-deportation-deterring-immigrants-reporting-crimes.

Amos, Deborah. “Biden Plans to Reopen America to Refugees after Trump Slashed Admissions.” National Public Radio, November 11, 2020. https://www.npr.org/2020/11/11/933500132/biden-plans-to-reopen-america-to-refugees-after-trump-slashed-admissions.

Amstutz, Mark R. *Just Immigration: American Policy in Christian Perspective.* Grand Rapids: Eerdmans, 2017.

———. “Two Theories of Immigration.” *First Things: A Monthly Journal of Religion and Public Life*, no. 258 (2015). https://www.firstthings.com/article/2015/12/two-theories-of-immigration.

Annunciation House homepage. Last updated August 6, 2020. https://annunciationhouse.org/.

Appiah, Kwame Anthony. "Cosmopolitan Patriotism." In *For Love of Country*, edited by Martha Nussbaum, 619–22. Boston: Beacon, 2002.

"Applying for Asylum: How Much Will It Cost." NOLO, accessed July 4, 2023. https://www.nolo.com/legal-encyclopedia/how-expensive-obtain-asylum-the-us.html.

Aquino, María Pilar. "Theological Method in U.S. Latino/a Theology." In *From the Heart of Our People*, edited by Orlando O. Espín and Miguel H. Díaz, 6–48. Maryknoll, NY: Orbis Books, 1999.

Araujo, Ana Lucia. *Reparations for Slavery and the Slave Trade: A Transnational and Comparative History*. New York: Bloomsbury Academic, 2017.

Arendt, Hannah. "The Perplexities of the Rights of Man." *Headline Series* 318 (Winter 1998): 88.

Association of Wartime Allies. "Our Story." Accessed October 19, 2022. https://www.wartimeallies.co/about.

"Asylum in the United States." American Immigration Council, June 11, 2020. https://www.americanimmigrationcouncil.org/research/asylum-united-states.

Atapattu, Sumudu. "'Climate Refugees' and the Role of International Law." Oxford Research Group, September 12, 2018. https://tinyurl.com/ytwbrsj4.

Bacon, David. *The Right to Stay Home: How US Policy Drives Mexican Migration*. Boston: Beacon, 2013.

Barnhill, John H. "Bracero Program." In *Multicultural America: A Multimedia Encyclopedia*, edited by Carlos E. Cortés, 389–90. Thousand Oaks, CA: SAGE, 2013.

Barokka, Khairani. "The Case against Italicizing 'Foreign' Words." Catapult, February 11, 2020. https://catapult-prod.herokuapp.com/stories/column-the-case-against-italicizing-foreign-words-khairani-barokka.

Baudouin, Mary. "The Encuentro Project: Encountering the Other on the El Paso/Juarez Border." Accessed January 20, 2021. https://www.jesuitscentralsouthern.org/stories/the-encuentro-project-encountering-the-other-on-the-el-paso-juarez-border/.

Baum, Gregory. "Structures of Sin." In *The Logic of Solidarity: Commentaries on Pope John Paul II's Encyclical on Social Concern*, edited by Gregory Baum and Robert Ellsberg, 110–26. Maryknoll, NY: Orbis, 1989.

Bellah, Robert N. "Civil Religion in America." *Daedalus* 96, no. 1 (1967): 1–21.

———. "Comment: [Twenty Years after Bellah: Whatever Happened to American Civil Religion?]." *Sociological Analysis* 50, no. 2 (1989): 147. https://doi.org/10.2307/3710984.

"Biden Administration in the Clear to End MPP." American Immigration Council, last modified August 9, 2022. https://www.americanimmigrationcouncil.org/news/biden-administration-clear-end-mpp.

Biggar, Nigel. *Between Kin and Cosmopolis: An Ethic of the Nation*. Cambridge: Clarke, 2014.

Birch, Bruce. *Let Justice Roll Down: The Old Testament, Ethics, and Christian Life*. Louisville, KY: Westminster John Knox, 1991.

Bova, Gus. "Shelter Director Ruben Garcia on How Struggling Nonprofits Carry the Load of the Migrant 'Crisis.'" *Texas Observer*, June 24, 2019. https://www.texasobserver.org/crisis-management-el-paso-interview-annunciation-house/.

Bradburn, Douglas M. "'True Americans' and 'Hordes of Foreigners': Nationalism, Ethnicity and the Problem of Citizenship in the United States, 1789–1800." *Historical Reflections / Réflexions Historiques* 29, no. 1 (Spring 2003): 19–41.

Branche, Jerome. *Race, Colonialism, and Social Transformation in Latin America and the Caribbean*. Gainesville: University Press of Florida, 2008.

Breitenberg, E. Harold. "To Tell the Truth: Will the Real Public Theology Please Stand Up?" *Journal of the Society of Christian Ethics* 23, no. 2 (2003): 55–96. https://doi.org/10.5840/jsce20032325.

Brest, Mike. "Estimated 450 Americans and Thousands of SIV Applicants Remain in Afghanistan: Defense Official." *The Washington Examiner*, October 26, 2021. https://www.washingtonexaminer.com/policy/defense-national-security/estimated-450-americans-and-thousands-of-siv-applicants-remain-in-afghanistan-defense-official.

Brewer, Kenneth W. "Wesley, National Sins, and Repentance: Does True Repentance Mandate Reparations?" *Wesleyan Theological Journal* 56, no. 1 (Spring 2021): 24–51.

Briggs-Cloud, Marcus. "Creation—The New Creation: A Maskoke Postcolonial Perspective." In *Coming Full Circle: Constructing Native Christian Theology*, edited by Steven Charleston and Elaine A. Robinson, 89–118. Minneapolis: Augsburg Fortress, 2015.

Brokenleg, Martin. "Church—Wocekiye Okolakiciye: A Lakota Experience of the Church." In *Coming Full Circle: Constructing Native Christian Theology*, edited by Steven Charleston and Elaine A. Robinson, 133–49. Minneapolis: Augsburg Fortress, 2015.

Brooks, Roy L. *Atonement and Forgiveness: A New Model for Black Reparations*. Berkeley: University of California Press, 2004.

Buff, Rachel Ida. "Sanctuary Everywhere." *Radical History Review*, no. 135 (2019): 14–42. https://doi.org/10.1215/01636545-7607809.

Burke, Kevin F. *The Ground beneath the Cross: The Theology of Ignacio Ellacuría*. Washington, DC: Georgetown University Press, 2000.

Burnett, John. "A Chapter in U.S. History Often Ignored: The Flight of Runaway Slaves to Mexico." NPR, February 28, 2021. https://tinyurl.com/2y9hymm7.

Burrough, Bryan, Chris Tomlinson, and Jason Stanford. *Forget the Alamo: The Rise and Fall of an American Myth*. New York: Penguin, 2021.

Buxton, Rebecca. "Reparative Justice for Climate Refugees." *Philosophy* 94, no. 2 (2019): 193–219.

Carlson, Elizabeth, Luis Guerra, and Tania Guerrero. "Supreme Court Holds That Biden Administration's Termination of the Migrant Protection Protocols Did Not Violate the Immigration and Nationality Act Authors." CLINIC, August 24, 2022. https://tinyurl.com/wz7z96vk.

Carroll R., M. Daniel. *Christians at the Border: Immigration, the Church, and the Bible*. Grand Rapids: Baker Academic, 2008.

Castles, Stephen. "Towards a Sociology of Forced Migration and Social Transformation." *Sociology* 37, no. 1 (2003): 13–34. https://doi.org/10.1177/0038038503037001384.

Charleston, Steven. "Articulating a Native American Theological Theory." In *Full Circle: Constructing Native Christian Theology*, edited by Steven Charleston and Elaine A. Robinson, 1–26. Minneapolis: Augsburg Fortress, 2015.

Chavez, Leo R. *The Latino Threat: Constructing Immigrants, Citizens, and the Nation.* Stanford, CA: Stanford University Press, 2013.

Cheng, Patrick S. *From Sin to Amazing Grace: Discovering the Queer Christ.* New York: Seabury Books, 2012.

Chishti, Muzaffar, Sarah Pierce, and Jessica Bolter. "Muscular Public Relations Strategy to Paint Immigrants and Immigration as Negatives Embedded Deep within Trump Executive Orders." Migration Policy Institute, March 22, 2017. https://www.migrationpolicy.org/article/muscular-public-relations-strategy-paint-immigrants-and-immigration-negatives-embedded-deep.

Clements, Chris. "KSJD Local Newscast—March 22, 2023." KSDJ, March 22, 2023. https://www.ksjd.org/podcast/ksjd-local-newscasts/2023-03-22/ksjd-local-newscast-march-22-2023.

Coates, Ta-Nahisi. "The Case for Reparations." *Atlantic*, June 2014. https://www.theatlantic.com/magazine/archive/2014/06/the-case-for-reparations/361631/.

Collier, Elizabeth W., and Charles R. Strain. *Religious and Ethical Perspectives on Global Migration*. Lanham, MD: Lexington Books, 2014.

"Commerce Clause." Cornell Law School. Accessed February 20, 2020. https://www.law.conrell.edu/wex/commerce_clause.

Cone, James H. *A Black Theology of Liberation*. Philadelphia: Lippincott, 1970.

———. *The Cross and the Lynching Tree.* Maryknoll, NY: Orbis Books, 2011.

Connor, Phillip, and Neil G. Ruiz. "Majority of U.S. Public Supports High-Skilled Immigration." Pew Research Center, January 22, 2019. https://www.pewresearch.org/global/2019/01/22/majority-of-u-s-public-supports-high-skilled-immigration/.

Copeland, M. Shawn. *Enfleshing Freedom: Body, Race and Being.* Minneapolis: Fortress, 2010.

———. "Marking the Body of Jesus, the Body of Christ." In *The Strength of Her Witness: Jesus Christ in the Global Voices of Women*, edited by Elizabeth Johnson, 270–83. Maryknoll, NY: Orbis, 2016.

———. "Wading through Many Sorrows: Toward a Theology of Suffering in Womanist Perspective." In *A Troubling in my Soul: Womanist Perspectives on Evil and Suffering*, edited by Emilie M. Townes, 109–29. Maryknoll, NY: Orbis, 1999.

Cox, Ronald. *Power and Profits: U.S. Policy in Central America*. Lexington: University Press of Kentucky, 2015.

Cuison-Villazor, Rose, and Ulrich Schmiedel. "'No More Deaths.' Religious Liberty as a Defense for Providing Sanctuary for Immigrants." In *Christianity and the Law of Migration*, edited by Silas W. Allard, Kristin E. Heyer, and Raj Nadella, 212–29. New York: Routledge, 2022.

Curran, Charles E. *The Catholic Moral Tradition Today: A Synthesis.* Washington, DC: Georgetown University Press, 1999.

———. *Christian Morality Today: The Renewal of Moral Theology*. Notre Dame, IN: Fides, 1966.

———. "Responsibility in Moral Theology: Centrality, Foundations, and Implications for Ecclesiology." *The Jurist* 31, no. 1 (1971): 113–42.

———. "White Privilege." *Horizons* 32, no. 2 (2005): 361–67.

Curtice, Kaitlin. "Dear Church, It's Time To Listen." *Sojourners*, May 25, 2017. https://sojo.net/articles/dear-church-it-s-time-listen.

———. "Decolonize Your Faith This Lent: A Reading List." *Sojourners*, March 6, 2019. https://sojo.net/articles/decolonize-your-faith-lent-reading-list.

———. "Have We Missed Who Jesus Is Altogether?" *Sojourners*, June 27, 2017. https://sojo.net/articles/have-we-missed-who-jesus-altogether.

———. "Is the Work of Deconstruction Violent or Fruitful?" *Sojourners*, February, 12, 2019. https://sojo.net/articles/work-deconstruction-violent-or-fruitful.

———. "It's Time to Prune Back the Unfruitful Parts of American Christianity." *Sojourners*, May 8, 2017. https://sojo.net/articles/it-s-time-prune-back-unfruitful-parts-american-christianity.

Daly, Mary. *The Church and the Second Sex*. New York: Harper & Row, 1968.

Denvir, Daniel. "Deporting People Made Central America's Gangs. More Deportation Won't Help." *Washington Post*, July 20, 2017. https://www.washingtonpost.com/news/posteverything/wp/2017/07/20/deporting-people-made-central-americas-gangs-more-deportation-wont-help/.

Deloria, Philip Joseph. *Playing Indian*. New Haven, CT: Yale University Press, 1998.

Department of Justice. "Remarks Announcing the Department of Justice's Renewed Commitment to Criminal Immigration Enforcement." Speech, Nogales, AZ, April 11, 2017. https://www.justice.gov/opa/speech/attorney-general-jeff-sessions-delivers-remarks-announcing-department-justice-s-renewed.

Devereaux, Ryan. "Humanitarian Volunteer Scott Warren Reflects on the Borderlands and Two Years of Government Persecution." The Intercept, November 23, 2019. https://theintercept.com/2019/11/23/scott-warren-verdict-immigration-border/.

Díaz, Miguel. "Outside the Survival of Community There Is No Salvation." In *Building Bridges, Doing Justice: Constructing a Latino/a Ecumenical Theology*, edited by Orlando Espín, 91–111. Maryknoll, NY: Orbis Books, 2009.

Douglas, Kelly Brown. *Stand Your Ground: Black Bodies and the Justice of God*. Maryknoll, NY: Orbis Books, 2015.

Dunbar-Ortiz, Roxanne. *An Indigenous Peoples' History of the United States*. Revisioning American History. Boston: Beacon, 2014.

———. *Not "A Nation of Immigrants": Settler Colonialism, White Supremacy, and a History of Erasure and Exclusion*. Boston: Beacon, 2021.

Dura, Nigel. "Arizona's Once-Feared Immigration Law, SB 1070, Loses Most of Its Power in Settlement." *Los Angeles Times*, September 15, 2016. https://www.latimes.com/nation/la-na-arizona-law-20160915-snap-story.html.

Edling, Max. "The US Fiscal-Military State and the Conquest of a Continent, 1783–1900." In *The Cambridge History of America and the World*, edited by Kristin Hoganson and Jay Sexton, 220–45. Cambridge: Cambridge University Press, 2021.

Edwards, Denis. *The Natural World and God: Theological Explorations*. Adelaide, Australia: ATF, 2017.

"El Paso: One Year Later." *The Commonweal Podcast*, July 31, 2020. https://tinyurl.com/nhft6t6j.

Estes, Nick. "Go Back to Where You Came From." Open Space SFMOMA, November 4, 2019. https://openspace.sfmoma.org/2019/11/go-back-to-where-you-came-from/.

———. *Our History Is the Future: Standing Rock versus the Dakota Access Pipeline, and the Long Tradition of Indigenous Resistance*. Verso Colophon, 2019.

"Evangelical Call for Restitution-Based Immigration Reform." Evangelical Immigration Table, accessed December 12, 2020. https://evangelicalimmigrationtable.com/evangelical-call-for-restitution-based-immigration-reform/.

Evangelical Lutheran Church in America. "Addressing Forced Displacement in Central America through Advocacy." Accessed December 12, 2020. http://download.elca.org/ELCA%20Resource%20Repository/Factsheet_Addressing_Forced_Displacement_2016.pdf.

———. "Family Separation." September 2018. https://tinyurl.com/yc75xm3r.

———. "From Ministry to Advocacy: A Guide to Advocacy after Visiting Lutheran Churches in Central America and Mexico." Accessed September 20, 2023. https://tinyurl.com/bdn4666f.

———. "Social Statement on the Church in Society." September 1991. https://tinyurl.com/4mptfecz.

———. "Support the NO BAN Act." Accessed December 12, 2020. https://support.elca.org/site/Advocacy?cmd=display&page=UserAction&id=1211.

"Fact Sheet: President Biden Sends Immigration Bill to Congress as Part of His Commitment to Modernize Our Immigration System." The White House, January 20, 2021. https://www.whitehouse.gov/briefing-room/statements-releases/2021/01/20/fact-sheet-president-biden-sends-immigration-bill-to-congress-as-part-of-his-commitment-to-modernize-our-immigration-system/.

"FACT SHEET: The Biden Administration Blueprint for a Fair, Orderly and Humane Immigration System." The White House, July 27, 2021. https://www.whitehouse.gov/briefing-room/statements-releases/2021/07/27/fact-sheet-the-biden-administration-blueprint-for-a-fair-orderly-and-humane-immigration-system/.

Fadal, Leila. "Columbus Day or Indigenous Peoples' Day." National Public Radio, October 14, 2019. https://www.npr.org/2019/10/14/769083847/columbus-day-or-indigenous-peoples-day.

Fernández-Armesto, Felipe. *Our America: A Hispanic History of the United States*. New York: Norton, 2014.

"Fighting to Save the Lives of Those That Served the U.S." Association of Wartime Allies, accessed October 19, 2022. https://www.wartimeallies.co/.

Fischer, Martina, and Olivera Simić. *Transitional Justice and Reconciliation: Lessons from the Balkans*. New York: Routledge, 2016.

Foley, Elise. "U.S. Left Most Afghans Who Helped Americans Behind." Huffington Post, September 1, 2021. https://www.huffpost.com/entry/afghanistan-siv-applicants_n_612fc097e4b0aac9c011d73b.

Folsom, Ralph Haughwout. *NAFTA, Free Trade and Foreign Investment in the Americas in a Nutshell*. St. Paul, MN: West Academic, 2014.

"Forced Migrant." Migration and Home Affairs, European Commission, accessed August 7, 2023. https://tinyurl.com/bdezf79w.

Francis, Pope. "Vigil of Pentecost with the Ecclesial Movements: Address of the Holy Father." Vatican, May 18, 2013. http://www.vatican.va/content/francesco/en/speeches/2013/may/documents/papa-francesco_20130518_veglia-pentecoste.html.

Frank, Andrew K., and Glenn A. Crothers. *Borderland Narratives: Negotiation and Accommodation in North America's Contested Spaces, 1500–1850*. Gainesville: University Press of Florida, 2017.

Frey, John Carlos. *Sand and Blood: America's Stealth War on the Mexico Border*. New York: Bold Type Books, 2019.

García Hernández, César Cuauhtémoc. *Migrating to Prison: America's Obsession with Locking Up Immigrants*. New York: New Press, 2019.

Gendelman, Rebecca. "Inadequate Access to Legal Representation, Rushed Timelines Impede Meaningful Opportunity to Seek Asylum under New Asylum Processing Rule." Human Rights First, September 14, 2022. https://humanrightsfirst.org/library/inadequate-access-to-legal-representation-rushed-timelines-impede-meaningful-opportunity-to-seek-asylum-under-new-asylum-processing-rule/.

Gevelber, Tevah. "Stuck While the World Moves On: Upwards of 160,000 Afghans Remain in Limbo." Responsible Statecraft, June 14, 2022. https://responsiblestatecraft.org/2022/06/14/stuck-while-the-world-moves-on-160000-afghans-remain-in-limbo/.

Giangreci, Leigh. "After 18 Months in Sanctuary at a Bethesda Church, This Undocumented Mother Has Been Granted a Stay of Removal." DCist, June 5, 2020. https://dcist.com/story/20/06/05/rosa-gutierrez-lopez-cedar-lane-ice-pandemic/.

Glaister, Dan, and Ewen MacAskill. "US Counts Cost of Day without Immigrants." *The Guardian*, May 1, 2006. https://www.theguardian.com/world/2006/may/02/usa.topstories3.

Gobat, Michel. *Empire by Invitation: William Walker and Manifest Destiny in Central America*. Cambridge, MA: Harvard University Press, 2018.

Goizueta, Roberto. "Beyond the Frontier Myth." In *Hispanic Christian Thought at the Dawn of the 21st Century*, edited by Justo J. González, Alvin Padilla, Roberto Goizueta, and Eldin Villafañe, 150–58. Nashville: Abingdon, 2005.

———. "Corpus Verum: Toward a Borderland Ecclesiology." In *Building Bridges, Doing Justice: Constructing a Latino/a Ecumenical Theology*, edited by Orlando Espín, 167–84. Maryknoll, NY: Orbis Books, 2009.

Golash-Boza, Tanya. "The Immigration Industrial Complex: Why We Enforce Immigration Policies Destined to Fail." *Sociology Compass* 3, no. 2 (2009): 295–309.

Gomez, Adam. "Deus Vult: John L. O'Sullivan, Manifest Destiny, and American Democratic Messianism." *American Political Thought* 1, no. 2 (2012): 236–62.

Gonzalez, Juan. *Harvest of Empire: A History of Latinos in America*. New York: Penguin Books, 2000.

Gonzalez-Barbera, Ana, and Phillip Conner. "Around the World, More Say Immigrants Are a Strength Than a Burden." Pew Research Center, March 14, 2019. https://www.pewresearch.org/global/2019/03/14/around-the-world-more-say-immigrants-are-a-strength-than-a-burden/.

Gorski, Philip. *American Covenant: A History of Civil Religion from the Puritans to the Present*. Princeton, NJ: Princeton University Press, 2019.

Groody, Daniel G. "Crossing the Divide: Foundations of a Theology of Migration and Refugees." *TS* 70, no. 3 (2009): 638–67.

———. "Jesus and the Undocumented Immigrant: A Spiritual Geography of a Crucified People." *TS* 70, no. 2 (2009): 298–316.

———. "Migration: A Theological Vision." In *Intersections of Religion and Migration: Issues at the Global Crossroads*, edited by Jennifer B. Saunders, Elena Fiddian-Qasmiyeh, and Susanna Snyder, 225–40. New York: Palgrave Macmillan, 2016.

Gross, Terry. "From Slavery to Socialism, New Legislation Restricts What Teachers Can Discuss." NPR, February 3, 2022. https://tinyurl.com/3svpww52.

Guardado, Leo. "Just Peace, Just Sanctuary." In *A Just Peace Ethic Primer: Building Sustainable Peace and Breaking Cycles of Violence*, edited by Eli Sasaran McCarthy, 77–92. Washington, DC: Georgetown University Press, 2020.

Gutiérrez, Gustavo. "Expanding the View." In *Expanding the View: Gustavo Gutiérrez and the Future of Liberation Theology*, edited by Marc H. Ellis and Otto Maduro. Maryknoll, NY: Orbis Books, 1990.

———. *A Theology of Liberation: History, Politics, and Salvation*. Maryknoll, NY: Orbis Books, 1973.

Gyory, Andrew. *Closing the Gate: Race, Politics, and the Chinese Exclusion Act*. Chapel Hill: University of North Carolina Press, 1998.

Haight, Roger. "Trinity and Religious Pluralism." *JES* 44, no. 4 (2009): 525–40.

Hall, Ryan. "The Two Hands of Yes and No." Campaign Nonviolence, October, 8, 2019. https://paceebene.org/blog/2019/10/8/the-two-hands-of-yes-and-no.

Hammond, Phillip E. "The Sociology of American Civil Religion: A Bibliographical Essay." *Sociological Analysis* 37, no. 2 (1976): 169–82. https://doi.org/10.2307/3709692.

Harris, Elise. "Central American Bishops Defend Francis over Amazon Synod, 'Pachamama.'" Crux, December 2, 2019. https://cruxnow.com/church-in-the-americas/2019/12/central-american-bishops-defend-francis-over-amazon-synod-pachamama/.

Heimbach-Steins, Marianne. "Migration in a Post-colonial World." in *Religious and Ethical Perspectives on Global Migration*, edited by Elizabeth W. Collier and Charles R. Strain, 87–108. Lanham, MD: Lexington Books, 2014.

Heimburger, Robert W. *God and the Illegal Alien: United States Immigration Law and a Theology of Politics*. Cambridge: Cambridge University Press, 2018.

Hernández, Arelis R. "She Was Supposed to Be Deported, Leaving Three Children. Instead, She Hid in a Church." *Washington Post*, December 12, 2018. https://tinyurl.com/tbwt3uyx.

Herrera, Allison. "U.S. Supreme Court Sides with Tribes in Stunning 5–4 Ruling." KGOU, July 9, 2020. https://www.kgou.org/politics-and-government/2020-07-09/u-s-supreme-court-sides-with-tribes-in-stunning-5-4-ruling.

Heyer, Kristin E. "Internalized Borders: Immigration Ethics in the Age of Trump." *TS* 79, no. 1 (2018): 146–64.

———. *Kinship across Borders: A Christian Ethic of Immigration.* Washington, DC: Georgetown University Press, 2012.

———. "Migrants Feared and Forsaken: A Catholic Ethic of Social Responsibility." *Interdisciplinary Journal for Religion and Transformation in Contemporary Society* 6, no. 1 (2020): 158–70. https://doi.org/10.30965/23642807-00601010.

———. "Social Sin and Immigration: Good Fences Make Bad Neighbors." *TS* 71 (2010): 410–36. https://doi.org/10.1177/004056391007100207.

Hoffmeier, James. *The Immigration Crisis: Immigrants, Aliens, and the Bible.* Wheaton, IL: Crossway, 2009.

Hogan, Linda. "Formative and Transformative." *JRE* 41, no. 2 (2013): 354–75. https://doi.org/10.1111/jore.12017.

Hollenbach, David, SJ. "Borders and Duties to the Displaced: Ethical Perspectives on the Refugee Protection System." *Journal on Migration and Human Security* 4, no. 3 (2016): 148–65.

———. *Driven from Home: Protecting the Rights of Forced Migrants.* Washington, DC: Georgetown University Press, 2010.

———. "A Future beyond Borders: Reimagining the Nation-State and the Church." In *Living with(out) Borders*, edited by Agnes Brazal and Maria Teresa Davila, 223–35. Maryknoll, NY: Orbis, 2016.

———. *Humanity in Crisis: Ethical and Religious Response to Refugees.* Washington, DC: Georgetown University Press, 2020.

———. "Internally Displaced People, Sovereignty, and the Responsibility to Protect." In *Refugee Rights: Ethics, Advocacy, and Africa*, edited by David Hollenbach 177–94. Washington, DC: Georgetown University Press, 2008.

Houston, Fleur S. *You Shall Love the Stranger as Yourself: The Bible, Refugees, and Asylum.* New York: Routledge, 2015.

"How Much Does an Immigration Lawyer Cost?" Upcounsel, accessed July 4, 2023. https://www.upcounsel.com/immigration-attorney-fees.

Ibrahim, Hudda. *From Somalia to Snow: How Central Minnesota Became Home to Somalis.* St. Paul, MN: Beaver's Pond, 2017.

Iftin, Abdi Nor. *Call Me American: A Memoir.* New York: Vintage, 2019.

Imperatori-Lee, Natalia. *Cuéntame: Narrative in the Ecclesial Present.* Maryknoll, NY: Orbis Books, 2018.

International Rescue Committee. "Evacuations from Afghanistan: What Is the Afghan Special Immigrant Visa (SIV) Program?" August 2, 2021. https://tinyurl.com/2zcb9zxy.

———. "Is It Legal to Cross the U.S. Border to Seek Asylum?" Last modified May 10, 2023. https://tinyurl.com/5n6vx6bk.

Isasi-Díaz, Ada Maria. "Kin-dom of God: A Mujerista Proposal." In *In Our Own Voices: Latino/a Renditions of Theology*, edited by Benjamin Valentin, 179–86. Maryknoll, NY: Orbis, 2010.

Jaimes, M. Annette. "Federal Indian Identification Policy: A Usurpation of Indigenous Sovereignty in North America." In *The State of Native America: Genocide,*

Colonization, and Resistance, edited by M. Annette Jaimes, 113–36. Boston: South End, 1992.

James, Thomas. "Responsibility Ethics and Postliberalism: Rereading H. Richard Niebuhr's *The Meaning of Revelation*." *Political Theology: The Journal of Christian Socialism* 13, no. 1 (2012): 37–59.

Johnson, Elizabeth. *Quest for the Living God: Mapping Frontiers in the Theology of God*. New York: Continuum, 2011.

———. *She Who Is: The Mystery of God in Feminist Theological Discourse*. New York: Crossroad, 1992.

Jordan, Miriam. "Court Widens Scope of Deportations." *New York Times*, June 25, 2022. https://www.nytimes.com/2022/06/25/us/immigration-enforcement-priorities-court.html.

Kanstroom, Daniel. *Deportation Nation: Outsiders in American History*. Cambridge, MA: Harvard University Press, 2007.

Keenan, James. "Proposing Cardinal Virtues." *TS* 56, no. 4 (1995): 709–29. https://doi.org/10.1177/004056399505600405.

Kendi, Ibram X. *How to Be an Antiracist*. New York: One World, 2019.

Kerwin, Donald M., and Robert Warren. "Putting America First: A Statistical Case for Encouraging Rather than Impeding and Devaluing U.S. Citizenship." *Journal on Migration and Human Security* 7, no. 4 (2019): 109–17.

Kilgore, Ed. "DeSantis Joins Trump's Call to End Birthright Citizenship." *New York Magazine*, June 27, 2023. https://nymag.com/intelligencer/2023/06/desantis-joins-trumps-call-to-end-birthright-citizenship.html.

King, Martin Luther, Jr. *Why We Can't Wait*. Boston: Beacon, 2010.

Klingle, Matthew. "Frontier Ghosts along the Urban Pacific Slope." In *Frontier Cities: Encounters at the Crossroads of Empire*, edited by Jay Gitlin, Barbara Berglund, and Adam Arenson, 121–46. Philadelphia: University of Pennsylvania Press, 2012.

Kohlhaas, Jacob M., and Ryan Patrick McLaughlin. "Loving the World We Are: Anthropology and Relationalioty in *Laudato Si*." *JRE* 47, no. 3 (2019): 501–24.

Koontz, Gayle Gerber. "Confessional Theology in a Pluralistic Context: A Study of the Theological Ethics of H. Richard Niebuhr and John H. Yoder." *Mennonite Quarterly Review* 61, no. 4 (1987): 413–18.

Kopan, Tal. "Sessions Criticizes Immigrants' Attorneys before Immigration Judges." CNN, September 10, 2018. https://tinyurl.com/3cphzfpf.

Kopinak, Kathryn. *Desert Capitalism: Maquiladoras in North America's Western Industrial Corridor*. Tucson: University of Arizona Press, 1996.

Krauthamer, Barbar. *Black Slaves, Indian Masters: Slavery, Emancipation, and Citizenship in the Native American South*. Chapel Hill: University of North Carolina Press, 2013.

Lessa, Francesca. *Memory and Transitional Justice in Argentina and Uruguay: Against Impunity*. New York: Palgrave Macmillan, 2013.

Liptak, Adam. "Is Half of Oklahoma an Indian Reservation? The Supreme Court Sifts the Merits." *New York Times*, November 27, 2018. https://www.nytimes.com/2018/11/27/us/politics/oklahoma-indian-territory-supreme-court.html.

Liptak, Kevin, Danielle Diaz, and Sophie Tatum. "Trump Pardons Former Sheriff Joe Arpaio." CNN, August 27, 2017. https://www.cnn.com/2017/08/25/politics/sheriff-joe-arpaio-donald-trump-pardon/index.html.

Lopez, Brian. "Republican Bill That Limits How Race, Slavery and History Are Taught in Texas Schools Becomes Law." *Texas Tribune*, December 2, 2021. https://www.texastribune.org/2021/12/02/texas-critical-race-theory-law/.

López, Paul. "Operation Wetback." In *Multicultural America: A Multimedia Encyclopedia*, edited by Carlos E. Cortés, 1652–53. Thousand Oaks, CA: SAGE, 2013.

Macalus, Austen. "Conversations Lead to Acceptance of Somali Refugees." Associated Press, November 2, 2019. https://apnews.com/f6621f7f15d048098c3779bcad75c947.

Marolf, Melissa. "The $63 Billion Dollar Reality Check." #UniteCloud, accessed January 20, 2021. https://unitecloud.org/the-63-billion-dollar-reality-check/.

Martin, David A., Daniel Kanstroom, and Peter H. Schuck. *Immigration Stories*. New York: Foundation, 2005.

Mathisen, James. "Twenty Years after Bellah: Whatever Happened to American Civil Religion?" *Sociological Analysis* 50, no. 2 (1989): 129–46. https://doi.org/10.2307/3710983.

Mattison, William C. *Introducing Moral Theology: True Happiness and Virtue*. Grand Rapids: Brazos, 2008.

McCrummen, Stephanie. "A Sanctuary of One." *Washington Post*, March 31, 2018. https://www.washingtonpost.com/news/national/wp/2018/03/31/feature/after-30-years-in-america-she-was-about-to-be-deported-then-a-tiny-colorado-church-offered-her-sanctuary/.

McDougall, Walter A. *The Tragedy of U.S. Foreign Policy: How America's Civil Religion Betrayed the National Interest*. New Haven, CT: Yale University Press, 2016.

McGee, Luke. "A Migration Crisis and Disagreement with Turkey Is the Last Thing Europe Needs Right Now." CNN, March 2, 2020. https://www.cnn.com/2020/03/02/europe/turkey-migrant-crisis-european-union-intl/index.html.

McKinney, Cynthia. *How the US Creates "Sh*thole" Countries*. Atlanta: Clarity, 2018.

McPherson, Alan L. *Encyclopedia of U.S. Military Interventions in Latin America*. Santa Barbara, CA: ABC-CLIO, 2013.

Mendoza, José Jorge. "Illegal: White Supremacy and Immigration Status." In *The Ethics and Politics of Immigration: Core Issues and Emerging Trends*, edited by Alex Sager, 208–19. Lanham, MD: Rowman & Littlefield International, 2016.

Metz, Johann Baptist. *Faith in History and Society: Toward a Practical Fundamental Theology*. New York: Seabury, 1979.

Michaels, Peter S. "Lawless Intervention: United States Foreign Policy in El Salvador and Nicaragua." *Boston College Third World Law Journal* 7, no. 2 (1987): 223–62.

Migration Policy Institute. "Legalization for DREAMers Would Result in Chain Migration of an Average of 1 Person or Less over a Lifetime—Far Fewer than Critics Suggest, MPI Estimates." November 30, 2017. https://www.migrationpolicy.org/news/legalization-dreamers-would-result-chain-migration-average-1-person-or-less-over-lifetime.

Miroff, Nick. "Biden Toughened Asylum Screening. It Won't Contain a New Border Surge." *Washington Post*, March 17, 2024. https://www.washingtonpost.com/immigration/2024/03/17/biden-migrants-asylum-new-restrictions/.

———. "Momentary Border Reprieve Rests on a Rickety Foundation, as U.S. Immigration Policies Are Put to the Test." *Washington Post*, July 13, 2019. https://tinyurl.com/2vm8atf2.

Morgan, Ted. *Wilderness at Dawn: The Settling of the North American Continent*. New York: Simon & Schuster, 1993.

Morin, Rebecca, and Dan Keemahill. "Biden Pledged to Fix a Broken US Refugee Program. Two Years Later He's Nowhere near His Goal." *USA Today*, March 2, 2023. https://www.usatoday.com/story/news/politics/2023/02/27/biden-us-refugee-cap-not-met-2022/11112116002/.

Morris, Amanda. "What Is Settler-Colonialism?" Learning for Justice, January 22, 2019. https://www.learningforjustice.org/magazine/what-is-settlercolonialism.

Morris, Glenn T. "International Law and Politics: Toward a Right to Self-Determination for Indigenous Peoples." In *The State of Native America: Genocide, Colonization, and Resistance*, edited by M. Annette Jaimes, 55–86. Boston: South End, 1992.

Morrissey, Kate. "Family Separations at the Border Continue under Biden." *San Diego Union-Tribune*, August 16, 2022. https://www.sandiegouniontribune.com/news/immigration/story/2022-08-16/family-separations-at-the-border-continue-under-biden.

Morrow, Maria C. "'Sensus fidelium': The Sense of the Faithful." Catholic News Service, 2018. https://catholiccourier.com/articles/sensus-fidelium-the-sense-of-the-faithful.

Moslimani, Mohamad. "Around Four-in-Ten Latinos in U.S. Worry They or Someone They Know Could Be Deported." Pew Research Center. February 14, 2022. https://www.pewresearch.org/short-reads/2022/02/14/around-four-in-ten-latinos-in-u-s-worry-that-they-or-someone-close-to-them-could-be-deported/.

Nagle, Rebecca. "The Treaty." Episode 4, *This Land* (podcast), June 24, 2019. https://crooked.com/podcast-series/this-land/.

Niebuhr, H. Richard. *The Responsible Self: An Essay in Christian Moral Philosophy*. New York: Harper∫& Row, 1963.

———. "War as Crucifixion." *The Christian Century*, April 28, 1943.

No One Left Behind. "About Us." Accessed October 19, 2022. https://www.nooneleft.org/about.

Oliphant, J. Baxter, and Andy Cerda. "Republicans and Democrats Have Different Top Priorities for US Immigration Policy." Pew Research Center, September 8, 2022. https://www.pewresearch.org/short-reads/2022/09/08/republicans-and-democrats-have-different-top-priorities-for-u-s-immigration-policy/.

Omar, Ilhan, and Rebecca Paley. *This Is What America Looks Like: My Journey from Refugee to Congresswoman*. New York: Dey St., 2020.

O'Neill, William. "The Place of Displacement: Ethics of Migration in the United States." In *Living with(out) Borders*, edited by Agnes Brazal and Maria Teresa Davila, 67–77. Maryknoll, NY: Orbis, 2016.

———. "The Place of Displacement: A Theological Locus." *Colloquium* 46, no. 1 (May 2014): 101–04.

———. "Rights of Passage: The Ethics of Forced Displacement." *Journal of the Society of Christian Ethics* 27, no. 1 (Spring/Summer 2007): 113–35.

———. "What We Owe to Refugees and IDPs: An Inquiry into the Rights of the Forcibly Displaced." In *Refugee Rights: Ethics, Advocacy, and Africa*, edited by David Hollenbach, 27–50. Washington, DC: Georgetown University Press, 2008.

O'Neill, William, and William Spohn. "Rights of Passage: The Ethics of Immigration and Refugee Policy." *TS* 59, no. 1 (1998): 84–106.

Ortiz, Paul. *An African American and Latinx History of the United States.* Boston: Beacon, 2018.

"Our Mission." La Mujer Obrera, accessed December 12, 2020. http://www.mujerobrera.org/.

"Our Story." Association of Wartime Allies. Accessed October 19, 2022. https://www.wartimeallies.co/about.

Pagnucco, Ron. "Editorial Counterpoint: There's More to the Other Side of the St. Cloud Story." *Star Tribune*, July 8, 2019. https://www.startribune.com/editorial-counterpoint-there-s-more-to-the-other-side-of-the-st-cloud-story/512438282/?refresh=true.

Palkot, Greg. "Afghan Translators, Families Fear Taliban Takeover as They Try Escaping to US." Fox News, August 4, 2021. https://www.foxnews.com/world/afghan-translators-families-fear-taliban-takeover-try-escaping-us.

Paquette, Gabriel B., and Matthew Brown. *Connections after Colonialism Europe and Latin America in the 1820s.* Tuscaloosa: University of Alabama Press, 2013.

Payan, Tony. *The Three U.S.-Mexico Border Wars: Drugs, Immigration, and Homeland Security.* Santa Barbara, CA: Praeger, 2016.

Perkins, John. *The New Confessions of an Economic Hit Man.* San Francisco: Berrett-Koehler, 2016.

Pineda-Madrid, Nancy. *Suffering and Salvation in Ciudad Juárez.* Minneapolis: Fortress, 2011.

"Polling Update: Americans Continue to Resist Negative Messages about Immigrants, but Partisan Differences Continue to Grow." National Immigration Forum, September 18, 2020. https://immigrationforum.org/article/polling-update-americans-continue-to-resist-negative-messages-about-immigrants-but-partisan-differences-continue-to-grow/.

Povoledo, Elisabetta. "Vatican Repudiates 'Doctrine of Discovery,' Used as Justification for Colonization." *New York Times*, March 30, 2023. https://tinyurl.com/33adm96t.

"Public Charge." Immigrant Legal Resource Center, accessed July 4, 2023. https://www.ilrc.org/public-charge.

"Q&A: Trump Administration's 'Remain in Mexico' Program." Human Rights Watch, January 29, 2020. https://www.hrw.org/news/2020/01/29/qa-trump-administrations-remain-mexico-program.

Raddatz, Martha, Cindy Smith, and Conor Finnegan. "Afghan Translators, Contractors Fear for Their Lives amid Taliban Offensives, US Withdrawal." ABC News. June 23, 2021. https://abcnews.go.com/Politics/afghan-translators-contractors-fear-lives-amid-taliban-offensives/story?id=78422573.

Rajendra, Tisha M. *Migrants and Citizens: Justice and Responsibility in the Ethics of Immigration*. Grand Rapids: Eerdmans, 2017.

"Respecting the Rule of Law." Evangelical Immigration Table, December 3, 2019. https://evangelicalimmigrationtable.com/respecting-the-rule-of-law/.

"A Restitution-Based Immigration Reform." Evangelical Immigration Table, accessed November 12, 2019. http://evangelicalimmigrationtable.com/a-restitution-based-immigration-reform/.

Riebe-Estrella, Gary. "Pueblo and Church." In *From the Heart of Our People*, edited by Orlando O. Espín and Miguel H. Díaz, 173–82. Maryknoll, NY: Orbis Books, 1999.

Robbins, Rebecca L. "Self-Determination and Subordination: The Past, Present, and Future of American Indian Governance." In *The State of Native America: Genocide, Colonization, and Resistance*, edited by M. Annette Jaimes, 87–121. Boston: South End, 1992.

Rodriguez, Cassaundra. "Seven Things to Know about Mixed-Status Families." Medium, June 5, 2018. https://medium.com/national-center-for-institutional-diversity/seven-things-to-know-about-mixed-status-families-92a18a714bb5.

Rodríguez, José. "Shaping Soteriology a la latina." In *Building Bridges, Doing Justice: Constructing a Latino/a Ecumenical Theology*, edited by Orlando Espín, 112–40. Maryknoll, NY: Orbis Books, 2009.

Rogin, Paul Michael. *Fathers and Children: Andrew Jackson and the Subjugation of the American Indian*. New York: Knopf, 1975.

Romo, Vanessa, Joel Rose, and Marisa Peñaloza. "Title 42, a COVID-Era Halt on Asylum Applications, Has Ended. Here's What to Expect." NPR, May 12, 2023. https://www.npr.org/2023/05/11/1175378000/title-42-expires-asylum-us-border-texas.

Rose, Joel. "Supreme Court Allows Trump Administration Rule for Immigrants on Public Benefits." National Public Radio, January 27, 2020. https://www.npr.org/2020/01/27/800158106/supreme-court-allows-trump-administration-rule-for-immigrants-on-public-benefits.

Ruiz, Jason. *Americans in the Treasure House: Travel to Porfirian Mexico and the Cultural Politics of Empire*. Austin: University of Texas Press, 2014.

Saiving, Valerie. "The Human Situation: A Feminine Viewpoint." *Pastoral Psychology* 17, no. 3 (1966): 29–42.

Saiving Goldstein, Valerie. "The Human Situation: A Feminine View." *JR* 40, no. 2 (1960): 100–112. https://doi.org/10.1086/485231.

Samuels, Brett. "Here's What the Supreme Court's Decision on Title 42 Means." The Hill, December 28, 2022. https://thehill.com/homenews/administration/3791054-heres-what-the-supreme-courts-decision-on-title-42-means/.

Sassen, Saskia. *Explusions: Brutality and Complexity in the Global Economy*. Cambridge, MA: Belknap, 2014.

Schmiedel, Ulrich. "The Theopolitics of the Migrant: Toward a Coalitional and Comparative Political Theology." In *Christianity and the Law of Migration*, edited by Silas W. Allard, Kristin E. Heyer, and Raj Nadella, 212–29. New York: Routledge, 2022.

Schreiter, Robert J. *Reconciliation: Mission and Ministry in a Changing Social Order.* Maryknoll, NY: Orbis Books, 1992.

Scribner, Todd, and J. Kevin Appleby. *On Strangers No Longer: Perspectives on the Historic U.S.-Mexican Catholic Bishops' Pastoral Letter on Migration.* New York: Paulist, 2013.

Seitz, Mark. "Night Will Be No More." October 13, 2019. https://www.hopeborder.org/nightwillbenomore-eng.

Semuels, Alan. "The Last Time the U.S. Seriously Considered Merit-Based Immigration." *Atlantic,* August 4, 2017. https://www.theatlantic.com/business/archive/2017/08/immigrants-merit-based/535974/.

Shivaram, Deepa. "What to Know about Title 42, the Trump-Era Policy Now Central to the Border Debate." NPR, April 24, 2022. https://www.npr.org/2022/04/24/1094070784/title-42-policy-meaning.

Smith, James Morton. "Alexander Hamilton, the Alien Law, and Seditious Libels." *The Review of Politics* 16, no. 3 (1954): 305–33.

Smith, Rogers M. *Civic Ideals: Conflicting Visions of Citizenship in U.S. History.* New Haven, CT: Yale University Press, 1997.

"Social Enterprises." La Mujer Obrera, accessed December 12, 2020. http://www.mujerobrera.org/.

"Special Immigrant Visas for Afghans—Who Were Employed by/on Behalf of the U.S. Government." United States Department of State—Bureau of Consular Affairs, accessed October 19, 2022. https://travel.state.gov/content/travel/en/us-visas/immigrate/special-immg-visa-afghans-employed-us-gov.html.

Staffieri, Kim, Matt Zeller, and Michael Trudeau. "The Left Behind Afghans One Year Later." Association of Wartime Allies, August 15, 2022. https://tinyurl.com/mr4a5wy6.

Suchlicki, Jaime. *Mexico: From Montezuma to NAFTA, and Beyond.* New Brunswick, NJ: Transaction, 2000.

Suls, Rob. "Less than Half the Public Views Border Wall as an Important Goal for U.S. Immigration Policy." Pew Research Center, January 6, 2017. https://www.pewresearch.org/short-reads/2017/01/06/less-than-half-the-public-views-border-wall-as-an-important-goal-for-u-s-immigration-policy/.

Sutcliffe, Ruth. "Learning Not to Sin: Repentance in Tertullian and Cyprian." *Colloquium* 53, no. 1 (2021): 73–97.

Tallbear, Kim. "DNA, Blood, and Racializing the Tribe." *Wicazo Sa Review* 18, no. 1 (Spring 2003): 81–107.

"Tech High School Expands World Language Opportunities." BARR, January 24, 2022. https://barrcenter.org/2022/01/24/tech-high-school-expands-world-language-opportunities/.

Telvin, Jon. "Untruths Fan Flames of Fear in St. Cloud." *Star Tribune,* October 23, 2017. https://www.startribune.com/jon-tevlin-untruths-fan-flames-of-fear-in-st-cloud/452139823/?refresh=true.

Tichenor, Daniel J. *Dividing Lines: The Politics of Immigration Control in America.* Princeton, NJ: Princeton University Press, 2002.

Tinker, George "Tink." *American Indian Liberation: A Theology of Sovereignty.* Maryknoll, NY: Orbis Books, 2008.

Torpey, John. *Making Whole What Has Been Smashed: On Reparation Politics.* Cambridge, MA: Harvard University Press, 2006.

Totiyapungprasert, Priscilla. "Annunciation House Helps Undocumented Immigrants Apply for Asylum." El Paso Matters, January 20, 2023. https://elpasomatters.org/2023/01/20/el-paso-migrants-apply-for-asylum-with-annunciation-house/.

Turnbaugh, Peter J., Ruth E. Ley, Micah Hamady, Claire Fraser-Liggett, Rob Knight, and Jeffrey I. Gordon. "The Human Microbiome Project: Exploring the Microbial Part of Ourselves in a Changing World." *Nature* 449, no. 7164 (October 18, 2007): 804–10.

Tutu, Desmond. *No Future without Forgiveness.* New York: Doubleday, 2000.

Ulanowicz, Robert E. "Mutualism in the Darwinian Scenario." Washington Theological Consortium Conference, April 14, 2012. https://washtheocon.org/wp-content/uploads/2013/12/Mutualism-Darwinian.pdf.

#UniteCloud. "Education and Speaking." Accessed December 12, 2020. https://unitecloud.org/education-speaking/.

———. "#UC Leadership." Accessed December 12, 2020. https://unitecloud.org/staff/.

United Nations Office on Genocide Prevention and the Responsibility to Protect. "Genocide." Accessed July 1, 2023. https://www.un.org/en/genocideprevention/genocide.shtml.

United States Conference of Catholic Bishops. "Asylum." Accessed December 12, 2020. https://tinyurl.com/h49mthpk.

———. "Binary Choice: Separation or Indefinite Detention." Accessed December 12, 2020. https://justiceforimmigrants.org/what-we-are-working-on/immigrant-detention/binary-choice-separation-or-indefinite-detention/.

———. "Call to Family, Community, and Participation." Accessed September 13, 2023. https://www.usccb.org/beliefs-and-teachings/what-we-believe/catholic-social-teaching/call-to-family-community-and-participation.

United States Conference of Catholic Bishops and Conferencia del Episcopado Mexicano. *Strangers No Longer: Together on the Journey of Hope.* Washington, DC: United States Conference of Catholic Bishops, 2003.

"US: Family Separation Harming Children, Families." Human Rights Watch, July 11, 2019. https://www.hrw.org/news/2019/07/11/us-family-separation-harming-children-families.

US Government Accounting Office. "North American Free Trade Agreement; Assessment of Major Issues." GAO/GGD-93—137, September 9, 1993. https://www.gao.gov/products/GGD-93-137.

US Immigration and Customs Enforcement. "FAQ on Sensitive Location and Courthouse Arrests." Last updated September 25, 2018. https://www.ice.gov/ero/enforcement/sensitive-loc#wcm-survey-target-id.

Veteto, Jeff. "Foreign Land Ownership on Mexico's Coasts: The Proposed Amendment to Article 27 of the Mexican Constitution." *Law and Business Review of the Americas* 20, no. 2 (Spring 2014): 325–34.

Villarreal, Alexandra. "The US Asylum Rule Replacing Title 42 Is Strict—Here's What We Know." *Guardian*, May 15, 2023. https://www.theguardian.com/us-news/2023/may/15/explainer-strict-asylum-rules-replacing-title-42.

Volf, Miroslav. *Exclusion and Embrace: A Theological Exploration of Identity, Otherness, and Reconciliation*. Nashville: Abingdon, 1996.

Walker, Margaret Urban. "Making Reparations Possible: Theorizing Reparative Justice." In *Theorizing Transitional Justice*, edited by Claudio Corradetti, Nir Eisikovits, and Jack Volpe Rotondi, 211–22. London: Ashgate, 2015.

———. "Restorative Justice and Reparations." *Journal of Social Philosophy* 37, no. 3 (2006): 377–95.

Warfa, Hasme. *America Here I Come: A Somali Refugee's Quest for Hope*. Makati City, Philippines: Sunshine, 2014.

Watson, Julie. "US Soldier Wins Long Fight to Get Afghan Translator Asylum." Fox 29, September 22, 2021. https://foxsanantonio.com/news/nation-world/us-soldier-wins-long-fight-to-get-afghan-translator-asylum.

Watson, Julie, and Andrea Rosa. "US Soldier Loses One Afghan Translator; Fights to Save Another." Army Times. August 27, 2021. https://www.armytimes.com/news/your-army/2021/08/27/us-soldier-loses-one-afghan-translator-fights-to-save-another/.

Waxman, Olivia B. "Anti-'Critical Race Theory' Laws Are Working. Teachers Are Thinking Twice about How They Talk about Race." *Time*, June 30, 2022. https://time.com/6192708/critical-race-theory-teachers-racism/.

Weber, Max. *The Protestant Ethic and the Spirit of Capitalism*. New York: Routledge, 2001.

"Welcome to the Table." Evangelical Immigration Table, accessed November 12, 2019. http://evangelicalimmigrationtable.com.

"What Is Indian Country." Tribal Jurisdiction, accessed February 20, 2020. https://tribaljurisdiction.tripod.com/id7.html.

Williams, Delores S. *Sisters in the Wilderness: The Challenge of Womanist God-Talk*. Maryknoll, NY: Orbis Books, 1993.

Worland, Justin. "How Climate Change Unfairly Burdens Poorer Countries." *Time*, February 5, 2016. https://time.com/4209510/climate-change-poor-countries/.

Young, Iris Marion. "Responsibility and Global Justice: A Social Connection Model." *Social Philosophy and Policy* 23, no. 1 (2006): 102–30. https://doi.org/10.1017/S0265052506060043.

Young, Thelathia "Nikki." "Queering 'The Human Situation.'" *JFSR* 28, no. 1 (2012): 126–31. https://doi.org/10.2979/jfemistudreli.28.1.126.

Younge, Gary. "Ambalavaner Sivanandan Obituary." *The Guardian*, February 7, 2018. https://www.theguardian.com/world/2018/feb/07/ambalavaner-sivanandan.

Zehr, Howard. *The Little Book of Restorative Justice*. Intercourse, PA: Good Books, 2002.

Zolberg, Aristide R. *A Nation by Design: Immigration Policy in the Fashioning of America*. Cambridge, MA: Harvard University Press, 2006.

INDEX